Beyond the Last Dragon

A LIFE OF EDWIN MORGAN

By the same author

Beyond the Last Dragon

A LIFE OF EDWIN MORGAN

James McGonigal

SANDSTONEPRESS
HIGHLAND | SCOTLAND

First published in Great Britain in 2010
Sandstone Press Ltd
PO Box 5725
One High Street
Dingwall
Ross-shire
IV15 9WJ
Scotland

www.sandstonepress.com

Editor: Moira Forsyth

The publisher acknowledges subsidy from the
Creative Scotland towards this volume.

ISBN: 978-1-905207-23-7

Front cover image: Simon Murphy Herald & Times Group
Cover design by River Design, Edinburgh
Index by Dr Ronnie Young, Glasgow

Typeset in Monotype Ehrhardt by Iolaire Typesetting, Newtonmore
Printed and bound by TOTEM, Poland

For EM –
expert, crackerjack, old hand

Contents

List of Illustrations

FAMILY PICTURES 1915–c1935

1. EM's mother's parents, the Arnotts
2. EM's parents, Stanley and Madge Morgan, on honeymoon in Torquay, July 1915
3. EM, aged one, with mother
4. On holiday at the beach
5. His favourite toy, a sailing ship for dry land
6. EM, aged six, with his father, June 1926
7. On holiday at Ascog, June 1926
8. On holiday, possibly on Arran or at Millport
9. On holiday, 1930s

UNIVERSITY PRE-WAR, NATIONAL SERVICE AND RETURN c1940–1946

1. As a student, prior to national service, 1940
2. The raw recruit, March 1941
3. Ready to embark, June 1941
4. Among the snow covered cedars of Lebanon, April 1942
5. 42nd General Hospital at Haifa, May 1945
6. Homecoming, Rutherglen

1950s

1. Some of the Departmental staff, 1951
2. In Dublin, July 1952

3. With Thomas Livingstone and colleague, 1952
4. Sydney Graham at Burnside, September 1954
5. At the Lenin Memorial, Kiev, Ukraine, May 1955
6. Building socialism in Moscow, May 1955
7. EM in Brighton, May 1958
8. EM in Dumbarton, 1959 (Iain Crichton Smith)
9. Iain Crichton Smith, Dumbarton, 1959

1960s

1. On the balcony of 19 Whittingehame Court, September 1964
2. John Scott, 1964
3. On the boat to Ireland, July 1965
4. EM and Marshall Walker, 1966
5. With Blue Bird typewriter, late 1960s
6. With George Macbeth, Nottingham Poetry Festival, February 1966

1970s

1. New Shirt. Carcanet publicity shot
2. Looking at a late scrapbook, 1975
3. With John Scott in Romania, 1976
4. Reading at Colpitts Hotel, Durham, June 1976

1980s

1. Reading tour of Israel with Michael Schmidt et al., 1981
2. With Aunt Myra and Dr Janet Hamilton at Buckingham Palace, November 1982
3. With George Mackay Brown and Peter Maxwell Davies, St Magnus Festival, Orkney, June 1985
4. On the balcony, August 1986

1990s

2000s

Preface and Acknowledgements

Edwin Morgan remains Scotland's best loved poet since Robert Burns. His work is widely read, making immediate contact through its humour, humanity, breadth and variety. He was Scotland's Makar, our other national poet, but not in the least parochial. On the contrary, he had a distinctly international outlook and was a renowned translator of poetry from many languages. Science, exploration, technology and modern city life are key themes in his poetry. Yet the man behind this diverse work is little known.

How his life and his writing interconnect is the subject of this book. I knew the poet for over forty years: he was my lecturer in the 1960s, research supervisor in the 1970s and friend thereafter. In his final years, as he had no immediate family of his own, I became his main 'contact person', the one to be phoned by his nursing home to help with any difficulties he was experiencing. He was very supportive of this biography and enjoyed reviewing the events and personalities of his own long life. On my weekly visits, we were able to discuss the cultural and personal contexts of his writing as it had developed from the late 1930s onwards.

Detailed research was carried out mainly in the substantial Edwin Morgan collection of papers and manuscripts held in the Special Collections Department of the University of Glasgow Library. It is one of three archives devoted to his work, so prolific was he in poetry, translation, drama, radio and television broadcasts, literary criticism and cultural journalism. He was also a prodigious letter-writer, replying diligently and winningly to correspondents from all over the world. Often he would make carbon copies of early letters that seemed to him significant for his emotional or creative life. Later, once he acquired a photocopier-fax machine suitable for a small business, he could copy and file much of what he sent out to friends and publishers.

All of this material is available in the University of Glasgow collection. It contains not only the record of a busy writing life but almost more than enough in letters, typescripts, photographs, reviews and personal papers for any biographer to cope with. Thus I had little time to examine in detail other riches, such as the 13000 books and early manuscripts of his that are lodged in the Mitchell Library in Glasgow, many with annotations; or the Edwin Morgan Archive in the Scottish Poetry Library in Edinburgh. The Mitchell collection was organised by Hamish Whyte when he was a Senior Librarian there. He was also Edwin Morgan's Scottish publisher from the 1980s onwards, as well as his bibliographer. The Scottish Poetry Library archive is essentially Whyte's own collection of all the poet's publications, painstakingly gathered from obscure and transient literary magazines, as well as the ephemera of his public career as a performer, now made available for new generations of readers.

In all my work, Helen Durndell, Glasgow University Librarian, and David Weston, Keeper of Special Collections and Assistant Director, provided a positive continuation of Edwin Morgan's long association with the institution where he first studied and later taught. Sarah Hepworth, Assistant Librarian, gave detailed attention to the many complexities that arose in a project lasting several years, and invaluable help with the poet's Scrapbooks and photographs. Details of the referencing system used for the Department's Morgan collection are to be found in the Bibliography, under SpecColl.

Edwin Morgan's publishers were similarly supportive. Hamish Whyte shared his own deep knowledge of the poet and his work, with insightful comment throughout and kind permission to quote from collections published by his Mariscat Press. Michael Schmidt of Carcanet Press also allowed full quotation from the various volumes of poetry, translation and drama that he has published since the 1970s, and supported the project with characteristic élan. Robyn Marsack, Director of the Scottish Poetry Library, and Gavin Wallace, Head of Literature at the Scottish Arts Council, were exemplary in their commitment to the poet.

I decided at an early stage not to rely overmuch on secondary work of literary criticism or reviews, although the key works used are listed in the endnotes and Bibliography. It seemed better to let Edwin Morgan's own letters, lectures and creative work tell the story of his life. The commentary of poets, friends and academics who knew him is also used, as discussion with them helped him to articulate his intentions as a poet, particularly in the early years. Sustained and generous contact was often maintained at a distance, and several of these individuals have shown his biographer a similar generosity, in conversation or by email, helping me to understand aspects of a complex personality.

Tim Cribb and Marshall Walker, friends and colleagues of Edwin Morgan when he taught in the University, have provided detail on his individual style and role within the Department of English Literature there. From the early 1980s onwards, Marshall Walker also worked with him to create a timeline of key events in his life, for which I was grateful, and some of his photographs are also used here. Present members of the Department, Nigel Leask and Paddy Lyons, were helpful, as was David Jasper, and Richard Finlay of the University of Strathclyde offered a vital perspective on social and economic change in Scotland during Morgan's long career. Poets such as Tom Leonard, Libby Houston, Alec Finlay, Valerie Thornton, Richard Price, James Robertson, Alan Riach, Donny O'Rourke, Peter McCarey and others have talked or written to me about his impact – both practical and liberating – on their lives as writers. Kevin McCarra, a renowned football journalist, has sharp eyes for this poet's agility as a performer, and I have borrowed from him what I could not emulate. I was also given access to taped interviews from 2002 that Hamish Whyte and Alan Riach undertook with the poet. I am indebted to all of these friends and enthusiasts.

Many people contribute their own skills to the making of a book. I would like to mention in particular Pam Luthwood's forbearance of my hand-written drafts over several years; Alex Boyd's combined enthusiasm for Edwin Morgan's poetry and the creation of new images; Ronnie Young's work on the Index; and the helpful comments of my editor at Sandstone Press, Moira Forsyth. The original idea for the book came from the publisher as did contact with Suzanne Gyseman, the creator of the fine cover image. Publication of the biography in paperback has allowed me to add a final chapter to the poet's life, to correct some small transcription errors, and to reflect the helpful comments received from several readers.

Finally, my wife's sustaining presence was vital throughout. Her research on Edwin Morgan's family history, much of which was unknown to him, informed the chapters on his early life; but she also showed understanding and care with regard to the poet's welfare in old age. Many kindnesses which people attributed to me were hers.

James McGonigal, July 2010 and January 2012

CHAPTER ONE

Dreams and Dragons

Edwin George Morgan, born in Glasgow in 1920, often signed himself as a poet with just three short equal horizontal strokes followed by three vertical ones. The reader's eye and imagination recreated this as EM, a readable sign with riddling gaps. This first book of EM's life will be like that, setting known and new facts alongside the unpredictability of a poet's mind that was always open to the mysterious gaps between questions and their various answers.

Beginning this biography, I therefore decided to call it 'a life', but not the full or only life. The varied characters and voices of his final major collection, *A Book of Lives* (2007), speak of a multiplicity of experiences, some historical, some actual and others that were powerfully imagined into a different sort of reality. This reminds us that no-one's life is simple, but a creative person's life is often multiple. In that late title *A Book of Lives*, there may be a hint that he has lived several.

His creative energies survived long into old age, perhaps because of an artistic tendency to play off against one another different facets of his life. To the outside observer these might seem deliberately kept apart – his family relationships from his gay identity; his academic work as lecturer in English literature from a radical and experimental poetry that he hesitated to analyse too closely; his political hopes for his city and nation from his essential privacy as a man.

Privacy was essential to his creativity. Contrasting or conflict-ing aspects of life may have provided the spark, but then a powerful imagination took over – so powerful, in fact, that it could blur a clear sense of the boundaries between fact and fiction. Asked in a late interview to respond to the criticism that his science fiction poetry 'hasn't been lived through, therefore in a way it's to be taken less seriously', EM countered with an appeal to the imagination and the creative act as themselves a lived and real experience:

> Once you're writing a poem [. . .] if the poem is going well, that *is* the experience, you're giving yourself that experience, and though many poems are personal, poetry is also a projection of yourself into other existences. The only thing that matters in the end is the intensity by which you do it.[1]

In the final years of his life, after he was diagnosed with terminal prostate cancer in 1999, he deliberately pitted the power of his imagination against death. He called death 'The Last Dragon'. In a poem with that title in the sequence 'Love and a Life', the centrepiece of *A Book of Lives*, he thinks back to the Anglo–Saxon epic, *Beowulf,* which he had translated half a century earlier, and exclaims:

> [. . .] may I never fail
> To guard my word-hoard before the dragon with his flailing
>   tail
>   Sweeps everything away
> Leaves nothing to say [. . .]

                                        (*A Book of Lives*: 93)

Imagination ensured that he had indeed much more to say between 1999 and his final days. On asking the consultant how long he had left, and being told that it could be six months – or six years, EM responded: 'Can I have the six years, please?' and outlived the best prognosis. Sometimes imagination is used therapeutically in work with cancer patients, who are asked to visualise the tumour, rather than dreading its unknown. In the poet's case, after research towards a BBC Radio Scotland commission in 2003, his visualisation became a full scale dialogue between Gorgo, a cancer cell, and Beau, a normal cell. Gorgo is flashy, cynical and gallus (in the Glaswegian sense of 'streetwise'). Beau is serious, thoughtful, sympathetic to the range of human suffering encountered in the cancer ward. Both 'cells' are aspects of the poet, or at any rate his mind must be home to both equally, if the poem is to go well.

Facing his death, EM's imagination often returned to the amazing voyages and fantasy landscapes of the books that he had loved in a lonely childhood. Beau says:

> I can see my cells as nimble stylish knights
> While yours are clumsy dragons on the prowl.
>
> (*A Book of Lives*: 62)

At times, however, that faculty of imagination could be overwhelming, particularly when in his last years he lost the strength of concentration necessary to turn visions or intuitions into literary works. It was in that period I came to know him best. He had been a senior lecturer when I studied English at the University of Glasgow in the late 1960s, and then was my supervisor for two research degrees in the 1970s. We kept in touch thereafter regularly if infrequently, perhaps three or four times a year.

In the early 1990s Hamish Whyte, his friend and Scottish publisher, became mine too, and when EM came to need increasing help after 1999, we tried to provide it. We were like two surrogate sons, both almost 27 years younger than he was, and called upon now for help or advice. The advice was always carefully considered, if not always taken. Hamish handled literary matters in the main, and I dealt with practical issues of clothing, food or bills, but there was an overlap and sharing of duties that was well understood. At this stage I usually visited EM every week, sometimes more frequently and sometimes less, depending on my work pressures and any particular help he needed. This was firstly in his flat at 19 Whittingehame Court in Anniesland, overlooking Glasgow's Great Western Road, where he had lived from 1962, and later in a care home where he moved in 2004, unable to cope safely on his own because he was falling and often unable to rise unaided.

In teacher education, which was my job, there were intensive periods of tutor visiting that took me to see students working in primary and secondary schools across central Scotland. During one of those periods, on Friday 7 December 2007, I had driven back in the mid-afternoon from Ardrossan Academy, and called by to see EM briefly, as I thought, before returning to my office in the University. As I was about to leave with some of his financial papers to be filed, he asked me to stay because, he said, he was worried about his own sanity. Did I ever wonder, he asked, whether a person could lead two utterly different lives, without either self being aware of the other? He was agitated and clearly distressed.

He had been having a series of dreams of such vivid intensity that he felt they must really have been part of his life experience, presenting themselves now in so disturbing a way that he needed to talk to someone. As he recounted them, I began to take notes of their detail so that I could comment, if asked. Narrating and discussing these took us almost two hours. All of them dealt with anxieties and fears that were part of him, not of some doppelganger. As will be seen, he was happy to have these nightmares transposed into readable form, so I will describe them here.

The first and most fearsome dream was set in his old flat. It was late on a winter's evening in the dream, and he was looking out of the window at all the familiar details of neighbouring houses when, under the street lamp at the corner, he noticed half a dozen plough horses and their men, whispering together. He knew about 'the horseman's word', that ancient language understood between beasts and men, and he had published a series of poems in 1970 called *The Horseman's Word*. But he could not speak it, and was disturbed by that obscure whispering as much as by their presence in the city. They were gathered there below his window with some obscure intent, and were whispering about it.

As he stared out at them, suddenly every light was extinguished, outside and in. Through the darkness, he heard with pounding heart the noise of hoof beats moving off.

What could it mean? I talked as straightforwardly as I could, since EM seemed to want this, about the numinous quality that attends horses in a Celtic culture; about the horsemen of the Apocalypse; and the half-rhyme of horse/hearse that had occurred to me as I listened. Was this dream a warning about the inevitable darkness, which might come on him suddenly one evening? On the positive side, there was the deep relationship of understanding between man and horse, and the language they had formed to express a bond between the human and natural worlds. Maybe the dream was an intimation of, but also perhaps an invitation into, another mode of being.

EM listened to all of this thoughtfully enough. The atmosphere of the dream had been nothing like the playful concrete and sound poetry of *The Horseman's Word*, but more like two later poems in his collection *Sweeping Out the Dark* (1994: 77): 'A Water Horse' which emerges suddenly and impossibly as 'a totality of water / dragonlike some force must surely have uttered [. . .]'; or the poem 'Whistling' that immediately follows, where horses ridden by 'half-stripped ramrod riders more like androids / than mercenaries [. . .] clattered across the courtyard for an airing', before being ridden off in search of fugitives. Neither of these threatening visions is in the earlier *Collected Poems* of 1990, so they are little known. Now it almost seemed that his own images had returned to haunt him, weakened as he was and, like one of the fugitives in his poem, frozen with fear.

The second dream related to his life as a university teacher. In it he was giving a lecture on sixteenth- and seventeenth-century writers, placing them all by date of birth and death and setting them in their cultural context. It was, he said, a scholarly lecture 'in the old style', non-theoretical and carefully prepared. He had just given out the year 1615 when a gruff voice from the audience shouted: 'Something wrong there.' Pause. And again: 'Something definitely wrong there!' – EM described the paralysis that gripped

5

him at the lectern, trying to take in what this meant, and to work out whether he had indeed, despite all his preparation for the lecture, made a mistake. The worst thing was that, if one date was wrong, then all the others might be too.

We talked about any teacher's normal fear of losing control of the class, and how we use knowledge and wit to control the volatility of our students' response to our teaching, whatever their age. Students at Glasgow University, in my time as an under-graduate, could be unforgiving of a weak lecturing performance. By that stage of his career, EM had a reasonably confident lecturing style, but with still a nervous habit of touching his upper lip sometimes as he spoke. Even after he retired from his university post in 1980, he continued to have nightmares about not being able to get examination marking finished on time. And he had memories of his own student days at the University before the war, when 'classes were big and noisy, probably noisier than they are now [. . .] some of the lecturers had a very bad time. I've seen one woman who was actually reduced to tears [. . .]'.[2]

We discussed also the way in which knowledge of facts does little to counter the knowledge that our lives are limited. The dream was possibly reminding him not to try to rely on what had worked so successfully for him in his academic career: study, preparation, clarity, and logical control of the revelation of his thinking. His life now was beyond such control.

The third dream was, for me, the most perplexing. It was retold with such conviction that at one stage I interrupted to ask whether the incident had actually happened to him as a child. He was slightly evasive about this, perhaps because it dealt with a gay encounter. In the dream he was on holiday with his parents on the island of Arran or perhaps Cumbrae on the Clyde coast, where they often went in his childhood in the 1920s and 1930s. He met someone he liked – an older man – and they walked some way round the island before stopping to rest in the shade.

At this point in the narration he broke off and told me in a serious and oddly paternalistic tone: 'Young girls don't under-stand how powerful a man's emotions can be. They need to be warned about this, and protected.' I was nonplussed: was this advice being given because he knew I have three daughters, now grown women, or was it in some sense a distraction from where the narrative was leading? What in his dream had begun as 'a pleasant affair' did not remain so, although it was ambiguously described. It ended with an awareness of his parents standing in the background.

This dream was more difficult to offer comment on, partly because it seemed self-censored, too personal or perhaps based on an actual childhood event. He was unforthcoming on it, although later some details would be added about the man on the island. At present, it seemed to say something about the nature of his homosexuality, manifested at a young age – he might have been 10 or 12 in the dream. The need to keep this secret from his parents was a theme, as was the sense of physical threat. All of the dreams appeared to be recording the tensions he had lived with, presenting them for appraisal now as he approached the final stage of his life. Perhaps he had lived by or through such tensions, rather than merely with them. We talked about the advantages of this in a writer's life.

The next dream was briefer. He had bought a comic book version of the Sumerian epic poem *Gilgamesh,* which he had translated several years previously. In the comic it had been updated to a space story, mystical and fast-paced. He noticed the title: *Tales of the Lords of Wallop.* I misheard this as 'Lords of Warp', distracted from the sexual connotation (in Glaswegian speech) by the science-fiction context, and took it to be a dream about how the creative writer and translator plays with form, transposes genres, or updates and refreshes the past. The dream evoked EM's characteristic desire to span ancient, modern and futuristic cultures, finding an almost boyish enjoyment in tech-nological (and scatological) detail.

The following dream returned to reality, and an obscure sense of threat. EM was on a bus travelling on Great Western Road in Glasgow. It had stalled opposite the entrance to the Botanic Gardens, near where the Silver Slipper Café formerly was before the building burned down in January 1970. There was no panic from the passengers, but anxiety grew. Three men and a woman, who was their ringleader, approached the bus – a bit drunk, rough and reckless. They were looking through the windows, 'looking for me', and started to beat on the locked door, shouting and pointing. The bus would not move, and he was paralysed by fear, expecting the glass on the door to break.

We discussed how EM, a non-driver, usually travelled by bus and in fact had written various poems based on incidents or people encountered on his journeys. This dream took place 'on his patch' in the West End, some ten minutes travel from his home in Anniesland and on the bus route he would use to travel to University in term time, or onwards into the city. The Silver Slipper had, for him, connotations of sensuality, dancing, to some extent an atmosphere of Glaswegian abandon. It was a scene he could only observe and not fully take part in, because of factors of social class, upbringing and sexual identity. Was this dream perhaps questioning his public role as laureate and recorder of Glasgow life? That the woman was the leader of the gang seemed significant, but we did not know why. This might have been some connection with his present state of 'entrapment' in the nursing home, unable to move without help, and cared for mainly by women. We were not sure.

The last dream returned to his work as an academic and translator. In it, he just could not call to mind the name of a Norwegian poet he had once referred to in a lecture on 'Non-Anglophone Modernist Writing'. He was, in the dream and in reality, frustrated by the lapse – and also as we discussed it by my ignorance of Norwegian modernism. He felt I should have known the poet he meant. What was astonishing in the dream, with a feeling of amazement experienced even as he slept, was that although the poet's name had escaped his memory he could recite whole stanzas of his work by heart.

Discussing this, we talked about the decline of some faculties but not of others, the vagaries of memory, the frustrating difference he now experienced in having lost the extensive reference library he had held in his flat. I did a little research on the missing poet and came up with several poets' names, the most possible being Olaf Bull. But even here there was a doubt: either my research was too cursory or the name had really vanished from his mind. But the idea of the deep underground reservoir of verses, still present in the heart of a poet's personality, remained as a positive thought for us both, and truer, somehow, than understandable fears about the loss of precise facts and figures with age.

As a whole, these dreams revealed something of the permanent issues in EM's life which this biography will explore: scholarship and poetic language, sexuality, isolation from parents and peers, and journeys through threatening landscapes, real or imagined. What happened next with the dreams, however, also showed a key characteristic of the man.

EM had been fretting for some time over his inability, because of painkilling drugs, to concentrate long and sharply enough to complete a poem. He had rashly said as much to a journalist from *The Times*, and the idea of a laureate with writer's block proved too piquant for her to resist. Thus the story was run in her paper and in others. As the dreams recounted in his own words seemed to have a certain shape and power, I offered to word-process a draft of each of them for him to amend.

This he did, adding significantly to the poem set on Arran, with details of the man's dark and heavy-set appearance, his corduroy trousers red with clay dust and his dog: he was a man 'close to the earth'. In discussing the changes, EM made reference to Jocelyn Brooke, a gay writer ('not much read now') who described 'unhappy middle-class sexual encounters with working-class men: ultimately frustrating'. Brooke's 1950 autobiographical *The Dog at Chambercrown* is the likely source of 'Clambercrown', a place-name in EM's dream. The man's dark and working-class appearance may remind us of John Scott, the great love of EM's life, whom he met in 1962 after various unsatisfying transient relationships. The dream, then, creates an early manifestation of a life-long preference, and links it to a youthful recklessness, open to what life offers.

Almost as soon as the dreams were in 'poetic' form, EM began to think about where and how they might be published. I had drafted them in an approximation to his voice and tone, using phrases from his account of the dreams, and making some decisions on layout. He entitled the series of seven poems *Dreams and Other Nightmares*, and seemed relieved of the burden they had presented, untold. He recalled, by way of contrast, an unsettling meeting he had with a psychiatric specialist on first coming into the care home: 'Do you have fear?' he was asked – and answered 'No', although rattled by the glum way in which the question was posed, and puzzled by the presumed difference between 'fear' and 'fears'.

He worried now only about whether the 'poems' needed some sort of prose introduction on the nature of dreams. As he talked, it was as if he had already imagined them into print, and I got a sense again of the younger man I had known in the 1970s, in his energetic mid-fifties, forever engaging himself in new poetic projects and commissions. He was pleased to have new work to show to visiting journalists, and also to friends such as the novelist and poet, Ron Butlin, who counselled him to revisit the poems and spend time with the detail of their language.

Hamish Whyte had already seen them at an early stage, had made some suggestions, and wanted to publish them in a further collection of unpublished or obscurely published Morgan poems. Beyond the substantial *Collected Poems* (1990) [CP] and *Collected Translations* (1996) [CT], there are many uncollected poems worth adding to the canon of his work, apart from the several collections published since 1990.

The relationship between EM's poems and his translations is an interesting one. The latter will play a key role in this book, as in his life. In a late interview, he spoke about looking on his *Translations* as 'Collected Poems Number Two':

> it wasn't exactly the same as the poetry I was writing off my own bat, but I really did take translation seriously – I found I would easily imagine myself to be, say, Montale, or Brecht [. . .] you're

beginning with a poetry that's not the same as yours, but it puts out little claws which latch on to your own poetry, and which end up influencing you. I felt I was pushing the art of translation a little further forward.[3]

This deeply imaginative identification with other poets' minds and voices suggests now that they can help identify EM's inner concerns at different stages of his life, and I will refer to the translations throughout. Another shaping device for this biography will be to see the progress of his life in decades, as he tended to do, born at the start of one in 1920. His *Collected Poems* (1990) closes with 'Epilogue: Seven Decades'. Ten years later, in *Unknown is Best: A Celebration of Edwin Morgan at Eighty* (2000), he added a sprightly coda:

> Mariners, keep watch always
> for that last passage of blue water
> we have heard of and long to reach
> (no matter if we cannot, no matter!)
> in our eighty-year-old timbers [. . .]. ('At Eighty')

EM's last voyage was undertaken bravely. In his poem 'The Last Dragon' he saw himself moving onwards like 'the grizzled warrior in Heorot hall', a man 'old in winters and stories', carrying with him the original words of the Old English epic, *Beowulf*: 'inne weoll / Thonne he wintrum frod worn gemunde' (ll. 2113–4). He had translated these lines in his 1952 version of the poem, his first substantial publication: 'His breast was vexed within him while the crowding / Memories came to him from so many winters.'

Now against the 'last' dragon of death, EM typically sets two others. One is the 'Dragon on Watch', the next poem in the sequence: a lucky bronze dragon that had belonged to his grandmother, which now 'straddles his mantelpiece like a guard'. Polished 'with respect, with a dry cloth', it will ensure 'the house will never be ill-starred'. This lucky dragon was given to Mark, a young friend who is celebrated in several poems in the sequence.

Later, once the house had finally been given up and all its contents sold or gifted, another dragon comes to the rescue in the care home. In 'The Old Man and E.A.P.', an old man's nap (as it seems to visitors or staff) conceals an imagined ride 'on dragon back':

> perched among its spikes and rolling folds
> as it swirled through cypresses, tapped them,
> kicked them, flicked them with a thundery tail [. . .].
>
> (*A Book of Lives*: 72)

In the poem the old man questions 'a brace of dragons', about the ancient times 'when they conversed with human kind'. Like the Edgar Allan Poe of his childhood reading, EM has sprung 'a tale of mystery and imagination': not sleeping, not dreaming, but releasing images from ancient treasuries – as much a solace in age as in his lonely boyhood, and itself a sign of a still vibrant and creative inner life.

I came to know EM best in age, and to admire him even more in his vulnerability than in his strength, partly for the positive effect that I could see he continued to have on other people. This was a question that genuinely puzzled him: why did people care about him? How was it that a somewhat private and self-absorbed gay poet, staying in one city for most of his life – and in one area of that city – had nevertheless come to make such a positive, life-enhancing impact on so many people in Scotland and beyond? To the end of his life they communicated this to him through letters, cards, emails, good wishes and visits. And beyond this personal impact arises the question of how the art of poetry itself comes to affect the life of a nation, as I believe his has done.

This book outlines 'a life', but other lives will follow, based on the mass of letters, papers, books and compositions of all sorts that EM wrote and collected without stint through most of his life. I have had access to much of this, but not the time and energy needed for a full study of all these sources, which will take years. When Hamish Whyte and I piled his files and boxes of papers for transporting to the Department of Special Collections in Glasgow University Library, their columns covered half of EM's ample study floor. A team of four librarians had earlier spent a long day sending van loads of annotated books from his shelves down to the Mitchell Library in Glasgow for storage and cataloguing. In both cases, the materials were joining substantial existing collections donated since the 1980s. In 2009, Hamish Whyte's own significant collection of EM memorabilia, with its first and rare editions, new and original work, press cuttings and essays from long vanished journals, all passed into a special archive area of the Scottish Poetry Library in Edinburgh. The John Rylands Library in Manchester University contains significant holdings of his concrete poetry, as well as the archives of Carcanet, his publishers since 1973. In addition to the uncollected poems already mentioned, there is a growing body of music, art and even architecture that has been inspired by his work still to be considered, as well as operatic and theatre productions in which he was involved.

All of this bears witness to EM's immense creative and linguistic energy, which emerged first when, in his forties, he sensed the stirrings of rebirth in *The Second Life* (1968). That new life was connected with love, but in its revelation he uncovered much that was buried, undiscovered or unarticulated, in Scottish life in the twentieth century. Without his creative journeys of exploration, a great deal of what we now think about the life of Scotland in the twenty-first century would have been, simply, unimaginable.

His early life, which was trammelled, lonely and in many ways frustrating, also tells us much about the limitations of the culture he lived in, and how he strove to explore through words, verses, fantastic fictions and a questioning of everything – ideas, codes, cultures, identities – the worth of his own inner life of poetic intuition. There was bravery in that, and an unswerving pursuit of an often frightening or lonely path over many years. It taught a self-discipline that served him well in his encounter – weakened yet still cunning, still alert – with the last dragon. He wanted to see, and if possible write, what was before him:

> When I go in I want it bright,
> I want to catch whatever is there
> in full sight.

(CP: 595)

That was why the dream of horses and sudden pitch black had scared him so much, and why he welcomed even a clumsy attempt to throw some light upon it. After that, the dreams ceased to bother him. Once they had been given a different life on the page, he moved on to other imaginings.

CHAPTER TWO

Silk and Steel 1920–1930

> At ten I read Mayakovsky had died,
> learned my first word of Russian, *lyublyu;*
> watched my English teacher poke his earwax
> with a well-chewed HB and get the class
> to join his easy mocking of my essay
> where I'd used *verdant herbage* for *green grass.*
> So he was right? So I hated him!
> And he was not really right, the ass.
> A writer comes to know what he needs,
> as came to pass.
>
> 'Epilogue: Seven Decades' (CP: 594)

What sort of child notices in the newspaper the suicide of a Russian futurist poet and revolutionary, and has begun to learn that language by the age of ten? One answer is: a gifted child. Another answer might be an only or a lonely child:

> [. . .] if you are an only child you tend to be by yourself and make up your own games. I collected stamps and then quite early on I began collecting words. I had a great list of words I would go through. My father would bring home gardening catalogues and I would make a list of the names of these strange, interesting plants [. . .]. I don't know what I was going to do with these things but it must have been some kind of early pointer to the fact that I was going to use words myself. That was a solitary thing.[1]

There are indications in the verse above of strong emotions in the young EM. The chosen word in Russian means: 'I love'. The

reaction to his inadequate teacher is passionately negative: 'So I
hated him! / And he was not really right, the ass.'

In one interview in the late 1980s EM described his childhood
as 'Reasonably happy, except with the kind of problems, perhaps,
that an *only* child has'.[2] Some twenty years later he admitted that
he was 'unhappy at school, where he was seen as a swot ("I wasn't
– I just happened to get good marks")', while at home he 'felt
himself a bookish anomaly in a house of desultory readers'.[3] For
this isolated child, reading provided an escape into a world of
legend and adventure:

> Perhaps some of the names are not very well known now. G.A.
> Henty [. . .] Edgar Rice Burroughs, and, later on, H.G. Wells,
> Jules Verne, Edgar Allan Poe. Tending to be either adventurous
> or a mixture of adventure [. . .] plus strong imagination, shading
> off towards fantasy and science fiction.[4]

In the Edwin Morgan Collection in the Mitchell Library in Glasgow, there is a diary listing the books he read between 1927 and May
1940. Begun in 1933, it also includes 'remembered reading 1927–33'.
Although the list is marked 'except poetry', later a few poetry
anthologies are included, in fact. Thus some of his earliest reading
can be reconstructed, adding J.M. Barrie, Kenneth Grahame, Lewis
Carroll, Grimm's and Andersen's *Fairy Tales*, and many more, to
those authors of mystery and imagination mentioned above.

A poet in the making responds as much to spoken words and
speech rhythms as to written narrative, of course. For EM at home
this was educated Glasgow speech, but with many traditional
Scottish words and phrases being used. He singles out the phrase
'As quick as a whittrick' used by both sets of his grandparents:

> It just means a weasel, but a weasel of course moves so quickly it's
> almost like a flash – you don't know whether you've seen it or not.
> It was a very common phrase. There were lots of words like that
> used in the family, without any thought that they were strange, or
> even Scottish; they were just the way people spoke.

To this family store of Scots words, he also added Glaswegian speech:

> We always used public transport because there was no car (my father didn't drive – we just used trams and buses and trains) – so obviously living in Glasgow your ear is attuned to the broadest kind of Glasgow speech as well as what you're using yourself. I've always liked listening to what I heard being spoken in the streets, in buses, and so on.[5]

EM was so fond of the word whittrick and its connotations that he used it to name an early sequence of poems: *The Whittrick: a Poem in Eight Dialogues* (1961, first published as a whole 1973. CP: 79–116). Yet the word is not so common in the West of Scotland. The *Concise Scots Dictionary* places it in Shetland, Ross and Cromarty and Sutherland (although its extended use to refer to a 'hatchet-faced person of an active ferrety disposition' is more widespread across Scotland). Perhaps its use among the Morgans gives a clue to family origins, of which EM was only dimly aware, and in which he claimed little interest. This was a surprising lack in someone who, to judge from his poetry, was interested in almost everything else.

When we were discussing his family background in the autumn of 2007, he recalled once being asked by the great Gaelic poet, Sorley MacLean, where his family had originated. EM had given his stock reply: he did not know, but the West Coast around Glasgow, probably – perhaps with some distant Welsh connection. No, the Gaelic poet replied, 'I have known many Morgans from Aberdeenshire and the East', and he was correct. The name, according to the Clan Morgan website, comes from early Celtic meaning *sea-bright* and is found in Breton, Cornish, Welsh and Pictish forms. In Scotland, it was at first mainly found in Aberdeenshire and Sutherland, gradually spreading down the East Coast as far as Fife.

This was where EM's grandfather, George Morgan, came from. He was born in Newburgh in Fife, on 15 October 1839, and was working in the silk trade by the age of 30 in Glasgow, where he courted and married his first wife, Jane Walker, in September 1870. The marriage was cut sadly short by her death in the following year, registered back in Newburgh. He then returned to Glasgow, having remarried in Fife in December 1873, and was re-settled in Glasgow by 1874. His eldest son, David Hepburn Morgan, was born in Cathcart in September of that year.

EM's father, Stanley Lawrence Morgan (b. 1886), was the seventh of the eight surviving children of that marriage: David, Albert, Jessie, Alice, Norman, Edwin, Stanley and Wilfrid. One child died at about one year old, Hector Lothian Morgan, born in 1889, between Stanley and Wilfrid. The first three were born in Cathcart on the south side of Glasgow and the rest in a house called Clunie Bank Cottage in New Kilpatrick, now Bearsden on the north side of the city. This house was likely situated in or near what is now Ledcameroch Road, not far from Bearsden Cross, but it was named after an ancestral farm between Newburgh and Abernethy.

EM was surprised to learn the detail of his Fife connections. He had wondered as a young boy about the link between the Clunie in the house name and that East Coast place. His father had, at some point in EM's teens, drafted out a family tree and taken him through their history, so far as he knew it. This family tree might exist 'somewhere in my papers', but EM did not know where. Some taint of scandal seemed to attach to the grandfather: something to do with a liaison with a French woman, possibly a silk buyer, but the details were hazy or obscured. He had died in 1912, eight years before EM was born, with his Christian name being recalled in his grandson's middle name: Edwin George Morgan.

EM's own birthplace was in a red sandstone tenement flat at 60 York Drive in Hyndland in the West End of Glasgow (now renamed Novar Drive). This is only about ten minutes walk from Clarence Court Care Home, his final residence, and about fifteen minutes walk from 19 Whittingehame Court in Anniesland, the modern flat where he spent the forty most creative years of his life, from 1962 until 2004. This is a circumscribed location, we might think, for a poet whose writing ranges through cosmic distances and variegated voices and forms. And yet a sense of Glaswegian reality certainly helped to ensure a rooted quality in his work, a rhythm of voyage and homecoming in the workings of a restless imagination.

EM was taken on an enjoyable 'field trip' on Sunday 7 September 1997 to revisit all the places where he had grown up, with Hamish Whyte and Marshall Walker. The first named was his Scottish publisher and bibliographer, and the second was EM's friend and former university colleague, then on sabbatical leave from his professorial post in New Zealand. They noted the middle-class solidity of the birthplace, with its dark wooden banisters and green and pink art nouveau tiles in the entry. Afterwards EM talked about his childhood memories, and the 'curious range from strong to faint recollections, to the blank of Novar'.

His earliest memory was of sheer delight in watching trees touching against the sky above his pram, but that was in the garden of a substantial red sandstone semi-villa at 245 Nithsdale Road in Pollokshields, where the family had moved when he was two years old. An abiding 'memory' of his birth, however, was the account of his mother that it 'went on forever', and 'never again'. There seems to be an unfortunate message here about the son being obscurely to blame for his own isolation.

His only-child status meant that he learned to adapt to adult expectations, whether in terms of politeness or performance. Compliance was expected, and yet he also had an audience for his verbal talents. His parents were, in his own words, a 'well-doing' couple:

> [. . .] church-going, with a strong sense of responsibility. They were the kind of parents who watched out for your moral progress and so as an only child I grew up with a pretty strong sense of what was right and what was wrong.[6]

I remember my own shock – having been brought up differently in a much larger and poorer, if equally 'well-doing', Catholic family – at his description of how his mother had dealt with a childhood 'crime'. EM had taken some threepenny bits being saved up for family funds. Even worse, he had used them to buy a racy thriller. Recriminations were swift and intense. His mother told him that, although he might do something secretly, and out of his parents' sight, there was a huge eye in the sky that could see everything, particularly any wrong-doing that he might commit, and so he could be certain of always being found out eventually: 'I was very young and I remember looking up and imagining that eye really was there'. His father threw the book on the fire and they watched it being consumed by the flames.

Thus he grew up with 'that sense of conscience pretty strongly implanted'. It was built on fear, which could recur in adult situations. After a quarrel and subsequent 'silent treatment' many years later while on holiday with his close friend John Scott, the childhood reaction is what returns, and the speaker is 'cast back into an ancient panic':

> You did not know it, but nothing you could do to me
> was worse than your silence when you were angry.
> Often when I did wrong as a boy, my parents
> refused the release of storming it out, pretended
> I was not there, went on talking to each other,
> brushing past me to wash and dry the dishes.
>
> (*Sweeping Out the Dark*: 70)

Looking back, EM related these parental attitudes to the Protestant work ethic that has famously re-shaped Scottish culture since the Reformation:

> My father worked with a firm of iron and steel merchants and he had, I suppose, a Calvinist businessman's idea. He took charge of the accounts and he was extremely hard-working, extremely honest, extremely conscientious and, perhaps going along with

that, nervous. My mother was the same. She had that conscien-
tiousness. I've got this nervousness still and I'm fairly easily made
to feel that something is right or wrong.[7]

As we saw in one of the dreams described earlier, the voice from
the audience paralysed EM's academic persona with a terrible
feeling that, if one detail in the lecture was wrong, then nothing
might be right. Growing up within that close-knit and nervously-
knit household, the boy's need to escape into his fantasy tales of
travel and brave adventure can be understood. He remembered
reading in his schooldays 'a rather bizarre' science fiction magazine called *SCOOPS*, published by Pearson's. He bought copies
(2d weekly) at a wee shop near Rutherglen Academy and smuggled
them into the house.

His mother shared his father's business ethic. Margaret Arnott
was a director's daughter of the firm of Arnott, Young and
Company, ship-breakers and iron and steel scrap merchants.
The firm supplied steel-making companies across central Scotland. When EM's father had started work there as a clerk, she was
already employed in the family firm as a secretary. Despite the
difficulty of quite severe deafness which came on him as a young
man, Stanley Morgan rose to become cashier and ultimately a
director of the firm, through steady and quite rapid promotion.
EM's family fortunes were closely linked, through this firm, with
the fate of Scotland's heavy industries in the years following the
Great War, and on through the Depression. Their various house
moves reflect a turbulent period in Scottish, and particularly
Glaswegian, life.

Yet neither side of the family 'belonged' to Glasgow, beyond a
generation or so back. Within themselves they embodied a
characteristic late nineteenth- and early twentieth-century movement of population in Scotland from rural to urban, from central
and eastern agricultural counties to western industrial ones, and
from lighter and local trades into the 'noise and smoky breath' of
Glasgow and Lanarkshire. In their case, it was a move from silk to
steel.

21

COMING TO THE CITY

George Morgan (1839–1912), EM's grandfather, a native of
Newburgh, a port on the River Tay. According to *Westwood's
Directory for the counties of Fife and Kinross* (1862), Newburgh
enjoyed 'good seaward communication' as well as being traversed
by the turnpike road from Cupar to Perth, and connected by rail
to Perth. The linen trade was the chief employer in the town.
Twenty vessels were registered there at that period, with regular
trade through Dundee, exporting lime, grain and potatoes.
George's father, Robert Morgan (1805–1889) was a draper, born
in Fossaway and Tullibole parish in Kinrosshire. His wife,
Margaret Hepburn (1810–1874), was a daughter of David Hepburn, a minister of the United Presbyterian Church. There were
two UP churches in Newburgh, and one Church of Scotland, and
this perhaps suggests some sense of radical commitment in the
family's approach to life.

As already mentioned, EM's grandfather was twice married.
His first marriage to Jane Walker (1843–1871) took place on
1 September 1870 in the mixed area of middle-class housing and
crowded tenement dwellings called Hutchesontown in Glasgow,
on the south side of the Clyde. They must have returned to Fife
when she became ill from consumption, because he gave notice of
her death in Newburgh in November of the following year. Two
years later, on 26 December 1873, he married Catherine Williamson (1851–1941), who was some 12 years younger than he was.
This marriage was also enacted 'according to the forms of the
United Presbyterian Church of Scotland', and George was
recorded as 'a widower aged 34 of Mount Florida in the Cathcart
parish of Renfrewshire', a warehouseman by occupation.

The couple then began married life in Cathcart, and their first
son, David Hepburn Morgan, was born there. By the 1881
census, the growing family with children Albert, Jessie and Alice
are recorded at Clunie Bank Cottage in New Kilpatrick, just
north of Glasgow. This suburban settlement had grown in the
nineteenth century as Glasgow businessmen built homes for

themselves a short distance from the city centre. In 1863 the Glasgow and Milngavie junction opened, with a station at New Kirk called Bearsden. This soon became the name of the village. The Morgans had two servants at Clunie Bank, one of them, Christian Wilkie, aged 16, born in Newburgh.

EM vividly remembered his grandmother, Catherine Williamson, for the strength of her personality as he took leave of her in Ayr just after he enlisted in the Royal Army Medical Corps in 1940. She would die there the following year, while he was in Egypt. She came from a farming family in Abernethy, and had been born in nearby Clunie, where her father, John Williamson (1813–1875), was recorded as a farmer and subsequently as a land owner. There was property on the Morgan side of the marriage too: George Morgan's grandfather, also called George Morgan, is recorded at Claysyke in Kinrosshire as 'independent', namely living off income either invested or saved. There were three agricultural labourers dwelling in the household, and he is recorded in the death certificate of Robert Morgan, his son and George's father, as a 'landed proprietor'.

Trade had brought George Morgan to Glasgow. He was a 'silk warehouseman' according to the marriage certificate of EM's father, in 1915, or a 'silk merchant' in Stanley's own death certificate. This would be EM's description, as he gave notice of his father's death on 25 November 1965. The family 'cottage' in Bearsden seems substantial, with eight windowed rooms being recorded in the 1901 census for New Kilpatrick. George Morgan retired to Port Bannatyne, on the island of Bute, and died there on 29 July 1912, in the Victoria Hospital in Rothesay. Thus EM never knew him.

EM's father, Stanley Lawrence Morgan, was born in Clunie Bank in 1886. The 1901 census records him at 15 years old as an 'iron and coal merchant's clerk'. Reporting his death, EM described him as a company director. His address then, at 89 Whittingehame Court, may surprise us as much as it must have dismayed EM, who had finally 'broken away' from his parents at the age of 42 to buy a newly built flat in Whittingehame Court, only to find them following him to this same development shortly thereafter, although residing in a different block. At some later point, his mother's married sister, Myra Parrot, joined them, but chose a flat in the same block as her nephew, number 16 near his own at number 19. The Arnotts seemed to function most comfortably as a unit.

EM's mother, Margaret or 'Madge' Arnott (1871–1970), had experienced even greater social change within her own family. Her connections were with Stirling, Lothian and Lanarkshire, and the movement from farming and carpet weaving to colliery, iron and steel working had been swift. Her father, William Hamilton Arnott (1857–1936) was born in the village of New Stevenston. By 1881 he was living at 73 Brandon Street, Motherwell, with his father and sister and working as a colliery clerk. Ten years later, he had moved to Millaig Place, Hamilton Street, in Motherwell, and was now recorded as a 'steel and iron Manufacturer's Clerk and Home Factor', in a dwelling with three rooms with windows. Madge was born here on 1 June 1891. By 1901 the family home in Wilson Street in the centre of Motherwell had four rooms with one or more windows. Their rise in the social scale can be traced in the glass and light they could afford in a smoky industrial town.

William Arnott had married Janet McGowan in 1887 at Stirling. She was a 24 year-old school teacher living at 24 Spring Kerse House, Stirling. Her own mother had been born in Kinross (a geographical connection with the Morgans) around 1832, and she herself was born in Lasswade, Midlothian, in 1863. Her father was a carpet weaver, rising to become at 66 years of age a 'Partner in A Carpet Manufactory', as described in the 1881 census. In terms of EM's own early life, this fact perhaps explains the family idea in the 1930s that he should aim for a position as an apprentice designer in Templeton's carpet factory in Glasgow. The link with teaching on his grandmother's side is also relevant, signalling an intelligent and aspirational ancestry.

Great great grandparents in EM's mother's family also make a connection with his Morgan ancestry. Andrew McKillop was a weaver in Kinross, and further back on the McKillop side there had been a Robert Faulds, recorded as a 'damask weaver', and married in Dunfermline in Fife. Thus there existed, unknown to EM, a strange touching of trades in fabric on both sides of his family, damask being a figured pattern woven especially on linen or silk.

But that seems far-fetched from the immediate context of Madge Arnott's early life in Brandon Street, Motherwell, a town where coal and iron in close proximity had brought a swift expansion of industry and workforce, and her father had already begun to make his way in business. Beginning as a colliery clerk, by the time of his death in 1936 William Arnott was described as an iron and steel merchant. He had become a director of Arnott, Young and Company.

EM's grandfather had entered working life at a time and place when tremendous developments in iron- and steel-making were reshaping the industrial landscape of Lanarkshire, and the town of Motherwell in particular. David Colville had founded a small works at Coatbridge in 1861 to manufacture malleable iron. David Colville and Sons began making steel at their Dalzell plant in Motherwell from 1881, and the business grew rapidly until by 1914 they were the largest steel-maker in Scotland. Two of the Colville sons died in 1916, and the third, John, became an M.P. The chairmanship of the company passed to John Craig, who had begun his career with the company as an office boy and, through his energy, intelligence and acumen finally took over and expanded the firm.

Within such an entrepreneurial climate, it is likely that William Arnott rose and prospered, before branching off independently to develop his own firm, recycling scrap metal, including the breaking of ships, within the context of war production and then its aftermath. His progress as a man of business perhaps explains something of the attraction between EM's mother and his father, who was similarly striving to rise through his own abilities from clerk to cashier and ultimately to director of a firm. The couple met as company employees and married on 30 June 1915 in her parents' home at 2 Maxwell Drive, Pollokshields, in a Church of Scotland ceremony. By that time Stanley was aged 29 and living nearby at 23 Nithsdale Road, his occupation being given as 'iron merchant'.

Arnott, Young and Company was a significant firm, with ship-breaking yards in Dalmuir near Clydebank, in Troon and latterly in Port Bannatyne near Rothesay on the island of Bute. EM claimed never to have visited his father's work, because his mother believed that it was 'a man's world', into which Stanley Morgan travelled by train or tram early each morning, leaving the domestic life behind. There are some indications, however, that the father attempted to share something of this world with his son during holiday trips:

> [. . .] when we went on a Clyde Steamer he would make a bee-line for the engine room, dragging me with him: to me, as a boy, the engines would have only a sort of hypnotic functional beauty, the sleek well-oiled movements, the various parts that always mir-aculously avoided hitting each other, but my father knew how the parts were made, how they fitted together, he could tell me how the boat actually moved, and somehow the whole industrial process remained human, despite all the problems, and I was never able to become a Luddite.[8]

He also fascinated his son on one Sunday walk by giving him a vivid outline of the process of iron- and steel-making. So the character-istic optimism in EM's poetry regarding urban life, technological change, and the interface of human minds and machine intelligence was established in him from an early age. This positive attitude to the modern world distinguishes him from other modernist poets who more often view the city as a place of alienation, and new technologies as tending to distort human values.

Another characteristic of his poetry is an enduring imagery of sea voyages. From the 1950s 'maelstrom of God's wrath [. . .] in the far flood of the north' that opens the first work in *Collected Poems*, to 'the ship with eighty / sails, oh what a sight that is to take to heart' in *A Book of Lives* (2007: 76), the sea ebbs, flows or thunders through his work. This artistic theme may also have originated in an ironic awareness of the distance between his own engagement with fantastic voyages and his father's daily concern for the profit and loss of breaking up ships for scrap.

Different dimensions of his life were caught up in the process of coming to terms with his own background. For example, HMS Jervis which had run supplies into Tobruk in 1941 when EM was a soldier in North Africa, and was damaged in an Italian human torpedo attack on the fleet in Alexandria, was sold for scrap to Arnott, Young and Company and broken up in 1954 at their yard in Troon on the Firth of Clyde. It was one of scores of navy and merchant ships 'recycled' in Dalmuir, Troon and Port Bannatyne in the post-war period's glut of shipping.

The company's pre-war work included the demolition in 1934–35 of the Solway railway viaduct that had bridged the Border estuary from 1868 until 1921. Some 2900 tons of cast iron and 1800 tons of wrought iron had been used in its construction, with cast iron piles 12 inches in diameter driven into the floor of the Solway Firth. Fifty years later, 'The Solway Canal' (CP: 455) was the first of EM's *Sonnets from Scotland* (1984) to be written, although finally printed as 45th of 51 poems in that sequence. The poem imagines a futuristic journey by hydrofoil along a waterway that now divides Scotland from England, under a 'high steel bridge at Carter Bar'. That is a fair stretch of time and space, but I can't help wondering whether the idea might not have originated in an adolescent awareness of this massive disassembling of an engineering achievement of the nineteenth century, with a later poetic desire to reshape such earlier technological ambition for twentieth-century Scotland, offering his nation the hope of a future separation from its powerful neighbour.

GROWING UP IN GLASGOW

EM's parents were united in matrimony and the family business from 1915 onwards. There was a gap of five years before their only son was born. This may have been because of the turmoil of war and the loss of family members. Madge Arnott's older brother, George Arnott, was killed on 1 July 1916, fighting as a private with the Highland Light Infantry at Serre, one of the fortified villages held by the Germans at the start of the Battle of the Somme. He was 28 years of age, and EM kept his service medal with his own. On the Morgan side, the second son, Albert John Morgan, who had been working as a silk warehouseman in Leytonstone, London, volunteered for the Territorial Force at Fulham in March 1915, but was invalided out with 'sickness' a year later.

There is a mystery about the sixth sibling, Edwin James Morgan, born in 1884, who 'disappears' from public record after the 1891 census, when he was living at Clunie Bank Cottage. Was he a military man? There was an Edwin James Morgan who was killed in May of 1916, and recorded on the Plymouth Naval Memorial with the rank of Stoker First Class, but whose name is then said to be a pseudonym for the true family name of Harris. Or he might have been the James Morgan recorded in the 1901 census in England in the Army Service Corps at the Aldershot Military Barracks in Hampshire, and said to have been born in Scotland. His age, given as 19 years, is approximately correct for the birth of EM's uncle and namesake. There may have been a family quarrel. Edwin James Morgan may have changed his name.

Almost as mysterious as his disappearance is EM's claim that his parents never discussed the uncle after whom he was named. He had been Stanley Morgan's immediate elder brother, and so there would have been a closeness there. EM's father often talked about his next younger brother, Wilfrid Lothian Morgan, who had emigrated to Saskatchewan and worked in a bank. Wilfrid signed an attestation paper for the Canadian Overseas Expeditionary Force there in 1916, but survived the war, dying in Vancouver in 1957. His relatives were in touch with EM into his old age.

But EM had no memory of his namesake ever being discussed. Was there some scandal – was he gay perhaps? EM thought that possible. Peculiar also is the fact that he himself, with a mind always full of questions, never seems to have raised this one to consciousness. Discussing the mystery, I teased him that this silence was all part of his own desire to be *sui generis*, self-fashioning, the one and only Edwin – and he wryly admitted the possibility.

His father did not enlist, presumably because of his severe deafness. It is possible that the years that passed between his marriage and the birth of his son were also when some surgical attempts were made to improve his disability. EM recalled with a shudder his father's description of the excruciating pain of these operations. Communication was clearly difficult in the home. Stanley Morgan often thought that people were laughing at him. One can wonder at the gap between the linguistic dexterity of the son and the misunderstandings and frustration of the father.

Broken communication is, of course, another theme in EM's poetry, and some of his best known poems exploit it, humorously in 'The Computer's First Christmas Card', 'Canedolia', 'O Pioneers!', 'First Men on Mercury' or 'The Loch Ness Monster's Song', and more seriously in the Emergent poems (CP: 133–6, 159, 176) and the 'Interferences' sequence (CP: 253–7). He renders creative, playful and exploratory what must in reality have been difficult and, in a sense, shaming.

EM was born on 27 April 1920. Two years later the family moved to a substantial red sandstone semi-villa at 245 Nithsdale Road, Pollokshields, near where his parents had separately lived before they married. This was the place of EM's first memories, not only of delight in the trees above his pram, but of terror when the dog belonging to the Hunters next door 'flew at me once'. He had some happy memories of poetry there. Marshall Walker, writing in *Unknown is Best* to celebrate EM's 80th birthday, recounted how 'Your mother laughed when you danced round the house as a boy, chanting your rhymes'. Family photographs show him usually as the centre of attention among adults, happy to perform for the camera when very young, but seeming to isolate himself through self-composure or an aware gaze as he gets older.

It is probably these earliest times which EM recalled in the 1990s in the poem 'Days'. Typically we find him playing with a boat on dry land that his imagination transforms into sea:

> I said the grass was waves, my toy boat bobbing.
> To get the swishing sound I thought was sea was
> steady tugs on the string.

> (*Sweeping Out the Dark*: 53)

A childish pleasure in forbidden working-class male company is also evoked, exotic to a middle-class boy:

> We'd hours with the roadmenders, their hut forbidden
> and so a place of great resort, a dusty
> sweaty sweary tarry magic caravan,
> they quizzed us, shared their cans of tea, felt our
> no muscles and laughed, surrounding us like a story
> of familiar giants we'd never be afraid of.

The poem ends in a parental call to order, with:

> [. . .] angry shouts from doorways, this minute,
> come in, until we too could sense the shadows
> advancing with what must be the end.

From 1925 he attended a private school run by Miss Mary Ross in a modest terraced house, 'Roskene', at 21 Larch Road in Dumbreck. He remembered plasticine and the taste of glitter wax; the medal on a blue ribbon awarded 'if you were good'; and a girl called Violet. She was always vying for this medal of goodness, and at about the age of 6 the prize was divided between them: 'Violet got the prize as well: she must have been very clever,' he said, and this became a family joke. He stayed happily there until the age of 8 or 9, when they moved to Rutherglen, which was cheaper than Pollokshields, leaving such glittering prizes behind. This was the time of the Wall Street Crash.

They were also leaving his maternal grandparents, who lived at 11 Maxwell Drive in Pollokshields: EM remembered their 'scented garden' and wrote about it in old age in 'Love and a Life', remembering 'the heady scents of other days – / Sweet pea mignotte wallflower phlox – recollection sees them shining in endless summer rays'. He writes about 'their erotic haze' and of himself in the midst of this: 'When I dreamed of lands / Untouched by hands.' Memories of roses came later, and possibly from another garden in Rutherglen, for the aging grandparents soon followed their daughter and her family there. EM's grandfather died at 38 Stirling Street, Rutherglen in January 1936, at the age of 79. There is perhaps a contrast here, and later in EM's life, between the 'centrifugal' Morgan and the 'centripetal' Arnott sides of his experience of family life, the former open to travel and trading, and the latter bonded within the industrial life of the West of Scotland. This may help us understand how basic to his life experience was the blending in his poetry of free-wheeling internationalism with constantly re-focused local engagement.

The Morgan family's move to Rutherglen was dictated by the Depression, which had a disastrous impact on a Scottish economy that was still largely based on the pre-war industrial structures of coal, steel and heavy engineering, particularly ship building. Richard Finlay's *Modern Scotland 1914–2000* (2004) provides the clearest perspective I know on the cultural and political changes that have shaped Scotland in the course of the last century. Reading it while reflecting on EM's life, I realised how literary study of the aesthetic or formal properties in his work has often ignored those elements of shared experience of national life that made his poetry accessible and relevant to readers. He reacted, as they did, to local and international events that affected Scottish lives, but found words or voices that could articulate a range of feelings and concerns – a sort of imaginary yet intense conversation with a history that twentieth-century Scots were living and sometimes making.

The Morgans, young and old, were caught up in the economic reckoning that followed the Armistice. A swift collapse of international economic confidence, a moratorium on naval construction, and loss of traditional markets for herring, coal and jute were combined with a squeeze on public subsidies, even on much-needed state housing schemes. Strikes and unemployment followed in the mines, shipyards and jute mills, with rioting and demonstrations against the levels of poor-relief in Fife, Edinburgh, Aberdeen, Greenock and Port Glasgow. A return to the gold standard stabilised financial markets, but at the cost of depressing the largely export-led Scottish economy further as manufactured goods became more expensive abroad. Reducing wages to increase productivity was one method employers could use to increase their competitiveness. Class conflicts were heightened, to emerge with full intensity during the General Strike of 1926:

> Students relished the prospect of driving tanks through mining villages. Those who drove buses were likely to find themselves subject to a barrage of stones, missiles and verbal abuse [. . .]. In Aberdeen on 6 May police baton-charged a crowd which was stoning tramcars. Rioting in Glasgow between 5 and 8 May resulted in hundreds of arrests [. . .].[9]

Scottish businessmen like EM's father believed in the market. Many of them had done particularly well from armaments and shipbuilding during the war, and Arnott, Young and Company would certainly have been well-placed to do so. There was now an expectation that the market would stabilise eventually. But any dream of a return to pre-war normality was a forlorn one. In Scotland there were endemic problems of structural unemployment, with about 100,000 men permanently surplus to economic requirements by 1930. Young or skilled workers emigrated to England and beyond, and there was a drift of business decision-making away from Scotland to more vibrant English centres. Traditionally-minded Scottish business men failed to develop any significant light engineering and chemical industries.

Even before the Great Crash of 1929, Scotland's economy was vulnerable and in decline. Its national culture too was now responding in defensive ways to the loss of so many Scots in the Great War. Finlay estimates a figure of 90,000 dead, with variations in the intensity of that loss in different towns and communities. In addition, he considers that probably 'some 150,000 to 200,000 Scots suffered some form of physical wound during the conflict. Some recovered but many did not and were forced to fend for themselves [. . .]'.[10] In this context of trauma, unemployment and economic uncertainty, it is understandable, perhaps, that anti-Irish sentiment – the so-called 'Irish Menace' which actual immigration figures reveal as a fiction – took hold.

It developed out of a poisonous combination of working-class Orangeism and middle-class freemasonry and 'scientific racism', focusing on the supposed defects of the Irish stock. As Finlay notes, 'their laziness, dirtiness and proclivity towards crime and squalor were explained as a form of genetic preference'.[11] Irish exemption from wartime conscription in their own country hardened such attitudes in the popular press. The Church and Nation Committee of the Church of Scotland had in 1922 published a document entitled *The Menace of the Irish Race to Our Scottish Nationality*, and expatriation of fictitious Irish immigrants was seen as an 'answer' to Scotland's problems well into the following decade.

As the son of church-going Protestant and conservative middle-class business people, it is clear that EM was exposed early to such views, and to some extent absorbed them. I remember clearly his account of his father saying at the breakfast table in the late 1920s that 'he would never knowingly employ a Catholic'. It was the word 'knowingly' that intrigued his young son. The implication was that 'Irish' Catholics would lie about their origins to get a job in a Protestant firm and, once through the gates, would pilfer with impunity, safe in the knowledge that they could confess to a priest and be forgiven the theft. The fearsome eye in the sky presumably could not work its power on such people, who were best kept out. One of the people who would not have got a job in Arnott, Young and Company was John Scott, the Lanarkshire storeman from a large but close and easy-going Catholic family, with whom EM fell passionately in love in his early forties

33

and continued to love for many years, even beyond his friend's early death.

There were other arguments at the Morgans' breakfast and dinner table, mainly about family finances: EM had memories of scenes, tears and anger, with his father shouting 'The money is not there!' and the son wanting to take sides, but scared to do so. In old age he clearly regretted his early negative judgement of his father. His own experience of being less able now made him more sympathetic towards his father's situation, almost to the point of tears, with an abiding sense of guilt.

EM retained aspects of his father's character into old age. He had a carefulness, almost a punctiliousness, about money which I, culturally shaped by those feckless Irish his father so despised and feared, could admire only up to a point, sensing an essential lack of trust and generosity in this attitude. From his perspective, using financial acumen was simply a way of being 'practical'. It is true that he had the responsibility of handling the inheritance of wealth earned by ancestors on both sides of the family.

He had learned the message of money early, although he could also use his own observation of life to counter its narrowing effects. Characteristically he connected one such counter-lesson with both Glaswegian dialect and male friendship:

> In the tram with my mother –
> I was five or six –
> drunk man leaned across
> offered me a sixpence.
> 'Ur ye a good boay?
> Sure ye're a good boay.'
> I was not so sure.
> My mother hissed
> 'Take it, take it,
> always take
> what a drunk man gives you!'
> I remember how nicely
> he clasped my hand round the coin.[12]

34

The generosity and touch of the drunk man are balanced here against his mother's 'hissed' advice about advantage or self-protection. It is unclear whether or not the drunk man was 'Irish', but he was certainly from another world in terms of class and attitude – a working man as spontaneous and earthy as the man in the dream of Arran, and with some degree of ambivalence attaching to him.

Economic matters at national level were less important to the young EM, of course, than the problems of moving to a new school: Rutherglen Academy, later renamed Stonelaw Academy, where he would be a pupil till the age of 14: 'I hated it'. He got off to an ill-judged start, when his mother kitted him out in buckle shoes, instead of the lacing shoes that all the other boys wore. Mocked, he refused to go back until he had normal footwear. Even his skill with words met with ridicule from his teacher, at least initially. Later he was encouraged in his writing by an English teacher, Mr Hutcheon, 'a small peppery man', who may or may not have been the teacher described in 'Epilogue'. He would embarrass EM by walking him home (they lived in the same street), talking about literature. This was presumably an improvement on his earlier experience, however, of being stalked by 'my well-named bully / Harry Maule', and punched repeatedly and irrationally:

> He was fond of winter,
> threw stones in snowballs.
> Not that I cried.
> But he never said why.[13]

The family moved twice within the Rutherglen area, staying first at 10 Albert Drive, Burnside, then changing to a more 'convenient' bungalow at 30 Broomieknowe Road for a few years, then back to 12 Albert Drive: a solid grey semi-villa attached to Number 10. EM would live there with his parents until 1962. At the age of eight or nine he became 'a member of an awful local football team called the Albertonians. I was never any good at football but you were expected to take part in group activities of that kind. I knew in myself that wasn't really my thing [. . .]'.[14] He played in goal, a position which might suggest that his team mates shared his self-evaluation.

'A writer knows what he needs' says the opening verse of the Epilogue, 'as came to pass'. What did the young EM need and what did he learn? He sensed that it was important to absorb a word-hoard and a style-hoard – even 'verdant herbage' has its place in the lexicon. That there were books to be read, and also recorded as having been read. That there was somehow a sense of the future, and of a model in writing worth following, in the person of Mayakovsky whom he later came to see as:

> [. . .] a kind of legendary heroic figure and I find him very attractive from that point of view [. . .] although people say his life was tragic because he killed himself relatively young, he was, in a deeper sense, optimistic, and I think that was one of the things that drew me to him [. . .].[15]

EM would contrast this optimism with the attributes of T.S. Eliot, whom he admired 'but didn't really like [. . .] from the point of view of the very deep-rooted pessimism [and] extremely conservatively traditional' elements of his mind. In Russian futurism, on the contrary, there would always be for him a sense that modernist experiments in the arts were to be linked with the future, not with the past. From EM's early urban industrial experience of life in Glasgow, one might have expected pessimism in the Eliot mould. This would be wrong:

> I'm drawn more, in that sense, to European modernism, especially Russian modernism, than to the modernism of Eliot and Pound although, obviously one learns, couldn't help learning, from what they've done about matters of technique.[16]

So there was a foreshadowing, in his early alertness to Maya-kovsky's suicide, of a radically different perspective on the modern. His sense of ambition regarding modernism, and of determination about his own difference, need to be viewed in parallel with the sensitivity to words already evident in EM's earliest school writing.

To that poetic sensibility can be added early intimations of sexual identity. Once when EM was with his mother and some of her friends in a Glasgow tearoom, a woman entered whose appearance was striking. It was not only that she was wearing a very expensive and well-tailored masculine suit, but it was the confidence with which she ordered tea, and then opened a journal and read, alone and aloof, that struck the boy. One of his mother's friends commented: 'I always feel sorry for people like that', and the description resonated with the young EM, even into old age: '*people like that*'. The woman clearly was able to shock the 'high bourgeoisie of Glasgow'. Yet she conveyed such elegance and strength of character that no-one dared to criticise her. She ate and read alone. 'I thought she was an intelligent person, and a lonely person,' he told me. Such a person of style, individuality and difference that a writer with enough steely determination might want to emulate in his turn – as came to pass.

CHAPTER THREE

Walking into War 1930–1940

> At twenty I got marching orders, kitbag,
> farewell to love, not arms (though our sole arms
> were stretchers), a freezing Glentress winter
> where I was coaxing sticks at six to get
> a stove hot for the cooks, found myself picked
> quartermaster's clerk – 'this one seems a bit
> less gormless than the bloody others' – did
> gas drill in the stinging tent, met
> Tam McSherry who farted at will
> a musical set.
>
> 'Epilogue: Seven Decades' (CP: 594)

Private Edwin George Morgan, Serial Number 11379, reported for duty in Glentress training camp in the Scottish Borders in early 1940. Germany and Russia had initiated their separate moves against Norway and Finland, but Britain had barely begun to respond. Winston Churchill was not yet appointed to succeed Neville Chamberlain as Prime Minister, when he would rally Britain for the blood and toil to follow. It was the end of a decade of political and social turbulence throughout Europe. For EM, these had also been ten years of personal exploration, a time of confusion and anxiety out of which there had gradually emerged a clarification of his talents and a sense of direction. Now he was walking into the unknown again.

He had volunteered for the Royal Army Medical Corps as a non-combatant soldier, willing to bear a stretcher but not a gun.

His unit, the 42nd General Hospital, had taken over a former work camp set up in the 1930s by the Ministry of Labour, one of many Instructional Centres designed to 'toughen up' young men who had been too long out of work. Digging ditches, road building and heavy labour in the forests of Glentress and Traquair, near Peebles and Innerleithen, had provided one official response to an unemployment crisis that in Scotland derived mainly from deep-seated problems of industrial and economic development. These problems were evident in the 1920s, when the forests were planted to redress a national short-age of timber following World War One. They were even more evident in the 1930s as the forests slowly grew. The onset of hostilities had finally begun to create new employment, and Glentress work camp was available to house recruits training for their new roles in the RAMC.

By a coincidence that might seem far-fetched in a novel, EM would serve in the same hospital unit as the great Scottish poet Hugh MacDiarmid (Christopher Murray Grieve) had done in the Great War. Both poets were also deployed in Quartermaster's duties, although EM had less access to alcohol than his pre-decessor had enjoyed. And both served in Mediterranean theatres of war which perhaps encouraged the distinct internationalism of outlook and a responsiveness to the forces of culture and history evident throughout their future writings.

Looking back at the 1930s from the present day, we tend to emphasise the economic and political crises that seemed to lead inexorably to war. It is easy to forget that for a bright boy growing up in favourable social circumstances this was equally a decade of exciting technological, scientific and artistic change. The gas turbine had been invented for use in jet propulsion and the cyclotron for accelerating atomic particles. Radio astronomy, kodachrome film, and television, as well as surrealism, construc-tivism, and the international Bauhaus style in architecture, had all begun to change the way the world was seen. EM had responded to all of this with a sense of wonder already heightened by a love of words and sensitivity to shape, surface and design. He remembered, at about the age of twelve or thirteen, someone coming to the house:

> who must have been very left wing, although my parents were very conservative, [who] left some magazines which [. . .] must have been early Soviet propaganda magazines with marvellous visual effects, really stunning effects, all concerned with building up the new Soviet State through technology.[1]

All of this would influence his future study of Russian at university, and his early poetic translation from that language. His breadth of interests across the arts and sciences was deep-seated:

> I've always been equally attracted by something that's intensely local and things which are international [. . .] I can always remember even at school, having a very wide range of interests. I would suddenly get interested in, well, Egyptology, astronomy, things like that, which weren't required learning at all – [but] which would take me to things which were either distant in time or space.[2]

These factual interests ran alongside his enjoyment of fiction. By the age of ten or eleven he was pestering his parents or grand-parents to buy him encyclopaedia magazines that were published in weekly parts. He loved especially the juxtaposition of subjects, flipping from archaeology to marine biology to Antarctic exploration, perhaps a dozen topics being unfolded from week to week.

This new knowledge in turn fed into scrapbooks that he began to keep in 1931 or 1932, into which he would paste cuttings from all sorts of sources. These began in exercise books but in his late teens he reshaped or edited them into larger books, now housed in the Department of Special Collections in Glasgow University Library.[3] These 'books' look suspiciously like unused ledgers brought home from a finance office, but with an artistic and scientific content that unbalances any notions of profit and loss.

EM continued to fill his scrapbooks through the 1930s and maintained the practice up until 1966. The final volume is unfinished, but the rest are chock-full of whatever printed or visual material caught his eye. They represent not just a viewing point from which to glimpse the growth of a poet's mind, but a precursor of his later poetic use of cut-outs from newspapers in *Newspoems* (CP: 117–30) and the imagined photo-journalism of *Instamatic Poems* (CP: 217–29). So much care is put into the selection, juxtaposition and overall decoration and design of these volumes, that they can be regarded as his most significant early creative work. They express the play, or possibly the conflict, between various dimensions of EM's creative personality at this stage – the artistic, the literary and the intellectual. The decision to study English at Glasgow University rather than painting in the School of Art was taken late in his fifth year of secondary school, and on the advice of others. Compared with the poems he was writing at the same period, the scrapbooks reveal a highly unusual sophistication and poise.

They are difficult to describe, being a sort of collage, or bricolage, of images, ideas, forms and discourses juxtaposed or contrasted, with care for the appearance or 'rhythm' of the double-page layout. Often there are little abstract patterns drawn in coloured ink, which decorate the gaps between cut-out texts and lead the eye on. The earliest books, begun in 1931 when he was eleven years old, were re-structured or re-edited in 1937, to include quotations from his reading of literature in his final year at school and his first year of university study. Thus they provide an eclectic guide to an eclectic mind: clever, responsive, visually acute, at once emotionally absorbed and coolly appraising. Perhaps it was also an acquisitive and determined mind, because he was by his own admission 'quite ruthless' in cutting up second-hand books and journals for the lines and images he had selected.

The principles for selection reveal that same inclusive, interested, sometimes quirky approach to wide-ranging aspects of existence that readers now praise in his mature poetry. The opening pages of the first book in the library contain, among other items, articles on Chinese mythography and Babylonian mathematical astronomy together with quotations from the Old English *Beowulf*: 'lagu drusade / waeter under wolcnum, wael-dreore fag'. No translation is given, but in his own later version it is: 'The tarn lay still, / The water with death's red stained under the sky' (ll. 1630–1). Newspaper clippings from, for example, the *Observer* of 25 September 1938 on 'The Ladybird in Folklore' take their place alongside more technical articles in zoology. e.g. on the gynandromorph ant, and there are stray quotations that have the effect of aphorism – ' Lust and forgetfulness have been amongst us' – or of humour – 'Nous sommes les tendres Lapins / Assis sur leurs petits derrières'. Architecture and sacred imagery from different religions make an impact, with illustrations of statues and reliefs from old churches and ruined temples. Arcane aspects of language are noted, such as examples from the Musée de L'Homme in Paris of the Tifinagh script, which is thought to be derived from an ancient Berber script and is used in North African languages such as Tamazight, Tamasheq and Amazigh. Scientific discovery is also present, in 'the first natural colour photograph of an eclipse ever produced', that was clipped from *National Geographic* in February 1937.

Two quotations in this volume encapsulate the motives of this encyclopaedic exercise. The first suggests the ferment of a young creative mind that is encountering, in a direct and emotional way, new words, images and ideas at an almost heart-stopping rate:

> The vortex of language comes up in my throat like a soft ball of blood.

The second suggests something of EM's later poetic skill in giving voices to a variety of objects, creatures and historical or imagined characters, through a powerful sense of identification with their viewpoint:

42

There was a child went forth every day,
And the first object he looked upon that object he became,
And that object became part of him for the day or a certain
    part of the day,
Or for many years or stretching cycles of years.

That idea (from Walt Whitman's *Leaves of Grass*) would surely have intrigued the young EM to try it out for himself and see what happened. It was a technique that would serve him well in poem after poem.

Other cuttings show a self-reflexive interest in his own mental facilities. There is a note on 'The Largest Human Brain on Record' from the *Bulletin* of 17 October 1936, or this article from *Chambers' Journal* in February of the same year:

> Mr Bernard Zufall, a resident of New York, has committed to memory the 1117 pages that make up the Manhattan Telephone Directory [. . .].

The overall effect, and possibly a shaping influence, is surreal. EM was studying art at school and had access in the Art Room to a library of artworks in reproduction. Surrealism interested him greatly, and the poetry of Dylan Thomas, who was also influenced by it, appears in these scrapbooks alongside stanzas from Edward Thomas ('Tall Nettles'), and by Gerard Manley Hopkins ('Tom's Garland: upon the Unemployed') whose work he first encountered in the *Faber Book of Modern Verse* around 1937 and found very striking indeed.

When I first studied Dylan Thomas with EM in the early 1970s, I was puzzled by his enthusiasm for this dense poetry that was so different from his own clear if experimental style of that period. I was ignorant then of his own early poems in *Dies Irae* (1952) which echo something of the Welshman's style. In the scrapbook, his pre-war taste had included this stanza from Thomas's 'A Saint about to fall':

Cry joy that this witchlike midwife second
Bullies into rough seas you so gentle
And makes with a flick of your thumb and sun
A thundering bullring of your silent and girl-circled island.[4]

Dylan Thomas is sometimes linked with the New Apocalypse movement, which in the late 1930s set itself in reaction to the rational and social poetry of Auden and others. Its poetry focused on non-rational impulses, weaving in strands of surrealism and expressionism. Its members' work in verse, prose and criticism was anthologised in *The New Apocalypse* (1939), followed by *The White Horseman* (1941) and *The Crown and the Sickle* (1943). The latter two volumes appeared while EM was on active service, of course, but it is interesting to think about the scrapbooks as a cognate response by a slightly younger contemporary to an artistic trend in which other Scottish and Welsh poets such as G.S. Fraser, Norman MacCaig and Vernon Watkins were also involved. The co-editor of these anthologies, J.F. Hendry, was also a Glaswegian poet, born eight years before EM. Like EM, he studied French and Russian at Glasgow University before national service and subsequent academic work as a translator and professor.

Although the scrapbooks can appear to be an amalgam, a kaleidoscope, a random assortment, EM would later speak up for randomness as a 'structuring' principle. He referred here particularly to the hundred poems that made up 'The New Divan' (1977), a major work that would eventually reflect his wartime experiences, and argued that it does have 'a *kind* of structure' but that it also uses

a kind of randomness in the sense that one is not following a story that really goes forward step by step. Characters appear and reappear. You're not certain whether the characters are autobiographical or not. That kind of randomness is something that did attract me. And, if you like, the idea of non-structure is almost a structural idea in itself [. . .]. In Arabic or Persian poetry they're rather fond of the idea that a 'divan' as they call it, a collection of poems, is something that you enter; you move around; you can cast your eye here and there, you look, you pick, you perhaps retrace your steps.[5]

Although he admits that this procedure is not something a critic could easily analyse in structural terms, nevertheless there would be 'something that in a mysterious, subterranean sense would be structure, an emotional structure, a structure perhaps relating to the life of the person who had written it'. A similar sort of deep relational structure makes the scrapbooks a fascinating collection. They provided a creative outlet that EM could not finally give up until his poetry came into its own in the 1960s.

Like the child who went forth each day able to identify with anything he happened to see and appropriate it to himself, EM seems a surrealist from the start. Discussing this artistic movement in Colin Nicholson's *Poem, Purpose and Place* (1992: 66), EM reached down his well-worn copy of Herbert Read's *Surrealism* (1936), containing the French poet Paul Eluard's essay 'Poetic Evidence' which states that every surrealist

strives to unite the imagination and nature, to consider all possibilities a reality, to prove to us that no dualism exists between imagination and reality, that everything the human spirit can conceive and create springs from the same vein, is made of the same matter as his flesh and blood, and the world about him.

GROWING UP

So much for artistic awakenings. But what of the normal flesh and blood issues of teenage years – of becoming alive to the world of sex, death, friendship and 'the meaning of life'?

Although his father and mother may have given the opposite impression in company, they were quite a loving couple at home. EM, who was always called Eddie in the family, had a memory dating from when he was about thirteen years of age, of his parents on a winter's evening sitting on opposite sides of a coal fire. From time to time his father would reach across and run his hand up his wife's silk-stockinged leg, which would crackle with static. Observing this erotic scene, their son thought to himself: 'So that is what married people do!'.

When his father was at work, EM was often in his mother's company. Madge Morgan got on well with her woman friends, particularly one whom her son knew as 'Aunt Rena', who was married to a 'wealthy' fruit merchant called Harry MacNeill and also had an only son, Eric (wealthy, in that EM remembers them going on a world tour). Through the MacNeills, he encountered another young woman called Mlle Rougerelle, a friend of the family. She had the air of being a 'fast' lady of the 'flirty twenties', and EM recalled that 'I didn't get any of my questions answered about her'. Thus he could see, if not always feel, that his life was 'lonely only up to a point' and that he did meet some interesting people.

At secondary school he was more fascinated by the sexual exhibitionism of some of his male classmates than by the developing sexual appearance of the girls in the class. This preference would become more pronounced when at fourteen he won a scholarship and left Rutherglen Academy for the all-boys High School of Glasgow:

> But even in this mixed school, I was aware of the fact that I was being attracted to boys more than to girls [. . .] so I knew at that age, twelve or thirteen, certainly fourteen, that there was something, although I couldn't really define it, you could hardly read about it at that time, there was little one could read about it.[6]

This preference would be one that later on, from the age of sixteen to eighteen ('seventeen especially') EM would begin to worry about, 'with very strong guilt feelings about it', but not so much before then: he was just enjoying the new world that was opening out for him. Nevertheless as a Scottish boy of the time he would have been subject to the social conditioning that pertained:

Parents looked upon gender confusion with horror [. . .]. A boy
who did not grow up with manly attributes was unlikely to make a
success of himself. Taunting, picking on, merciless teasing and
social ostracisation awaited the effeminate boy or man. It was a
hard society, and boys had to be tough to survive.[7]

Even into his old age, EM considered that his parents did not
really know much at all about homosexuality. He may have
mistaken their reticence for ignorance. There seems an element
of anxiety in their encouragement of a bookish son into the local
football team and tennis club. Later, his mother would intervene
on her son's behalf, unasked, during a period of unhappy
separation from his friend, John Scott.

It is true that they appear to be conventional Scottish adults of
their period, even to their preference of holiday venues on the East
and West coasts. As Richard Finlay notes, family holidays were
becoming increasingly common at this time, as industries closed
down for the fortnight of the local fair and there was an exodus of
city workers to seaside resorts on the west and east, seeking freedom
and fresh air. This normality did not prevent new or shocking
experiences, however. At about the age of twelve, EM had his first
sight of a dead body on the beach at North Berwick:

> I saw an enormous
> sudden freak
> wave pound
> a swimmer down
> and crashing cast him
> limp on the sand.
> Amateur hands
> ran to pump him.
> Blue; too late.[8]

Back at home, parental anxieties focused mainly on their son's
progress at school, and a growing apprehension that the standard
of teaching at Rutherglen Academy was not very good. This

centred on Mathematics and Science, both important in the sort of careers they knew best and had envisaged for EM. His father was a businessman and most of their friends were also in business and, as he remembered it, their talk tended to be about industry or finance or current affairs or the most popular records they would play on the gramophone – the immediate events of the day. His parents could clearly see that EM was interested in art, however, and so it came about that he almost left school at the age of fifteen:

> I had no thoughts of an academic career at that stage at all, but they knew I was good at drawing and painting. There was a chance of a job at Templeton's carpet factory. I would have been a kind of apprentice designer, I suppose. I was attracted by this idea [. . .] but perhaps in the end they thought it was a risky thing to do and wouldn't lead to much [. . .].[9]

The alternative plan was for EM to sit a scholarship for the independent High School of Glasgow. He was successful, and completed the last three years of his schooling there from 1934 to 1937, specialising in French, Art and English. There was more emphasis on sporting activities, never his strong point. Instead, EM used charm and wit to find acceptance. For example, when a classmate was talking about the metallic safety strip embedded in a pound note to prevent forgery, EM accepted this as a challenge to split a note in two. He kept the two halves as proof of the feat, in the current scrapbook, but then took it further:

> I seized another note
> washed my hands
> examined my nails
> took chair to table.
> In best midday light
> made one note two
> removed metal strip
> made two one again.[10]

This time he retained the metal strip and re-circulated the note, with a schoolboy's sense of bravado. There could have been a subversive enjoyment here in undermining the laws of profit and loss that his parents lived by. By the age of 16 he had also told them that he no longer had sufficient belief to attend church with them. They seem to have respected his views, although his father continued to press the case for his son to join him in the freemasons as an alternative. In Scotland, this might have proved useful for future business connections.

In 1935, his mother thought that EM should learn to play the piano which they had in the house, and engaged a music student at the University, Lex Allan, to teach him. He was about six years older than his pupil and lived near them in Rutherglen, with a reputation as a good teacher of beginners. EM immediately recognised that here was an interesting person from whom he could learn a great deal, as they talked about contemporary writing and politics. The Spanish Civil War was then being fought, in which many writers and intellectuals had enlisted on the republican side:

> I remember him saying to me when I was about sixteen [. . .] you know, if you were a couple of years older you could have been going to Spain, have you ever thought of that? The thought hadn't struck me actually – I suppose I read the papers but I hadn't thought of going there like some of the English poets [. . .] and I had to think about that.[11]

There was a gay undercurrent to the relationship, perhaps signalled from the start:

> He came up to the house, and after he went away my father said, 'He's all right, but he's a bit of a jessy.' He didn't mean it in a very negative way – just that his manners were slightly effeminate. He didn't say, 'Don't darken my doorstep again'. And he did come and teach me the piano.[12]

EM found him very intelligent and widely read, interested in all the arts but especially in the writing scene of the 1930s, including gay authors:

> Whether he knew or guessed that I was already somewhat knowledgeable about it, I just don't know. He was quite open about it. Though I remember the first time he talked about all these gay authors, he said at the end of it, 'I don't know how we got onto this subject!', joking about it.[13]

The gay Spanish poet, Federico García Lorca (1889–1936) who was killed soon after the Civil War began, also came up in conversation, although really in a political connection. Already committed to his university studies, Lex Allan did not himself want to volunteer to fight in Spain:

> but he was aware of the fact that very important political things were happening, and Lorca came up in the context of that conversation. I remember getting hold of some of Lorca's work after that and having a look at it and being quite surprised, I suppose, that there seemed to be so little about it that one would identify with writing about being gay or writing on gay subjects [. . .]. So I was left wondering a great deal about Lorca, but being very much impressed by him, liking his work a lot.[14]

We can see here how EM's self-development combined responsive listening, research from original sources and a willingness to engage with people and politics that were beyond the ambit of his family. To his parents, to be political meant to be left wing, conservatism being for them the natural scheme of things.

He got some awareness of right-wing politics during a school trip to Germany in 1937. The boys were briefed beforehand about what to do or not to do. Because they were going to be to some extent the guests of the *Hitlerjugend*, the Hitler Youth Movement, the pupils had been warned always to shake hands and never to give the raised arm salute when meeting their

contemporaries from German schools. Staff from the High
School accompanied them. They visited Bonn and Koblenz
and travelled along the Rhine. EM took lots of photographs,
including one of an aeroplane in a field when he was out walking
beside the river. At which point he and his friends were speedily
surrounded, arrested and taken to an army camp for questioning.
The camera was confiscated, but EM was told that it might be
returned the following day. He found his way back to the camp
and retrieved it – minus the film – but with a clearer understanding of the new German State.

The trip was also memorable to him in terms of his sexuality.
All of the boys had been told to wear kilts, and that true Scotsmen
wore nothing under the kilt: an order which they duly obeyed
with great pleasure, as he recalled. Sexual play was not taken very
seriously, and seemed to be viewed by teaching staff as a phase
that the boys would grow out of.

In the year prior to the trip to Germany, his earliest published
poems appeared in the *High School of Glasgow Magazine* XXXV
2 & 3, as well as a story entitled 'Kyriof: a mystery', a drawing
called 'View from the Art Room', and also Art Club notes on the
term's activities in volume XXXVI. EM was noted as secretary
of the Art Club and also a sub-editor of the magazine. 'Kyriof: a
mystery' opens in a rocky sea-girt landscape that would remain
the setting for many of his future poems of quest and exploration:

> Kyriof bounded lightly across the remaining ravine and paused,
> expectantly, at the edge of the cliff. A moment's intense gaze
> dispelled any doubts he had had. This was the place, and the time
> was drawing near [. . .].
>
> Storm-petrels and seagulls wheeled and shrieked over his head,
> shattering the silence of that lonely spot with the thousand echoes
> of their wild, raucous clamour.

His poems and story are signed KAA, after the rock snake in
Kipling's *The Jungle Book*. EM would retain this pseudonym for

his poems published in *GUM* (*Glasgow University Magazine*) in his two and a half years of study before being called up for national service. That he kept the name suggests it was in some sense a significant expression of his writing self. The list of 'Books I Have Read' places *The Second Jungle Book* first, in his early teens, and *The Jungle Book* shortly thereafter.

Both books chart the growth to maturity of the boy, Mowgli, as he experiences his divided allegiance between the responsible code of the animals, with their stoical sense of duty, and the undignified variability of human society. This sense of doubleness of identity may well have attracted the young EM. Kaa, the powerful and ancient snake, is one of Mowgli's mentors – totally opposite to the devious comic villain of the Disney cartoon version. The original Kaa represents wisdom and strength, as well as conveying a coiling sensuous quality, as when he and Mowgli bathe and wrestle.

There is a combination of mythic wisdom, exoticism and mature guidance here that EM had already sought to gather in his scrapbooks and, somehow, to express in his still immature writer's voice. In Kipling's story 'The Spring Running', Kaa tells Mowgli as he prepares to leave the jungle and return to human duties that 'It is hard to cast the skin'. But the teenage boy must lose the skin of his old life in order to grow into a new identity, and EM would take on poetry to express that glimpsed 'maturer' and wiser self.

It was not yet certain, however, that he would study literature at university. The original plan had been for him to go to the School of Art but, as with the early idea of the carpet factory, his parents were unsure. It was a side of life they knew nothing much about, and it seemed risky. The decision was finally taken on the advice of a 'left-wing' lecturer in the School of Art, who visited the house to give an appraisal of EM's portfolio of work, both visual and literary:

He said I was a very good drawer, that I could represent things very well but he didn't think there was enough there to make a

52

career out of it [. . .] he read my stories and essays and thought they were much better.[15]

So we have this unnamed lecturer to thank for the ultimate poetic direction that was taken. EM considered that he liked drawing and writing 'about equally' at that time. He went on to study English without much of a career plan, putting down the Civil Service 'as the kind of thing I might do, not that I had any hope, desire, wish or longing'. Some examples of his art work are preserved in the Mitchell Library in Glasgow, and show the influence of Art Deco and the 'Glasgow Style' of artists and designers such as Charles Rennie Mackintosh (1868–1928) and his wife, Margaret Mackintosh (1865–1933). Although EM did not 'keep up' his skills as a painter, his designer's eye clearly helped him later to respond to and explore the possibilities of concrete poetry, print and calligraphy in the 1960s.

In about 1948, shortly after he began lecturing in the University of Glasgow, EM took part in a test organized by a member of the Psychology Department who was interested in perception and looking for 'achromotopsiacs' or colour-blind subjects. His experience in Art classes at school had made EM suspect he might be one, and he volunteered to take the Isahara test:

an elegant book of colour plates where arrangements of dots are read to give different numbers by normal and colour-blind people – very convincing. [. . .] He also tested me with skeins of silk. With green in my hand, I confidently said 'Pink!' to the gasps of my colleagues.[16]

This may explain some of the 'surreal' effects of his early paintings, and of those colourful shirts for which he became well known on campus. On the poetry reading circuit as years went by, his yellow, pink or powder-blue jackets often matched the brightness of his performance. Whenever I bought him clothes in later life, I had to 'explain' what the colour they were, often by reference to features of the natural world which we both knew he might well be seeing differently. He was also interested in this from a gender perspective, since about 10% of men are supposed to be colour blind, but almost no women.

THE EARLIEST POEMS

EM's early poems in the Department of Special Collections in Glasgow University Library are fair copied on to the blank back pages of unused stamp albums, rather as his scrapbooks were recycled ledgers.[17] His first extant literary works thus back on to Victoria, Venezuela and Upper Volta. The poems are less exotic and much more 'impressionist' than his 'surrealist' collection of visual imagery, reflecting his early exposure to a traditional kind of poetry:

> It was mostly Romantic poetry we got at school – Keats and Tennyson and Shelley. That was the first poetry I liked and it wasn't realistic. It wasn't the kind of poetry I should have been reading as a person living in Glasgow in the thirties [. . .]. It took me a while to understand that you could write about anything – ugly things, dirty things, painful things. It can all be written about but no-one told me that at school.[18]

'The Pond' (May 1936) is well observed in two contrasting weathers or moods. 'The Willows' (June 1937) describes morning mist vanishing 'in dove-grey wings' to reveal 'Each tiny leaf gold-flecked'. In 'The Opium Smoker' published in the school magazine in the same month, he enjoyed trying to imagine what this man's life would be like:

> Pathetically raising bloodshot eyes
> To watch the swinging lamp's smoke-misted glare.

There is a certain amount of formal experimentation with line length in 'Rain'. Elsewhere a tendency towards the adjectival and conventionally poetic continues into his earliest work published in

Glasgow University Magazine in December of the same year, 'Nocturne: Ruins and Music':

> Darkling, pale-fluted,
> Soft columns silhouetted mistily
> Against the night sky's velvet [. . .].

A gloomier and introspective mood is evident in these university poems, however, possibly connected with the guilt he was feeling about his own identity at this stage. 'Evening Light' published in *GUM* in December 1937 at the end of his first term evokes something of the mood of such post-war works as 'The Vision of Cathkin Braes' (1952. CP: 43–9) or 'Glasgow Green' (1968. CP: 168):

> I walked quickly through the darkening wood
> And in my mind was darkness.
> The black-armed trees were symbols of the mood
> In which my thick thoughts, crowding
> Sought a breath of freeing air – and all around
> The mocking shapes were crouching,
> Shapes of bushes which I always found
> Half-human in the twilight.

The poem ends with a wished-for poise or calm:

> Into my heart this wondrous stillness crept:
> Into the cloister of torment
> Where dark-winged desires flocked together and leapt
> Into my darkness came light.

The setting of this poem probably derives from Cathkin Braes, a wooded hillcrest stretching along the south-eastern edge of the Glasgow conurbation, rising above Burnside. When the atmosphere at home grew too stifling or tense, EM would walk there, mainly alone in his early or mid teens. But once he became a university student, he often went with George Hunter. He was EM's intellectual equal, and would often share top examination or competition placings with him. In 1938, EM came first in the Coalter Prize essay on 'The Uses of Words', with a prize of £10, and G.K. Hunter came second and gained £5. He would ultimately become a renowned Shakespearean scholar and professor at Warwick and Yale universities. And he was instrumental in encouraging his friend to enlist in the armed forces. As war approached, EM still inclined to a pacifist, or at least non-combatant, position:

> I think in the late 1930s, just before war, politics, whether left or right, were strongly bound up with the peace movement. The Peace Pledge Union and pacifism was talked about, as I remember it, possibly more than fascism, communism or socialism [. . .]. There was a strong desire not to have war and it was this I was interested in more than politics itself. I think I was a socialist but not a member of any political party.[19]

The hesitancies and qualifications here are characteristic of EM's way of speaking, but honestly reflect what was a conflicted or confusing time for him.

The subjects he had chosen to study reflected his academic strengths and interests: English, French, History, Political Economy, and Russian. But Russian was chosen in part because a friend, Frank Mason, was a communist at that stage and studying the subject from a political point of view. He was heterosexual, but EM 'was bowled over about him', and chose the Russian course partly as a reason to be in his company. They may have met in one of various university societies. Although EM would always claim not to be particularly happy with group activities, he had joined the Literary Society, the Zoological Society and several others. More probably, as both were studying Political Economy, they first met at lectures.

Frank Mason also shared his interest in film. Some of EM's most vivid early memories were of films his parents had taken him to see: Fritz Lang's *Metropolis* (1926) with its nightmare vision of futuristic urban living, and *The White Hell of Pitz Palu* (1929), in which Leni Riefenstahl acted, with its powerful images of a chase across ice and snow. One of the poignant memories of this unrequited love for his straight classmate was of being 'stood up' at the *Cosmo*, which was, and remains, the city's essential art house cinema, now renamed the Glasgow Film Theatre. In fact, the arrangement had merely slipped Frank Mason's mind, but that did not lessen the emotional impact that EM later recalled in 'Tram Ride 1939 (F.M.)', in *Sweeping Out the Dark* (1994: 76):

> How cold it is to stand on the street corner
> at nineteen, in the foggy Glasgow winter,
> with pinched white face and hands in pockets, straining
> to catch that single stocky gallus figure
> who might be anyone but was one only [. . .].

It would all end in tears, we might say, and it does:

> ridiculous but uncontrollable tears, a choking
> you gulp back instantly, no one has heard it,
> shameful – shameful – to be dominated
> by such emotions [. . .].

At that stage, in the second year of his course, EM found himself in love with both Frank Mason and Jean Watson. She was a very intelligent young woman, who after the war took triple Honours in English, French and Latin. EM would later claim that this was mainly a platonic relationship, possibly emanating from his own 'self-repression': 'I knew there was something wrong somewhere, and that I would have to deal with this as well as I could, but I tried to deal with it by getting rid of it, at that age'.[20] But there is no doubting its sincerity on her part. Her long letters to EM in Glentress army camp reveal an articulate and emotional person, vibrantly committed to him even to the extent of losing a sense of her own worth in admiration of his. In 'Love and a Life' he hears again 'her ringing laugh / Cut through the draff and chaff / like a knife-edge' (*A Book of Lives*: 88).

Intellectual stimulation at university matched the complexity of the emotional life he was leading. EM gained first prize in French and English, somewhat to his surprise: no-one had told him how well he was doing. He won a prize in Political Economy too. His list of 'Books I Have Read' reveals, however, a deepening interest in philosophy, psychology, science and religion in addition to standard literary studies. He enjoyed new encounters with the French symbolist poets, Mallarmé and Rimbaud, and in particular Baudelaire:

> I got into [Baudelaire] before I got into Eliot and it seemed to me that he was one of the few who had, at an early date really, the sense in poetry of what was going to be a modern city and I liked that tremendously. I think subconsciously I had been looking for that and not finding it, but it seemed to be there in Baudelaire.[21]

Baudelaire's combination of classical poetic form with dark or damaged modern subject-matter may well have influenced EM's later focus on the sonnet as a vehicle for exploring contemporary Scottish issues in his 'Glasgow Sonnets' (CP: 289–92) and 'Sonnets from Scotland' (CP: 437–57). In the Russian class he also discovered Mayakovsky, and recalled discussing his poetry with the left-wing Scottish poet, Morris Blythman.

At the same time, he was returning to the *Faber Book of Modern Verse*, and learning from the work of Gerard Manley Hopkins, Hart Crane and Laura Riding. An *Anthology of World Poetry*, edited by Mark Van Doran in the early 1930s, with translations from many different languages, also made an impact. Hafiz, the Persian poet whose example he would follow in 'The New Divan' (1977), his belated war poem, also figured in this influential pre-war text.

In his second year at university there was the further stimulation of a trip to Paris over the summer of 1938, with his mother and her sister. There was the chance to practise his French and to see at first hand some of the works of art and architecture that he had continued to paste into his Scrapbooks. They stayed at the Hôtel Roblin, near the Madeleine, and he always remembered its dark rooms with flagstone floors. He also visited the *Empire Exhibition, Scotland*, which was held at Bellahouston Park from May to December. It attracted twelve million visitors, and featured, to EM's delight, much modernist architecture in the design of its pavilions, including the Palace of Engineering, the Palace of Industry and the Tait Tower, or the 'Tower of Empire'. This was later demolished in July 1939, in case it might be used as a landmark for German bombers – or so it was claimed. It is possible to see the Festival buildings in digital reconstruction from contemporary film footage, and imagine the impact that their confident modernism would have made on Scots who had lived through years of economic uncertainty. EM responded with particular enthusiasm to this vision of the architectural future in a Glaswegian context.

Another part of his temperament was reacting just as positively to Anglo-Saxon poetry:

> I was one of the few who positively liked Anglo-Saxon. It was generally thought to be a hard part of the course and wasn't very popular. But I liked it and fairly soon I suppose got into the way of being able to read the language and enjoy it. The poetry appealed to me very, very strongly. I liked both the [. . .] elegiac side of it which is pretty strong, but also the heroic side of it [. . .] and I thought I would like to have a shot at it. I had read various translations, and it didn't seem to me that any of them really met the case, and I thought I would just go through the whole thing, and do it.[22]

There is a remarkable ambition here in an eighteen year old, as well as a confidence in his own linguistic and poetic skills. This is also evident in EM's steady submission of poems for publication in *GUM* and also in *Poetry Today* (1) 1939:51, a quarterly supplement of *The Poetry Review*.

At the same time, EM also developed a friendship with a

young poet of equal talent and ambition. W.S. Graham had left
school at fourteen to take up an apprenticeship as an engineering
draughtsman in his Clydeside home of Greenock. He had
followed up on his interests in art and literature through evening
classes at the University, however, and was introduced to EM
through a mutual friend, Norman Thomson. This led to a strong
friendship between the two poets, and they sustained a correspondence across many years in which their lives diverged.
Graham seemed 'a very dashing, good-looking person then',
as well as being poetically gifted, and they provided each other
with engaged and careful responses to the verse they were
writing.

Graham gained a bursary to study at Newbattle Abbey, an
adult education college in Dalkeith near Edinburgh, where he met
Nessie Dunsmuir, his future life partner. She came from Blan-
tyre, a mining town on the other side of Cathkin Braes, and EM
visited them there, fascinated by the energy of another sort of life,
working-class and bohemian combined:

> Sidney Graham
> sitting up in bed
> pyjama jacket
> open to the waist
> tearing into a steak
> clutched in both hands:
> the poet at home.
> I watched fascinated
> as gobbets of grizzle
> splattered the sheets.
> 'Christ', cried Nessie,
> 'we *have* got a plate!'[23]

INTO WAR

When EM was called up in 1940, he was in a turmoil of
uncertainty, with his broadly pacifist views about the war now

adding to the strains of his emotional and sexual life. In the English Language exam of this Junior Honours year, instead of addressing the question on the paper, he wrote an essay on time, life, war and identity. Ritchie Girvan, whom he admired tremendously as a scholar and lecturer, simply commented: 'You must have been very unhappy when you wrote that essay'.

EM first registered as a conscientious objector, and then waited months before being called to a tribunal. Meanwhile Frank Mason had gone into the artillery, and George Hunter was set to enter the Royal Navy. His other love, Jean,

> said yes to war; she had a very Latin word
> about coming back with your shield or on it [. . .].
>
> (*A Book of Lives*: 88)

During that intervening period he came to the personal view that it would be wrong to 'stand aside' as a conscientious objector, as Norman MacCaig would ultimately do. He had a desire to take part, in some capacity, in great events:

> I think I felt it was wrong to stand aside from what was happening. It wasn't just simply a capitalist war that the worker wouldn't support. There was an actual enemy over there.[24]

When EM had at first put his name down as a conscientious objector, his father had taken him to the family lawyer who examined him on the sincerity of his motives, and he had passed that stringent test. But by the time he came before his official tribunal, he had made up his mind to ask to join the Royal Army Medical Corps. There he could play his part in the war effort, but in a non-violent capacity. That was accepted, and so matters moved forward towards Glentress camp and its cold winter of training for Private Morgan in basic military discipline and medical aid.

Before he left, he saw his Granny Morgan for the last time in Ayr. She was a 'ladylike' woman whom he did not see often, although he did not know why this was. On his last visit there with his father, they found her arguing with a lawyer who was trying to sort out details of her will, and she seemed to EM a strong-minded character. His father had brought her a bag of plums, and he remembered her 'taking a plum with her bony fingers and putting it in her mouth with a glint in her eye, as if she was in a Vermeer painting'.

In preparation for a war from which he might not return, EM burned personal letters. He gave his Scrapbooks to Jean, as a token of their love, or of himself. They parted on a note of tension:

> With my call-up papers
> I stood at the tram stop
> talking to Jean.
> 'Don't know when I'll see you,
> everything's uncertain.'
> 'I don't know' she said
> very sharp 'if I like
> to be included in everything.'
> 'Well – ' I said,
> turned on my heel
> and quickly walked off.[25]

George Hunter meanwhile went into the navy. In many ways the university friends and rivals would follow opposite trajectories:

> [He] had a pretty bad time as regards the weather and scary assaults on the convoy but he came through it [. . .] it always struck me that when I was in the Middle East in a very hot place and he was in the desperate cold of the very north of Norway, that was very interesting, the kind of comparison there.[26]

After convoy protection, Hunter worked in naval intelligence in Sri Lanka, operating throughout the Pacific and learning Russian, Japanese and other languages. He then became a 'career academic', proceeding directly to Oxford University after the war for a B.Litt. in lieu of an honours degree and then doctoral studies. Subsequently he taught in Hull, Reading, Liverpool and Warwick universities, becoming pro-vice-chancellor in the last of these before gaining an inter-disciplinary chair in Renaissance Studies at Yale. EM's own military and academic careers would be far less varied.

The two men had entered the services as intellectual equals and they remained friends after the war. EM did not dwell on comparisons that might be drawn between their careers, since his main ambitions were directed otherwise. These were much more creatively focused, if no less intense. Perhaps they would necessarily be slower in realisation. He would finish the war with the same rank as he started, and return to Glasgow University freighted with experience that might some day be turned into poetry.

EM had not yet found a voice that, like Baudelaire's, would encompass both classical poise and the paradoxes of modern life. His study of economics and his conversations with Frank Mason had led him to a greater understanding of the poverty, unemployment, blighted lives and loss of hope that Scotland had experienced in the 1930s, and from which his own upbringing and intellectual interests had largely shielded him. But he was not blind to these matters, or to his own creative inadequacy in this regard:

> There are the houses of this dark,
> Silent cells of this monstrous city;
> I move among them like a ghost
> My silence pity.
> Dwellings of man, made by man,
> Factories of the blind spirit,
> These, I thought, are the halls of death
> Our souls inherit.

> ('Lazarus Gate' March 1939)

63

The poem ends with an aspiration that the writer will:

> [. . .] move among these houses like a flame
> Silent, amid snow.

But the decade in reality ended with the young poet trying to coax fire from damp sticks for the cooks, so that breakfast for the awkward squad of raw recruits could get under way.

CHAPTER FOUR

A Universe Unbroken 1940–1950

At thirty I thought life had passed me by,
translated *Beowulf* for want of love.
And one night stands in city centre lanes –
they were dark in those days – were wild but bleak.
Sydney Graham in London said 'you know
I always thought so', kissed me on the cheek.
And I translated Rilke's *Loneliness*
is like a rain, and week after week after week
strained to unbind myself,
sweated to speak.

'Epilogue: Seven Decades' (CP: 594)

This stoical chapter title is challenged by the near despair of the epigraph: 'At thirty I thought life had passed me by'. Extremes of life were experienced by EM in war and uneasy peace. In his mid-twenties he had come home from the heightened life of the senses that came with the scope and danger of army life. On the crescent of coastline from Egypt and Suez through Palestine to the Lebanon, in the landscapes whose artifacts and ruins he once researched and pasted in his schoolboy scrapbooks, he had explored new cultures and relationships, encountering aspects of his own identity. Now he had returned to the different risks of sexual encounters in Glasgow's wild, bleak city-centre lanes.

Yet he never quite lost the intuitions or intimations gained in those wartime experiences, even though he would find himself unable to 'unbind' and express them openly for thirty years, until 'The New Divan' (1977):

> On guard, I climb the water tower. Strengthening
> stars are thick in absolute black. Who ever mourned
> the sun? A universe unbroken
> mends man and the dark. No northern mists envelop
> me, there's nothing but the silent metal, the pack of stars
> from
> zenith to horizon blazing down
> on mile on mile of undulating sand. (CP: 328)

Far from the northern mists of Glentress, EM experienced a clearer sense of living within history:

> One star moves, drones. Position
> on a map's the universe. The night is Rommel's tree:
> searchlights cut it, history the secretion.
>
> (CP: 328)

He had travelled to this point in one of many merchant ships converted into troop carriers, sailing round the Cape of Good Hope in 1941 to avoid the dangerous Mediterranean:

> South then, south round Africa, months of sweat, daily deck
> drills to make
> us leaner and lanker – [. . .].

The same poem in 'Love and a Life' recalls:

> Hundreds of hammocks swaying and snoring – time for
> ribaldries, no
> space for rancour – [. . .].

The memorable voyage would, in his mind, turn this unlikely band of newly trained soldiers into something akin to the Anglo-Saxon seafarers he had left behind in his Old English texts at University. He recalls them in alliterative verse:

A Universe Unbroken 1940–1950

> Water-watchers all
> Through sun and through squall
> In case some sleekit dark sub from Kiel should pull an eerie
> flanker.

(A Book of Lives: 88)

With him on the journey EM had taken some books and also the love letters from Jean Watson, which he 'could reread even when slightly beer slurred'. Yet he was living now in a mainly male world. For the middle-class only child this was 'a culture shock [. . .] absolutely overcrowded, over-packed to bursting and the conditions pretty dreadful – but you deal with it. That was the first time I'd slept in a hammock'.[1] Slipping free of the familial and social disciplines of Scotland, he was able to experience the 'libertinism' (as he would later call it in *The Cape of Good Hope*, 1955) of a more hedonistic military life. This was constrained in some senses, of course, not only by military discipline but by 'an aspect that most of those who take part in war must be familiar with – non-heroic, not enormously dangerous, potentially boring yet not always so, physically uncomfortable, concerned chiefly with the minutiae of survival under difficult conditions'.[2] And yet for young men living on the edge of danger, sexuality might be heightened by risk. In EM's case he had entered a world 'where other loves were not to be ignored' (*A Book of Lives*: 88).

Arriving in North Africa in temperatures well over 100 degrees Fahrenheit ('you hadn't time to worry about it or meditate on it') he found himself:

> part of a huge body of people in the unit all talking together and just doing what you were told. [. . .]. The tents were already put up, everything was ready for us, so we had to float out to the tents and get our kitbags stowed away and get used to using mess tins and so on, a kind of series of little practical things that had to be done [. . .].[3]

A contemporary account of the conditions at the 600-bed 42nd General Hospital where he was based at El Ballah can be found in

67

an official war history of the 2nd General Hospital of the New Zealand forces in North Africa. This was established alongside the four British hospitals on the same site in 1941:

> El Ballah – meaning a date palm, though no one ever found it there – was a stretch of desert south of Kantara, some three miles from the Suez Canal and almost alongside the Sweet Water Canal [. . .]. Most of the wards were in Nissen and Army huts, some were tented, and there were also administration and departmental buildings [. . .]. El Ballah was within easy reach of Cairo, while Port Said and Ismailia also made good shopping and leave centres.[4]

This history confirms the enemy flights against which EM was on watch in the poem already cited: intensive but sporadic nuisance raids were being launched on the Canal Zone from aircraft based in Crete. The Germans also attempted to sow mines in the Suez Canal. The 54th General Hospital was severely damaged in early September 1941.

Because he could type, EM's main duties were as Quarter-master's clerk, but occasionally he was called upon for stretcher bearing and to help in the operating theatre, including assisting at the amputation of limbs. He did not keep any diary or notebook at the time:

> I knew that my memory was pretty strong: you don't have to lose things, you don't have to write them down, they're still there if you can just withdraw them later on [. . .]. I was quite glad in a way that I hadn't taken notes, my memories were [. . .] visual and were quite real. I can remember things thirty years later that were as if they had been the day before – they were very strong.[5]

Of course, we have already learned something of the creative power of EM's visual imagination, and also that 'The New Divan' sequence blends fictional characters, memories of his reading, and actual people or events in a deliberately unstructured Middle Eastern form of verse. Sinbad and the Old Man of the Sea figure early in these Arabian tales, and the poet sees himself as a story-spinner within an ancient tradition. Nevertheless, as the sequence nears its end point, actual recollection appears more vividly in the last twenty or so of the poems:

> I dreaded stretcher-bearing,
> my fingers would slip on the two sweat-soaked handles,
> my muscles not used to the strain.
> The easiest trip of all I don't forget,
> in the desert, that dead officer
> drained of blood, wasted away,
> leg amputated at the thigh,
> wrapped in a rough sheet, light as a child,
> rolling from side to side of the canvas [. . .].
>
> (CP: 329–30)

Poems 86–90, 95 and 97–9 seem largely based on the realities of military life as experienced by EM.

He had a good working relationship with the lieutenant who was his Quartermaster: 'an ugly little man like a monkey and with a vile, a violent tongue, a real soldier's tongue – his vocabulary was searing'.[6] The pair got on well because EM was accurate and efficient in the work of recording, filing and accounting for all of the resources that a field hospital demanded. He suggested that EM should apply for promotion to corporal, but held no grudge when he refused: 'maybe he thought that someone who was a conscript wasn't meant to be a corporal anyway, so it wasn't brought up again'. But EM's main reason for refusing this chance of promotion was that: 'it would have driven a wedge between me and the other boys that I got on with. I just wanted to keep the situation I was in [. . .] talking to all sorts of people, learning all sorts of things and a way of life that I'd never thought of before'.

He enjoyed being accepted as one of the group, and got along well with most people. It was as if this rather extraordinary young man was learning how to live as most other men do. There were disadvantages, of course, so far as his creative ambitions went:

I couldn't write anything, during the war. I tried but couldn't write a thing, maybe because I couldn't be alone. You are always in a tent or a barrack room with other people. That confirmed the feeling that if I was going to write I would have to be by myself.[7]

As we will see, this might not be quite accurate. In addition, it may make us wonder how other soldier-poets managed. Sorley MacLean, George Campbell Hay, Robert Garioch and Hamish Henderson are Scottish poets who come immediately to mind, all of them fighting the Axis forces west of Egypt. However, the first three of these poets were some five to ten years older than EM. His near contemporary, Henderson (b. 1919) is now remembered as a poet mainly for one volume, *Elegies for the Dead in Cyrenaica* (1948), which EM admired very much indeed. In North Africa, however, he himself was still gathering experience of new cultures and places:

> Domes, shoeshines, jeeps, glaucomas, beads –
> wartime Cairo gave the flesh a buzz,
> pegged the young soul out full length,
> made pharaohs in the quick electric
> twilight, strutting brash as hawks.

(CP: 329)

His sense, as an only child, of now being part of a 'band of brothers' was also significant. In old age he linked this also to the warrior bands of the Anglo Saxon epic that he loved, as well as to groups of real and fictional explorers on their quests into the unknown:

The idea of a band of fairly close-knit persons – maybe that's why I like *Beowulf* so much – appealed to me [. . .]. I liked that idea of a band of soldiers or explorers, and the sense of going in search of something – maybe I'm not sure what [. . .]. Perhaps, if it's a gay poem then the quest is for the impossible perfect partner.[8]

In the same interview, he mentions that in a male society like the army there were certain kinds of friendships that created 'a strong bonding'. These could be at the level of shared identity, ease or admiration. This was the non-physical bond that he experienced with Cosgrove, the named person who exists most powerfully at the end of 'The New Divan', and beyond that in 'Love and a Life'. The same sort of bonding is described with the soldier Tommy Cosh, in EM's breakthrough collection, *The Second Life* (1968):

> When the troopship was pitching round the Cape
> in '41, and there was a lull in the night uproar of seas and
> > winds,
> > and a sudden full moon
> swung huge out of the darkness like the world it is,
> and we all crowded onto the wet deck, leaning on the rail,
> > our arms
> > on each other's shoulders, gazing at the savage outcrop of
> > great Africa,
> And Tommy Cosh started singing 'Mandalay' and we joined in
> with our raucous chorus of the unforgettable song,
> and the dawn came up like thunder like that moon drawing the
> > water of our yearning
> though we were going to war, and left us exalted,
> that was happiness [. . .].
>
> > (CP: 182)

The title of this poem, 'The Unspoken', is echoed in the interview with Christopher Whyte in which EM finally 'came out' at the age of 70. Poetry can gain 'Power from things not declared'.[9] Possibly because he was talking to another gay writer in that interview, EM was much more explicit here about many aspects of his sexual experiences. He described the 'breaking down of inhibitions' during the war, and the risks run ('and it was serious, sodomy, that would have been a court martial offence').

Ultimately one of his affairs seems to have been discovered or was strongly suspected, and the other soldier, who worked in the Dental Corps, was given a new posting: 'One of the officers must have said "We'll just break it up, without making a great thing of it"'.[10] In retrospect EM considered that they were treated leniently because both of them were doing specialised work in a conscientious way. This might have been so, or it may just have been the simplest way of handling a complex issue of discipline and morale. The social history of homosexuality in military life, and of institutional attempts to regulate it, is now a developing field of academic study.[11]

In the same interview, EM described his intensely emotional but non-physical relationship with Cosgrove, and he returned to this in 'Love and a Life':

> Cosgrove my closest companion that burning year on the
>   Lebanese coast,
> I have written about you already but raise you this last
>   toast.
> Nothing happened between us and that might seem a boast
> Since there is pain in silence, but I never deserted the post
> Of our vibrant daily intimacies even if the best and the
>   worst
>   Tore me for all to see
>   Eyes down in decency.
>
>   (*A Book of Lives*: 88)

Both these relationships took place in 1944, when the hospital moved to Sidon in Lebanon, and in 1944–45, when the unit was in Haifa, Palestine. In the earlier years of his war service, something of his emotional and intellectual state can be tracked through letters from his university friends, Frank Mason, George Hunter and Jean Watson. Most of it has to be inferred, of course, since only their side of the correspondence is available.[12]

Reading such letters now between three separated friends in different theatres of war, one is struck by just how young they were, how serious and perplexed, as they try to bring their intelligence to bear upon experiences and moral ambiguities beyond anything encountered in their academic studies. Frank Mason, in particular, puzzles over his changing perspective on earlier communist sympathies in the light of new loyalties to his fellow soldiers in the Artillery. All of EM's friends clearly respect his judgment and wide reading, or perhaps mistake wide reading for good judgment. There is interchange of news of friends and family, and of gifts: George Hunter sends EM copies of Edwin Muir's poetry and of the journal *Horizon*.

Both were shocked when EM confessed in a letter to his homosexuality. Of Frank Mason, he later commented:

> [. . .] I was stationed in Egypt and his unit was going to be in Egypt, and there was a chance of a leave for both of us. We might actually meet in Cairo or Alexandria. We'd kept a correspondence going, and I wrote to him. It was partly being separated, and this possibility of meeting a couple of years later made me, probably very foolishly, confess my feelings, and that was the end of that! He just said that while he could understand my feelings, he could not sympathise with them.[13]

In fact, they met after the war, but 'on an ordinary level', and the matter was not discussed. Frank was married by then, and the friendship waned.

George Hunter reacted with misunderstanding to EM's (possibly ambiguous) attempts to describe his emotional life by confessing to his own horror and fear of homosexuality. As an officer in the Royal Navy he may well have had to deal with, or at least consider, the disciplinary issues involved, apart from any personal considerations. It was through Hunter that EM learned that Jean had married. He and Jean possibly knew each other through their shared university study of Classics. EM had given 'clear hints' about his sexual preferences in his letters to Jean, he told me, and I imagine that this would have been while he was still in Egypt, in 1942 or early 1943.

When I asked EM about his mother's view of Jean, he told me that she felt that Jean was 'too strong' a character, and that he would have been overwhelmed by her. This he justified by referring to Edwin Muir and Robert Louis Stevenson, whose creative work had not been improved, in his view, and indeed had been held back, by their respective marriages to Willa Muir and Fanny Osbourne, both strong-minded and clever women. EM's mother was herself equally strong-minded, and he certainly thought her clever.

There is a touching vignette in one of Jean's letters to EM when she describes being invited for tea with his mother and grandmother shortly after EM had entered the army. After the meal, as old Mrs Arnott brushed the crumbs from the table and Jean set about doing the washing up, the older women's mournful comment was: 'This would have been his job'. Their words suddenly made Jean aware of just how insignificant her own feelings for the son of the house were to them, and how far outside the inner circle she was being kept. Yet as the daughter of a Stock Exchange cashier who had risen to Company Secretary, and living locally in Rutherglen, she might seem exactly the sort of suitable young woman one joined the tennis club to meet.

In her letters at this time she seems emotionally vulnerable, possibly needing more affection than EM could ever have given. A year younger than he was, she was possibly over-awed by his intelligence and breadth of reading. She persevered at university for a while, before leaving to become a Land Girl, working in Strathyre. She was married in Rutherglen in September 1943, to an English accountant serving in the Royal Army Ordnance Corps. She and EM would meet again in changed circumstances after the war.

Contact with the university life left behind came through visits to the parents of both EM and G.K. Hunter by Tom Livingstone, a young lecturer in English Literature. He too was a pacifist and had been placed in a non-combatant service unit, serving in England. On leave he would try to keep in touch with some of his

former students, or send maximum postcard messages in minis-
cule handwriting. He searched out books to send to EM, and had
taken his photograph before he left. EM thought that his own
handwriting might have been influenced by his tutor's. He also
enjoyed wearing the kilt, as Livingstone did. He never married,
and EM speculated in old age that he might have been gay. On
one occasion he had seemed on the point of saying something
about his feelings, but had not risked it.

Only one poem may be recorded as being written in the wartime
years. 'A Warning of Waters at Evening' is dated October–
November 1947 in his early compilation of typescripts, Poembook
1936–1961[14] but with the 47 so distorted as to seem like 43:

> What river-growl appals my flesh?
> Night shakes the hounded streams with fear.
> What waters roaring plunge, burst, crash
> This chafed and shuddering weir?

(CP: 26–7)

This would be EM's first poem to be published internationally in
the post-war years, in the American journal *Accent* IX:2 (Urbana,
Illinois) in 1949. It was reprinted in the Jesuit journal *The Month*
3:5 in May of the following year. Some of the imagery such as
'sparkling mountain-spring', 'The birth of snow' and 'rain dark
gulf' may place it in the Lebanon landscape of that wartime year,
as well as its haunted, hunted sense of guilt: 'I fear the bitter salt
far out / where sin and wrath must meet'.

Some of EM's anxieties about his own poetry, or the lack of it,
may have transferred themselves into critical reaction to the work
of his friend, W.S. Graham. One letter survives of their wartime
correspondence, but Sydney Graham, as EM knew him, was a
fitful correspondent, and in any case was often living in poor or
impermanent lodgings. He had been excused the draft on medical
grounds, and did war work in a torpedo factory near Greenock,
before leaving to teach for a short while in Kilquhanity House, a
progressive school in Galloway, in 1942. He had then left for

Cornwall, staying in the caravan that was to be his home until 1947. On 22 September 1943 he wrote:

> I am pleased to hear from you and sorry you are disappointed for I mind what you think of my poetry [. . .]. For me, Edwin, your letter goes on so much a stream of vague and complicated ingredients that poetry must have that maybe it is different things we want to make out of words [. . .].

Responding to EM's critical comments on poetry that is 'unreal, without meaning, severed from time and naked emotions and shy of true thought', W.S. Graham rejects poetry that is overworked in order that:

> something worthy and valuable to humanity [. . .] some compara- tive wisdom is tortured into the world [. . .]. The poet does not write what he knows but what he doesn't know [. . .].[15]

Graham stands by his own talent ('because I am potentially a greater poet than most today which does not make me very great but I am') and concludes: 'Christ it's a great letter Morgan you can fairly write like a wee minister of a good gospel'. Both of these are acute estimations of himself and his friend, for he possessed innately poetic gifts to a very high degree. EM would need to work for years to attain something comparable, and that from his own intellectual or thought-out position. Graham's rural and wayward life, his poetic intelligence and relatively early success with Faber and Faber, where T.S. Eliot admired his work, would be a spur and challenge to EM over the rest of the decade and beyond: 'I fish and gather mushrooms and write and cook'.

Lebanon meanwhile offered a rich contrast to both Scotland and Egypt. Many British soldiers retain memories of the striking landscape, colours and climate of its coast and mountains, and of the vibrant French-inflected atmosphere of Beirut.[16] Recalling that period in 'The New Divan', EM blends location with imagination in his Arabian tales of journeys and encounters (poems 32, 35, 39, 49: CP: 305–11). The spiritual history of this landscape haunts him, with contrasting elements of demonic (poems 63, 82) and transcendental imagery (81, 85, 90). The final poem ends on a crag that is partly reminiscent of Cathkin Braes: ridge and escarpment imagery is found frequently in EM's work, signifying a range of aspirations:

> The dead climb with us like the living to the edge.
> The clouds sail and the air's washed blue. For you
> and me, the life beyond that sages mention
> is this life on a crag above
> a line of breakers.

(CP: 330)

Not quite transcendental then, except as all good poetry transcends its origins in fragmentary human lives. Here 'a shred of sailcloth / relic of a gale' is lifted from the rock where it has dried in the sun to be used by the poet in binding the leaves of his poem.

During the war, EM was also consciously looking for a religious perspective that might replace the conventional and social Christianity which he had already rejected. When the hospital moved to Palestine in 1945, he visited Jericho, Jerusalem and other religious sites, as many soldiers did, but found this counterproductive. He experienced nothing on a spiritual level there:

> The power and the glory walked
> here? Buy some statuettes,
> blue and white, nothing looking
> blander ever shot from the mould.

(CP: 316)

In the late forties and early fifties he would feel more of an inclination towards religion, reading the Bible carefully as a text along with detailed commentaries. He thought deeply about the figure of Christ and his historicity. In later life he wondered whether he was then, around 1946, in the process of becoming, belatedly, a Christian. Something continued to 'needle him' about Christ, he told Marshall Walker. He would re-explore or challenge Christian ideas throughout his creative life, feeling drawn to sublimity in a sense, but repelled by religious systems.

Towards the end of the war, when the US military dropped atomic bombs on Hiroshima and Nagasaki in August 1945, EM and four or five others were so horrified that they protested in a petition to their commanding officer. As members of the medical corps, they wanted to disassociate themselves from this destruction. EM and Lesley Rose, a Londoner, led the protest. Again, he had to consider court martial if matters were taken further, but the petition was accepted. Things were drawing to a close.

RETURN TO GLASGOW

EM returned to Britain the following month, and was demobilised in January 1946. He had been away from home for five years. His parents found him altered and did not quite know how to react. This sort of awkward homecoming must have been a common experience for many men returning. Later that year, Private Edwin Morgan (Clerk BII) was awarded a Certificate for Outstandingly Good Service, signed by the Commander in Chief of Middle East Forces.

Re-adjustment was difficult. In the records it appears seamless: he had left university at the end of the first term of his Junior Honours year, and now he rejoined the course at the start of the second term, but five years later. He had been doing well before, but experience of war had unsettled him:

> It was very, very hard, starting again after being away doing completely non-intellectual things for such a long time, and I didn't do well at all, to begin with, when I came back. I wondered, in fact, whether I should go on with university work [. . .]. I just had this terrible restlessness and not knowing whether I wanted to settle or not to any one job.[17]

78

He thought about going back to the Middle East, or to another foreign country, or of rejoining the Army in the manner of T.E. Lawrence. After being mostly in the open air and doing physical or straightforward work for so long, his mind did not take easily to reading books, even, or especially, books of poetry. In this unliterary frame of mind, Romantic poets such as Keats seemed totally removed from life, and he could hardly bear to read them.

He began to keep a series of commonplace books, which he called Gnotelibrik 1–4.[18] In them we can trace some of the impact of his reading, and what seemed worth dwelling on intellectually: this from Keats, for instance: 'I think poetry should surprise by a fine excess, and not by singularity'. Or from Johnson: 'I will be conquered; I will not capitulate'. These books are more word-based than the Scrapbooks, but gradually come to use a similar cut-and-paste approach to reviews or long quotations, so dating is possible. The final book ends in the late 1960s.

The first book contains many Renaissance sonnets copied out in French, from Ronsard, Du Bellay and Maurice Scève. The latter seems to be particularly important in terms of self-identification, and EM translates part of the Introduction from the 1916 Hachette edition:

> Scève himself courted anonymity or veiled authorship by signing in initials only or enigmatic mottoes [. . .] and by never presenting dogmatic ideas from which an adequate picture of a personality might be derived.

Many of the ten line decasyllabic 'dizains' from Scève's *Délie* are copied out, some of them ticked, and EM follows the order of these in his translations which finally appeared in his *Fifty Renascence Love Poems* of 1975 (CT: 166–76). In his introduction to that selection, EM discusses how lines of a dizain 'though reminiscent of a sonnet in general effect, seem to pack more meaning into less bulk, mainly as a result of their involuted, much less open syntax' (CT: 161). He refers also to Scève's enacting of a state of mind in which the lover 'is dissolved, like his purely physical longings, in an abyss of nescience, a gulf of oblivion'. He admires too the way that Scève can bring his widely varying moods into the traditional Petrarchan structures of imagery, and so renew and extend these. For a gay person in search of an 'impossible perfect partner', the poetic convention of unattainable distance between poet and beloved must also have retained a particular resonance into modern times.

This reminds us that EM's unresolved feelings of love and loss still vexed him at this time, and possibly even more intensely since he had returned to the context of his early friendships. In February 1946 he wrote a poem of renunciation for Frank Mason, now distanced by marriage and incompatibility:

> Upon your heart I will not walk,
> Your body I myself fence round,
> The garden where I may not walk,
> The happy lots and dazzling ground.[19]

Into another poem, in the veiled manner of Scève, EM inserted the words *frank* and *mason* in their ordinary meanings, so that the name was recorded in a hidden way. One day by chance he met up with Tommy Cosh, the singer of 'Mandalay', now married. They had been good army friends, with no physical attraction on either part, but had now both gone their separate ways. EM considered briefly whether they might all be friends, but 'the wife obviously didn't like me'.

At this time, too, EM met up with Jean again, but mainly to retrieve his Scrapbooks. Although he had presented them as a parting gift, he now had to argue that they had only been given to her for safe-keeping. He told me this in July 2008, and had the grace still to feel ashamed of the lie. She was at that point living in Anniesland, another odd example of EM's pattern of voyage and return. She sent him instructions on which tram to take. I asked how he had carried them home, since they are heavy volumes, but he did not respond. Perhaps he had a taxi waiting on the street. I thought of several women I know who would have invited him to reclaim his scrapbooks from the nearest skip.

Of course, there were far fewer volumes to carry at that stage, but in new Scrapbooks of the late 1940s and early 1950s he began again to create a visual record of the paradoxes and anxieties of post-war life. Photo-images of atomic weapons counter more optimistic images of human endeavour such as the Russian space programme or the ascent of Everest; the vagaries of human behaviour are juxtaposed to the exuberance and scale of nature. The tone is notably more satirical in his use of captions, but he also pasted in photographs of his time as a soldier, including a picture of Cosgrove, and of Jean in her Land Army uniform.

He would keep extending his Scrapbooks till the early 1960s. Some entries suggest that a key theme in all of this effort was the exploration of time. In particular, the pages practised a use of coincidence with images and texts from widely separated eras – a sort of synchronicity that also interested him at an intellectual level. In an entry dated 2 April 1946 he records his thoughts under the heading: *Do Events Cast Back Shadows in Time?*

> About a week after I had finished writing my poem *Dies Irae* I began to read the journal of Gerard Manley Hopkins. Under the date 25 October 1870 I was startled to find references in one paragraph to the Aurora Borealis as a sign of *God's Anger*, to *Hailstorms*, and to the *Solar Halo*, all of which had been connected in my poem. Such 'coincidences' or clusters of events seem relatively common and yet they never fail to have a striking effect on the mind.

He then goes on to mention occasions when he had encountered rare words in quick succession in different texts, or had un-expectedly met with people whom he had just mentioned in conversation, or the startling effect, many years before, of seeing in Glasgow all on the same day three people whose noses had been eaten away. He concludes:

Some such things might be explained by heightening of attention which flare up and die again, but not all. Are these 'clustered events', I wonder, sufficiently rare to be natural according to the laws of probability affecting all happenings? And if not, *then* what?

Thus the frequent theme in his poetry of time-travel, and of all-seeing visitants from another world co-existent with our own, are established in the Scrapbooks almost as a manifesto, long before he had found the poetic language to express them.

ACADEMIC WORK

Although academically he got off to a hesitant start, EM began to make good progress in his Senior Honours year, and in fact came second *(proxime accessit)* for the Thomas Logan Prize for the most distinguished graduate in Arts in 1947. He won a scholarship to Oxford, probably the annual Snell Exhibition for high achieving graduates of Glasgow University to pursue postgraduate studies at Balliol. Adam Smith is often cited as an early recipient. The original intention of the bequest was to educate clergymen for the Scottish Episcopal Church, Snell having been a Royalist and secretary to the Duke of Monmouth, but this stipulation had now lapsed. EM did travel to Oxford and stayed in the College, but told me that he found the whole atmosphere of hierarchy and privilege distasteful. Nor could he face the thought of three more years of study before starting work.

He did not mention that G.K. Hunter had already started his B.Litt. degree at Balliol in October 1946, focusing on Shakespeare and his contemporaries. Hunter booked accommodation for his friend for five nights, from Monday 19th to Friday 23rd of May 1947, and advised him to bring emergency ration cards, although the College would provide breakfast and Hunter would buy him dinner. All seemed amicable, and their intellectual and personal friendship was re-established and would continue for many years. But EM returned to Glasgow where another opportunity had in any case arisen: to join the English Literature staff there and begin his academic career as a junior lecturer.

His father and mother did not altogether approve of this decision, he thought, as they would have preferred a 'safer' career for him in banking or the Civil Service. However, within a few years there is a note of congratulations dated 12 August 1950 from a Glasgow solicitor, David Hutchison, about EM's success in publishing an academic article in a journal: his father had mentioned this to the lawyer in the midst of his own business matters.[20] The article was probably EM's 'Women and Poetry' in the *Cambridge Journal* III:11, August 1950, which posits a basic incompatibility between the two. Of this essay, his friend and colleague Jack Rillie remarks that it 'would blow the mind of Shere Hite', and admits that reading it again in the 1990s he was 'required to blink, if only for my friend'.[21] He asks that contemporary readers remember the 'unreconstructed' era of its composition. The views there may also reflect EM's own sense of isolation and creative sterility at this period, and his awareness that the men he admired and cared about were becoming taken up, as G.K. Hunter was, in all the contentment and cares of marriage and children.

EM brought typical determination and some ambition to his new role as lecturer, with letters to the *Times Literary Supplement* on 'Russian Transliteration' (2 August 1947) and 'A Hopkins Phrase' (27 May 1949); book reviews of W.S. Graham's *The White Threshold* in *Nine* II:II [No.3], May 1950, and of L. and E.M. Hanson's *The Four Brontës* in *Cambridge Journal* IV:1, October 1950; and articles on the poetry of William Dunbar sent to the *Scottish Periodical*, which ran into financial difficulties before publication, and on the prose style of Browne and Johnson to *Scrutiny*. The latter drew a scrawling letter of refusal from F.R. Leavis, on the grounds that someone else had promised them an article on Browne. EM, undaunted, found a home for this essay in the *Cambridge Journal* IV:8, May 1957, and for the Dunbar piece in *Essays in Criticism* II:2, April 1952. 'Dunbar and the Language of Poetry' was reprinted in EM's *Essays* (Carcanet 1974: 81–99).

Such academic research and publication would become a bit more extensive in the following decade, as EM settled into the lecturer role. As it was, he had to find his own way forward in those pre-Quality Assurance days. The Head of Department, Professor Peter Alexander, was a noted scholar and editor of Shakespeare, but with a light touch on staff development and mentoring for new staff, who were expected to get on with the job. He had a standard question in one paper that was so studiedly opaque that even his staff, who had to do the marking, did not know what the expected response was. It is, however, possible to read EM's draft lecture notes for those first years in the job and marvel at his organisation of detail in what looks like high speed handwriting.[22] This would be a draft for typewritten final versions, according to his later practice.

More interesting from a creative point of view is evidence of his thorough-going attempt to link himself to developments and people in the literary scene. Thus we find Norman MacCaig writing to him on 5 August 1948 on behalf of the editor of *Scottish Periodical*, apologising for a delayed response to his 'Dies Irae', since the editor was now living in London and the journal about to cease publication, but praising his poem:

> [. . .] it is full of more excellent lines, phrases and images and has a fervour and vigour of utterance all too seldom met with in these days of reason and cynicism and doubt and despair [. . .] your work interests me very much.[23]

The two poets arranged to meet in McVittie's in the West End of Edinburgh, in 'the small room for men only': 'I'll be there at 11 o'clock,' says MacCaig, ' – grey tweed jacket, flannels, tallish, thin, and looking out for you'.

Also looking out for EM, but in the other sense, was Edwin Muir. EM had written to him just after his Finals, sending him some poems for comment. Edwin Muir was then working in the British Institute in Prague, and with Willa Muir was engaged in their translation of Kafka's novels. On 20 June 1947 he sent EM a

84

balanced and supportive letter, in my view, praising his high aim and desire to write significant or 'major' poetry. At the same time, he gently points out EM's current distance from his aim. The younger man's poems gave Muir the feeling of being 'the result of will rather than of inspiration'. He counselled him to wait for the poetry to come, and not, on any account, to force it.[24]

This advice is, of course, precisely what EM ignored according to 'Epilogue', as he 'week after week after week / strained to unbind [himself], / sweated to speak'. There was often a driven quality about his approach to the creative life, despite a mild-mannered appearance. Muir commented on the monotonous effect created by EM's 'hammering' at some images in his 'Dies Irae', and directed him towards development of movement as 'one of the means of containing energy in poetry'. And he pointed him again towards the actual originals of EM's Anglo-Saxon translations as positive examples of poetic movement that created energy in a continuous stream. Finally he advises him to write more simply: 'You are too involved, in both senses of the word. You are in your own whirlpool [. . .]'.

This seems to me to be judicious and accurate advice, and the whole letter expresses the combination of gentleness and insight that later students such as George Mackay Brown would discover in Muir. And EM took his advice to the extent that he could at that stage. For example, his first major essay on Dunbar opens with a discussion of poetry as 'the manifestation of energy as order' (*Essays*: 81). He may also have been stimulated to begin his translation of *Beowulf* within the next year or so. He had already begun to translate the shorter Anglo Saxon poems. His Transla-tions folder has Anglo Saxon riddles dated February 1946, with first drafts of 'The Seafarer' and 'The Wanderer' in May and June of 1947.[25] A revised version of both would follow in February 1950.

The earliest versions of EM's translations of Maurice Scève's poems are dated October 1945 to January 1946, just before he re-entered civilian life. His early choice of this complex syntax as a poetic challenge, perhaps matching his own experience of a

85

tangled emotional life, suggests the aptness of Muir's description of the young poet as 'too involved'. Of course, it is with the clarifying of that labored syntax into the more open verse that EM began to write in the 1960s as his emotional life became more joyous, that readers really began to respond.

I wonder, however, to what extent Muir was ever forgiven for this early critique. EM's later essay on Muir emphasises that he 'was little interested in technical innovation', had 'a scrappy education' and 'never did develop an entirely sure-footed technique'. And that even his last poems 'are liable to be flawed by some awkward rhythm, some clumsy inversion, some flatness of vocabulary'. All of this judgment before the opening paragraph is barely half way done. The essay ends with the faint praise: 'Muir of course has many drab, dull poems which don't come to life at all [. . .]. But the best of them have a quiet, persistent, winning quality which overcomes the occasional stammering of the voice' (*Essays*: 186).

This was published in *The Review* (5 February 1963), and we can understand that what was mainly at issue here was Muir's retreat, as EM saw it, from the challenge of science and the future, into an idealised and rural past that seemed to him 'to be more insulting than comforting to man's restless spirit and aspiring brain'. Yet there is an echo of Muir's earlier comments to EM about learning to contain his poetic energy, and perhaps too a feeling of satisfying riposte in this hammering on at the older poet's lack of this quality. Maybe here was a second elder Edwin, who, like his lost uncle and namesake, could not really be countenanced in EM's aspiring mind. He never failed to be annoyed at the confusion that their identical first names and same initial surnames sometimes caused.

Given EM's poetic ambition and the ultimate range of his output, the critic and poet Chris Jones suggests that his translation of *Beowulf*, undertaken at the very beginning of his career, is 'a deliberate laying down of a foundation stone for a personal *ars poetica*' that reaches back to the epic origins of English verse.[26] The ambition is seen in the unflinching way that he sought publication for the work. When E.V. Rieu at Penguin Classics declined to take it on 21 October 1948, despite recognising that 'In many aspects your version of Beowulf is the best I have seen',[27] EM immediately sent it off to Cambridge University Press. When they regret they are unable to make an offer of publication on 10 November 1948, off it goes to Oxford University Press, who also decline it by 23 November 1948. In every case the reasons are sound enough in publishing terms: lack of potential sales, heavy congestion of existing commitments and a competing prose version already on the publisher's list, respectively.

Eventually, EM found a publisher in Erica Marx at The Hand and Flower Press in Kent, and through her contacts ultimately reached an international readership for the poem with the University of California Press, who republished it in paperback and sold over fifty thousand copies before it was discontinued in 1999. Carcanet brought out a new paperback edition in 2002. It is a poem that was with him, therefore, from his earliest creative experiments in the scrapbooks, and which had accompanied him into and out of the war. As Jones suggests, his 'far-flung peripatetic seafaring may well have put him in mind of the section of *Beowulf* that describes the voyage of the Geats to Denmark in order to deliver Hrothgar from Grendel'.[28] He links the deadly underwater monsters of the Anglo Saxon poem with German u-boats in 'War Voyage' and finds old and new kennings for the sea in 'Cape Found': 'the whale's road, the gull's acres' (*A Book of Lives*: 88, 87).

In fact EM came to feel that this translation *was* the war poem that he had been unable to write in the 1940s. Out of the confusion of war and a sense of dislocation and sterility, he recovered a means of giving expression to war's themes 'of conflict and danger, voyaging and displacement, loyalty and loss. *Inter arma musae tacent*, but they are not sleeping'. His poetic silence as a soldier then was not to be taken for creative inactivity.

These words from the brief Preface to the Carcanet edition of 2002 have no echo in the original Introduction, which is a scholarly examination of both 'the translator's task in *Beowulf*' and 'the art of the poem'. But as Jones points out, his translation of Old English works in two directions, as EM both creates new and vital versions of Anglo Saxon poems and at the same time is created by them. He is remade or healed as a poet, not only in being enabled to write energetically and at epic length, but also because the mainly male warrior context of the poem allows him to deal with homosexual possibilities, albeit in a coded way.

When I interviewed him in May 2003 for a volume I was co-editing on ethics and identity in modern Scottish writing, he referred to the work of Queer Theorists, and in particular to Eve Kosofsky Sedgwick:

> She's written a lot about this in the general context of human relationships. She uses different words: words like homosexual, homoerotic and homosocial. It's a sort of ladder from homosexual to homoerotic (is it homosexual or is it not?) down to homosocial, which is just boys or men together, in an army or in a band or whatever. I suppose the *Beowulf* society would be regarded by her as homosocial. There are overtones of something, but you're not quite sure.[29]

Thus when EM writes in 'Epilogue' that he 'translated Beowulf for want of love', one can sense his need in the late 1940s for the homosocial context of the army life that he had lost, and which the poem helped him to retrieve or reshape. The art of the *Beowulf* poet, with its alliterative drive, its difference from other poetic norms of rhyme and regular rhythmical patterns, and its blending of heroic quest narrative with severe moral commentary, are all factors that had a deep influence on EM's later practice. They resonated with his temperament in a profound way.

As ever, he tracked reviews and sales very carefully. I have the clippings and accounts in one of his file boxes, which will eventually be housed in the University's Department of Special Collections with other new material. Although it charts his first public success as a writer, there is the rather sad inclusion of a letter from Ritchie Girvan, his Old English lecturer, by then Reader in English Language. The translation was dedicated to him 'with respect and affection', and EM had sent him a copy on publication. While very gracious in expression, Girvan studiedly avoids any comment on EM's literary effects (and, indeed, extensions to the original's meaning at times), claiming to be competent only in philological matters.

He also sent a copy to Ezra Pound, whose modernism had increasingly turned towards fascism and paranoiac anti-Semitism in the 1930s. During the war he had made radio broadcasts from Italy in support of Mussolini, and was then interned by the American military forces before finally being held as a mentally ill patient in the St. Elizabeth Hospital, Washington. The gift was acknowledged first by Dorothy Pound, and shortly afterwards by Pound himself, on a postcard from St. Elizabeth's:

> He seems to have added 'ound' in pencil after his E.P. just in case – though it's unlikely anyone would mistake him! There is what looks like a censor's or a doctor's initials above the stamp, though I'm only guessing, as I don't know how free his correspondence was at that date.[30]

The card is now in the Mitchell Library in Glasgow. He also sent a copy to Hugh MacDiarmid, who praised its 'meaty Introduction'.

Beowulf was published in the early 1950s although written in the previous decade. EM's original copies also date both 'Dies Irae' and 'The Vision of Cathkin Braes' as March 1946 (CP: 21, 43), when he was still an undergraduate. 'Stanzas of the Jeopardy', 'The Sleights of Darkness' and 'Harrowing Heaven, 1924' were all written in 1949, and 'Sleights of Time' and 'Sleight-of-Morals' in early 1950. At least some of these along with translations from Italian, German and Old English were beginning to be published by the end of the 1940s, in *Horizon*, *Poetry London* and *Nine*. Details are given in Hamish Whyte's essential checklist in *About Edwin Morgan* (1990: 140–255).

So although he perceived a lack of success, EM had begun twin careers by the end of the 1940s, as lecturer and as poet. There is no doubt that there was much darkness and ambiguity in his personal life, and we will return in the next chapter to the city underworld in which he also moved. Guilt, tension and terror are features of some of the poems cited above. Sydney Graham was one person whom he felt accepted by. In a verse letter to him, dated 29 October 1950, he talks clearly about the plain expression of feelings that he had found so costly in life and difficult in his poetry:

> And if all the imagery and congestion and turgidity
> Round a simple thing could have been swept away
> I would have swept it away, but it is hard, hard
> To say the simple things that involve a life and a friend,
> And to me friendship is like others' love,
> The most of life; and for this called, in pain, 'love'.
>
> Aberration draws on rebuff, rebuke, contempt.
> At thirty one has built a shell, or been beaten.
> The shell is complex to guard a simplicity
> Or hard to guard a reproved gentleness.
> In penalty, sometimes like a live thing
> Feeling unaccountable or at a sight of a boy's face
> In a city street stirs in me crying or
> Trying rather to cry and to stretch outward [. . .].[31]

In an earlier letter dated 30 April 1950, typed and carbon copied, in reply to a postcard from Sydney Graham, EM describes such intermittent communications from his fellow poet as doves and ravens knocking at the window of a storm-tossed Ark, in which he floats. The Ark transmutes into a sort of broch settlement, that is also near a mountainside observatory: 'The crags and plateaux are incredibly recalcitrant to all good walking; hail and snow are frequent, the summits are high, and many of us are swept down by the avalanches [. . .]'. We are back, it seems, in the heady landscapes that EM loved as a boy, both in film or fantasy. And yet when he continues:

> Very remarkable are the visions we have of the moon, and of the stars, and of all the icy properties and manifestations; but something has been done to the sun, it never appears more than smouldering, an ochre, a snarling crimson, even a monstrous purple [. . .]

we cannot help but be reminded of another night watcher of the moon and stars in 'The New Divan', and of a desert landscape where 'Moonlight coming down hard converted / dunes to memories of snow' (CP: 328, 324). The contexts differ, but the watcher is the same. To that extent the universe remained unbroken, and a source of hope.

It was not until 25 November 1978, in the year after his belated war poem was published in *The New Divan*, that EM applied for the 1939–1945 war service stars and medals he was entitled to. He was informed that there would be a delay of two years, because so many of his generation were now applying for public recognition of the hardships endured. He signed his request: Professor Edwin Morgan. It is true that he had been thinking over those times for several years. I recall my surprise, when I first began postgraduate study with him in 1972 at how, after a late afternoon tutorial, he put on a blue Royal Army Medical Corps beret and a military-looking trench coat before heading out into the damp November gloom. I can't recall now whether it was on that occasion or another that we had looked at poetry of the Second World War, including Keith Douglas, Hamish Henderson and others from the North African campaign.

CHAPTER FIVE

The Dark Decade 1950–1960

The years between 1950 and 1960 were EM's bleakest. At one point in mid-decade he considered suicide, harried as he was by frustrations in his personal, academic and creative lives. To the outside world, he must have seemed to be 'making his way', busy with teaching, writing, translating, revising – never short of ideas and always able to produce interesting and well-crafted material against the tightest of timelines. And yet within each of these different spheres, he sensed himself to be an outsider. The decade was tense partly because so much of his life had to be kept censored and separate.

So far as his poem 'Epilogue' is concerned, those years remain obscured. The poem provides no stanza as an epigraph for this chapter but overleaps the 1950s in a single bound, like some comic-book hero, to alight in the brighter 1960s. Nevertheless these hidden years of turmoil and frustration were crucial in shaping the multifarious poet who would seem suddenly to emerge with the new decade, as if reborn.

In discussion with Christopher Whyte in 1988, EM for the first time openly recalled the experience of being gay in Glasgow thirty years earlier. His memories of the period were still as clear, or dark, when I interviewed him fifteen years later. The publication of the *Wolfenden Report* on homosexuality and prostitution in 1957 meant that the subject was more widely discussed, but still with significant disapproval. There were also several high profile prosecutions, of Lord Montagu, Peter Wildblood and John Gielgud, which were widely publicised:

The Dark Decade 1950–1960

In the 1950s people were genuinely shocked by Gielgud. How could a man who was a famous actor do things like these? He was charged with 'importuning' in a public place. How could he possibly do that? People had to grasp a new fact. It took a long time, in Scotland especially, for this to come across.[1]

Although the law was liberalised in England in 1967, in Scotland this was not done until 1980: 'I always think of it as a Calvinist thing. Maybe it wasn't – maybe it was the general religious background of the country. It was thought to be in some way very difficult to move forward in any reasonable way at all'.[2]

EM read about these things with great interest, 'a painful interest, and also various worries and apprehensions whether the fact that people like that were getting into the papers and having their lives disrupted would apply to me too'.[3] He knew that if something like Gielgud's situation had applied to himself, he would have been sacked. There would also have been a social ostracism. Thus there was a stark divide between his respectable professional life as lecturer in an ancient university and his night life of gay activity in bars, cafes, parks, toilets and waste ground.

Many of the venues he recalled have gone. There was the Oak Café which was 'probably in St Vincent Street, or perhaps West George Street', the Good Companions which was 'further up towards Bath Street or possibly Blythswood Square', and the Royal Bar on West Nile Street. The Oak Café 'was somewhat louche, even very louche, but very interesting, you never knew what was going to happen there!'.[4] Despite his anxieties, there was also an enthusiasm or recklessness in being absorbed in a range of sensory experiences:

the curious business of public activity, semi-orgies, no doubt very much disapproved of, but it's surprising how much of that there was going on, even at that time just after the war. I never seemed to have any hesitation in joining in that kind of activity. There was a café, near Buchanan Street bus station, gone now [. . .] an upstairs place with a toilet, and really pretty well anything went

93

on, it was obviously very very risky, but people did go there and enjoy this, and you could see a dozen or more people there at any one time [. . .].[5]

The atmosphere of this alternative existence is well caught in the underworld echoes of one of the 'Pieces of Me' published in 2002:

> A man like a shade
> fastened onto me
> along Gordon Street.
> 'Gie's a pound.
> Hink Ah don't know ye?
> Ye'll no shake me aff.
> C'mon, c'mon, c'mon.
> Right. That's be'er.
> You know the score.
> Try Buchanan Street Station,
> toilet's busy therr.'
> Janus, blackmailer
> of the friendly city.[6]

Of course, wandering in this world EM was courting real danger. The homosexual rape described obliquely enough in his poem 'Glasgow Green' (CP: 168) was a reflection of several experiences, including one with

a real kind of hard man, young, very good looking, but no expression, that strange, blank, good-looking expression you often get in Glasgow [. . .] he threatened me, he said if I didn't do exactly what he wanted he would get the boys to me. I used this in the poem, 'get the boys t' ye'. And he meant it too [. . .].[7]

EM eventually came to see 'Glasgow Green' as a plea for some kind of acceptance, a gay liberation poem written before that term had been invented. The poem asks 'How shall the race be served?' by such activity, and asserts that:

94

It shall be served by hunter and hunted in their endless chain
as well as by those who turn back the sheets in peace.

(CP: 169)

And yet there is also the recognition that 'the beds of married love
/ are islands in a sea of desire', and a sense that the poet finds
himself adrift, despite assertion to the contrary.

As ever, EM used intellect and reading to explore his situation.
He belonged to various short-lived gay discussion groups, one of
which was known as the Bachelor Clan, which would meet to
discuss homosexuality and gay writing. He also joined a book club
which had an exchange scheme for gay publications, and so had
access to such novels as Fritz Peters's *Finistère,* Rodney Garland's
The Heart in Exile, Charles Jackson's *The Fall of Valour* and Gore
Vidal's *The City and the Pillar*. Such group developments were
still tentative in the 1950s, with no sense of gay liberation as yet,
but 'just a feeling in the air [. . .] that something could possibly be
changed, that this oppression of people's real feelings couldn't go
on forever'.[8] There was still no activist movement, and it is
doubtful whether EM would have joined one, even if it had
existed: 'You tended to be a series of solitary people who were in
fact gay, but there wasn't much of a sense of solidarity [. . .] at
that stage'.[9]

What was intriguing to him was that, in Glasgow, homosexuality was a cross-class activity with considerable working-class
involvement, and that among married men bisexuality was quite
frequent, in his experience. He was involved in several relationships of this kind, and some are recalled in 'Love and a Life'
('Harry', 'G' in *A Book of Lives*: 93, 99). To that extent he was
aware of coming to know more about his society than those who
ignored or denied these strata of Scottish life, even although he
had not yet found a poetic language in which to deal with such
relationships openly.

His correspondence from this period reveals a wide range of
contacts, several of them in the army, some of them working-class
judging by the style and content, some of them seeking advance-

ment through education, others whom EM helped by advice, references or books. He was quite frequently in London or in Brighton, combining visits to theatre, publishers or the British Library with socialising there.

What did his parents make of all this daily and nocturnal experience – the steady arrival of letters and books, their son's absences and returns, his endless commitments and anxieties? EM still stayed in the family home, so it seems unlikely that they were not aware of his moods. Family routines may have provided a way of avoiding discussion. They tried their best. In September 1951 we find a note from William Sloan Smith, writing from Dalmuir Dockyard, inviting EM to accompany him, two of his sons and a Police Superintendent from Kirkintilloch on a four day cruise in the Company's motor boat, the *Northern Kiwi*: 'I understand from your father that you are keen on sailing'. The boat would be crewed by a captain, an engineer and one of the company salvage men, and would depart from Helensburgh for Northern Ireland and return by Cairnryan. But EM had no recollection of ever having accepted the invitation: it may have been too near the start of the university term, or he might have had other commitments, or have been sailing other waters.

In his isolation from close relationships at this time, he told me, he identified keenly with Gerard Manley Hopkins: as a poet 'who made as much as you can make of frustration'; as a priest whose superiors failed to help him; and as a human being who was not given a decent job but was always left on the fringes, 'scrubbing the floor'. He admired him tremendously because of the difficulties he had come through. In his 1955 copy of *The Letters of Gerard Manley Hopkins to Robert Bridges* (ed. Claude C. Abbott), EM has marked pages where a similarity of experience has struck him: 'His face was fascinating me last term. I generally have one fascination or another on' (p.8); or 'I always knew in my heart Walt Whitman's mind to be more like my own than any other man's living' (p.155). We have seen that EM published his early post-war work in the Jesuit periodical, the *Month*, which had consistently refused Hopkins' poetry.

There was also a Glasgow connection. Hopkins had been sent as an assistant to St Joseph's Church in the north side of Glasgow in the summer of 1881, and wrote warmly of the poor Ulster Irish Catholics there: 'They are found by all who have to deal with them very attractive, for, though always very drunken and at present very Fenian, they are warm-hearted and give a far heartier welcome than those of Liverpool'. When EM came to write about Hopkins in Glasgow in his 'Sonnets from Scotland' series of 1984, the sense of identification was so close that he pictures the young Jesuit in terms that might well have described his own younger self in darkest Glasgow:

> Earnestly nervous yet forthright, melted
> by bulk and warmth and unimposed rough grace,
> he lit a ready fuse from face to face
> of Irish Glasgow. [. . .]
> He blessed them, frowned, beat on his hands. The load
> of coal-black darkness clattering on his head
> half-crushed, half-fed the bluely burning need
> that trudged him back along North Woodside Road.
>
> ('G.M. Hopkins in Glasgow'. CP: 445)

Of course, EM remains a little fuzzy as to Catholic ritual here, focusing more on the human need, or lack of warmth. That at least he understood from experience.

UNIVERSITY WORK

This Hopkins sonnet is dedicated to J.A.M.R., Jack Rillie. He and EM had begun teaching English literature at about the same time in the University, and shared a room for years:

> Shared the most threadbare
> carpet in the university.
> Shared the hilarity
> of our joint bibliography

97

of literary articles
'Knoepflmacher?'
'Knoepflmacher!'
                    (*Thirteen Ways of Looking at Rillie*)

These lines are from a tribute to his old colleague, published in a limited edition by Enitharmon Press in 2006. Its title glances at Wallace Steven's famous poem, 'Thirteen Ways of Looking at a Blackbird'. All of this might seem to risk bordering on academic self-regard, but the sequence is saved from that by the genuine warmth and a sense of the sharing of intelligence and wit that the poem recalls, and also by the way that it is flanked by two other significant late works. 'Conversation in Palestine' continues EM's argument with magisterial Christianity in a conversation between Jesus and a contemporary on the topic of the future Wittgenstein ('If you want processions, hierarchies, / he's not your man'). Then 'A Birthday: for IHF' is a witty celebration of the poet and artist Ian Hamilton Finlay at 80, with a sense of enduring energy and beauty expressed in the imagery of sea and ships that both he and EM had loved. The book is a sort of triptych on the theme of time, and on what remains significant and respected across the years, with a deep sense of enduring creativity even into old age.

The author's note recalls Rillie's broad humanism: 'Several generations of students will testify to his brilliant but never pedantic qualities'. Certainly as a student in the 1960s, I clearly recall his inspirational qualities as a teacher, particularly of poetry, particularly on Hopkins and on modernism: 'Einstein in Xanadu – ', as the poem describes him, 'hair floats, eyes flash – '. And in contrast to EM's ambitions always to publish, here was his closest colleague's 'goal without hubris', and the daily play of his intelligence:

> Philosophy, theology
> – I'm a theist, he said –
> were great streams flowing
> into the ever enrichable
> delta of literature.

The Dark Decade 1950–1960

He had married his sweetheart, Ann Scorah, in 1940, while still a twenty-two year old student at Glasgow University, just before National Service, and by the 1950s the couple had two young daughters. Like EM he had served in the RAMC; unlike him he was promoted to corporal. Together the two young lecturers went along to a discussion group, called 'The Group', on contemporary philosophical writing: Martin Buber, Karl Jasper, Camus and other existentialists. The psychiatrist R.D. Laing was a member, but Rillie 'didn't like Laing / so that's a plus'. On the other hand, in EM's view, he 'praised Camus / too much – that's a minus'. EM was never unreservedly a member of any group, being essentially an individualist, if not a loner. And yet he could appreciate warmth and sociability in others, and respond in kind.

His reservation also applied in the 1950s to the profession in which both he and Rillie were engaged. EM did not possess his friend's charm and confidence as a teacher, even by the stage when I was an undergraduate a decade later. He was always interesting and sometimes surprising or humorous in the links he made, yet he convinced more by his clarity, sincerity and good sense than by any 'stage presence' in the lecture theatre, or by that penetrating yet seemingly unforced dialogue between lecturer, listeners and the text under scrutiny that memorable teachers create. I believe that EM did achieve this sort of impact after retirement in 1980, when he continued to lecture widely and when his own poetic reputation and insight accompanied him, as it were, on to the platform.

His friend and colleague, Marshall Walker, had been his student in this decade. He attended the university from 1956 to 1960, and recalled the Department as it then was:

The English Department was headed by Professor Peter Alexander, probably the foremost Shakespearean scholar of the day with an edition of Shakespeare to his name. His staff portioned out the curriculum. John Bryce walked with Milton, had clearly read everything and made literary theory inspiring without recourse to jargon. Sean Purser and Hannah Buchan were Wordsworthian

99

though it was rumoured that Mr Purser would have preferred a career in football. Tom Livingstone gave the impression he had just come from a chat with Tennyson, and Philip Drew, being Dickensian, was thereby omniscient, like the other Shakespearean, Ernst Honigmann, whose youthful appearance couldn't disguise formidable scholarship. Charles Salter was iconography and Augustans.[10]

But Jack Rillie and Edwin Morgan, in their shared office, were recognisably different to their students of the late 1950s:

They were the Moderns, the now men, from T.S. Eliot to the Beat generation. We called them 'The Rillie–Morgan Axis'. They were hip. Intimate with existentialism and the writings of angry young men. A whiff of danger on Gilmorehill. A cell.

The subversive impact can be guessed at through notes EM made for a talk to the University's Literary Society on 27 November 1957. Entitled ' "Angry Young Men" in Poetry?', it makes connections between that current British literary movement and American experimental poetry. Thom Gunn, an English poet who had recently moved to California, is noted for dealing with Marlon Brando, Elvis Presley and James Dean in his poems. But EM's main enthusiasm is for Allen Ginsberg:

The main thing abt Ginsberg is the directness of his language, the way he gives things their real names, the xtraordinary impression his verse makes of a person actually speaking to you, gettg something off his chest, an angry frustrated person, an outsider, a wild one, a lone wolf who raises this 'howl' of his against the most widely-cherished prejudices of his country. Ginsberg is like J. Porter, then [the main character in John Osborne's play, *Look Back in Anger* (1956)] in striking us as being in some ways an intolerable character, *but* absolutely *alive*, and he is also talking abt things that are really happening, & taxing us to take up some attitude to these things.[11]

There is a sense of frustrated identification here with the gay and bohemian American poet, who has the freedom to speak out creatively against prejudices in ways that a Scottish poet could not yet dare to. At this early stage of his professional life, academic work actually conflicted with EM's artistic ambitions. This was partly to do with the size of classes in English Literature at a big urban university, with the number of courses to be taught and the hundreds of essays and examination papers to be marked on a yearly basis.

He gives an outline of this in 'Notes on the Poet's Working Day', written for a symposium organised by *Ambit* magazine in 1972 (reprinted in *Nothing Not Giving Messages*: 196–9). Even at that later stage of his career, by which time he had been promoted to Reader, EM carried a significant load of teaching, on four out of the five main courses, with five lecture series and a special option course on Scottish literature, group seminars and individual tutorials to take, plus postgraduate research supervision. Some days were relatively free, with only several hours of seminars or tutorials, but 'others are really packed on a ten-till-five basis'.

The sample November day he describes is certainly full, with much of what we might now call multi-tasking in its academic, administrative and social aspects. There is also a side-lining of any creative work: 'this is always difficult to do within the university's surroundings and I seldom in fact do it'. The one idea for a poem that crosses his mind is later worked up as a sonnet and appears in *Nothing Not Giving Messages* next to his 'working day', as 'Cantus Interruptus'. The worst part of the job was always the marking of essays and exam papers:

> even with a substantial staff this is a heavy and soul-battering operation. There's often a real clash between the desire to write poetry and the necessity to get so many papers marked by a certain deadline. And there's no way out except burning the midnight oil [. . .] it is at these moments that you feel like giving up the job.

Here too his sense of identification with Gerard Manley Hopkins was confirmed. Writing to his mother from Dublin in July 1888, Hopkins complained: 'It is great, very great drudgery. I can not of course say it is wholly useless, but I believe that most of it is and that I bear a burden which crushes me and does little to help any good end'.[12] One way of coping, in EM's case, was to take a sort of revenge against drudgery by recording the most unintention-ally amusing or silly responses given by exam candidates in English, categorising and then publishing them in a thought-provoking, but also in some ways shocking, essay that appeared in two parts in the journal *The Twentieth Century* in December 1956 and January 1957. Here are just two of 'A Hantle of Howlers':

> 193. It was in Greece that Caesar crossed Egypt and became enarmoured of Cleopatra.
> 194. Burns was very good to small flowers [. . .]. The poem goes on to address the mountain daisy and then cuts it down.

EM's essay could be said to be arguing for a change to the traditional sustained diet of written examinations as a valid assessment of understanding. These were a sort of cross-country race through the muddy landscape of memory for too many of the candidates. As an invigilator EM could sense and sympathise with:

> the whole examination-room ferment of disorganised recollec-tions, and the painful attempt to organise them which issues in broken logic and bad grammar. The heads of the writers lie open, and we can gaze into them at the jumble of knowledge they contain. The scene may perhaps shock and surprise, as well as amuse.

A former colleague of mine, one of his students in the late 1950s, still vividly recalls EM's kindliness of expression in the examina-tion hall. But if this article was a plea for a more humane university examination system, it was in advance of its time. The Finals for my year group, a decade later, were five and a half days of writing, morning and afternoon without stint, producing no doubt its own share of howlers to add to the heap. And in any case, was improvement in assessment practice really his main intention? Most teachers off-load their frustrations about pupils' unpredictable minds to staffroom colleagues, often amusingly. But not often to the general public, or to such of its intellectuals as happened to read *The Twentieth Century*. It may be simply another example of EM's delight in wordplay and the serendipity of life and language. He republished this piece in *Essays* (1974). That's possibly a minus, though I'm willing to be convinced otherwise.

Nowadays, a fairer balance of timing and types of assessment is to be found in the University of Glasgow, as elsewhere. There is more continuous evaluation of lecturers, too, not only as to the quality of their teaching but also of their research 'output'. The 1950s were not highly productive years for EM in this regard, at least from the sort of academic perspective of present-day 'research assessment exercises'. These take place every four to five years, with varying formats, and grade university lecturers in terms of the significance and originality of their books, chapters or academic papers published in that period.

In 1950 EM published 'Women and Poetry' in the *Cambridge Journal* III:11. ' "Strong Lines" and Strong Minds: reflections on the prose of Browne and Johnson' (*Cambridge Journal* IV:8) followed in 1951; and in the following year 'Dunbar and the Language of Poetry' in *Essays in Criticism* II:2. 'Dryden's Drudging' appeared in the *Cambridge Journal* VI:7 in 1953 (and would be reprinted in *Dryden: a collection of critical essays* ed. B.N. Schilling in 1963). There is a year's gap and then 'A Prelude to *The Prelude*' in *Essays in Criticism* V:4 in 1955 (which would also be reprinted in *British Romantic Poets* ed. S.K. Kamar in 1966 and 1967). In 1956, his 'Jujitsu for the Educated: Reflections on Hugh MacDiarmid's poem *In Memoriam James Joyce*' appeared in *The Twentieth Century*: 160, in advance of his 'Hantle of

Howlers' later that year – although it is highly doubtful that this last would 'count' as an academic paper in such an exercise.

For the rest of the decade, there is an increase in publication rate and diversity, with many brief articles, book and theatre reviews, translations and poems in mainly Scottish literary reviews, newspapers or little magazines, more or less fugitive. His real artistic interests were clearly beginning to lead him away from the academic lecturer's career record of publications, in which a focused research specialism tends to be expected and valued. EM was working towards a different and wider cultural and creative horizon.

Something else got in the way of his academic productiveness in the late 1950s. In 1957, along with Jack Rillie, he began to provide a 'Summary of Periodical Literature' that appeared thrice yearly in the *Review of English Studies*, from volume VIII:29 in February 1957 to volume XVI:64 in November 1965. This was another kind of drudgery, and is the 'bibliography' referred to in *Thirteen Ways of Looking at Rillie*, good-humouredly in retrospect. They had to categorise and document in one convenient list for other scholars every article that had appeared in the most important learned journals of English Studies.

When I asked EM in old age why he had got involved in this work, whether or not it was a serious attempt at building an academic CV, and if he had actively sought the commitment, he had forgotten the exact circumstances. But since his professor, Peter Alexander, with Norman Davis also of the University, had become co-editors of the *Review of English Studies* in 1954, and then joint editors from 1955 until 1964, it seems likely that this was a semi-official request. After 1964, EM and Jack Rillie continued to fulfil their commitment for one further year under the new editor before bowing out.

In the first three years, their work appeared anonymously, and this must also have rankled. It seems likely that their professor had taken them on as foot soldiers in his own particular academic campaign. It could be said that he was inducting his young colleagues into academic responsibilities, and certainly some credit is attached to such scholarship. But we have also seen its impact on the diminution of EM's original research publications, and perhaps also Rillie's, towards the end of the 1950s. There's a postcard from Rillie to EM, sent at the end of his brief summer holiday, making arrangements to pick up half of the heap of journals piled on the desk in their room with the threadbare carpet, and return to the grind.

EM was also reviewing regularly for this same academic journal, among others, in areas of particular poetic interest: one example is his review of *Articulate Energy* by the poet and academic, Donald Davie, in *Review of English Studies* VIII:30, in May 1957. Thus he was perfecting his ability to work accurately to different deadlines in the clear and forthright style that made him invaluable to numerous editors. His manuscript versions of articles reveal a sense of confident speed in still-elegant but hasty handwriting, with few crossings-out or second thoughts. Using secretarial skills retained from his army years, these would then be speedily typed and sent. Sometimes the time and cost of posting is noted.

A drawback to such varied productivity was that he began to feel he had not yet found an academic niche. Literature in translation and comparative literature, where he had genuinely new expertise, were not yet recognised as separate disciplines in UK universities at this time. His interest in Russian literature might also have taken him in a new direction.

In a sense it did. On the 18th of April 1955 he paid 40 pounds, 2 shillings and 8 pence to the Scotland–USSR Friendship Society as a delegate on a month's study tour of Russia. Leave of absence had been granted by the Principal of the University, provided that Professor Alexander did not object. The visit coincided with the busiest period of examination marking, but permission was given. This release from the normal grind must have contributed to the sense of enthusiasm conveyed in two pocket notebooks in which EM recorded precise details of visits to a state vegetable farm at Kiev, an orphanage and kindergarten, the impressive Moscow Metro, the new University, which was a skyscraper 32 storeys high, and the Ministry of Education, as well as cultural excursions to ballet, opera and art exhibitions. He noted down everything from academic syllabuses to the prices of everyday goods, and was struck by the contrast between sixteen-lane main streets and meagre shop windows with shoddy domestic items for sale.[13]

The delegation was five strong: Anne Simpson and her husband, a teacher, from Edinburgh, Professor Ferguson Rogers of the Department of Psychological Medicine at Glasgow University, a journalist called Meg Munro, and EM. They travelled by boat to Helsinki and then, because of ice in the Gulf of Finland, by First Class Sleeper to Moscow. The trip had been organised by VOKS, the state organisation for cultural relations, and EM told me that he had no idea why he was approached to join it, except that he was known to be interested in Russian literature. He was in steady correspondence with Hugh MacDiarmid on literary matters from at least July 1953 onwards, inviting him to speak at the University Literary Society, and had met up with him at a USSR Society Conference in the summer of 1954. The older poet praised EM's use of 'a species of Scots' in his 'Dialogue 1: James Joyce and Hugh MacDiarmid', the opening of 'The Whittrick' (CP: 79–116). Both men shared a deep interest in Scottish nationalism and Soviet socialism. However, EM had no sense of any attempts made to 'turn' him to communism on the Moscow trip. He recognised of course that there must be a propaganda element involved. This he was willing to fulfil in talks and writing after the trip.

On his return he gave lectures on his experiences to the Rutherglen Rotary Club and the Busby and Clarkston Literary and Debating Society, and wrote a two-part article for *The Glasgow Herald* (12 June 1955), which had to be cut because of competing demands. There he focused on the paradoxes of the socialist revolution:

> Here is a country where the ordinary citizen of Moscow can easily
> buy a seat for theatrical productions which in ballet and opera are

probably the best in the world, and yet where he can hardly buy a decent pair of shoes or a well-cut suit.

He commented on the confusing effect of the contrast between 'the drab outward appearance of things and the obvious animation and happiness of the people', and was struck – as in the poetry of Mayakovsky and in Russian futurist work in architecture and in film generally – by the sheer energy of what was going on:

> Everywhere you go you will see the silhouette of giant cranes above unfinished walls, and the whole country seems to be stirring, humming, constructing from morning to night, and during the night as well.

This feeling would be re-awakened in him by Glasgow's slum clearance and high-rise building in the 1960s, which he celebrated in 'The Second Life':

> writing as the aircraft roar
> over building sites, in this warm west light
> by the daffodil banks that were never so crowded and lavish –
> green May, and the slow great blocks rising
> under yellow tower cranes, concrete and glass and steel
> out of a dour rubble it was and barefoot children gone –
>
> (CP:180)

However, any illusions that he might have had about progress under the soviet system were dispelled somewhat when the editor of the *Soviet Weekly* cut out any reference to the 'drab outward appearance' in an article EM had sent in, leaving only the 'obvious animation and happiness of the people'. His subsequent letter of protest was, of course, not published.

There are some photographs taken on the tour, showing an EM eager, bespectacled, wearing a jerkin, and 'kilted in Kiev' as he later wrote in 'Pieces of Me':

Beyond the Last Dragon

A crowd gathered
From nowhere like filings
to a magnet, muttering,
whispering, pointing,
man in a skirt – [14]

His fellow delegates had abandoned him for a joke and he was left alone for several alarming minutes among the proletariat.

Back in Scotland at this time, too, he felt oddly isolated and out of place, lacking a clear direction. He considered becoming a librarian, a job which might leave him more time or opportunity to balance learning and creativity. If he imagined a role for himself, it would be that of the *doctus poeta*, the learned poet bearing an epic responsibility for his nation's history and identity. And yet poems composed in a distinctive voice were slow to be written, and even more slowly published.

POETRY AND TRANSLATION

In a sense, EM's frustration in constructing a poetic role for himself ran parallel with the halting reconstruction of Scotland after the war. In 1951 a quarter of the population still lived in dwellings of two rooms or less, a third of these sharing a toilet. Although not on a Russian scale, shortages and rationing held back the sale of goods in a climate of austerity, with domestic production falling and greater reliance on imports. Heavy engineering and shipbuilding were again in decline after an immediate post-war surge of rebuilding, and Scotland seemed locked into low-value industries with far less investment than elsewhere in the United Kingdom, or in post-war Germany for that matter, in new areas such as pharmaceuticals, machine tools, telephones, cars and light engineering. By the early 1950s, as Richard Finlay points out, average incomes in Scotland were about ten per cent lower than elsewhere in the United Kingdom, hindering the kind of vibrant domestic economy that might in turn attract new industry.[15]

The Dark Decade 1950–1960

There was also a sense of frustrated nationhood following the signing of the National Covenant in 1948, exemplified in the raid on Westminster Abbey by Glasgow University students on Christmas Day 1950, to bring back the Coronation Stone or Stone of Destiny that had been taken from Scotland by Edward I. The stone was eventually returned at Arbroath Abbey in April 1951, making the connection with the Scots' declaration there against English overlordship in 1320. There were also protests in Scotland after the Coronation in June 1953 about the designation Elizabeth II appearing on postboxes, since there had been no previous Scottish queen named Elizabeth.

Although Scottish productivity continued to decline through the decade, paradoxically social indications did begin to show more prosperity in the second half of the 1950s. Wages and house building increased under a Conservative government, and new estates were built on the periphery of Glasgow: Easterhouse, Pollok and Castlemilk. And yet their monotonous design, the inadequate social planning for shops and leisure, and the poor workmanship with materials unsuited to Scotland's climate all meant that the centralised modern vision of the planners failed to live up to its promise on paper, much as its soviet equivalent would do. EM was keenly aware of such social and economic changes, through his family's involvement in heavy industry, through his own encounters with men of different social backgrounds, and through his engagement with Scots language and poetry as one crucial marker of independent identity. We can sense here the beginnings of the social or political edge to his poetry, that runs from his 'Glasgow Sonnets' of the early 1970s through to his great poem for the opening of the Scottish Parliament building in October 2004, which combined a celebration of the event and place with stern warnings to the parliamentarians in equal measure.

Although never a joiner of political parties, he came to see his role in Scotland as being to inform its literary culture about American and European perspectives, movements and writers. Increasingly he wrote for Scottish journals such as *Saltire Review*,

The Voice of Scotland and *Lines Review*. He favoured others such as *Jabberwok*, and its continuation *Sidewalk*, both based in Edinburgh but with a marked interest in 'anti-provincialism' and an American and European focus. *Sidewalk*, for example, published work by William Burroughs, Robert Creeley and Gary Snyder, with translations of Alain Robbe-Grillet and Tristan Corbière, among others. At the very beginning of the 1960s, EM published translations of Pasternak, Michaux, Mayakovsky and Quasimodo in *Sidewalk*, as well as an article on Jean Genet. He was reviewing Scottish drama regularly in the late 1950s for *Encore*, a London-based journal, and also reviewed Russian literature for the *Anglo Soviet Journal*. In Scotland, he was a regular *Glasgow Herald* reviewer on a range of literary and cultural topics.

In all of this, EM seemed to be participating in the somewhat more positive social and economic climate of Scotland in the late 1950s. Yet it might also be said that all this activity was perhaps a displacement for his frustrated sense of poetic destiny. His early poems of this decade can be read as a creative reworking, almost a pastiche, of the literature he was having to teach. 'The Vision of Cathkin Braes' (CP: 43–9) is a comic version of the medieval dream vision poem, and 'Ingram Lake' (CP: 50–5) is a stylistic critique of the dramatic styles of, in turn, Tennessee Williams, T.S. Eliot, Jean-Paul Sartre, Konstantin Semeonoff and Christopher Fry. 'Verses for a Christmas Carol' conflates James Joyce and Gerard Manley Hopkins (CP: 56) and 'A Courtly Overture' converts the Glasgow gay scene extremely obliquely into an Elizabethan setting of elegance combined with menace (CP: 49–50). The question of his individual poetic voice and role remains unanswered at this point, despite signs of advancement in his ventriloquial skill with other voices, and of lessons learned from engagement with other poetic minds through the steady act of translation.

The commentary of friends was also helpful, although it may well not have seemed so in the bleakest times. G.K. Hunter was constant in his support, and also in his criticism where he reckoned that EM fell short of his true potential: 'You have vast gifts, but sometimes seem to me to spend them on matters (?whittricks) of remote importance and minimal interest [. . .]'.[16] This was on 30 December 1957, in response to *The Whittrick,* a poem in eight dialogues which EM had been working on since late 1954. That seems harsh comment but it is true, in comparison with the quality of the poetry that he would later write.

In early 1956, Hunter had also offered judicious comment on *The Cape of Good Hope,* which was finally published by Peter Russell's Pound Press in 1955 in a limited edition of 195 copies, after many delays and accidents to which Russell's enterprises seemed prone – in this case, a fire at the printing works. He praised the poem, liking especially the beginning and the lyrics throughout, but taking issue with the portrayal of frustrated artists in Section III which showed, he felt, a kind of 'inverted sentimentality':

> the episode selected was not typical in any case of the total vision of any one of them, but was distorted by your determination that only the worst would do. And conversely I find something like ordinary sentimentality in the lovers with the faithful dreams and the dreaming child in its cot [. . .] you are saying (I believe) that the creative artist has to suffer the horror of separateness and dehumanisation but is compensated by the patient detachment he acquires in his work; but I cannot feel myself that the last section answers the challenge of Section III – the sense of order is conveyed weakly and conventionally, whereas the sense of horror and anti-humanity is strained and powerful. I say I am quarrelling with your meaning here, for I think your assumptions are *wrong.* The great artists are not anti-human, except to the same extent as they are pro-human. Their suffering can only be said to be *for the sake of humanity,* if they show humanity to be worthwhile, if their extraordinariness hinges on ordinariness and comes to rest just there.

Sensing the likely impact on his friend of this astringent judgement (yet an accurate judgement, as it transpired, since it was

111

precisely in a celebration of ordinary human experience that EM's poetry would soar in the 1960s), he adds:

> If I am not honest with you I ought to be completely silent, which I am not willing to be, or indeed able to be, for even my silence would be a kind of (unkind) speech.[17]

Presumably EM was sensible enough to take such an argued criticism seriously, and it must have recalled the range and sharpness of their pre-war undergraduate conversations along the slopes of Cathkin Braes. Ultimately it was a more helpful comment than Hugh MacDiarmid's response in July 1955, on being sent a copy of the poem. He finds it splendid, and notes the resemblance to W.S. Graham's *The Night Fishing,* while also quoting a *Times Literary Supplement* review on the 'intellectual muddle' at the heart of that poem, to EM's advantage. We might see this either as evidence of MacDiarmid's real loss of lyric sensitivity with age, or as his genuine recognition of EM as a fellow poet of ideas.

It could well be that *The Cape of Good Hope* was written in rivalry of Sydney Graham's poem. He had sent EM a copy of it for critique, which was provided on 13 May 1950: 'a fine and moving experience (though I know myself so *near* many of the ideas that my liking is more of an expected identification than the quite objective comment you're after)'. EM pointed out that Graham had contacted him in 'just the most packed and hashed week of the year at the university – examinations, marks, class tickets, prize-buying, meetings, dinners', and that he had mostly read the poem in bed from midnight onwards. Nevertheless, the response is detailed, helpful in pointing out several spelling errors, and positive:

> One thing, I am glad I called my *Nine* article 'Graham's Threshold', for here you are cast off from the shore and sending back something brighter than herringshine. You become the sea bell or the sea light, and there is something about both these things that fairly shakes the light in the blood and the tolled heart.[18]

EM's article, a review of Graham's collection *The White Threshold*, had just appeared in Peter Russell's magazine, *Nine* II:II (No.3) in the same month. The praise here is sincerely meant, but his friend's achievement probably spurred him on to begin *The Cape of Good Hope*, which he then worked on from August to December of 1950.

G.K. Hunter continued to support EM's poetic ambitions. In March of 1956 he was in the process of moving from Hull to Reading University, and had arranged with his new Head of Department, Professor D.T. Gordon, to publish a slim volume of EM's translations of Eugenio Montale, through Reading School of Art. Matters dragged on, partly as a result of Gordon's absence through illness, with Hunter acting as a negotiator on EM's behalf. Finally by May 1958, EM was given a free hand to decide on the contents of the book, which shortly appeared in an edition of one hundred and fifty copies, with the Italian text printed with facing translations. In the introduction, several people are thanked 'for help and encouragement of various kinds', but not G.K. Hunter, surprisingly, who had done most to initiate and sustain the project.

Silences, as Hunter himself had remarked earlier, are a kind of speech. Another remarkable silence is to be found in the case of Attila József, a Hungarian poet born in Budapest in 1905. EM considered him one of the major poets of the century. His many translations of József from the 1960s onwards were collected in *Attila József: Sixty Poems* (Mariscat Press, 2001). EM always wrote that he 'came across' József's work originally in Italian translation in the 1950s. In fact, Hugh MacDiarmid had the booklet, and asked for EM's help in translating the poems in 1959.[19] He also directed the younger poet to *The New Hungarian Quarterly* where essays on József's work and further versions in French and English were to be found. Working on these translations from the Italian spurred EM on to learn some Hungarian. But having received them, MacDiarmid was unable to make poetic use of them and by 17 July 1961 he gave EM a free hand to work on József's poetry, and make it his own.

This sense of 'owning' the foreign poet derived from EM's frequent sense of empathy and imaginative identification with the particular vision of the world held out by the original text. He thought deeply about what was happening in the process of translation throughout the 1950s, lecturing on it, for example, at a conference in University College of North Staffordshire, now Keele University, on 29 February 1956, and at Bristol University Literary Society on 7 December of the same year. He referred to contemporary experiments with machine translation in Russia, England and America, and was aware of the complex interplay of elements and patterns of grammar, word connotations, sound and visual elements in any poetic text. But a crucial element for him was absorbing the atmosphere of a particular poem or poet:

> For example, long before one fully understands a difficult poem by Eugenio Montale, his world stirs and reveals itself: there is shimmer, a play of light on water and on crumbling buildings, a face glancing in a mirror, an accordion being played in the twilight [. . .]. Absorbing that atmosphere is a step in comprehension, and one grasps at this point not only the tone of the particular poem but the signature of the author's style; one begins to sense his 'hand', his way of putting things.

This is quoted from EM's later article 'The Translation of Poetry' in *The Scottish Review* 2:5, 1976, but the passage is in fact extrapolated from a talk with the same title, given to the Durham University English Society on 1 November 1957; and some phrases here also appear in his Preface to *Poems from Eugenio Montale* in 1959 (CT: 3). So this view emerged from his immersion in the act of translation in the 1950s, and remained his considered position. As the translation overlays the 'grid' of meaning with the 'web' of atmospheric impressions, something strange happens:

> Translating is searching for the English (or Scots) equivalent, but an equivalent of what? Not, apparently, [. . .] the words of the

foreign language so much as the words of *the poem itself*, which has attained some sort of non-verbal interlinguistic experience in the mind [. . .]. Without desiring to be mystical, I believe there does seem to be some sense [. . .] in which the poem exists independently of the language of its composition.

('The Translation of Poetry': 22)

He then goes on to quote from Walter Benjamin's essay 'The Task of the Translator' (1923), to the effect that the poem is written not in its original language nor in its translated language, but in a third 'true language' which exists behind these actual languages, and which both the poet and the translator attempt to release through their individual expressions of the hidden original. This was why EM came to see his *Collected Translations* as another *Collected Poems*.

The process was helped in EM's case whenever he felt a particular interest in the personality of the poet he was translating. Discussing translation with Tim Parks at the Edinburgh Book Festival in August 1999, he re-emphasised that sense of personal involvement with Mayakovsky:

Some people were put off either by his outrageous behaviour or by his political beliefs or both; he was said to be a loudmouth, a propagandist, a *fugleman* for the Revolution and nothing more. I didn't believe that. I found him a fascinating, complex, eventually tragic figure with whom I could readily empathize. If I had not found this, would I have been able to translate him? Perhaps not!

In the 1950s, that involvement and identification was not only with Mayakovsky, but with József and with Montale, and when he writes about them, and as he translates them, he is revealing something of his own deepest longings in those years. In Eugenio Montale he had encountered a parallel EM:

speaking more particularly of his own feelings of isolation, a theme to which he often reverts, and which is compounded almost equally of a desire and a fear to be swept up in the exhilarating but confusing flux of twentieth century experience. Uprooting [. . .] exile [. . .] and absence [. . .] are painful, yet nothing is more remarkable in other poems than the author's instinctive (and life-giving) yearning for abandon, change and movement, expressed in evocations of the great natural forces of the wind and the sea.

(CT: 4)

Perhaps it was this intensity of self-recognition, or a sense of his own 'co-authorship' with Montale in deciphering the 'true language' that lay behind the Italian's poetic experience, that caused EM to neglect the role of his friend G.K. Hunter in bringing the partnership to print.

Translations kept his poetic talents occupied when his own poetry was unforthcoming. In 1955, to take a single year as an example, we find him translating poems and madrigals by Théophile de Viau, G.B. Marino and Torquato Tasso in January and February, Guillaume Apollinaire in February and stanzas from Saint-Amant in March, with two poems by Pablo Neruda in April. Perhaps inspired by his trip to Russia, or using books purchased there, he turned to Pushkin and Lermontov in July, along with work from the Ukrainian poets Lesya Ukrainka, Taras Shevchenko and Yekaterina Shevelyova. In August came two poems by Vera Inber, and in September poems by Boris Pasternak and Anna Akhmatova. Single poems by Ukrainka and Leopardi followed in November and December, as his output slows in rhythm with teaching demands, before the new year opens with six poems by Heine in Scots.

Apart from working in the major languages of the European poetic tradition, in all sorts of forms, EM was clearly marking out a terrain in Russian and East European poetry. Peter Russell, his publisher, was supporting himself at this time as a bookseller and found many original Russian texts in prose and verse that EM purchased from him. A disadvantage of all this effort was that frequently editors would keep his translations for publication, and return his own poems. And yet it did at least mean that once he began to be published in his own right, he had a stock of translated work that could be published alongside his own collections in the 1960s and 1970s: *Sovpoems* (1961), *Sándor Weöres: Selected Poems* (1970), *Wi' the Haill Voice: 25 Poems by Vladimir Mayakovsky* (1972), *Fifty Renascence Love-Poems* (1975), *Rites of Passage* (1976) and *Platen: Selected Poems* (1978). Thus the reading public gained an impression of tremendous energy, diversity and success – which was at odds with the slow and often dispiriting progress which he actually experienced in the 1950s when much of this work of translation was done.

His first collection of poetry was published by the Glasgow publisher, William MacLellan in 1952: *The Vision of Cathkin Braes and other Poems*, twenty six pages in length. A companion volume, *Dies Irae and Other Poems and Translations* was intended for publication by Lotus Press in Hull. Again there may have been a Hunter connection, since he was working in the university there. EM's contact was Robin Skelton, who would later teach in the University of Victoria in Canada and support W.S. Graham in various ways, but he was now the one to break the news to EM of financial difficulties which prevented publication. EM had already designed a cover for the projected volume, although the editors reckoned that its severity would actually discourage potential buyers.

William MacLellan notified EM on 16 October 1952 that his *Cathkin Braes* had 'done fairly well in John Smith's [bookshop], but the incidence of reviews has been too low to raise interest'. In the following months, it was included ('Mr Morgan's madcap vision') in a Books for Christmas feature in *The Scotsman* newspaper. Like most young poets, EM was struggling to make his name through limited editions with limited sales. In June 1953, he was approached by the literary agents, Christy and Moore, for a publishing project and offered them the Scrapbooks as 'a Whitmanian reflecting glass of "the world" [. . .] refracted through one personality'.[20] But nothing came of this.

In such circumstances, contact with a poetic equal was valued keenly. As he wrote to Sydney Graham in April 1950:

You know, apart altogether from my natural desire to hear from you as you, I relish your communication as doves and ravens sent out from the Real, and they have I assure you plenty of waste rolling world to cross and cover, but when they come, when they do reach me and knock on the glass of whatever half or three-quarter-reality I am living in, I feel less like a forgotten survivor of godly flooding [. . .].[21]

In December of the same year, Graham asked EM for a loan of £5 'for about three months' to help him travel to a friend's farm, in order to recuperate from a leg injury that was taking too long to heal. In May 1954 he wrote: 'Dear Edwin, I know I owe you £5 that I will pay sometime [. . .]', but mentioned that he had been asked to select poems by young writers for a BBC Radio programme. EM immediately sent him some of his poems, but on 6 June 1954 received a reply from his friend:

This is ridiculous somehow but I just don't like those poems at all and I can't use any in the program [. . .] what disconcerts me most is – an over loudness, a clamour, a welter of too many objects containing (each one) political and moral overtones, too many 'high shock' content words too close together so that I long for it to be more quiet and for the ear to regain its full sensitivity [. . .]. I find the rhythms very often ridiculing the sense of the words.[22]

The effect of this, coming at the end of EM's most exhausting period of teaching and assessment in the academic year, can be imagined. Disappointment was compounded by the harsh honesty of a friend whose poetic talents he admired. If there was one period when he was tempted to suicide in a bleak decade, this would be the time. The thought was in his mind. 'Northern Nocturnal', written earlier but then revised in September 1954, powerfully evokes a dark Glasgow cityscape:

A late train blazes and shrieks past. I watch
As its train of sparks rides off into the darkness

Among the freezing stars, and over the Clyde's dark streams
 [. . .].
    And then to blackness, silence, cold, my sense
Chokes blind in breaking death, death like this night will
    free
My fire and verve of desire to the stone and the steel and
    the sea.

                                                            (CP: 565)

Sydney Graham came up to Glasgow to visit EM in late September 1954. He had trouble finding the house in Burnside on a bitterly cold night and arrived very late, having been misdirected by some of the passers-by (he may have been drunk, and would certainly have looked out of place in the neighbourhood). In his wanderings through Burnside, he wrote, 'the wind seemed to go right into my spine' – and it seems his reception was also frosty. Harsh words were spoken, and EM felt obliged to send him a long typewritten letter on the 15 November, with the gift of a pen: 'It was exciting, as always. If it was too exciting, and I was a little on edge, and said things I shouldn't have said, I hope you'll forgive in the circumstances'. He then recounts a curious experience that happened as he tried to fall asleep that night:

> I kept being startled by a succession of the most astonishingly vivid visual images I have ever seen sleeping or waking [. . .]. I saw a series of bursts of energy: great curtains of rain coming suddenly down, rockets hurtling past, brilliant fusings and crystallizations, savage animals [. . .]. I suppose my mind was very much awake, and yet there was no intellectual content in the imagery – at least, if there was, it had all been turned into pictorial and kinetic terms [. . .].

This vision is reminiscent of his childhood involvement with fantasy fiction, and also of his late startling dreams, looking far forward. At all three stages of life, he seems to be attesting to the powers of his own imagination, especially when in a position of relative weakness. In this case, EM seems to recognise the disparity between his own poetic achievement and Sydney Graham's, but in terms of an identification that reminds us of his practice as an identifying translator:

> I still find [your poetry] more interesting than most of the poetry that is being written, and in a curious sort of way, because of the strongly continuing (no matter how superficially interrupted) involvement of each of us with the other (which I would never give up) I find myself wanting or willing you to make certain changes and developments, as if I was more concerned with poetry you have yet to write than what you have written.

The focus on willpower here is symptomatic of EM's approach to poetry: he is ambitious even for those with a lyric power he does not yet himself possess.

Whether or not the summer and early autumn of 1954 were the nadir of EM's sense of his own worth as a poet and person, things began gradually to open up for him thereafter. Through Erica Marx of Hand and Flower Press who had published his *Beowulf* translation, he appeared in the PEN anthologies for 1954 and 1955. He began the series of 'Whittrick' dialogues which would occupy him until 1957, and which she wished to publish until, as before, lack of funding made this impossible. In a long letter to her on 21 August 1957, he attempts to explain the meaning that this sequence had for him:

> The Whittrick in general stands for truth or reality, but seen especially under its fleeting or revolutionary aspect, which is in any case how it impresses itself as most people's minds (say when they fall in love or have some experience in wartime or just in everyday life have something happen to them which they cannot forget), and is also how it tends to appear in the arts, each work of art being like a 'flash' of something passing, whether a great sheet of lightning that lights up a whole tract of life (*Macbeth* or *The Canterbury Tales*) or a bright-eyed weasel running along a wall and

darting across the country road in front of you in a striped flash of vitality and unexpectedness (*The Jolly Beggars*, perhaps, or *The Whittrick*?). I have been startled by a weasel myself in this kind of way, not far from Loch Lomond [. . .].[23]

EM then goes on to show how each dialogue shows an aspect of this central idea, pointing particularly to the opening dialogue of James Joyce and Hugh MacDiarmid (CP: 79ff) and to the Zen dialogue that is number seven in the sequence (CP: 106ff) as the clearest expression of it. He relates it to his admiration of the Russian revolutionary spirit of 1917, 'as opposed to Stalinist monolithic gradualism', and suggests that it is useful to keep facing the West with this revolutionary ideal: 'the daring, the unusual, the whittrick-like, the tykish [. . .]'. The final dialogue, which he had not, at that point, written, was to deal with scientific attempts 'to control or even create the whittrick, by man himself, the science of cybernetics [. . .]'. The whittrick thus finally becomes a machine that is made to think and talk creatively.

This poem sequence, then, is in many ways a statement of intent by EM, who would continue to explore poetically the interface between human creativity and machine intelligence in the modern world. *The Whittrick* was eventually published as a whole by Akros Publications in 1973, but its final focus on science was clearly in tune with events that were taking place in the late 1950s. In October 1957, for example, the USSR launched Sputnik I, and then in the following month Sputnik II, with a dog on board. The progress of these satellites was tracked by Jodrell Bank radio telescope. This was also International Geophysical Year, with scientists concentrating on Antarctic exploration, oceanographic and meteorological research. In the following year, the United States satellite Explorer I was launched from Cape Canaveral to study cosmic rays, and the nuclear submarine *Nautilus* passed under the ice cap at the North Pole. In 1959, Lunik II and III reached and then photographed the moon. All of this, and other developments such as the British hovercraft that crossed the Channel in two hours in July 1959, lifted EM's spirits, and resonated with scientific interests that had moved him since childhood.

He was beginning to be recognised as a poet in Scotland too, not only through his critical articles and reviews but by his inclusion in *Honoured Shade: An Anthology of New Scottish Poetry to Mark the Bicentenary of the Birth of Robert Burns* (1959), edited by Norman MacCaig. This book would generate its own literary controversy, as we will see, since it excluded some of the younger, more experimental poets with whom EM tended to align himself. Yet he had worked hard to win acceptance among 'the establishment' too. For example, he was called upon to write the article on 'Scottish Literature: In Scots and English' for the *Encyclopaedia Britannica* in the same year.

Another young poet included, like EM, in the anthology but also somewhat distanced from the largely Edinburgh-based mainstream was Iain Crichton Smith. The two were in contact from 1956, EM having sent him a copy of *The Cape of Good Hope* in the late summer of 1956. Iain Crichton Smith was teaching in Oban at that point, but later moved to Dumbarton. In letters, EM discussed the possibilities of a communist society, but they also shared opinions on literature and their own poetry. At the end of January 1957, Iain Crichton Smith sent EM a collection of two years' worth of poems (31), asking his friend to help him separate out the best from the worst. This was done, using a system of one, two or three stars. Once Smith had moved to Dumbarton to teach in Clydebank High School, they would occasionally meet and discuss the authors they were reading. EM took photographs, including one of him chewing a match in gangster fashion, and sent copies to his friend. He thanked him but said: 'The one with the match is hellish, really, really hellish. That of course is not the fault of the photographer – it is the fault of the match.'[24] The two poets would remain trusted friends.

As the decade ended, there was also for EM the energising contact with contemporary American poetry, partly through his links with Migrant Press. This most influential, most fugitive operation lived up, or down, to its name. It was run from his garage in Ventura, California, by a remarkable Scottish doctor and poet, Gael Turnbull, educated in both England and North America. The hand-duplicated publication *Migrant* that he edited and produced there was sent out to friends and experimental poets across North America and Europe. As the poet Richard Price puts it, 'quietly, exploratively, and with the invaluable British editing of his old school friend Michael Shayer, *Migrant* heralded the decade of ideas and creativity now thought of as the 1960s'.[25]

Through his contact with *Migrant*, EM would make new connections with poets otherwise working in isolation from one another: Anselm Hollo, Ian Hamilton Finlay, Hugh Creighton Hill, Roy Fisher. Creating such a network of British poets, and linking them with the Black Mountain poets and other significant new American writers, such as Cid Corman, Charles Olson, Robert Duncan, Robert Creeley and Denise Levertov, with the continuing influence of an older modernist generation represented by William Carlos Williams and Louis Zukofsky, had been Gael Turnbull's hope. EM was already predisposed towards such poetry through his attraction to the Beat poetry of Allen Ginsberg, Gregory Corso, Lawrence Ferlinghetti and Gary Snyder, and the prose of Jack Kerouac, with their provocative, anti-hierarchical explorations of off-beat and forbidden dimensions of modern life. These were in part aspects of his own life. There was also the influence on these writers of Zen Bhuddism: if he described *The Whittrick* as a sort of Zen poem, it was also influenced by his reading of the Beats.

EM probably came across *Migrant* in a London bookshop and made contact with Michael Shayer, its English editor, offering poems and translations – in particular his translations of Maya-kovsky. Shayer was a scientist as well as a poet, at that point school teaching in Worcester, although he would later become an influential professor of psychology in London. At first he could make little of the Scots language versions of Mayakovsky, but eventually came to appreciate the significance of what EM was attempting to do. And in their correspondence at the turn of the decade, we can hear EM trying to articulate both the problems and the potential that he had wrestled with throughout a difficult decade:

> A writer can overcome, in the actual production of his works, deficiencies and frustrations which are real enough – and perhaps criticisable enough – in his private and sexual life. He might have 'difficulties with women' and yet write an epithalamium. All depends on his attitude and spirit, his deepest desires and hopes. Even a greatly frustrated creative artist like the homosexual Tchaikovsky or Michelangelo can make his artistic appeal and impact at a wide and universal and even popular level, although the tensions which lie at the back of the work are a matter for psychologist.

The letter is typed and carbon-copied, as EM tended to do when he was conscious of making a strong and reasoned statement of his position, as if to preserve it for posterity, although it may also have been part of the normal self-reflectiveness of the artist. *Migrant*'s mode of operation encouraged such intense but long-distance discussion by letter, sustained over time:

> And science: science must somehow someday be brought into literature to a far greater extent than it has been [. . .] in fact one of my strongest feelings is that of being on the threshold of a great epoch of history, and I only hope I live long enough to see the developments that are coming. I am very susceptible to the 'epic' feeling, to the idea of exploration, adventure, endurance, discovery, and I think that this feeling is very important to man as a species [. . .].[26]

This was a credo which would shape and inform the surge of EM's poetry for the rest of his long creative life. Here it marks the light which was beginning to shine for him at the end of a decade whose darkness must have seemed, in his worst moments, un-relieved. But two night poems, one from the start of the decade and the other from beyond its dark midpoint, show how far he had come psychologically. 'From Cathkin Braes: a View of Korea' is dated 1951 and begins with the speaker on 'a quiet ridge', gazing over the city that lies calm 'In its streetshine and smoke below [. . .]'. But what fills his mind are images from Bloody Ridge and Heartbreak Hill in Korea:

> [. . .] a night of flares and blood,
> Shadows, the shriek of jets
> And men like shadows running
> From thicket to stunted thicket
> Gaining a tree, an ambush,
> An outpost, a shelter, a bullet [. . .].

(CP: 570)

The poem, although deeply felt, has to remain at a distance from its theme of war's inhumanity. There is a sense of agonised stasis. The watcher can only imagine.

'Night Pillion' is dated 1956 and begins with the motorbike taking off as the traffic lights turn green:

> The shuddering machine let out its roar
> As we sprang forward into brilliant streets.
> Beyond your shoulders and helmet, the walls rose
> Well into darkness, mounted up, plunged past –
> Hunting the clouds that hunted the few stars.

The energy and involvement continue on this night ride through Glasgow:

> We lost the shining tram-lines in the slums
> As we kept south; the shining trolley-wires
> Glinted through Gorbals; on your helmet a glint hung.

The poet suddenly realizes that 'what we flashed past was life / As what we flash into is life, and life / will not stand still until within one flash / Of words or paint or human love it stops / Transfixed [. . .]'. This is the sort of whittrick-moment of inspiration and suddenly glimpsed significance that EM felt sustained by:

> And my blood quickened in me as I saw
> Everything guided, vibrant, where our shadow
> Glided along the pavements and the walls.

They have turned for home, and 'roared in a straight line for Rutherglen'. There is a confusion of emotions as 'tenements and lives, the wind, our wheels, / the vibrant windshield and your guiding hands / Fell into meaning, whatever meaning it was – ', and the poem ends with a realistic sense of the ambiguities of all human relationships:

> Perhaps I only saw the thoroughfares,
> The river, the dancing of the foundry-flares?
> Joy is where long solitude dissolves.
> I rode with you towards human needs and cares.

> (CP: 461)

Some of the ambiguities may have related to the friendship between the pillion passenger and his driver here. He was a young art student from Burnside, either at the Glasgow School of Art, or about to go there, who would sometimes come to EM's house to discuss painting. So their relationship had echoes of the earlier one with Lex Allan who tutored him in piano and Latin, although EM was now the older person, and the age gap much wider than the five or six years of that 1930s friendship. But it is likely that he saw in his driver a younger self, an alternative self, someone who would not be persuaded against an artistic career.

Their joint shadow glides along pavement and walls, and the poem works through that balanced sense of distance and closeness, physical movement and reflection, and a deep engagement with technology on journeys out and back that would become the mark of EM's mature poetry, 'Hunting [. . .] the stars'. There was the promise, too, that solitude might occasionally dissolve into another existence, a second life.

CHAPTER SIX

The Singing Sixties 1960–1970

> At forty I woke up, saw it was day,
> found there was love, heard a new beat, heard Beats,
> sent airmail solidarity to Saõ
> Paulo's poetic-concrete revolution,
> knew Glasgow – what? – knew Glasgow new – somehow –
> new with me, with John, with cranes, diffusion
> of another concrete revolution, not bad,
> not good, but new. And new was no illusion:
> a spring of words, a sloughing,
> an ablution.
>
> 'Epilogue: Seven Decades' (CP: 594)

Those of us who came of age in the 1960s are now in our own sixties, and the experience of that era's music has echoed through life ever since. Thus although Richard Finlay suggests that 'The swinging sixties passed Scotland by [. . .]. There was no flower power, few hippies, no love and peace nor anything usually associated with western decadent youth culture',[1] the times did feel different to those living through them. Not decadent, particularly, but charged by the energies of change. Fundamental attitudes seemed to be shifting alongside the new styles of music and fashion.

Scots of EM's generation who had come of age in the 1940s and early 1950s were now beginning to enter positions of responsibility or influence. They probably felt the new politics more powerfully. At the time, he expressed his own frustration at the lack of response of the Scottish establishment, as civic and cultural leaders failed to react to the excitement and significance of changes that were international:

> Yes, it is too cold in Scotland for flower people; in any case
>   who would be handed a thistle?
> What are our flowers? Locked swings and private rivers –
> and the island of Staffa for sale on the open market, which no
>   one questions or thinks strange –
> [. . .]
> and a Kirk Assembly that excels itself in the bad old rhetoric
>   and tries to stamp out every glow of charity and change,
>   most wrong when it thinks most loudly it is most right –
> and a Scottish National Party that refuses to discuss Vietnam
>   and is even applauded for doing so, do they think no lesson
>   is to be learned from what is going on there? – [. . .].
>
>   (CP: 203)

EM wanted Scotland to wake up from its sleepwalking, as he himself felt awakened by love, by music, by world movements in the avant-garde, by the 'spring of words' that seemed to pour from his pen in the 1960s. Like the Beatles, he was 'on song' throughout this still remarkable decade. And like them, the success that seemed assured for him by the end of 1969 had been won by earlier years of practice in obscurity.

Malcolm Gladwell has recently analysed our modern understanding of the process of becoming successful. In *Outliers: The Story of Success* (2008), he acknowledges personal talent, but also emphasises the figure of 10,000 hours of practice that researchers have reckoned to be the price of true expertise. He cites the Beatles' eight-hour sets seven days a week in Hamburg nightclubs, or the luck of Bill Gates in having unusual access to a school computer in his teenage years. In EM's case, working for an average of two to three hours a day, say, on his translations and poems through the 'unsuccessful'

1950s had provided him with the poetic skills to respond sharply and memorably to the new world opening up for him in the 1960s.

He was involved in the main love relationship of his life during this period, as well as a series of intense artistic relationships, so it is difficult to provide a simple year by year account. Projects begun in one year might come to fruition not within the expected twelve months but two or three years later, because of the vagaries of small press and magazine publication. Even working with an established firm such as Edinburgh University Press towards his break-through collection, *The Second Life* (1968), proved a frustrating experience.

Meanwhile his engagement with international writers and movements continued, particularly with concrete and sound poetry in Brazil, Switzerland and Austria as well as with Ian Hamilton Finlay's avant-garde Wild Hawthorn Press. Some of his best known poems come from this period, and unite national content with new international form: 'Canedolia', 'Message Clear', 'The Chaffinch Map of Scotland' (CP: 156, 159, 179). He became involved in public controversy in the 'poetry wars' between younger Scottish writers and the Scottish Renaissance 'establishment', epitomised in Hugh MacDiarmid's dogmatic stance on the content and style of modern Scottish poetry. EM tried to steer a rational course through the values and strengths of various factions. While he was clearly experimental in approach, he not only used Scots language well in poetry but was also keen to work with such establishment bodies as the Arts Council, the British Council, Collins the publishers and Edinburgh University Press.

He was not easy to categorise, having the widest possible interests. Throughout the decade his international work of translation continued to extend, with new and direct contact with East European writers, particularly the great Hungarian poet, Sándor Weöres. EM also helped to found and co-edit a new Scottish journal of cultural and political analysis, *Scottish International*, and he reviewed literature and drama for the *The Times*, *The Listener*, the *New Statesman* and the *Times Literary Supplement*, as well as for several Scottish newspapers and journals. By the end of the decade he had written his first film script and a libretto for an opera broadcast on BBC Radio.

Meanwhile, too, his normal work of teaching and assessment went on, together with his scholarly compilation for the 'Summary of Periodical Literature' for the *Review of English Studies*, at least until the end of 1965. Just listing all this, and more, could leave you breathless. Yet in his teaching, as experienced by my generation of undergraduates from the mid-1960s onwards, there was no sense of strain or impatience.

In all this activity he was buoyed up by the atmosphere of the era, particularly its music and especially the songs of the Beatles. These seemed fresh and joyous, with a clear sense of creative development that could be felt in each of their LPs: their lyrics influenced his poems, beyond the obvious title, but obscure lyric, of his 'Strawberry Fields Forever' (CP: 139). It was a validation of the impact that could come from celebrating ordinary life creatively, with optimism and wit. It was also popular music that had developed in a non-metropolitan industrial city and port, with a Celtic mix of population and an inspiration part-Irish, part-American, similar in many ways to Glasgow. This music, and the name of the band, ran parallel to the new energies and rhythms EM had found already in Beat poetry, and it communicated across classes and generations – again as he longed to do.

MEETING JOHN SCOTT

Even more supportive of EM's creative life, however, was the relationship with John Scott, whom he met in 1962. After the despairing series of physical encounters in the 1950s, this was 'a very absorbing kind of relationship and I didn't want to go back to the [gay] scene and didn't much do so. It was both very physical and it was a love affair'.[2] They met in Green's Playhouse, a huge 4368-seat cinema on the corner of Glasgow's Renfield Street and West Nile Street. It also had tearooms, a putting range and a ballroom that could cater for about 6000 dancers. Opened in 1927, with its Broadway-style sign lit up by hundreds of bulbs that featured a crazy unlit 'U' in PLAYHO*U*SE – their slogan was 'We want "U" in!' – it was Britain's biggest ever cinema, constructed on American lines, and a well-known gay meeting place.

By the 1970s the cinema had become the Apollo rock music venue, and then mysteriously burned down in 1987, just as it was being considered as a listed building. Revisiting that vanished world in his 2002 collection *Cathures*, EM recalled his lonely 1950s experiences:

> Community of shadows on the screen,
> Community of shadows in the stalls,
> Great coming and going – Patrons Who Persist
> In Changing Their Seats Will Be Ejected – [. . .].
> Those lost ones sitting in the smoky dark [. . .].
>
> (Cathures: 29–31)

In fact, he had once been barred from the cinema for misbehaviour – although he made his way back there after a week or so.

The new relationship gave a different sort of stability and tenderness. In many ways it was an attraction of opposites, with both the sense of fulfilment and the tensions that this phrase implies. John Scott was two years older than EM, small and wiry, extrovert, working class, a keen Celtic fan from a large and close Catholic family. He lived in the village of Law, near Carluke in Lanarkshire, and worked as a store man in various factories. He was a skilful and prize-winning dancer, in contrast to EM's noted lack of co-ordination in sport, and was a fairly heavy smoker. Hence the erotic charge in the poem 'One Cigarette': 'I am drunk on your tobacco lips' (CP: 186). EM, a non-smoker after he returned from the army in 1945, always had cigarettes in a hand-painted Russian box on his table, even after John's death.

The Singing Sixties 1960–1970

The poet John Burnside has praised 'the clarity and honesty of "One Cigarette" – surely one of the best love poems ever written in these islands' (*From Saturn to Glasgow*: 86). For EM, there were various levels of feeling involved:

> To me the act of smoking and the smell of a cigarette, perhaps just because of the fact that this person smoked and I didn't, became very erotic, became very loaded with all sorts of feelings and emotions which were quite strong, and positive, not anti.[3]

EM also associated smoking with what he called the 'poetry before poetry' – those things that stirred his imagination in boyhood and that he remembered vividly:

> My uncle Frank, who had a good tenor voice, sitting at the piano to sing 'Pale hands I loved beside the Shalimar' or 'Ramona' or 'Charmaine', the strange longing filtering out over the playing-cards, bobbed heads and cigarette smoke [. . .].[4]

Both EM and John Scott had grown up in the same county, but John regarded himself more as a Lanarkshire than a Glasgow person. He tended to be the one who would come to Glasgow, but EM did sometimes go to John's house to meet his family. His mother, Rose Ann Malone, was originally from Anderston in Glasgow, in fact, and had worked as a shirt machinist before marrying William Scott, a colliery stoker who lived in Law with his widowed mother. They had married in St Patrick's RC church in Anderston in 1904, possibly having met through the Gaelic-speaking Scotts who were the Malone's neighbours. EM was impressed by the relaxed and accepting nature of John's family life:

> They were always meeting each other, a very affectionate family. I was an only child, very different in that sense. He had brothers and sisters and all sorts of cousins and nieces and so on, whereas I had only my mother and father and a few aunts and uncles.[5]

They also accepted him very readily, and his clearly close relationship with John. Two of his sisters visited Whittingehame Court, to see how their brother's friend lived.

The two men met mainly at weekends, and went on holidays, but never lived together. EM always felt that he had to be alone to write: 'even just the presence of somebody, not just in the same room but in the same house, puts me off my stride'.[6] Although he said that John accepted this too and that it did not worry him, there were strains that occasionally flared into quarrels. In old age, EM told me that he admired the way that John recognised the social class differences between them and had said that if EM ever met someone he preferred, from his own sort of background, then he would understand. That freedom worked both ways, perhaps. EM recalled with amusement how one evening, during the period of their relationship, they had met by chance in Green's Playhouse, each man having secretly made a date with someone else.

The relationship continued, however, and it sustained both partners. It was not just, from EM's point of view, a merging of the physical and the emotional sides of his nature that had been previously kept separate. It also had an impact on his creative life, even if this did involve a necessary separation so that his writing could be done:

> It changed my life in so many ways. My writing just took off from the time I met him and the great doubts I had about myself in the Fifties just disappeared and, touch wood, will never come back. I owe everything, in a sense, to that relationship.[7]

This sense of liberation in his personal and creative life also chimed with a new sense of international freedom in literature, both in the USA, with the Beats and Black Mountain poets, and in Russia, as a partial thawing of censorship allowed younger writers such as Voznesensky and Yevtushenko to come to the fore, and to travel in the West.

The Singing Sixties 1960–1970

DOM SYLVESTER HOUÉDARD

Internationalism was central to EM's approach to writing in the 1960s. If Scotland was slow to thaw in literary matters, he found congenial writers in Europe and Latin America to admire and translate. In a sense, the decade had started off for him with an international aspect. In March 1960 he was invited to meet the Italian poet, Salvatore Quasimodo (1901–1968), a Nobel Laureate and professor of literature in Milan. He was speaking at the Dante Alighieri Society in Glasgow on the 21st of that month, and EM may also have met him earlier in the university's Italian Department. He offered Quasimodo his translations of some of his work. With that sense of identification that was always a powerful factor in drawing him to certain foreign poets, EM could appreciate the older writer's movement from his early symbolist and 'hermetic' style to a later poetry showing deep concern for social issues and the fate of his native land.

Such was to be EM's chosen path in this decade too. *The Second Life* (1968) would be remarkable for its blend of social and political poetry, such as 'King Billy', 'Glasgow Green' or 'The Flowers of Scotland', quoted at the start of this chapter, with more personal love poetry and avant-garde experiment. He absorbed some of this from foreign writers. His translations of Quasimodo (CT: 212–21), first published in *Rites of Passage* (1972), reveal what might at first sight seem a typically 'Morganesque' iconography of moonlight, horses, marshalling yards, snow, and even a poem on the launching of the first Russian sputnik in October 1957. We can see why he was drawn to the older poet's work.

Two months after meeting Quasimodo, EM was in Germany, as visiting lecturer at the University of Freiburg. He gave talks on Burns (20 May 1960) and on modern Scottish literature (23 May), with some time given to a well-organised excursion into the Black Forest. The impression was of Germanic thoroughness, but he would soon also be engaged with German avant-garde developments, in the concrete poetry of Eugen Gomringer in Switzerland and the sound poetry of Ernst Jandl in Austria.

Concrete poetry flourished in the 1960s, with Gomringer in Europe and the Noigandres group in Brazil being the leading exponents. It concentrated on apparently isolated aspects of poetry: visual patterning of layout and typography, or sound effects and repetition, or kinetic movements of the eye and mind in the act of reading. It has been variously linked to structuralism, semiotics, constructivism, or earlier examples of pattern poetry in English from the 17th century onwards. But to 1960s practitioners such as Gomringer, its aim was to recover for poetry an organic function in society, through its new focus on flexibility and freedom of communication. EM was also in touch with its foremost proponents in Scotland and England: Ian Hamilton Finlay (1925–2006) and Dom Sylvester Houédard (1924–1992), who signed his poems 'dsh'.

Dom Sylvester, or Don Sylverstarre as EM named him, was a Benedictine monk who was a member of the community at Prinknash Abbey in Gloucestershire. However, having 'the biggest address book in the universe', according to his fellow concrete poet John Sharkey, enabled him to be at the heart of many experimental developments, through letters, articles, lectures and the organising of poetry exhibitions in Cambridge and Oxford, for example. He combined heterodox learning with a deep and ecumenical spirituality, and had some connections with the Samye-Ling Buddhist centre at Eskdalemuir near Lockerbie in Dumfriesshire. To him, concrete poetry was related to the hieroglyphs and ideograms of ancient writing systems, and EM must have been reminded of his own early fascination with these in his scrapbooks.

All of this learning was lightly carried, however, with an arch and gossipy humour in his letters that was very engaging. In one letter of November 1963 he refers to EM's poem for Edith Piaf, 'Je ne regrette rien' (CP: 146) and recalls that her song 'La vie en rose' was played again and again at gay post-war Oxford parties. His letters and poems were also typographically adventurous. EM invented the word 'typestracts' for the concrete poems where 'dsh' achieved new linear and almost tactile effects on typewritten sheets. In fact, EM offered this neologism to the Oxford English Dictionary compilers, who declined it citing lack of printed evidence.[8]

When Dom Sylvester referred in a letter of July 1964 to the origins of British concrete poetry in the work of Gomringer and the Brazilians, EM replied that this was

> loosely correct, but in my case the initial knowledge and impetus came from the Portuguese concretist E.M. de Melo e Castro in Covilha to whom I wrote in May 1962 after he had a letter in TLS about concrete poetry; he sent me the anthology *Poesia Concreta* published in Lisbon through the Embaixada do Brasil and containing of course the Brazilians' work: that was what set it off.[9]

He records the first concrete poetry in Scotland as being published in 1963, in Ian Hamilton Finlay's avant-garde journal *Poor.Old.-Tired.Horse.* issue six (March 1963), in which the Brazilian poets featured. Two of EM's own concrete poems ('Dogs Round a Tree' and 'Original Sin at the Waterhole') appeared in *Fish-Sheet* 1, from Finlay's Wild Hawthorn Press in June 1963.

Dom Sylvester was staying at Pluscarden Abbey near Elgin in November 1964, working on biblical translation, but was also in contact with a postgraduate student in Edinburgh, Robert Tait, who wanted him to give a talk there. Dom Sylvester visited EM for tea in his new flat at Whittingehame Court at that time, and made a striking impression in his black Benedictine cloak on Great Western Road. He gave him a handful of his typestracts. They also met the following evening in Robert Tait's flat. A year later, after a visit by Gael Turnbull and Michael Shayer of Migrant Press to Prinknash Abbey, we find Dom Sylvester suggesting the need for a critical magazine in Scotland, and also that Robert Tait ('fresh sincere original and impeccable academic standards') would be the person to be involved in it. This would come to pass, when EM and the Edinburgh poet Robert Garioch co-edited *Scottish International* with Tait from 1968 until 1970, continuing thereafter as editorial advisors until 1974.

In the 1960s, it seems that EM was rethinking the negative impression of Catholics that had been a 'normal' part of his Church of Scotland upbringing in the West of Scotland in the 1920s and 1930s, probably the worst period for sectarian bigotry in Scotland since the influx of Irish migrants in the Famine years. It was not only his experience of ready acceptance by John Scott's family that now gave him a new perspective. There were also highly intelligent, creative and urbane people like Dom Sylvester who were not only Catholic but committed and celibate members of religious orders. Late in the decade he would encounter Anthony Ross, a remarkable Dominican friar who was Chaplain at Edinburgh University, as well as being a penal reformer, Scottish historian, the first Catholic student to study in New College, founder of the *Innes Review* and future Rector of Edinburgh University. He provided premises for the new journal *Scottish International* as it came into being. Robert Tait, and various other talented student writers such as Tom Leonard and Stephen Mulrine whom EM supported in various ways, had also arrived at university via Catholic schooling – all intelligent, thoughtful and independently-minded people.

Earlier in the 1960s EM was also in contact with Sister Marie Vianney of the Sisters of Notre Dame. The Order ran a college of education close to the University, for women who wanted to teach in Catholic primary schools, and she was Head of English there. She is the nun visiting Istanbul in his poem 'The Domes of Saint Sophia' who:

> sends me a postcard of St Sophia –
> church, mosque, and now museum –
> speaks of its 'supreme beauty'
> and forthright as always, adds
> 'Its perfection of form
> would delight the eye eternally' [. . .].

(CP: 148)

'I wonder' responds the poet, and begins to make the case for the ultimate boredom of any perfection of form, and for the attractions of some of his favoured ruins – brochs, pyramids, 'giant Baalbek / with its foundered columns / where I wandered in wartime / in the Lebanese sun'. For him, the religious dome is silent but 'The ruin speaks'. He feels compelled at this stage to restate his reservations about religion generally, and perhaps Catholicism in particular.

He kept the postcard, however, and later helped her review the English curriculum in the College of Notre Dame. He supported her by being a speaker at a 1962 summer school for English teachers held in Chesters House in Bearsden (later the Scottish seminary for priests in training). Another speaker was the Edinburgh-born critic, Karl Miller, who was a literary editor at the *New Statesman*, and would shortly help him to negotiate a particularly awkward turn in the cultural politics of the 1960s Scottish literary scene, involving Hugh MacDiarmid and some of the younger experimental Scottish writers.

Those politics largely depended on divergent views of language, nationalism and internationalism. EM's interests encompassed all of these. His Portuguese contact had sent him, besides the anthology of *Poesia Concreta*, the address of Augusto de Campos, one of the two brothers who were key members of the Noigandres group in Saõ Paulo. When EM wrote to him, the Brazilian replied that he already knew of his work through POTH (*Poor.Old.Tired.Horse.*) and had been about to ask Ian Hamilton Finlay for his address in Glasgow. He mentioned that his brother, Haroldo, was good at Russian – both brothers studied it – and had translated Mayakovsky and Khlebnikov. He sent EM *Noigandres 5*, which collected ten years of concrete and pre-concrete poetry by their group.[10] EM sent Augusto back English translations of some of his poems in that collection by August 1963, and he responded with suggestions for improvement. This sort of networking by letter was typical of the way that the avant-garde continued to explore new poetic territory, and is reminiscent of Gael Turnbull's approach with his *Migrant* authors.

IAN HAMILTON FINLAY

EM was fond of citing the original sense of the term *avant-garde* as an advance guard or band of scouts sent out to test the strength of opposing forces. In Ian Hamilton Finlay, he found a courageous comrade, perhaps too quick to anger, and prone to be combative where the good scout needed stealth. Nevertheless, or therefore, he became the foremost British exponent of concrete poetry, and the most widely recognised internationally. EM admired his work very much, and supported him in various ways.

They first met in the summer of 1961. Finlay had written to him in response to the Migrant Press pamphlet of EM's Russian translations, *Sovpoems* (1961), inviting him to his house in Edinburgh. He hoped to persuade EM to do a *Selected Poems of Attila József* (of course, he would need little persuading) but admitted that at present he and his publishing partner, Jessie McGuffie, had no money. However, he would play him 'a lovely Elvis Presley record' when he came to tea.

The two poets got on well, and Finlay contrasted the Glaswegian writer who saw poetry as being of the people and the world and who was open to experience, with Edinburgh writers he knew who behaved like headmasters, or gamekeepers with a gun. So already the battle lines were drawn in his mind. EM told him that he was normally Eddie to his friends, but that his Professor, Peter Alexander, always called him 'Yedward'. So in letters, he became 'Dear Yedwin' or 'Yeddie', and this name was taken up by Dom Sylvester in his letters too.

Jessie McGuffie, a part-time teacher of Classics whose work provided financial support to the Wild Hawthorn Press, was an attractive and energetic person. She suggested that EM ask Arthur Koestler, born like József in Budapest in 1905, to write an Introduction to the book. He did contact Koestler from the University at the end of August 1961, and got a reply by 5th September, suggesting that they could use quotations from his *The Invisible Writing* (1954) but to clear it with the publisher Collins first. EM commented to Jessie McGuffie: 'from one point of view I am not really sorry, as I have never liked Koestler, either his mind or the way he writes: everything he does is twisted and gritty'. Koestler also claimed to have forgotten his native Hungarian language.

Jessie McGuffie became a co-editor of *Poor.Old.Tired.Horse.* along with Paul Pond in Oxford (aka Paul Jones, of Manfred Mann band). They hoped to be able to use some of EM's translations of Fyodor Tyutchev in the first issue (CT: 462). Translations from Giacomo Leopardi (CT: 229–44, 326–30) were also accepted for publication, but nothing came of them. EM had reviewed Charles Tomlinson's *Versions from Fyodor Tyutchev 1803–1873* in the *Anglo-Soviet Journal* XXII:I in Spring 1961, and may have been spurred by this towards his own translations.

He was also writing occasionally for the *Scottish Daily Express* around this period, reviewing Isaak Babel's *Collected Short Stories* (6 May 1961) and *Gibbon's Journey from Geneva to Rome* (17 June 1961) and also declaring, as guest critic in the newspaper's *Viewpoint* feature, 'Poetry in rock 'n roll sends me, says Edwin Morgan' (29 April 1961). So he was obviously picking up the vibes of a new age even pre-Beatles, whose 'Love Me Do' was released in the following year.

In November 1961, in a review article for *New Saltire* 2 entitled 'Who will Publish Scottish Poetry?', he raised an issue that was to align him with Ian Hamilton Finlay as an antagonist to MacDiarmid's vision for Scottish poetry. Scottish publishers replied in *New Saltire* 3 in the Spring of 1962, and EM answered them in the *Scotsman* Weekend Magazine on 12 May 1962. EM's original review had been of work by younger and 'non-Establishment' Scottish poets (for example, Alan Jackson, Alan Riddell and I.H. Finlay). A quarrel had smouldered on between poetic generations ever since Norman MacCaig's anthology *Honour'd Shade* appeared in 1959. In the correspondence columns of the *Scotsman* there had been claims of the existence of a 'Rose Street Group', based in Edinburgh and biased towards poets writing in Scots. Some of the 'excluded' younger writers, including Ian Hamilton Finlay and W. Price Turner, produced a tape of readings of their own poems and called it *Dishonour'd Shade*. They wrote in English, although clearly with a Scottish accent of mind.

Norman MacCaig also wrote in English, of course, and his selections from both MacDiarmid and EM in the anthology mix English and Scots poems by both poets. Nevertheless, EM felt provoked enough by critical comments on Edinburgh Festival Fringe events in *New Saltire* 2 (November 1961) to enter the quarrel. He had begun to take part in Festival poetry readings in New Town cellars with Migrant and other poets, and had seen how the 1960s movement towards performance poetry, pop poetry and the spoken word involved a different relationship with the poet's audience – and that his own serious earlier style did not 'work' in this context, compared with the performances of poets such as Pete Brown, Christopher Logue, Ian Hamilton Finlay or Gael Turnbull. It was not only a matter of style, but of content, relevance and engagement with people's ordinary life experience, and the language in which they lived their lives.

So he wrote an extended essay for *New Saltire* 3 (Spring 1962), 'The Beatnik in the Kailyard' (*Essays* 1974: 166–76). It is a reasoned exploration of the tensions, indeed the self-contradictions, that tends to swirl around the issue of language in Scotland. In the opening pages EM provides a scholarly perspective, demonstrating that he has read widely and thought deeply about the language of Scottish literature as an expression of its society across the centuries. He is particularly critical of the literary void of 19th century Scotland:

> Where were the *real* writers, when Scotland was being industrialised? [. . .] A crucial imbalance developed with the intellectual decline of Edinburgh and the enormous growth of Glasgow, and the swing of work and population to the Clyde area. The imbalance may have been felt, but its full implications – in terms of cultural centrality and continuity – were not faced.

This was, of course, the very shift of population and production through which his own parents had arrived in Glasgow. It also

142

crucially depended on an underclass of mainly Catholic Irish labour, as well as Highland Gaels, to sustain that production. This was John Scott's ancestry, and that of other young working-class men EM had met. The emotional connection perhaps adds fire to his argument, as he goes on to suggest that whereas MacDiarmid had been able to develop a Renascence movement in which modern subject matter could be tackled in new forms, that same movement was now being limited by both its leader and his followers. For MacDiarmid wanted the Renascence to be clearly *Scottish* in attitude and language, and too many of his followers focused on traditional language rather than truly modern and contemporary content and form:

> There is a new provincialism [. . .]. Almost no interest has been taken by established writers in Scotland in the important post-war developments in America and on the continent. Ignorance is not apologised for. The Beat writers are dismissed as a throwback to the 1920s. The Italian poet Quasimodo visits Edinburgh and Glasgow and is greeted with something like indifference – though his ideas on the future of poetry, to say nothing of his creative work, are highly relevant at the present time.

The tone here may remind us of Sydney Graham's war-time comment on EM's preaching mode when in full flight on a topic about which he cared personally and passionately. What he had found in Quasimodo was a writer who had placed his lyric gifts at the service of expressing and sustaining the socio-political life of post-war Italy. In contrast,

> Too much of the experience of living in Scotland [. . .] is not being reflected by novelists and playwrights. Life in a 'new town' like East Kilbride – in some of the huge suburban housing estates – on a hydro-electric construction scheme – at Dounreay or Hunterston – in a recipient town for Glasgow 'overspill': there is so much experience that seems to cry out for literary embodiment, for the eye of a sharp but sympathetic observer to be turned upon it.

The huge social changes that were taking place in 1960s Scotland seem to push and heave at the syntax here. And it is no coincidence that within the year EM would write some of his best known poems on contemporary Scottish life: 'The Starlings in George Square' (17–19 November 1962), 'Glasgow Green' (August 1963), 'King Billy' (July–October 1963), 'The Unspoken' (30 December 1963–1 January 1964). And in the following year, 'In the Snack-bar' (August–September) and 'One Cigarette' (7 October). In both critical and creative modes, he was driven by a growing commitment to his nation, its urban landscapes and its literature. And he was appalled by the second-rate and backward-looking art that would come from refusing to confront the gathering change:

> A desperate unwillingness to move out into the world with which every child now in school is becoming familiar – the world of television and sputniks, automation and LPs, electronic music and multi-story flats [. . .] paperbacks and water-skiing, early marriage and larger families: a world that will be more fast, more clean, more 'cool' than the one it leaves behind.

Although EM gets a couple of things wrong here – being rather out of his depth in the area of heterosexual relationships and the impact of the contraceptive pill – he was mainly correct in the challenge that the 1960s, and also future-oriented artists like himself and Finlay, were presenting to the Scottish tradition as defined by MacDiarmid's successors. He realised crucially that for poets to matter, they had to speak in the same terms as their audience. This meant using a range of Scots language, including urban Scots: in his case, the Glaswegian blend of Lowland Scots with Irish and Gaelic forms of speech.

The battle lines were being drawn for a famous confrontation at the Edinburgh Festival Writers' Conference in late August 1962, where EM and MacDiarmid would share a platform. In June, MacDiarmid published a pamphlet, *The Ugly Birds without Wings*, against 'a few younger writers who see themselves as representatives of the beat poets and who accuse the writers of the Scottish Renaissance Movement, and Hugh MacDiarmid in particular, of having formed an Establishment [. . .]'. It was printed by Allan Donaldson of Morningside Park, Edinburgh, and EM sent a 4/3d postal order for a copy on 25 June.

Ian Hamilton Finlay did not see a copy until a month later, and was typically incensed. He assumed that the real publisher was Kulgin Duval, an Edinburgh bookseller and publisher. EM knew him well, in fact, and remained a life-long friend: Kulgin Duval had hoped at an earlier stage to publish *The Whittrick* and the Quasimodo translations. It is unclear to what extent Finlay knew of their connection.

Things were made more complicated by the fact that Kulgin Duval was a co-editor with Sydney Goodsir Smith of *Hugh MacDiarmid: A Festschrift*, to mark MacDiarmid's 70th birthday in 1962, and that EM had contributed an essay on 'Poetry and Knowledge in MacDiarmid's Later Work' (*Essays*: 203–13). EM was, I think, the earliest critic to appreciate MacDiarmid's later and more 'difficult' English poetry of facts, as compared with the early lyric poems in Scots. He was interested above all in the older poet's fusion of scientific data and artistic realisation, and in his sense of the transformative power of knowledge in advancing the human spirit. MacDiarmid's focus on language itself as the main vehicle of this transformation was, of course, exactly the sort of affirmation that EM needed at this stage of his own poetic career, when translation and linguistic experimentation were paramount.

Thus we see, in his letters of the time, EM trying to placate, or at least head off, Finlay's anger at the *Ugly Birds* attack, merely declaring it 'well off beam'. At the same time he was writing to Karl Miller at the *New Statesman*, offering an article on the controversy. But this offer was declined because of the forthcoming festschrift and EM's conflict of interest. Miller himself wrote an article, 'Allagrugous Auld City' (*New Statesman* 10 August 1962), having promised to treat the issues 'very charily'. The Scots word 'allagrugous' means 'grim, discontented-looking', and that was Finlay's reaction. To him the article seemed metropolitan and dismissive, and he responded trenchantly, citing the range of international authors – Mayakovsky, József, Leopardi, Trakl, Apollinaire, Prévert, Zukofsky, Niedecker – who were published in *Poor.Old.Tired.Horse.*

ALEXANDER TROCCHI

So the stage was set for the Edinburgh Festival Writers' Conference that was to take place over five afternoons from 20–24 August 1962. EM had been invited in March to be one of the Scottish representatives. The chairperson was to be Dr David Daiches, and writers from over eleven countries were being invited to discuss, under the broad theme of *The Novel*, the following issues: Contrasts of Approach; Is Commitment Necessary?; Censorship; Style and the Future; and Scottish Writing Today. In early April, Andrew Hook, then lecturing in English at Edinburgh University although he would later become a Professor in Glasgow, invited EM to provide a conference briefing paper of 2000 words on 'Problems facing the young writer in Scotland today'.

In this paper he highlighted issues which had been increasingly in his mind. Practical problems of the shortage of literary periodicals and Scottish publishers narrowed the scope not only for Scottish writers, but also for Scottish culture:

> There are people in Scotland quite as competent to write on cultural affairs as the majority of those who cover London (and occasionally even 'the provinces') in the pages of the *Spectator* and *New Statesman*, the *Observer* and the *Sunday Times*, yet the would-be Scottish critic or reviewer rarely has the chance of saying what he has to say when he wants to say it. Cultural events in Scotland tend to drift past like a gesticulating frieze which never quite engages with those who sense they are being waved at.[11]

The effect on creative writers was that they lacked contact with 'a knowledgeable range of opinion', and so they were sometimes reduced to 'fighting shadows, discovering what has long been known, or clinging manfully to traditions which have now no relevance [. . .]. We want to see the issues of our time submitted to young and vigorous pens'. Like his own, or Ian Hamilton Finlay's, was the inference. This leads him into the language situation in Scotland:

> Although I want to see – and do see – Scottish writers working on a straightforward Standard English basis, I would also like to see more experiments towards a 'Scotch English' which would move, paradoxically enough, in the two directions of more truthful naturalism and freer manipulation, but in both cases with the aim of infusing a new vitality into the 'English' language, as American and some West Indian and African writers have done in recent years. We have rather neglected the importance of the speech basis ('the current language heightened', in Hopkins's phrase) in the excitement of developing an eclectic or synthetic Scots.

Against the rural, the parochial, the traditional for tradition's sake, EM makes a radical and prescient case for an urban and 'post-colonial' Scots, and links this with international writing in a range of 'Englishes'. This new poetic language is intimately linked with new media and performance poetry: 'The poem is jumping off the printed page into the gramophone record and the concert hall, and with it goes the poet [. . .]. The concept of a living and reacting audience revives. Qualities weakened for centuries – vibrancy and warmth, immediacy, tonal indication, subtlety of emphasis – are being regained'. And he links such advances in poetry with the vigour of the spoken dialogue in recent drama he was reviewing at this time: by Miller, Beckett, Pinter and Osborne.

Also in his mind must have been the impact of radio. EM sent *The Young Writer in Scotland* to Andrew Hook on 4 June 1962. Early in May he had sent Ian Hamilton Finlay a copy of part of a BBC broadcast he had made relating to his work: 'It is time for the poet to appear in a more open relationship to his reader (or hearer). There are many ways of doing this, and Ginsberg's breast-beating oyez is not Finlay's whistle in the dark, though both loud and quiet methods are valid'. On the 27th of May, he wrote again, having just returned from London where he had recorded readings of translations of Russian poetry, which the BBC would broadcast on the 4th, 11th and 18th of June. In July, in response to Finlay's ideas for putting poetry on tape, EM noted that the Canadian Broadcasting Corporation intended to broadcast a version of his *Beowulf*, and contrasted this sort of 'openness to new experiences' across the Atlantic with the BBC's reluctance to take risks.

Towards the end of his article, EM makes a plea for a Scottish literature that is more open to, and more thoughtfully engaged with, current international trends:

> Anyone who thinks I am asking for Robin Jenkins to write like Robbe-Grillet or Ian Crichton Smith to write like Ginsberg misunderstands an essential point [. . .] the main thing is simply to get our country to break out from its prickly isolation and have the self-confidence to measure its creative life against the best and vividest examples from outside. Many young writers in the past have felt that it was impossible to do this and at the same time remain in Scotland, with all the demands living in Scotland makes on one's becoming a 'Scottish writer'. There is something wrong with the literary society which cannot keep a W.S. Graham [. . .] an Alexander Trocchi [. . .].

Alexander Trocchi (1925–1984) was, like Graham, something of an alter-ego for EM. He was a radical and non-conformist figure, working outside the Scottish avant-garde in the very years when EM was trying to establish or sustain it. Trocchi's career and his own had overlapped fleetingly. Born in Glasgow of Italian-Scots parentage in 1925, Trocchi had left Glasgow University at the end of his first year for national service in the Navy, returning in 1946 to complete a degree in philosophy. This was the very period of EM's own unhappy readjustment to civilian and undergraduate life, but their subjects were different and there is no record of them ever having met as undergraduates. As a young lecturer EM did come to know of him, at least by reputation. In 2002, writing to Alec Finlay (son of the concrete poet) about a planned book called *Justified Sinners*, he described the impact of Trocchi on a traditional university:

> What was he? Brilliant, wayward, charming, passing exams on benzedrine, starting up a pig farm shortly before his finals. Everyone knew he would make his mark sometime, somehow, somewhere.[12]

After graduation, Trocchi left for Paris, where he edited the avant-garde literary journal *Merlin* (publishing Beckett, Sartre, Genet, Ionesco, Henry Miller and Christopher Logue), and then, in the late 1950s, writing in New York and San Francisco as part of an alternative and drugs-related cultural movement – 'a cosmonaut of inner space', as he described himself. EM later provided a balanced overview of his work for the *Edinburgh Review* in 1985: 'Alexander Trocchi: a Survey', republished in 1990 in his second essay collection, *Crossing the Border*: 300–11.

Trocchi's work had been banned in Britain as too erotic, or pornographic, and he championed the work of William Burroughs, also banned in Britain. Both Trocchi and Burroughs joined the international and UK writers gathered at the Edinburgh Festival in August 1962 to debate the state of the novel, along with Norman Mailer, Henry Miller, Laurence Durrell, Angus Wilson, Muriel Spark, Naomi Mitchison, Rebecca West, Mary McCarthy, Robin Jenkins, the Indian writer Khushwant Singh and the Austrian Erich Fried. The Russian delegation had failed to appear, and this meant that the planned discussion on censorship focused on sexual rather than political censorship. The presence of the authors of books banned in the UK, such as Miller, Durrell, Mailer as well as Burroughs and Trocchi, meant that newspaper reporters had ample opportunity to focus on the scandalous. This set the scene, unfortunately, for the debate on contemporary Scottish writing, where MacDiarmid angrily linked contemporary experimental writers with decadence, and, if Scottish, with a shameful abandonment of their native language.

Several accounts of the occasion exist. Of the journalistic articles, Hugh C. Rae's in the *Scottish Field* of October 1962 was able to combine a positive outline of the conference contributions of Mailer, Burroughs, Spender, Angus Wilson and Mary McCarthy with unsparing critique of the cultural attitudes of the Scots, as displayed in the debate on Scottish writing which he called one of the 'backcourt cock-fights which have substituted for genuine creative effort for so long' in Scotland. Metropolitan writers, such as Spender in his 'Letter from Edinburgh' in *Encounter* (October 1962), could dismiss the 'curious' occasion as 'a few grains of salt and a fearfulness of haggis'. Visiting writers were amazed. According to Neal Ascherson in the *Observer Weekend Review* (26 August 1962), 'Norman Mailer said with awe on the day after the Scottish eruption that they were certainly committed men'. The *Glasgow Herald* took a sour view of the proceedings, and saw the conference as pandering to authors' vanity.

Perhaps it was this journalistic misrepresentation that led EM to give a talk about the conference to the Rutherglen Rotary Club shortly afterwards. Perhaps his father wanted his son to set the record straight in the local community. Or it may be that EM was conscious of how much he needed to explore his reasons for breaking free from various father-figures. He respected MacDiarmid but needed to create space for his own poetic aspirations. The new flat he had bought at Whittingehame Court in Glasgow's West End was set for completion in August, and he was (over-)due to leave his father's house. His account of the conference to these local businessmen is balanced and yet committed, focusing on the 'genuine interest' of the audience of 2000 people 'packing the McEwan Hall day after day', as well as on what those writers demonstrated, as opposed to the *Glasgow Herald*'s negativity.

He dealt head-on with the 'lurid reports of the Scottish day in the newspapers [. . .] you might get the impression it was Scotland's worst disgrace since Flodden'. It emerges that part of the problem was that:

> At the speakers' table the water carafe was filled with whisky. This was the only day on which the speakers got whisky, I don't know why, unless the organisers thought that the dour Scots wouldn't speak if our tongues hadn't been artificially loosened? Anyhow, the results were as might have been expected. Speakers began to shout and reasonable discussion became impossible.[13]

Yet EM refused to see it as a wasted afternoon. Rather, it was extremely useful 'in airing, out in the open, certain important and long-smouldering Scottish literary matters' through the clash of personalities and generations that took place:

> Trocchi attacked MacDiarmid for encouraging an old-fashioned and reactionary view of Scottish literature – he called it 'turgid petty provincial stale cold-porridge Bible-clasping nonsense', and he said MacDiarmid's opinions, especially his scorn for the novel, were just 'too crummy to be commented on'. Of course Mac-Diarmid was furious about this and replied that Scottish literature wasn't provincial and even if it was this was better than submitting to wicked American influences represented by people like Trocchi (or me . . .).

The argument for or against an unadventurous and conservative Scottish culture failed to materialise, however, as first the drunken poet Sydney Goodsir Smith came on to the platform in support of MacDiarmid, and then the left-wing poet Morris Blythman entered to publicise his anti-Polaris ballads. The audience were already leaving as

> some of the ballads were sung amidst general exodus by Josh Macrae with his guitar. There was such a hubbub by this time that

151

I doubt if people could have heard the words if they wanted to. A fantastic scene – could only have happened in Scotland?

In the rest of his Rutherglen talk, EM reveals what had meant most to him during the conference, focusing on two American writers. Firstly, there was Norman Mailer on the earlier topic of 'commitment'. Countering another of MacDiarmid's fiery speeches, about himself as the only really committed writer in the hall and the proud recipient, moreover, of a telegram for his 70th birthday from the Writers Union in Moscow, Norman Mailer argued that 'the writer should only be committed to "the other" – anything outside himself, other people, the world, the universe, he should always be looking OUT' – and at this point he asked the audience to look up at the McEwan Hall's barrel of a ceiling, and to see beyond it.

On the day devoted to the future of the novel, the second 'star performer' for EM was William Burroughs, 'American author of *The Naked Lunch* and *The Soft Machine*, both banned in Britain and the United States, hardly known to the general public at all but generally thought by those who have managed to get hold of his books as one of the most powerful writers now living'. His theme was that 'the future of the novel is in space not in time', and instead of a story that moves steadily along chronologically, he tried to create 'an exploration of life in all its dimensions, using techniques like the flashback of cinema, what he calls the cut-up and fold-in methods'. EM was fascinated by this exposition of Burroughs' own craftsmanship, and doubtless by how it tuned with his own desire for a multi-dimensional literature close to the experience of living in an age of cinema, relativity and space exploration. It reminds us also that, as a narrative poet, EM constantly plays with space, time, perspective and continuity. Two 1960s examples would be 'In Sobieski's Shield' and 'From the Domain of Arnheim' (CP: 196–9). In the 1970s, his long war poem 'The New Divan' would use a similar technique.

He very quickly set out to see if he could mimic Burroughs' style, writing an account of 'The Fold-In Conference', then sending it to *The Outsider* (New Orleans) and *The Review*, as well as copies to John Calder, George MacBeth at the BBC Third Programme, Jack Rillie and Magnus Magnusson. It was eventually accepted by the Edinburgh University-based journal, *Gambit* (Autumn 1962). It is a long piece, but gives an authentic-seeming record of his attraction to Trocchi's ideas and energy, as a fellow rebel against a heavy-handed literary father-figure:

> *Trocchi* sharp lean Glasgow-American voice theme fragmentation McEwan of junk and destruction of object forget drugs remember loneliness questioning identity modern barrel of exile cosmonaut of INNER space read passage Cains Book fragmentation not evident [. . .] expatriate Paris America Canada agreement Keir Morgan violent disagreement other speakers MacDiarmid love and respect but an old so-and-so old fashioned quaint ideas contempt for novel just too CRUMMY for words national provincial Scottish petty turgid Scottish stale national cold-porridge Bible-clasping literature that's any good last two decades I've written [. . .] Mind the carafe. Audience stirred air charged statues blush Presbyterian junkie cameras shorthand races next morning's column.[14]

A deadline-driven reporter's role was also part of EM's self-chosen fate at the Festival. He was covering drama for *Encore* theatre magazine, as he told the editor of *The Outsider*, who had just published his article on Jean Genet, and so he 'had really no time left for social contacts as I was rushing about from place to place [. . .]'.[15] Perhaps he felt safer as a moving target, being harder to hit. He was certainly conscious of being part of an international movement of creativity and change. It was in June of that same summer that he had made his first contact with concrete poetry from Brazil, via Portugal, and this would make his own work radically different from the poetry of his Scottish contemporaries, including Finlay.

Yet it might be more accurate to say that all this forward momentum of the 1960s was like that of a high-wire artist, working on several wires – as poet, translator, critic, teacher, friend, antagonist – and only able to keep upright by gliding smoothly into the next move. No wonder his later poem 'Cinquevalli', celebrating the art of a great performer, would become a personal favourite at readings:

> Cinquevalli is practising.
> He sits in his dressing-room talking to some friends,
> at the same time writing a letter with one hand
> and with the other juggling four balls.
> His friends think of demons, but
> 'you could all do this,' he says
> sealing the letter with a billiard ball.
>
> (CP: 433)

Sometimes only poetry could leap across contradictions. In *The Second Life* EM would finally place his poems 'To Hugh MacDiarmid' and 'To Ian Hamilton Finlay' deliberately side by side (CP: 153–5). In ranging lines that echo the intellectual sweep of the older poet, he celebrates that 'out of scraps of art and life and knowledge / you assembled that crackling auroral panorama / that sits on your Scotland like a curly comb [. . .]'. Finlay, in contrast, is a craftsman, domestic and humane, and the spare construction of the poem reflects this poet's preference for clean-cut classical forms:

> You give the pleasure
> of made things,
> the construction holds
> like a net; or it
> unfolds in waves
> a certain measure,
> of affection.

Years later, in a lecture on the tensions between the critical and creative intelligence, given on 16 November 1979 to first year

The Singing Sixties 1960–1970

English Literature students at Edinburgh University, EM described the two poems as companion pieces, written close together in July and August of 1962. He proposes that it is possible to write a 'critic's poem' by writing 'from a position of knowledge and warmth, about writers who have very distinctive qualities, and to allow the concentrating power of poetry to say something that critical prose might not reach'.[16] Both knowledge and affection are the essential combination. Regarding Finlay, there is a wonderful ambiguity in the phrase 'a certain measure'.

EUGEN GOMRINGER

EM and Finlay supported each other throughout the 1960s, although the latter's movement was increasingly towards 'made things' and what he called 'avant-gardening' on his land at Stonypath by the end of the decade. EM continued to explore both sound, concrete, formal and code poetry, and at the same time to write the poems of city life and relationships for which he became best known, and which Finlay did not esteem so highly.

They had, however, shared all their hopes and disappointments as developing writers. There was the hope in October 1962 that the University of California Press would co-publish an edition of the József poems along with Wild Hawthorn Press – only to be dashed by November 1963: 'The mood will pass, but at the moment I feel like just locking everything up in a drawer', EM wrote.[17] Wild Hawthorn Press had already been staggered by Jessie McGuffie's sudden leaving of Edinburgh for New York in October 1963, by Finlay's account, to marry a sailor who had been sent to Scotland by the modernist poet Louis Zukofsky to meet the Scottish writer.

More positively, it was Finlay who gave EM the address in Switzerland of Eugen Gomringer, whom he felt was closest to his own interests in art and purity of line. Both Scots poets were taken up with the joy of concrete poetry: Finlay said that he could not imagine himself ever writing non-concrete again, and that he was completely and hopelessly in love with the new forms.

155

Writing to him in March 1968, EM likewise stressed what this form of poetry gave him personally:

> [. . .] a sense of release, or perhaps it could be called a species of joy, which cannot entirely be obtained by other means, though something similar happens (I think) when I use Scots inventively for translation purposes [. . .]. [But] I still want to write poems such as (for example) 'In the Snack Bar' which is a kind of opposite to the concrete poem and is doing something [. . .] that concrete cannot do.[18]

He was astonished at an attack on his concrete poetry in the *Times Literary Supplement* by Mike Weaver, who described them as 'literary jokes'. Writing a few months earlier to a young Swiss scholar from Neuchâtel University who wanted information on concrete poetry for an arts magazine, EM took issue with the view that this was an 'inhuman', narrow or intellectually abstract art:

> Again, there is a great range of effects in concrete poetry from 'warm' to 'cold'. Some of it is outgoing, joyous, humorous, witty; some of it is stark, hermetic, forbidding; some is political; some is religious; some is mathematical; some is sculptural; some is two-dimensional, some three-dimensional; some abstracts concrete forms such as animals, some concretises abstract forms such as grammatical relationships. I myself incline to the 'warm' rather than the 'cold' end, but I recognise that there are other points of view.[19]

Discussing the divergent paths, and the artistic arguments, that were starting to appear in the concrete movement in the mid 1960s, EM suggested to Finlay that 'my humour and your boats may be of some use, both tying concrete to certain bollards of human life and human pleasure'.

An example of EM's use of concrete approaches in a serious situation is 'Message Clear', which is placed beside his political 'Starryveldt' in the *The Second Life* (CP: 159). It was one of his 'emergent poems', first published in 1967 in a limited folded single sheet format by Edition Hansjörg Mayer in Stuttgart. The form ends with a recognised quotation: in this case, Christ's statement in John's Gospel: '*I am the resurrection and the life*'. The poem extracts the permutations of meaning from those letters, finding different sets of words embedded in the phrase (for example, 'i am here / i act / i run / i meet / i stand / i am thoth / i am ra'). It spreads these letters out along each line to match their location in the final phrase, in which all the meanings rest. The strategy is rather like code-breaking, but it seems both to construct and deconstruct meaning as it goes. The reading of the phrase is made more halting but also more thought-provoking.

Its personal significance for EM adds a human dimension. It was conceived and largely completed during a bus journey home from Robroyston Hospital in Glasgow, where his father lay dying. He had been admitted in the early summer of 1965. On 10 June EM wrote to Finlay, who had moved to a farmhouse in Ardgay, Rosshire: 'My father is in hospital again and due for an operation, and my mother is in a pretty nervous state about it. It is cancer and of course serious.'

By this point, his parents had moved to 89 Whittingehame Court, in a block of flats near his own, which was number 19. His father died on 25 November 1965, at the age of 79, and as he visited him over the summer EM was clearly reflecting on his father's religious principles and their distance from his own eclectic and individualistic views. So there is a striking sense of filial rebelliousness or self-affirmation here in the face of his father's death. Not merely playing games with words, then – which might have been his father's view of concrete poetry, as well as that of TLS reviewers and at least some of EM's university colleagues – but seriously questioning death, faith and affirmation.

He sent the poem to the *Times Literary Supplement* almost immediately, and it was published on 13 January 1966, generating significant correspondence over the following three weeks. He also published it in the German journal *Feuilleton* (71, 26/27

March 1966) and in the *Chicago Daily News* (9 April 1966). The newspaper editor sub-headed it 'A Poem for Easter', suggesting more piety than it possesses.

Sister Vianney of Notre Dame College sent him a supportive letter on his father's death, saying that EM's character and professional progress must have been a source of considerable satisfaction to his father. His reaction to this may have been mixed. The line from his poem on her visit to the church of St Sophia in Istanbul comes to mind: 'I wonder'. Certainly in old age he came to regret his own emotional distance from his father when younger. Many sons do.

His father's death involved EM, as the only child, in new financial and emotional responsibilities. Finlay, feeling isolated and always sensitive to slights, rebuked him two months later for what he thought a muted defence of himself in some journalistic controversy or other in the *Glasgow Herald*, and for a lack of contact. EM replied at once: 'My father died, and with various difficulties that had to be dealt with, I couldn't get round to writing – but you were being written to invisibly [. . .]'.

And he sent him some poems for a Tea-themed issue of POTH (*Teapoth*), which appeared in July 1967. EM included these in his *Selected Poems*, 1985 (CP: 462), and they show a resilient return to his customary wit. Definitions from *The Dictionary of Tea* include:

tea hod	small hod for carrying tea bricks in Tibet
tea square	an impotent Dervish
tea cloud	a high calm soft warm light gold cloud, sometimes seen at sunset
grey tea	used of a disappointment. E.g. 'Harriet got her grey tea that night'.

He was also expanding the range of his concrete poetry through serious translation. On 6 February 1965 Haroldo de Campos wrote to him, having persuaded Lawrence Ferlinghetti to publish some Brazilian concrete poetry in his *City Lights* journal. Haroldo had decided to use EM as his translator, and EM replied almost immediately, asking for poems to work on.[20] The most important text translated was his 'Servidão de passagem', or 'transient servitude' (CT: 286–92). They worked on the detail of this translation from November 1965 onwards. Its blend of concrete techniques and a complex sound poetry of alliteration and assonance with a strong political sentiment was taxing, and EM had to draw on all his translation skills, some of them honed on *Beowulf*'s metric, to express the Brazilian poet's intentions:

> this bone grind
> with flesh
> this bloodgut
> with bone
> this baregear.

On 27 February 1967, Haroldo sent EM a copy of the Mexican magazine *el corno implumado* (*The Plumed Horn*) containing his finally 'excellent' translation, as well as versions of two other poems not in CT: 'Alea I' and 'Semantic Variations'. They continued to correspond, sharing an interest in modern Russian poetry: Haroldo also translated Voznesensky's work. In June he mentioned a contact at the Museum Mayakovsky in Moscow, who worked with 'Guenadi Aigui who seems to be the most experimental of Russian young poets'. This was, of course, the Chuvash poet, Genady Aigi, whose allusive, rather mystical poems EM went on to translate and publish in 1994 in *Sweeping Out the Dark* (CT: 364–9).

Thus the world came to Whittingehame Court, either in person or on paper, and creative communications went out from Glasgow to the world.

In February 1965, Ernst Jandl, a Viennese poet specialising in sound poetry and over-laid recordings, contacted EM via Ian Hamilton Finlay to ask for help in finding a venue in Scotland to give a talk on Austrian poetry. EM suggested the Scottish-German Centre at 3 Park Circus in Glasgow and also gave Jandl the name of W. Walker Chambers, the Professor of German at the University. Jandl arrived in Glasgow in April 1965, having asked EM to spare a few hours to meet him. He was feeling attracted to Glasgow 'as it is said to be a big and ugly industrial town'. Back in Vienna, he later contrasted Glasgow's energy with 'this strange place of backwardness, arrogance and sleep'.

Jandl also praised EM's 1965 collection *Starryveldt* from Eugen Gomringer's press at Frauenfeld in Switzerland as 'very witty and utterly original', seeing it as proof of concrete poetry's individuality, as compared with dismissive critical complaints about its supposed barrenness. The title poem 'Starryveldt' uses sound-play on the 's' and 'v' consonants of the town of Sharpeville in South Africa, to commemorate the shooting there of 67 Africans during a political demonstration against Apartheid's pass laws in March 1960. As in de Campos' long poem 'transient servitude', the engagement with politics is not absent from concrete poetry. Rather, this poetry's sharpened focus on language easily cuts through the false rhetoric of corrupted power.

The collection came about after initial contact by EM in the spring of 1964. Gomringer offered to publish a collection of his concrete poems, which he admired: 'I wanted to have written them myself'. The deal was that each published author was offered one hundred copies of an edition of five hundred to sell at cost, so EM worked out the value of a Swiss franc, plus postage and packing, reckoned he could sell them for two and sixpence and sent a cheque for ten pounds and ten shillings. It was to be a stapled pamphlet on twenty-four unnumbered pages, in orange paper covers. The first print run was ready by the beginning of September 1964, but problems with the paper meant that production values were poor, and Gomringer asked him to retype the twenty-three poems cleanly enough for a photographic print to be taken.

Once he had these new versions, EM sent out review copies to the *Times Literary Supplement*, *Guardian Review*, *Glasgow Herald*, *Scotsman* and *New Saltire*, as well as personal copies to Ian Hamilton Finlay, Dom Sylvester Houédard, Andrei Voznesensky, Haroldo de Campos, George MacBeth and George Bruce at the BBC, Edinburgh contacts such as Giles Gordon, Robert Tait and Kulgin Duval, and others. By May of 1965, he was reporting 'quite a lot of interest' in *Starryveldt,* and asked Gomringer for more copies. By June, he had arranged for some of them to be sold through Finlay's Wild Hawthorn Press.

Gomringer was planning to take a holiday in the Austrian Tyrol in July 1965, reawakening EM's enthusiasm for mountain landscapes. He had recently seen on television a climbing party reach the top of the Matterhorn, probably Mme Vaucher, the first woman to climb the North Wall, on 14 July 1965, the centenary of the first ascent. Now he wrote to Gomringer: 'Very small mountains I can do, but rock-faces I leave to the dedicated. There is, however, a great beauty in snow ice sun and sky to which I am very susceptible'. He himself had his holiday that year in the Irish Republic with John Scott. On 12 August he wrote to Gomringer:

> While you were among the mountains I was in the green valleys of Eire and walking along the Joyce-haunted Liffey [. . .] and in Dublin I heard many Glasgow voices. The overnight boat from Glasgow to Dublin has become quite an institution, with much drinking, singing, watching the stars, etc [. . .].[21]

However, the following summer John and he made the trip to the mountains at Achensee in the Tyrol. EM described the not wholly successful holiday in a letter to Ian Hamilton Finlay on 15 August 1966 just after returning from 'Ach on Sea'. It had rained so much that they had fallen back on Tyrolean Evenings, bingo, rummy, and watching the World Cup on German television:

> On the last but one evening there was a great Schuhplattler competition which John (the friend I was with – he's in fact a champion dancer) won, his reward being a bottle of wine with a golden monkey embossed on it [. . .]. I think both of us should have got a golden monkey for doing the Schuhplattler in the kilt.[22]

A chairlift ride up into the mountains was a memorable occasion, perhaps especially because it was experienced in his normal solitary state:

> each person isolated in his own little rickety chair, swinging slowly and steeply up through the huge pines and space to the summit [. . .] you feel as if you were cast adrift, it is exhilarating and yet in a sense it is too free, almost frightening [. . .].

Holidays together after much of the year apart did create a certain tension. There is a poem called 'The Quarrel', dated October 1966, and published in the journal *Form* 1 three years later, which refers to a holiday in the mountains, although the action is set in the north of Italy:

> Over the chill of the Dolomites, clouds
> like basalt cooled in air, a wet
> sundown going black quickly.
> After you avoided me all that day
> I turned on you [. . .]

Assuming that at least some of the poem is based on a true incident, it appears that social class differences are at the heart of the quarrel: they end up screaming at each other on the stairs, then

> – Give me the key, you said.
> I know I'm common as dirt.
> Go on with your fancy friends
> I know I'm nothing. Go on
> I'm nothing, you don't need me.[23]

It ends in tears, of course, and a sort of reconciliation. Too sentimental perhaps, or not fully realised enough in its final lines for publication in the *Collected Poems*, it is nevertheless a touching reminder of the realities of differences that no amount of love or passion could wash away. It ends with the 'common' man mending a rip in the other's coat.

CAVAN MCCARTHY AND VERONICA FORREST-THOMSON

Literary relationships at a distance could be safer, if no less engaging. EM's regular correspondence over several years with Cavan McCarthy, a student of Russian at Leeds University and later a librarian in England, Nigeria and Brazil, is typical of the way in which the network of those working in avant-garde poetry was extended. He had first written to EM in May 1964, asking for some poetry to publish in a new literary magazine. He had seen some of his translations from Russian in *Poor.Old.Tired.Horse.* (POTH 8, August 1964), 'Slow Song' by Yury Pankratov (CT: 301), 'Parabolic Ballad' by Andrei Voznesensky (CT: 188–9) and 'Poem' by Velimir Khlebnikov (CT: 335–7). By the time EM had replied, he had left the original magazine over an editorial disagreement and set up a new one called *TLALOC*, with experimental interests in 'pop poetry', influenced by the 1960s pop painters, and involving woodcuts and coloured inks in its production.

They swapped Russian texts, EM lending him a volume of Soviet poetry *(Den Poesii)*, and providing a list of authors and titles for Cavan to find, if he could, on a summer study trip to Moscow. He had difficulty with this task, it turned out, since most new poetry there was funded by subscription and soon sold out. Cavan was also in touch with Dom Sylvester Houédard, who was then working in Pluscarden monastery in Morayshire, and who gave a reading for the Literary Society in Leeds on his way back south to Prinknash.

Letters provided EM with opportunities to articulate his own particular vision of poetry to sympathetic but not uncritical readers. Cavan McCarthy took a fair bit of convincing about concrete poetry at the start, although he went on to practise and publish it. He offered a critique of 'Spacepoem 1' (CP: 194) and

its original layout, on 3 January 1965: 'it must have more space'.
EM replied agreeing with much of his criticism, and went on:

> I think what I am doing can be done on a (horizontal rather than
> vertical) page. I know this mixture of different types of poetry
> which you refer to was a risk, but it was a calculated one. Be not
> afeard, the isle is full of voices (or noises) – I wanted a succession
> of different noises/voices mechanical/human scrambled/clear all
> the way through; perhaps the answer is simply different type
> spaces [. . .].[24]

There was shared networking with other groups – with Bob
Cobbing's sound poetry in London and with Finlay, who agreed
to send out *TLALOC* with POTH mailings.

As Cavan McCarthy said, things were happening everywhere,
'in fact, the sheer amount is sometimes terrifying'. He was
responsible for two very important connections that EM made
in the 1960s. One involved retrieving from a university notice
board in June 1965 a letter from Hungary addressed to EM.
Other letters to *TLALOC* seemed to have been stolen by
McCarthy's lodger, and he had no idea how this one ended
up where it did. The Hungarian contact wanted to include some
of EM's Attila József translations in a 'poetry yearbook' to be
published in Budapest later in 1965, and also wanted him to
translate other contemporary Hungarian poets for this book,
'working from prose versions and existing translations in French,
which is a second best method, but I may do it; they seem unable
to get anyone to do it direct into anything that looks like poetry'.
EM thanked Cavan 'for being my good angel with the letter'.
Other Hungarian contacts were beginning to come his way about
this time, and he would go on a British Council tour there the
following summer.

The second significant link came when Cavan, after working on
a Directory of Little Magazines, trained as a librarian and got a
post in Blackburn Technical College. He continued his magazine
connection through *Small Press Review*, and in March 1967 he

asked EM to write a review of a first publication by Veronica Forrest-Thomson, *Identi-kit*. He himself did not want to do it as she was 'a close friend', a second year student at Liverpool University and 'mad keen on concrete poetry (and concrete poets)'. She came from the West End of Glasgow, and had originally been 'switched on to concrete poetry by hearing a lecture you gave maybe two-three years ago in Glasgow'.

This may have been the lecture EM gave to the English Association in Glasgow one Friday evening in December, shortly after Dom Sylvester's visit to his flat in late November 1964. With no time to prepare slides, he duplicated the material for an audience of about one hundred and thirty people: poems by Finlay, Houédard, Augusto de Campos, Pedro Xisto, Ernst Jandl and Eugen Gomringer, as well as his own work. It is more likely that contact came through her hearing one of EM's radio broadcasts on concrete poetry on the Third Programme. She wrote him 'an amazingly mature letter' in response, stating that she considered the movement to be 'the first healthy development in poetry since the war' since it showed 'responsibility towards the exploration of language instead of the usual egotistical watered down angst-dichten which seems to monopolise the Third Programme readings'.[25] In June of the same year, she came to one of his readings, sat in the front row and asked searching questions, following this up with a letter where she talked about Ian Hamilton Finlay and his Wild Hawthorn Press, and compared the style of the two poets. Thus EM already knew something of the young poet whose work he was asked to review.

Her letters to him dated from February 1965 to August 1974, the first contact therefore being when she was aged seventeen, in her final year at school. In June 1965, she wondered whether she should send work to *Poor.Old.Tired.Horse.*, but said she 'would be apprehensive of committing [her]self to one label'. So she sent poems to EM instead for an opinion; he replied and the correspondence grew from there. She shared his enjoyment in the international, surprising and paradoxical nature of Finlay's magazine, which seemed to EM in retrospect 'very un-English

165

(but really quite Scottish and Bakhtinian)', as well as his interests in language and science.[26]

Veronica Forrest-Thomson would go on to do postgraduate research at Cambridge on 'Science and Modern Poetry', and later teach at the Universities of Leicester and Birmingham. She was both a poet and a critical theorist and died tragically young in 1975. Her *Poetic Artifice: A Theory of Twentieth Century Poetry* (1978) and several collections of poems were posthumously published. EM liked and admired her work, and kept in touch, mainly by letter but sometimes meeting her, generally in London during the summer months.

By one of life's ironies, Cavan McCarthy became firstly a university librarian in Leeds, and then lectured in library science in Saõ Paulo, settling and marrying there to become 'more or less Brazilian', but giving up his British life as a concrete poet in the very place where one key strand of the movement began, and to which EM had posted his 'airmail solidarity' to its poetic-concrete revolutionaries. To the best of my knowledge and Cavan McCarthy's recollection, he and EM met only once, at a reading of concrete and sound poetry. The relationship was one of those Migrant-inspired epistolary partnerships in the exploration of poetic values – an intense but distanced conversation towards a credo.

It may be that the concrete poets were a set of surrogate brothers (I've seen no sisters) offering a combination of playfulness and rivalry within a shared context of creative growth. Their distance from the mainstream was also an attraction, although EM was determined that they should be recognised more widely. By June 1966 he had successfully sponsored Finlay for an Arts Council bursary of £350. In December of the same year, he advised him to explore whether his growing interest in the public use of poetry in combination with image and sculpture might find an outlet on the campus of the new University of Warwick, where there was 'a vast long term programme of building over a huge site near Coventry'. EM had been invited to give a lecture there by G.K. Hunter, who had become its founding professor of

English in 1964. He had been able to make radical changes to the traditional English curriculum, which was now to be studied in the context of world literature and other languages.

Perhaps it was this experience that made EM apply for the chair of English at the new University of Stirling early in 1967. In old age, he recalled being encouraged by colleagues that this was 'the expected thing to do'. But the combination of rivalry and radicalism offered by G.K. Hunter's position may have been influential. EM was not successful in his application, and he came to think that, as a campus university, Stirling became too inward-looking and somewhat detached from its nearby town. Urban was better for a university, he decided.

But when Warwick failed to take up Finlay's suggestion of public art works, EM offered to write to Dr Tom Cottrell, the Principal at Stirling who had interviewed him, to make a case for his work. This was one way of bringing the avant-garde into the daily life of the next generation of students.

PUBLISHING THE NEW POETRY

A different stratagem for bringing avant-garde writing to students' attention was to create teaching materials that would reflect new cultural perspectives, as in his *Albatross Book of Longer Poems* (1963) for Collins, the Glasgow-based publishers. The volume begins traditionally enough with Chaucer's 'The Nun's Priest's Tale' but ends with MacDiarmid, Charles Olson, Dylan Thomas, Robert Lowell, John Wain, Christopher Logue and Allen Ginsberg. The presence of a 'safe' English poet like Wain, usually associated with the formalist Movement style, is explained by the poem itself. His 'A Song about Major Eatherley' is based on the mental turmoil suffered by the pilot of the aircraft that carried the second atomic bomb to Nagasaki. This particular selection recalls EM's own part in a soldiers' protest about the bombing in the last months of his military service.

The anthology is a scholarly one, of course, with conscientious attempts made by EM as editor to gloss, for example, the naval terminology in Rudyard Kipling's 'McAndrew's Hymn' (and its Glaswegian background), and Robert Lowell's 'The Quaker Graveyard in Nantucket'. He wrote to the British Indian Steam Navigation Company, the Royal Yachting Association and the Department of Naval Architecture at Glasgow's Royal College of Science and Technology in his quest for definitions of obscure terms.

It is unclear whether the suggestion for the volume came from him originally, but by August 1961 the publishers were asking for notes to be sent to the typesetters as soon as possible. There was a rush on to try to get the book out for the start of the university term in October. In fact, it was subject to various delays and was finally published as a companion volume to the Collins *Albatross Book of Verse* in the Spring of 1963. EM had not been involved in this earlier anthology, but the delay now gave him the chance to add Charles Olson and Allen Ginsberg to his own book at the last moment, and he wrote to Ginsberg (who was in India) on 22 November 1962, asking permission to use his recent poem 'American Change'. His editorial note quotes the poet's argument against cold 'academic' poetry, in favour of the 'rhythms of speech and rhythm prompted by direct transcription of visual and other mental data'.[27]

The anthology became an academic set text in the University's Ordinary English Literature class in 1965–1966, and this would have helped sales. Maurice Lindsay's anthology *Modern Scottish Poetry* (1966) was set in the following year, when EM lectured on it. This was my first experience of him as a lecturer, and he was particularly clear and memorable on Hugh MacDiarmid's poetry. His own poems in the book were not dealt with in the lectures. Nor was his assistance acknowledged by the book's editor, who thanks Douglas Young, George Bruce and Alexander Scott for suggestions, but not EM who had written to him in March 1965 putting the case for Burns Singer (who was published in *Glasgow University Magazine* during the war), Sydney Graham and Ian Hamilton Finlay, who were all included, as well as for Tom McGrath and Giles Gordon, who were not.

Lindsay's Preface states that he had not included concrete verse 'because much of it seems to me to be simply a play-about with typography which, however interesting visually, is in no way memorable as poetry'. EM is represented by his Glasgow poems 'To Joan Eardley', 'King Billy' and 'Good Friday', and also by 'Aberdeen Train'. This last poem he wrote just after a journey to Aberdeen University to give a poetry reading to students there.

Maurice Lindsay was a positive influence, however, on the *Scottish Poetry* series of annual volumes from Edinburgh University Press. EM co-edited the series with him and George Bruce from 1966 until 1972. Lindsay had written to Donald Mather of the Scottish Committee of the Arts Council of Great Britain in December 1964 proposing a Scottish Poetry Society that would publish two half-yearly anthologies for a trial period of two years. This was to be supported by subscription and by sales of books through the stationers John Menzies and independent booksellers, as well as by Arts Council assistance. A grant of £225 was given to support the first issue, and the link with Edinburgh University Press was made by George Bruce, who knew Archie Turnbull, Secretary of the Press.

By March 1965 the enterprise was under way as an annual volume. EM wrote to Finlay requesting poems for the first one, 'as I want you to be represented'. Editorial decisions were made by a consensus judgement, of course, achieved by the time-consuming process of swapping the typescripts by post. The first volume was a success, and the process was continued until *Scottish Poetry 6*. Both new and recently published poems appeared in the annual selection. In Number One, EM had 'Strawberries', 'The Death of Marilyn Monroe' and 'In the Snack-bar', and some of his now best-known poems gained their first substantial readership in this series: 'From the Domain of Arnheim', 'Absence', 'From a City Balcony', 'For Bonfires', 'Floating off to Timor'. These collections represented a lively and authentic view of contemporary Scottish poetry, and helped create a wider readership for younger poets such as Tom Leonard.

EM took care to encourage those whose poetry he regarded

positively. When Sydney Graham wrote to him in the autumn of 1967, asking about current Scottish outlets for poetry, EM referred to *Lines Review*, *Akros*, his own new enterprise *Scottish International*, and also the EUP annual anthology. He asked him to send some 'newish' poems for Number Five, preferably not already selected for his soon to be published *Malcolm Mooney's Land* (1970). Graham had sent EM an advance copy of the poems, with a friendly letter:

> [. . .] let me say that I have followed your good real flight with great pleasure. You have my best respect, Edwin, and if that sounds pompous I say it at that risk [. . .]. Cheerio child of Lanarkshire – Love Sydney.[28]

EM's response was also a warm one, although he was reluctant to rush into judgement on the new poems. He ends: 'I often think of you. The years are nothing when it comes to that. Love Edwin.'

At this time, EM was well placed to give his old friend advice. He had just been asked to join the Literature Committee of the Scottish Arts Council. The organisation, newly established as an autonomous body by a royal charter in 1967, was at the stage of developing its structures and policies, and so EM gained an 'insider' view of how writers' bursaries and prizes would be awarded. He gave advice, too, to a working group on 'Recorded Literature', suggesting authors and texts that should be made available on disk, and making the educational case for material that would be useful at both school and university levels, and also show 'the range of linguistic usage from Scots to English'.

By the end of August 1968, however, less than a year after joining the Literature Committee, he had decided to resign. He had come to feel that it was 'not a healthy situation when creative people also have to make financial decisions from which they stand to gain', as he told Ian Hamilton Finlay. This involved not only his fees for editing the sponsored *Scottish Poetry* volumes, and the fees, which he would at first refuse, for editing *Scottish International*. He may also have been thinking about awards that might follow from the publication of *The Second Life* in that year. His letter of resignation proposed an alteration to the structure of the Council:

> The conclusion that I have come to is that people who have some particular knowledge in one of the arts should be called on as members of a panel but not as members of an inner Council which administers funds and makes policy decisions. [. . .] I do not think it is a healthy situation that permits practising artists, writers and composers to take financial decisions affecting not only their own contemporaries but in many cases inevitably their friends and acquaintances and even (as happened to me on more than one occasion) themselves.[29]

He offered to work hard and make his contribution on any such advisory panel. Involved as he was in such a range of literary activities, it was almost impossible for him not to know those whose work was being funded. He sponsored Ian Hamilton Finlay and Robert Garioch for writers' bursaries, and as a committee member approved a publication grant for the poet Robin Fulton, and financial support for Duncan Glen's *Akros* publications as well as *Scottish International*. In the following year, *The Second Life* did in fact win a publications award for Edinburgh University Press.

PHILIP HOBSBAUM

EM both responded to and encouraged the creative atmosphere in the University of Glasgow and in the city itself in the second half of the 1960s. The atmosphere seemed altered, not only because of changes in music and fashion and in student political movements, which were now more radical. The leadership of his Department had also changed, as Peter Butter had come from Queen's University, Belfast, to succeed Peter Alexander as Regius Professor. He was soon followed by Philip Hobsbaum, who had worked with him there, as Senior Lecturer. In Northern Ireland,

Hobsbaum had continued the practice of 'The Group', which he had developed in London with Edward Lucie-Smith, Peter Redgrove, George MacBeth and others. This was a monthly poets' workshop, where poems were subjected to robust professional close-reading by peers. At Queens University, members of the Group had included the notable young talents of Michael Longley and Seamus Heaney, and Paul Muldoon would join soon after its founder's departure for Glasgow.

Arriving there, Hobsbaum was at first nonplussed by what he failed to find – a creative energy commensurate with the size of the city. His combative and provocative approach as a tutor and lecturer, his actor's RP accent and his emotional style as a poet did not get the best response from local students. He found them tongue-tied, and conservative in their literary judgements. Local poets too would be cautious about him. Out of the Jewish East End of London and industrial Yorkshire, then back via Cambridge to London's Royal Academies of Music and Dramatic Art, chock-full of attitude and argument, he was both odd and formidable, squinting through the bottle-lenses of spectacles that barely helped his semi-blindness. He seemed not to notice the crushing impact of his critical comments on many students.

Nevertheless he persevered, and started a Glasgow Group which included Tom Leonard, Stephen Mulrine, Robin Hamilton and others. I was a member for a year or so. Hobsbaum was my tutor in 1966–1967, and, if you could get behind the unusual mixture of RP accent and East End tough to the vulnerability beneath, he was a stimulating presence. He felt himself to be an outsider – as a Jew, as a Londoner in Yorkshire and a Yorkshireman in Cambridge, with his weak vision further isolating him from the crowd. Like EM, he was tremendously hard-working as a lecturer and literary critic, was well-connected among publishers and the BBC, and was genuinely and generously supportive of beginning writers. Later members of his workshop would include Alasdair Gray, Aonghas Macneacail, Liz Lochhead and James Kelman.

The Group approach helped make the act of writing less

isolated and subjective by bringing the individual poet's aesthetic experience into a public arena. It is interesting how gladiatorial metaphors tend to crowd in when considering Hobsbaum's approach. Chosen work had been photocopied and circulated in advance, and the writers had to be able to explain or justify each stylistic choice of word or form – in the process learning a great deal from the responses of fellow practitioners to work that might otherwise have had little scrutiny. At the same time, Hobsbaum emphasised constantly the need to stay close to personal experience in the shaping of a poem.

Although he was never close to Hobsbaum, who 'went his own way', EM watched the progress of these workshops keenly and was eager to see what would come of them. The two men differed significantly in almost every aspect of character, and EM preferred to offer support to student writers in a quieter and, he believed, more sustaining way. Their lecturing styles also could not have been more different. EM felt that the new Professor had brought his Queens University colleague across to Glasgow in order to stir things up, to add 'intellectual backbone', to encourage publication and productivity, and to make the Department better known.

Creative writing as part of the degree structure was another area where the two poet-scholars disagreed. Hobsbaum was much keener on this, and did a great deal to develop it within the University. EM always had reservations about the extent to which people could be taught how to write creatively, and about the real comparability of traditional academic essays and portfolios of creative work. His position had not shifted much from what he had written in 1959, in a symposium for *Universities Quarterly* XIII:4:

I am opposed to the American experiment of complete rationa-lisation of the creative writer's position and function within the universities, because it has produced [. . .] a generation of tech-nically advanced and professionally cultivated poets [. . .] whose response to life itself has atrophied and whose poetry is impotent to make and inspire the human heart.[30]

He saw Ginsberg's *Howl* as the inevitable counter-attack to this, and admired the way his 'angel headed hipsters' got themselves thrown out of the academies for being crazy. Yet he recognized, both as a person and as a poet, that he needed to be where his vast intellectual curiosity could be sustained by academic life. And he could see that poets might still be useful teachers and researchers, while also adding 'a quirky leaven to the discipline'.

Philip Hobsbaum continued to develop creative writing courses in the University of Glasgow, and then a highly successful degree programme from 1995 onwards. This extensive activity was focused around the new Edwin Morgan Centre for Creative Writing in 2000. EM always remained slightly at odds with this recognition, however, which felt, somehow, even though he had been asked, like identity theft.

Both EM and Hobsbaum perhaps mellowed as colleagues over time. In the late 1970s, by then Professor and Reader, they even lectured together to present their differing responses to the work of Ian Hamilton Finlay and Roy Fisher, for example, thus demonstrating that both dialogue and difference are part of the process of literary criticism. And both men recognised the sharp intelligence of Tom Leonard, supporting him through some early difficulties in his career as a student and writer.

In the late 1960s, Tom Leonard edited *Glasgow University Magazine*, and brought a new radicalism and humour to it. The University Literary Society published the magazine *Epos*. Alan Spence was involved with a cyclostyled student production, *Nik*, and another student magazine was called *Henry*. The dramatist and poet Tom McGrath had returned to Glasgow with experience of 'counter-culture' in London. So it did really feel, as EM wrote to the small-press publisher and graphic designer, Duncan Glen, in late 1966 that there was 'definitely something "happening" in Scottish poetry in the Glasgow area at the moment'[31] despite Hobsbaum's claims to the contrary.

At the end of 1966, EM was suggesting to Duncan Glen that he bring out a collection of work by some of the Glasgow's new student poets, whom he had already helped into print. Robert

Tait, Colin Kirkwood and Alan Hayton had appeared in *Scottish Poetry* 1, and Stephen Mulrine in *Scottish Poetry* 2. This collection came out as a booklet, *Four Glasgow University Poets*, from Glen's Akros Publications in May 1967, EM having selected the poems, organised the author notes and written a brief introduction.

Duncan Glen was too stretched financially to publish a separate *Whittrick* collection, which EM had requested, but he suggested that he could create a booklet of concrete poems, using this as a practical exercise for students on his Typographic Design course at Lancashire Polytechnic. Glen, a gifted book designer and also a poet, had been born in Cambuslang near Rutherglen in 1933. He became Head of Graphic Design at Lancashire Polytechnic, and was later Professor of Visual Communication at Nottingham Trent University. From south of the Border, his publishing and editing activities had a significant impact on the poetry being written and read in Scotland.

So while his student poets' collection was being produced, EM put together a selection of twelve concrete poems for a limited edition booklet of three hundred copies. Entitled *gnomes*, it included several pieces that failed subsequently to make it into the *Collected Poems*. These included the title poem 'gnomes', which EM found impossible to type and so had to write out by hand. He asked Glen to print it 'very much as I have it, i.e. difficult but not impossible to read. It reads diagonally upwards from left to right, and makes a series of *gnomic* statements, "Fast bets best", "Cast fits fist", "Zest jets jest", "West eats east" etc . . .'. The poem was meant to be 'a puzzle, but with a solution'.[32] It is little wonder that the senior generation of Scottish poets, and English poets such as Hobsbaum now resident in Scotland, did not know what to make of EM, or felt that the solution to his poetry was not worth their puzzling.

SÁNDOR WEÖRES

To that extent at least, EM was without peer: a rather isolated, quietly defiant writer. But not truly alone, he thought, from the international perspective which was crucial to him. In the autumn of 1966 EM was one of a British Council group of writers attending an international poetry conference in Hungary. George MacBeth, the Scots-born poet and BBC radio producer, was also part of the group. It was a tightly-packed fortnight, with 'days spent with earphones listening to broken French' in the first week (there was no English translation available, but only Russian, French and Hungarian). EM gave a paper on translation, and then in the second week lectured on modern British poetry at Budapest University and at the British Embassy. He told Robert Tait: 'I slipped some (phonic) concrete into my lectures and this caused something of a sensation'.[33]

But there was also a Hungarian poet, Sándor Weöres, who had 'already written quite a bit of both visual and phonetic poetry though outside the concrete movement as such', as EM reported to Ian Hamilton Finlay on his return. EM tried without success to find and bring back examples of his books, but, as in Russia, poetry books were published in short runs and sold out almost at once. Even Weöres himself had no spares to give him, but EM vowed that 'someday and somehow I shall get hold of it and see if it is possible to translate it'.

Weöres encouraged him in this. Recalling in old age their brief meetings in Budapest, EM sparkled with enthusiasm and admiration:

> He knew, he surely knew what he was: I think he was a genius. He knew he was a great poet and therefore ought to be known in the English language [. . .]. He had, of course, a humorous impish quality, which was very attractive – almost a kind of child-like quality. He would think of something quite entertaining, quite funny, and just say it, even though it had no tremendous depth to it. I liked that about him: there was a kind of innocence perhaps [. . .].[34]

In this interview in 2000 with the Hungarian critic Attila Dósa, EM described a meal he had with Weöres and his wife, who was also a poet and translator. Weöres would use the menu card to scribble jokes and drawings or snatches of poetry, and make political comments, even although he knew he was regarded in this Communist state as not entirely a 'safe' writer:

> But he would come to a point and say 'Oh, I shouldn't be saying that, should I?' He was very interesting and his wife too was an interesting person. Both were extremely cultured, civilised persons. I liked the way the conversation flew very freely back and forward [. . .] nothing was taboo, or difficult or awkward, it just flew very naturally.

The conversation used a variety of French, German and Hungarian, as Weöres had little English, yet both men recognised a deep affinity:

> We seemed to get on very well and we were to some extent on the same or a similar wave-length. I liked his linguistic virtuosity – because he wrote in many different styles and obviously with a tremendous command of language – and I too have used different styles [. . .]. Sometimes in writers workshops teachers will say: 'Well, you must find your voice!'. I don't agree with that. I think you can have many voices – well, I have many voices. I think Weöres also had many voices. Yes, I felt a kind of kinship with him.

There were, it is true, differences between them: of culture, life experience and literary success. Born in 1913, Weöres began his career as a child prodigy of poetry, with a virtuoso mastery of form and technique. He had been a librarian, a museum administrator, a farmer, a forced labourer during World War Two, a translator and a scholar. He had won Hungary's highest literary award twice in his early twenties, whereas EM when they met had yet to see his own first full collection of poems published. Marxist critics had branded Weöres a Nihilist in the post-war years of the Iron Curtain, and for some time he could make a living only from his translation and his poetry for children, which has also had a long-lived national impact in schools through its rhythms and sounds.

There was a spiritual depth and complexity in Weöres very different from the values EM had developed through a Scottish upbringing, or in antagonism to it. Both men, however, shared interests in mythology, anthropology, aesthetics, the translation of Ukrainian verse, epic poetry and a thousand other topics. And both had the sort of vivid, questing imagination that, even in old age, never seemed to grow old. It is clear, however, that EM recognised the superiority of his older Hungarian contemporary, as he seldom did with others, and with a sort of wonder that had no envy in it.

A year later he had the opportunity to put that admiration to a practical use. At the Budapest conference he had met Miklós Vajda, then editor of the *New Hungarian Quarterly* (*NHQ*) who had formed the impression that EM had 'a good kind of touch with translating Hungarian poetry'. They agreed that rough literal translations of poems would be sent to him in Scotland, and he would try to turn them into good versions in English. In 1967, EM had translations in the Spring, Summer and Autumn issues of *NHQ*. None of these was of work by Weöres, but the critic Al Alvarez, who was an advisory editor for the Penguin series Modern European Poets in Translation, had taken note. He wrote to EM at the beginning of October, asking whether he had enough József translations to fill fifty pages, plus a general introduction of two thousand words. But he also asked him about Weöres translations, as Peter Redgrove, the poet commissioned to do these, was unhappy with his own results. The intention was to feature both Hungarian poets in one volume.

EM replied almost immediately that he had about twenty József poems and was happy to do more. He would also be willing to work with Peter Redgrove's Hungarian collaborator, and contacted the English poet himself in the following week. His keenness was obvious, even at the hectic start of the university teaching year. The two poets corresponded and swapped some versions, and by the end of the month it had been agreed that EM would do half the Weöres and all the József poems, for fees of seventy five and one hundred and fifty guineas respectively.

By December 1967, EM had received some versions from Redgrove, and asked for a postponement of the original deadline. There had now been a proposal to have a separate József book, and a joint volume featuring Sándor Weöres and Ferenc Juhász. By March 1968, Redgrove was trying to retrieve his versions from EM, to take further advice from a Professor Gömöri, who taught Polish and Hungarian at Cambridge University. EM too contacted György Gömöri, who was also a poet, in an attempt to get a sight of the original Hungarian texts, and was given details of a Paris publisher and a fortnight's loan of one of Weöres' recent collections, *Tüzkút* (*Well of Flames*, 1964). Gömöri in turn asked for any reprints or new translations that EM had available for a proposed anthology of Hungarian poets in English translation. He replied that he was able to supply versions not only of József and Weöres but of Kassák, Pilinszky, Jékely, Kormos, Csoóri, Szabó and Füst. To Alvarez, Gömöri also expressed his dislike of Redgrove's translations: they seemed to him simply to be the English poet's variations on Weöres's themes.

However, the two translators proceeded in tandem over the summer. EM provided guidance on points of detail, to the extent that by December of 1968 Redgrove wrote to Nikos Stangos, his Penguin editor, that he was prepared to have EM retain or adapt whatever seemed valuable in his own versions, and complete the task on his own. He recognised EM's genuine translator's gift, and fine ear. Although EM wrote to him about feeling guilty 'about seeming to appear as a sort of cuckoo in the nest in this situation', and promising to acknowledge any use made of Redgrove's versions, no such reference appears in the book as published in 1970. Possibly nothing much was retained. The additional work meant that he requested an extension of the deadline till the end of April and an increased payment for the extra translations. In fact he completed the task by the end of May, and was then in contact with Weöres, through his wife, who spoke English, for help over the summer with some of the obscure mythological references in the poems. These turned out to be from both actual and imaginary mythologies.

Níkos Stangos thought the translations were 'terrific'. At the start of the year it seemed that the József section of the volume was still being considered, but this was replaced by David Wevill's translations of Ferenc Juhász, presumably to provide variation in the translator's voice.

The page proofs were ready by the end of May 1970, in time to be used at a Poetry International festival being held for the first time in Scotland that summer, which Weöres attended. EM's translations were first read aloud by Charles Osbourne of the Arts Council, and then, as Stewart Maclennan described it in the *New Edinburgh Review* (No.9, November 1970), 'Weöres released an unbridled cataract of syllables which broke over each other like waves, picking up an intricately textured sonic structure'. The reviewer linked this effect to the sound poetry of Ernst Jandl from Austria, and also recognised the close affinity to Weöres in EM's poetry (citing 'Spacepoem 1: from Laika to Gagarin', CP: 194). EM met Weöres and his wife after this performance, and again communicated across the language barrier the warmth of his enthusiasm.

Coincidentally with that strong imagery of breaking waves that occurred to Stewart Maclennan, EM had commissioned a similar artwork from Ian Hamilton Finlay immediately on his return from Hungary. This was a 'wave/rock glass poem' which he had first seen on the cover of the *Beloit Poetry Journal*. The etched letters of 'wave' collide with those of 'rock' on an oblong of glass. He thought the piece would be the right size for an ordinary living room, 'big enough to be distinctive but not overpowering', and able to take advantage of the position of his Whittingehame Court flat:

> my room faces south and gets a lot of light, stands high, looks out mostly to sky and roofs, hills in the distance, and then by a stroke of luck water (the boating pond in Great Western Road, with two swans on it).

Finlay wrote back to him over the Christmas holidays, offering the work free. But EM was determined to pay him eighty pounds, sharing the windfall fees he had earned, over and above those from the British Council, from interviews, translations and readings in Budapest. He had already had to leave half the money in Hungary, being obliged to open an account there in a different name. He chose Robert Burns:

> Burns doesn't know it, but he now has a few thousand forint which I suppose are helping to build up the Hungarian economy. Unfortunately neither he nor I can use them.[35]

While all this work of translation and publication was going on, EM was bearing his normal load of teaching and assessment. Occasionally it all got too much, as he complained to Finlay in March of 1967:

> Term has just ended and I come up for air [. . .]. Life is really very difficult – one in the morning, two in the morning, trying to catch up but never quite making it [. . .]. And even though it is the Easter vacation, I have two hundred papers to mark.

Totting up sales and royalties perhaps gave some sort of justification for all the additional creative effort, and was the sort of hard evidence of success that his father would have recognised. Sales for the Penguin translations peaked at 8702, with only small numbers selling thereafter. This sort of close accounting was a feature of his approach to writing throughout his career.

He was meticulous in his approach to teaching too. Tom Leonard remembered him as a teacher who was always

> very full of detail, and particular to detail [. . .]. He was very specific and very assiduous. [. . .]. Where there was Edwin, there was never any sloppiness and there was never any bluff. He would have read through thoroughly everything he was talking about [. . .].[36]

EM was shaken, therefore, to receive a hate letter from a male student during the late 1960s. In the account given to Marshall Walker, this had come about because EM was one of a panel judging a poetry competition, who had failed to recognise the young man's talents. But that was a confusion with a later event of the 1970s. In the story as retold in old age, he was sure the student's complaints were general ones, made against the Department as a whole, and in particular at his poor grade in an assessment, which EM may possibly have marked. He consulted his colleague, Dr Sarah Davies. She told him: 'I think when this sort of thing happens, one should examine oneself'. EM wrote to the student, therefore, but received no reply. The matter remained as unfinished and therefore disturbing business over the years. The punctilious approach evident in his normal teaching must have made the marking of essays by the hundred a particular worry for him.

The contrast between EM's unassuming manner as a lecturer and his dynamic effect as a creative writer on campus was evident to the 'Young Turks', new lecturers recruited by Peter Butter as part of government-funded expansion of higher education. The appointments he made show how deliberately the professor was extending the range of his Department's traditional curriculum. Marshall Walker joined the Department after a three-year stint at Rhodes University in South Africa, and would later teach in New Zealand. Tim Cribb joined the staff for the second half of the Sixties, having taught in the United States and France. He would also teach briefly in universities in Tunis and Nigeria, and have a continuing interest in what was then called Commonwealth literature but is now postcolonial literature. He was my tutor, a stimulating lecturer and a gifted actor.

Tim Cribb admired Jack Rillie as an inspiring teacher, but EM 'as inspiration itself'. He attended one or two of EM's lectures but concluded that they were 'bread and butter' presentations, 'sufficient to the purpose'. What in his view made EM central to the dynamism of the Department, however, was that:

he gave meaning to the curriculum through his remarkable extracurricular activity [. . .] his activity creating new literature gave meaning to the teaching of the rest of us of what had already been written, thus gearing the past to the creation of the future now. That was truly energising.[37]

Without any hint of posing or poetic factionalism, EM seemed to his younger colleague to be a living exemplar of many Modernist principles, putting the emphasis on craft and experiment rather than personality and expression. His very Scottish internationalism was evident not only in his translations of Mayakovsky into Scots and his engagement with concrete poetry, but in the row of dictionaries in a surprising variety of languages above his desk:

> And all of these riches were made available as if it was the most natural thing in the world to any student who wanted to discuss poetry, launch an ephemeral magazine, stage an event, or whatever.

It is also true that he could in the midst of the most 'bread and butter' lectures provide unexpected and stimulating links between disparate writers. I remember how, during one rather heavy lecture in 1968 on 17th-century prose stylistics in polemical works on religion and the state, he suddenly made cross-reference to contemporary Polish poetry and the work of Zbigniew Herbert. Almost forty years later, when I had a chance to see his typed notes, it was clear that he occasionally but deliberately left paragraph-size gaps in the text, as a space for improvisation. This helped him to create a lecturing style that Marshall Walker memorably described as 'springy'.

SCOTTISH INTERNATIONAL

In the same month as he was complaining to Finlay about the stresses of work, EM was in discussion with Peter Butter, Alex Scott in the Department of Scottish Literature, and Alisdair

Skinner of the Arts Council about co-editing a new journal of Scottish culture and society. As yet it had no name, but EM rejected both the suggested publication by the Edinburgh firm of Blackwoods and any title involving the word 'Saltire'. Both would have a 'backward-looking' connotation that was definitely not what was needed in a decade of major social and scientific change. This was precisely the sort of journal he had been agitating for since the early 1960s, but now, presumably because of his many other commitments, he was uncertain about the extent to which he could be involved.

He may also have been made wary by his earlier and ongoing experience with *New Saltire* journal. He had been involved since 1962, first as Poetry Editor and then as Literary Editor. This was where his early salvo against the establishment had been published, 'The Beatnik in the Kailyard'. The journal had been running at a loss almost from the start, and had the normal problems of sustaining the quality of articles. The editor, Magnus Magnusson, resigned at one low point after Issue 5, but was persuaded to return. The journal was finally wound up in 1970. So EM knew what he was letting himself in for, if he took a leading role in the new journal.

Peter Butter, however, with his institutional aim of bringing the department into greater public focus, had taken up the idea energetically. In tutorials he gave the impression of taking a rather languid Oxbridge approach, which was confirmed for students by his habit of arriving at University in a vintage car driven by a chauffeur, and yet his lectures showed a sharp textual awareness. He would chair the board of trustees to guide *Scottish International* through its difficult early years. The first problem was to get his colleague engaged.

EM was unwilling to be seen to be taking Arts Council subsidies for both the Scottish Poetry series he was co-editing and for the new journal. The significant amount of new work involved must also have been a consideration, and at first he proposed alternative editors, such as Norman MacCaig, who declined the offer, and Jack Rillie. Another area of difficulty was that Robert Tait was intended from the start to be the managing editor, and he had already riled the literary establishment by some trenchant comments as a contributor to the Edinburgh-based magazine, *Feedback*. Alex Scott, in particular, had a negative view of Tait, and perhaps of the whole enterprise. He suggested privately to Peter Butter that EM was overstretched, but at the same time declared that he was also unwilling to support two suggested alternative co-editors: the Scots language poet, Robert Garioch, or the more experimental poet, D.M. Black. Both of these were based in Edinburgh, as it was thought politic to balance the West Coast Tait and Morgan – if he agreed – with someone from the capital.

Scottish International finally got started, incorporating *Feedback*, which had built up a circulation of fifteen hundred, and with EM and Robert Garioch as co-editors. Tait was to be a full-time editor, based in an office in the Dominican house in George Square, Edinburgh. The Dominicans staffed the Catholic chaplaincy of Edinburgh University, and Anthony Ross O.P., a member of their community, was a well-known social reformer and cultural activist. He became Treasurer to the board of Scottish International Review Limited, which Professor Butter chaired, with Professor John MacQueen of Edinburgh University as vice-chairman. It later emerged that the editorial accommodation was given free of charge, which was typical of Anthony Ross's unorthodox and free-wheeling generosity. Official grants were made by the Arts Council, the Saltire Society and Scottish Television.

The journal's title had also caused problems for Alex Scott. He thought it 'injudicious', and declared that Hugh MacDiarmid had made a public denunciation of the new enterprise and everyone connected with it. He wrote to tell Robert Tait that his articles in *Feedback* and EM's 'concrete-mixing' had created intense dislike. The editorial team moved swiftly in the autumn of 1967 to counter this negative propaganda. Robert Garioch contacted Sydney Goodsir Smith, Douglas Young and Tom Scott, all 'establishment' Edinburgh poets who wrote in Scots and had been involved in the public disagreements with Finlay and EM in the early 1960s. Meanwhile EM tried, with some success, to draw in Maurice Lindsay, seeking an article from him on the Scottish Civic Trust, and also George Bruce, who suggested an autographical piece. Even Alex Scott was grudgingly open to persuasion, and 'willing to show willing' once he learned that Norman MacCaig had agreed to send poems for the first issue.

Robert Garioch seemed an unexpected choice for third editor. A retired schoolmaster, best known for his poems and translations in a lively, demotic Edinburgh Scots, he appeared to lack the range of intellectual interests of his co-editors. But EM learned much from him whenever they shared a platform at poetry readings:

> it was quite a study to see how well he understood the poet-audience situation – the fact that somehow, although it's partly a case of people being there to be entertained, it's also a kind of self-revelation – it's both performance and truth.

Reflecting on Garioch in a 1981 tribute tape recorded by George Philp of Scotsoun (*In Mind of a Makar*, Scotsoun SSC 061), EM recalled his contribution to *Scottish International*:

> the two Roberts used to come through from Edinburgh to my place in Glasgow for editorial meetings. Time and again I noticed how unexpected, and sharp, his comments were, even though he liked to project the image – and after all it wasn't entirely an untrue image – of a conservative and distracted person unaccountably brought into the cut and thrust of contemporary ideas.[38]

Scottish International is part of the cultural history of 1960s and early 1970s Scotland, and it is impossible here to do justice to its contribution to that 'cut and thrust of contemporary ideas'. Robert (Bob) Tait provided a short outline of the journal's work with respect to poetry in '*Scottish International*: A brief account' (Scottish Poetry Index Volume 6: 63–5). But the editors were not short of ambition. Drafted by EM, the first issue's Editorial takes forward the vision, outlined years earlier in 'The Beatnik in the Kailyard', of a Scottish cultural awareness that was informed by a real understanding of the social and economic background that had shaped it. The Scottish arts could not exist in a Scottish world of their own, he argued, hence the 'international' emphasis of the title, but on the other hand a 'colourless and promiscuous internationalism' would be to nobody's advantage. Against 'bad habits of stereotyped thinking and unwillingness to look at the situation as it really is' the new journal would aim to look at what was really there, and to call people's attention to it:

> Everyone is aware [. . .] of how cultures other than Scottish impinge on us, through publishing and the mass media. It is important that this awareness should be sharpened and extended critically, so that more opportunity can be given to compare Scottish work with work done elsewhere. To define ourselves, we believe it is necessary to define many other things, for that is the nature of the world we live in.[39]

As is the way with new journals, some people had promised copy material that did not arrive, or was of variable quality and needed redrafting. Perhaps this was the reason that each of the editors supplied an article: Robert Tait's 'Ma, Your Dreams are on TV', Robert Garioch's 'The Use of Scots', and EM's 'Heraclitus in Gorky Street: The theme of metamorphosis in the poetry of Voznesensky' (reprinted in *Essays*: 71–8). In a positive review of the new journal in *The Guardian* (1 February 1968), Cordelia Oliver said it was worth buying for this article alone, untainted as it was 'by the urge felt by many writers on art to analyse at all costs, rather than to feel'. *The Scotsman* ran with a correspondence of complaints about the new journal not being available in local shops.

Other material in Issue One involved '*Current Topics*': articles on Perth Theatre and on Scottish Publishing; '*Trends and Anti-trends*': articles on violence in the arts by D.M. Black and on Stravinsky's 'The Rake's Progress', a major operatic performance in the previous Edinburgh Festival; '*A Commemoration*' on the composer Francis George Scott, seen as 'the Dante to Hugh MacDiarmid's Virgil' in his musical exploration of the Scottish nether-world; and pieces on 'The Spelling of Scots' by A.J. Mackie and 'The SNO on Disc' by Robin Fulton. These latter pieces, together with Garioch's article and the celebration of F.G. Scott, are carefully placed to forestall criticism of the journal's 'un-Scottish' avant-gardism from MacDiarmid's supporters. The selection of poetry also places better known voices such as Norman MacCaig, Alex Scott and George Scott-Moncrief along-side newer or more radical poets (most of them well known to EM): Colin Kirkwood, Tom Leonard, Mark Hill, Ian Hamilton Finlay, George MacBeth, Alan Jackson. The new voices out-number traditional ones.

The first issue was set to appear on 26 January 1968, 'the morning after the nicht before' (which was Burns Night) as the *Glasgow Herald* pointed out in a feature interview with Bob Tait in the preceding week. Tait outlined the balance that was aimed for in *Scottish International*:

> My job is trying to make people in the arts aware of each other and what's happening here. There's a lot happening in the Scottish scene. That is what we try to show in the first issue. Yet Scotland remains an unmapped area. We don't know enough about our-selves. Take the effects of new industries like electronics [. . .].[40]

The second issue was already in an advanced planning stage, with articles expected on George MacBeth's poetry by D.M. Black; on younger Scottish artists by David Irvin of the Fine Arts Depart-ment in Glasgow University; on the Citizens and Close theatres in Glasgow by Christopher Small; and on Shostakovitch by Robin Fulton. EM had already provided a draft editorial by 10 Decem-ber 1967. A fortnight later he received his six author's copies of

The Second Life, with a proposed publication date of 4 January 1968.

Early in March, the directors on the board of *Scottish International* wrote to Ronald Mavor, Director of the Arts Council, asking for a guarantee against losses for the financial year of 1968–1969, with an estimated deficit of £4319. This loss had been expected with a new and minority venture. Positively, it was argued that sales had been good, with only between two and three hundred left of the original print run of 2500, and hopes that even these would be used up as libraries began to take out subscriptions. The aim was to increase sales to three thousand per issue by the end of 1968.

But the negative feelings of the 'old guard' continued to surface. Maurice Lindsay and George Bruce were thought to be behind adverse comment from the Saltire Society, which was partly funding it, on the new journal's minority appeal. When Emilio Coia joined the Board in July 1968, there were tensions regarding the relative lack of features on art, and on the overall design quality of the journal.

Perhaps most interesting from the perspective of EM's life during this period are the occasional comments he adds to the many editorial letters that went between Glasgow and Edinburgh. Responding to an invitation from Bob Tait to join a dinner and discussion club in Edinburgh, EM wrote:

> I am not really a wining and dining sort of person (anyone can give me an inordinate amount of pleasure by presenting me with a well-boiled free-range egg, a fresh slice of toast on which the butter just slightly melts though without running, and a newly-poured cup of tea).

Plain food, then, but to be prepared with some precision. And he did join the dinner club after all.

His attitudes to technology were not as overwhelmingly enthusiastic as some of his poems of the time would suggest. He had bought an early colour television set, but in July of 1968, just after its return from a month in the workshops, it went on fire. Fortunately he was in the room watching it and managed to unplug the set 'while it was still at the smoking stage'. But he described the smell as 'out of this world [. . .] hot; acrid; intense; pervasive; frightening. It's when it smells that you feel its power for the first time'.

The renewal of Glasgow, as well as being exciting, also unnerved him:

> Multi-level roads (Los Angeles approaches, say), large airports like Heathrow, even the disappearance of Anderston Cross under as yet ill-defined impositions of alien functions (partly industrial) – all these arouse ambiguous feelings compounded of the pleasure that things are stirring plus the uncertainty of knowing how to relate oneself to them. The nightmare of never getting *down* from the flyover. Hell as a place where there is nothing but magnificent flyovers, clover-leaf fields forever.[41]

EM never learned to drive, and tended to view the world as a passenger – often with interesting results. In late September 1968 he was in a bus that slowed down at a fruiterer's shop where

> a girl in the absolute mini was standing looking in at the fruit; two Glasgow bodies behind me with their shoppers started noticing her – 'Wid ye luik at yon!' 'If she bends she's had it.' At that precise moment the girl bent smartly down to prod an apple. Quite everything was revealed. It was wholly ridiculous, like the flamingos upending themselves in a zoo pond. One of the women screeched 'O Jesus Christ!' and the two of them began cackling non-stop like something out of William Dunbar.

Here EM seems caught between generations and social classes with regard to one item of 1960s culture. He also listened differently to its music. In an editorial discussion of a submitted article on 'para-pop', he comments to 'the two Roberts' that its author could have added:

a reference to the bisexuality which is a Beatles feature [. . .]. Not only are women not needed to sing Beatles songs, they spoil them if they do [. . .]. If the Beatles songs are in a sense sentimental, it is an extraordinary pure and detached (while at the same time 'real' and affecting) kind of treatment they produce, and this may be because the bisexuality thing puts the song in a strange area of its own.

EM was determined to bring different aspects of his life as far as possible into the public domain. When Bob Tait devised a survey of Scottish people's daily work, as it affected their identity, asking respondents to focus on a single day – 15 December 1970 – and on particular hours within that day as well as writing about their attitudes to their jobs, EM encouraged John Scott to complete one. He typed up John's handwritten survey verbatim, and also mentioned to Bob Tait 'two other pals that I'd like to give the questionnaire to'. One of them, a truck driver, was 'somewhat elusive', and the other was 'a young Irish faith-healer and cooker-repairer who is quite a character (he lays on hands and it seems to work)'.

The truck driver was 'Harry the van man', described many years later in *A Book of Lives* (2007: 93): 'Wayward paths can be affectionately led'. His picture was beside John's on EM's desk in old age, within the same paperweight frame. The comment above about getting both men to complete the survey suggests that they coincided in EM's life at that point, and his late 1960s diaries confirm this. But the Irish cooker-repairer with the healing hands seems to have vanished back into the mists.

The John Scott that emerges from his response is a friendly, middle-aged, energetic personality in 'brown overall coat, blue jeans and Toe-tector boots', who likes to have 'a friendly atmosphere at work. I am happy-go-lucky. I like a joke with my mates and I have a smile for everyone who comes to my store.' We see him at the designated hour being taken to a different store to help out with a rush assignment of meters for a factory in England: 'My job is to feed the Assy Line, putting the materials in different benches for the girls to assemble, which takes about an hour –

plus a few chats with the girls.' He prefers the older women in the canteen who seem 'more tolerant than the young girls, they always have time when passing the dinners for a laugh', and he also chats to nightshift nurses and orderlies from Law Hospital near Carluke, when waiting for the early bus to work. The journey takes him via Wishaw and past the Ravenscraig Steel Works to his factory, opposite the Motherwell Bridge Works and a huge railway siding.

What appeared in *Scottish International* of 13 February 1971 is an edited selection from the completed surveys, of course, and EM commented to Bob Tait on the 'self-consciousness' of most of the respondents there, and on the essential lack of representativeness of the teacher, engineer, social therapist, crofter, librarian, journalist and storekeeper who were included:

> although I remember you smiled when I suggested it was an odd 'work' feature which didn't represent the wurrkers, now that I've read the pieces I feel the lack more strongly [. . .]. It might seem to an outside observer as if we had gone out of our way to avoid occupations where sharp/controversial issues would arise. A car worker. A docker. A miner. A policeman. A shop steward. A University principal![42]

Shortly after this work feature appeared in *Scottish International*, both EM and Robert Garioch became 'editorial advisors' rather than co-editors. This was a decision of the Board, who seemed keen to allow Bob Tait more scope to handle socio-political issues, particularly as the journal moved to a monthly format, in hopes of building on a slow but steady rise in sales income. The journal would ultimately founder in 1974, amid recrimination on matters of public funding, debt, counter-claims on circulation figures, and changes of editorship. But by the end of the 1960s, it had already achieved, in its own terms, the same blend of sharp-eyed observation with social concern, and of wide-ranging cultural exploration with humane engagement, that would be the key features of EM's first collection, *The Second Life*.

THE SECOND LIFE

This book took years to see the light of day. EM signed a memorandum of agreement early in December 1966 with the University Court of the University of Edinburgh, ultimate owners of Edinburgh University Press. It was witnessed by his colleagues, Professor John Bryce and Jack (John A.M.) Rillie. But the idea for the book had begun a year and a half earlier.

On 15 July 1965 Tom Maschler, the Editorial Director at Jonathan Cape, had invited EM to contact the firm whenever he had a collection of poems ready for publication. He received forty poems by return, including 'The Whittrick' to which EM had remained attached since his wounded 1950s. Indeed the suggested title was *The Whittrick and Other Poems*. EM had not included any of his concrete poems. The editorial team at Jonathan Cape were equally speedy, replying by the first week in August that the collection as it stood was 'too varied, and just misses being sufficiently strong in any one direction'. This is an explanation that is still sometimes heard to account for EM's 'ranking' as a poet in the United Kingdom, which is below that of more 'monologic' writers possessing a clearly identifiable style.

Undaunted, EM immediately sent the returned collection to Archie Turnbull at Edinburgh University Press, in the midst of their correspondence regarding the *Scottish Poetry* series he was co-editing for them. Turnbull already knew of the Cape reaction, but said that quite a strong recommendation had gone in from one of his own reviewers, so that he had expected that Cape would publish it. Edinburgh University Press would be quite keen to do so, he said, but not at this particular juncture. In his reply, EM referred to the criticism made about being 'too varied', which rankled: 'the use of different modes and styles is very much part of what I am doing in poetry and I would want this to be represented to some extent'.[43] He said that he had excluded concrete poetry 'apart from one or two poems that verge on the concrete area' – but stuck by the Whittrick sequence initially.

Six months later, in April 1966, EM was pressing for a firmer signal about publication, and this was finally given. By July, he wrote asking to include the concrete poems from his Gomringer pamphlet, *Starryveldt* (1965), which was now out of print, and almost half of these became part of *The Second Life*: 'Bees' Nest', 'Summer Haiku', 'Chinese Cat', 'The Computer's First Christmas Card', 'Starryveldt', 'O Pioneers', 'Orgy', 'Unscrambling the Waves at Gilhooly' and 'French Persian Cats Having a Ball' – nine of the original twenty-four poems.

He also made the case for some already published in magazines, such as 'The Chaffinch Map of Scotland', 'Opening the Cage', 'Siesta of a Hungarian Snake' and others. In particular, he wanted to include 'Message Clear', the emergent poem that had been 'in the TLS and has been reprinted in America and Germany'. The inclusion of these meant that by the beginning of August he had pruned out some poems, including the Whittrick dialogues, added one or two recent ones, and used the concrete poems in four clusters, printed on grey paper, to divide the collection into thematic groups.

It opens with poems about precursors and contemporaries: Hemingway, Marilyn Monroe, Edith Piaf (the gender of this poem's voice is a useful mask: 'No! let the men that had me go their ways. / I regret nothing, nothing. Some were kind. / But I don't care if they were kind!'). The builders of the speaking ruins of Baalbek, Caernarvon, Carnac and the Pyramids also appear here, and wild animals such as the White Rhinoceros and the Canadian timber-wolf also inhabit the poetic world that EM is mapping out, along with the Scottish pheasant 'in a field of mist' in the Mearns. This section is completed by three poems for Scottish poets, Hugh MacDiarmid, Ian Hamilton Finlay and Maurice Lindsay – the last of which modulates into the first group of concrete poems. 'Canedolia', subtitled 'an off-concrete Scotch fantasia', was the first of these. This positioning of the musical, but definitely un-concrete, Lindsay next to a poetic form he disliked intensely is surely deliberate, although the tone of his 'own' poem is affectionately domestic. We might see a pragmatic balancing act being displayed here.

The section that follows the first group of concrete poems deals with Glasgow themes: 'To Joan Eardley', 'Good Friday', 'The Starlings in George Square', 'King Billy', 'Glasgow Green', 'In the Snack-bar', and 'Trio' – poems which made an immediate impact on readers through their combination of dark realism and urban violence together with a clear celebration and affirmation of the human life of the city. Fourteen of the 'Fifty Favourite Poems by Edwin Morgan' selected for *From Saturn to Glasgow* in 2008 were from *The Second Life*, including most of those just mentioned. They were also poems that were readily 'teachable' in schools, and so made their way into the consciousness of young people across Scotland, and stayed with them into adulthood.

More concrete poems come next, in a range of the tones of which EM had argued that concrete was capable – from 'Summer Haiku' to 'Seven Headlines', from 'The Computer's First Christmas Card' to 'Opening the Cage'. Then the title poem, 'The Second Life', gives its introductory testament to a section of poems on love, and the rebirth that love brings, set against 'the slow stirring, a city's renewed life / that stirs me [. . .]':

> Many things are unspoken
> in the life of a man, and with a place
> there is unspoken love also
> in undercurrents, waiting its time.
> A great place and its people are not renewed lightly.
>
> (CP: 181)

These poems of 'unspoken love' were deliberately ambiguous, as EM 'generally used the pronoun "you" instead of "he" [. . .]. But they were coded in such a way that it left people to make up their own minds as to what was going on there'.[44] It will be remembered that the law on homosexuality had been liberalised in England in 1967 but real changes in Scottish law did not come about until 1980. Yet it was clear to people 'who had worldly experience, or a good imagination, or who knew me' that these were gay poems, EM thought. He mentions Tom McGrath and Tom Leonard as people 'who jaloused what was happening'.

Something else was happening, even for those who did not see this, but would read and respond to them as 'straight' love poems. Once EM officially 'came out' at the age of seventy, and even earlier when the Scots law was finally changed, his poems of love and longing had already redefined for his readers the human nature of homosexual love, with the full range of love's vulnerability and joy. Such love was now more easily accepted, therefore, because already imagined at an emotional level through his poetry.

The love poems are followed by a section of technological concrete and sound poems, 'O Pioneers!', 'Construction for I.K. Brunel' and 'Spacepoem 1', among others, leading into a final set of science fiction poems. 'In Sobieski's Shield' and 'From the Domain of Arnheim' are particularly powerful (CP: 196–9). An early poem about *Paradise Lost* seems oddly placed, except in so far as EM always admired Milton's cosmic vision, and would admit the possibility, at least, of an identification of free-floating astronauts and fallen angels. The collection ends with a kick of the heels, in 'A View of Things' and 'The Flowers of Scotland', where this chapter began. These bravura listings of personal loves and hates and of political betrayal or narrow-mindedness act in counterpoint to provide an upbeat yet also serious ending to the book.

Its design and production were now in the hands of Walter Cairns at Edinburgh University Press, who liked the balance between concrete and traditional poems, and in fact asked for more of the former to make the sections even. He envisaged a 'fairly large and squarish' format, to accommodate the more extreme typographical features of line-length and layout involved. He also planned for it to be the first computer-set book in Scotland. This pleased EM enormously, at first. Delays with the new technology at the printers in Manchester meant that inputting of the text was postponed until January 1967, then March.

At the start of April, EM was asked to come over to Edinburgh to help with proof-correcting this new fangled book. With his liking for codes and writing systems, he became quite adept at deploying the different alphabet and signs involved in computer language. And he took advantage of the delays to add new poems, or substitute others. 'The Ages' and 'A View of Things' (CP: 200–2) were late arrivals in the collection. From August to October he was still picking up errors, and discovered that new ones, alarmingly, were beginning to creep in. Even in the final proof he found that the printers had somehow or other confused the alignment of 'Message Clear'. Typewriter and computer did not simply transpose.

However, once published, the book proved a great success. It was widely reviewed and had sold 523 copies by 31 March (royalties: forty-six pounds, five shillings and one pence) and about 700 copies by mid-May. It also won him the 1968 Cholmondely Award, which honours two or three distinguished poets each year. He shared his place with Harold Massingham, each poet getting a sum of £450. Seamus Heaney, Brian James and Normal Nicholson had preceded him in 1967, and Derek Walcott and Tony Harrison followed in 1969. *The Second Life* must also have been instrumental in gaining EM his place in the *Penguin Modern Poets* series (number 15, 1969, with Alan Bold and Edward Brathwaite).

Perhaps even more influential on EM's later career was the way that poems from *The Second Life* were re-published in the Penguin school anthology series: *Voices*. Educational publishers McDougal, Littel and Company in the United States also picked up on the book's popularity, and suggested an American edition of *The Second Life*, perhaps excluding some poems and adding others to suit an American audience. By 1970, EM was writing to Edinburgh University Press about poems that had been used, as he thought, without prior permission in the Penguin English Project series: *Things Working* ('O Pioneers!'), *Creatures Moving* ('The Third Day of the Wolf') and *Junior Voices* 3 and 4 ('The Computer's First Christmas Card' and 'The Starlings in George

Square'). In fact, he discovered that Edinburgh University Press had granted permission without informing him, and now sent him a cheque for seventy pounds, seventeen shillings and six pence. They were equally unforthcoming in promising a second volume of poems, which he now began to push for as the new decade began.

KEEPING IT NEW

While his first major collection was in preparation, EM continued with his avant-garde work. This involved, as *Scottish International* also intended, an exploration of the ways in which the verbal art of poetry intersected with painting and sculpture on the one hand, and music or sound patterns on the other. He experimented a little on his own part, with *Sealwear* from the Gold Seal Press in Glasgow, based at the dining table in Whittingehame Court: a twelve-leaf poem handwritten in different coloured inks and stapled into a gold card cover. The title was taken from an advertisement for an actual brand of all-weather wear, which had intrigued him.

Creative partnerships with professional artists proved more fruitful. John Furnival was a friend of Dom Sylvester Houédard, teaching at Bath College of Art and living in Woodchester, some ten miles from Prinknash Abbey. He had founded Openings Press in 1964, and EM probably met him through arrangements for the Brighton Festival of Concrete Poetry in 1967. EM had written a 'Festive Permutation Poem-Happening' for the event. This included ninety three-word phrases for posters or postcards: different combinations of eighteen adjectives and thirty-six nouns relating to a festive theme:

> green symphony terrace
> gay pavilion cats
> loud boat bucket
> tingling sand diva [. . .][45]

And so forth. There followed nine longer units of six words each, with each of the fifty-four words occurring only once; and two larger units of twenty-seven words in two groups. EM wrote a comment on the poem for the journal *Form* 4 and two photographs of the event appeared in *Poor.Old.Tired.Horse*. 24, one of them of a Brighton bus window with a section of the poem printed on it.

Now Furnival and his students at Bath Academy collaborated on *Proverbfolder* (1969), published by Openings Press. EM sent them his versions of original proverbs, such as 'A stitch in time saves nine':

1 ST2TCH 3N T4M5 S6V7S N8N9

(which did not make it to the final selection) or 'Every dog has his day':

DOG	day
DOG	day
DOG	day
DOG	day [. . .]

(repeated another eight times, which did). The students then went on to develop their own visual extensions of these concrete patterns.

Another connection with John Furnival was through Thomas A. Clark, a young poet from Greenock who was interested in concrete poetry. He had written to EM in October 1964, and they had several meetings and discussions. EM put him in contact with Hansjörg Mayer, who would later publish the 'emergent' poems, and who was at that point interested in bringing out a little anthology of British concrete poetry. EM had shown him some of Thomas Clark's poems. Later, Clark moved to Woodchester, renting a room in John Furnival's house, and becoming part of the group around Dom Sylvester. The Scot developed his own style, which was spare, lyrical, contemplative and close to the natural scene. With the artist

Laurie Clark, he would found Moschatel Press in the early 1970s, publishing work by Ian Hamilton Finlay and the American poets Jonathan Williams and Cid Corman, as well as his own poetry inspired by walking in the living world.

Other artists with whom EM was in contact in the 1960s included Joan Eardley and Alasdair Gray. He bought four of Eardley's paintings, including 'Sweetshop, Rotten Row', which inspired his poem 'To Joan Eardley' in *The Second Life* (CP: 163), and he wrote to ask her about their provenance. The children in this painting may have reminded him of those featured in a Ministry of Health film for Glasgow in 1963–1964. EM had written the commentary for its producers, Templar Films:

> The children are our new Glasgow. It is for them that the tower-cranes are straddling the building-sites and conjuring a new world out of the rubble. For them, new houses and schools where they can breathe and grow. [. . .] Our children are the real untapped wealth of this city.[46]

EM first contacted Alasdair Gray in March 1962, having got his name from a mutual friend. He wanted him to provide the cover illustration for his hoped-for Whittrick plus Quasimodo collection from Wild Hawthorn Press. Because of his 'shameful ignorance of most modern writings', Gray suggested that they meet either in EM's home in Rutherglen or at his own flat at 158 Hill Street, Garnethill, in Glasgow. He was interested in illustrating the collection, and tentatively enquired whether there would be any money involved, especially if other artists were being paid. Both Finlay and Jessie McGuffie quickly replied that there was no money for anybody, all 'profit' going towards postage, advertising and the next book (although the cost of materials could be refunded). However, Jessie had disliked the only mural of Gray's she had seen, and wanted to consider other examples of his work before agreeing to any arrangement.

As co-editor of *Scottish International*, EM later wrote strongly in support of an excerpt from Alasdair Gray's *Lanark*: 'I don't quite know what we can do with this, but it is surely a find of some importance. I am greatly impressed by it [. . .]. Remarkable stuff, a Kafka of Garnethill.'

In the months following publication of *The Second Life*, EM was also involved in a new musical project: writing the libretto for an opera by Thomas Wilson, a composer who lectured in Music at the University. It had been commissioned by BBC Radio, with a deadline of St Andrew's Night. By 12 May 1968, EM was writing to Finlay that he had finished the first part of the libretto: 'I suppose the summer will largely be devoted to tinkering it into singability'.

The Charcoal Burner was based on a story he had been interested in for a couple of years, about a good man who commits a brutal murder. He had first read about it in a *Times Literary Supplement* article on a lost poem by Wordsworth, which contained a version of the story. Psychologically EM found it fascinating that a mother would force her son into marrying an unsuitable and unstable girl, who mistreats and taunts him to such an extent that he loses control, murders her and is hanged – his body being displayed in a caged gibbet as an example.

EM and Thomas Wilson were interviewed about the opera for *Scottish International* 6, April 1969 (15–17). EM asked Bob Tait to tone down his negative editorial comment on the weakness of Scottish Opera provision, citing the fact that this one had actually been commissioned. In the libretto he had used 'free range verse', as he described it to Finlay: 'We want the music to hit people both above and below the belt. (Can music do this?)'. In the more formal interview, which was mainly devoted to musical decision-making, he describes the way in which most of his first-draft rhymes and repetitions were found to be unnecessary, as 'the music in fact did it better'. The choice of text for the opera, Wilson's first, was surely suggested by EM. As he delved deeper into the various characters, he felt that his sympathies

were shifting all the time. [. . .]. Wordsworth altered the character of the mother to a step-mother because he couldn't believe a mother would behave in the way this woman did. But of course she *did* behave in this way – and we've kept it as the mother.

It may be that playing the role of 'man of the house' since the death of his father three years earlier had awakened certain tensions, fears or expectations in the son. He did not know then how short this new relationship with his mother would be.

I remember that my Senior Honours tutor, Dr Sarah Davies, who was both motherly and resolute, and I would guess about twenty years EM's senior, once remarked: 'Mr Morgan works extremely hard'. When I told him so in old age, the comment pleased him, not only because she had 'a very level head', but because it was true: 'I did work extremely hard!'.

True for the astonishing sixties, certainly, and also for the decade to come. But the real and more far-reaching work in the 1970s was probably going on at a hidden level.

CHAPTER SEVEN

Unconscious, underground 1970–1980

At fifty I began to have bad dreams
of Palestine, and saw bad things to come,
began to write my long unwritten war.
I was a hundred-handed Sinbad then,
rolled and unrolled carpets of blood and love,
raised tents of pain, made the dust into men
and laid the dust with men. I supervised
a thesis on Doughty, that great Englishman
who brought all Arabia back
in his hard pen.

'Epilogue: Seven Decades' (CP: 595)

Looking back, EM claimed that the 1970s were 'a blank' in his mind, compared with the marvellous 1960s. This was the infamous decade 'when the lights went out' in Britain, the years of the miners' strike in the winter of 1972, of the three-day working week in factories following the disruption of fuel supplies during the Yom Kippur War in the Middle East, of a remorselessly rising death toll in Northern Ireland, of tumult in the economy and strikes in essential services that left refuse uncollected and the dead unburied in the 'Winter of Discontent' of 1978–1979. So there was much to blank out in the social and political world of the time. Like the rest of the adult population, it was a matter for EM of just trying to get by – struggling to get his examination papers marked in the intervals between power cuts or discovering the problems of typing by candle-light (an excess of shadows).

But there was more than just coping with inconvenience. This is perhaps signalled in 'Epilogue' in the odd way he transposes into the 1970s 'a thesis on Doughty' that was actually begun in the mid-1950s and presented in the early 1960s. Mohamed Kaddal was an Egyptian student who was forced to return in haste to be with his family during the Suez Crisis of 1956. All of the Egyptian students at the University of Glasgow were leaving, and one had lost his entire family in an air raid on Cairo. EM gave Kaddal his own copies of books by Doughty to take with him in the hope that he might complete his thesis in Egypt. He finally returned to Glasgow in April 1960 and, helped by fortnightly and even weekly meetings with EM, completed the thesis in less than two years, submitting it in February 1962.

The original title of the research was *C.M. Doughty: Search for the Form of an Epic*, and it is this focus on form, as well as the Arabic background of Doughty's best known work, *Travels in Arabia Deserta* (1888), that links this research supervision with EM's own later attempt in the 1970s to find a suitable quasi-epic way of writing about his war experience. This would be his 'hundred-handed' long poem, 'The New Divan' (1977). He had been unable to use this experience artistically at the time, and now its memories were returning to haunt his imagination. The appearance of his Egyptian student in the context of a new war in the Middle East, and as EM was still trying to readjust in the mid-1950s to civilian life, may well have kept those memories alive.

Charles Doughty is not much read now, perhaps because of his curious style that combines Chaucerian or Elizabethan English with metaphysical speculation and wild landscape. But EM knew how deeply Hugh MacDiarmid admired this Englishman. In *Scots Unbound*, MacDiarmid asserted that Doughty's significance 'dwarfs all other English poets since Elizabethan times', and praised his 'marvellous penetration' into an ancient Celtic aware-ness. His own poem 'Stony Limits (In Memoriam: Charles Doughty, 1843–1926)' strongly identifies with the English poet-explorer's 'lonely at-one-ment with all worthwhile'. Inter-penetration of identity, language and deserted landscapes, of course, and a questing need to explore beyond normal social and linguistic boundaries, was EM's poetic territory as much as MacDiarmid's, although they disagreed about the most fitting way to write about this for the contemporary world.

At a personal level, EM's decade was shaken by four deaths. His mother was approaching 80 when she died of a stroke on 28 April 1970, the day after EM's fiftieth birthday. Next Veronica Forrest-Thomson, the young avant-garde poet from Glasgow whom he had met through the concrete movement, died in 1975 at the age of 27, in accidental but somewhat doubtful circumstances. And then the love of his life, John Scott, and his poetic father-figure, Hugh MacDiarmid, both died within days of each other in early September 1978.

His mother's death was shocking and unexpected. EM was called from the University where he was teaching and told to go home at once. By the time he arrived, his mother was unconscious from a cerebral haemorrhage. He went with her in the ambulance to the Western Infirmary, where she lingered for about half an hour, he recalled, without ever regaining consciousness. This was in a tiny waiting room

> [. . .] still on the stretcher she was wheeled in on, with loud clattering and hammering from workmen at the door, and another stretcher wheeled in almost up against hers, with an old wandered woman from whom the nurse tried in vain to extract name and age. It seemed an awful way to die – to me: but as my mother was not conscious it didn't really matter, or so I thought afterwards, and at least I was there.[1]

The experience gave him an enduring suspicion of the idea of 'dignity', having experienced its absence: 'I suspect we have to "slip past" dignity as often as not.'

The death of his mother released a variety of emotions that were difficult to deal with. Whereas the death of a father might also give a sort of freedom and new responsibility, the death of a mother might entail, in some sense, a deeper loss of 'soul'. Poetry did not directly help, and EM was unable to write openly about his mother until the end of the decade. But the death of older women does appear in several translations he worked on in the following years: as in this extract from 'Interview', a poem-cycle by Göngey Gabor which appeared in the Budapest journal *Arion* 3 in 1970:

> But if I can't distinguish –
> because I can't remember –
> which in all the swaying column of souls
> was once my mother:
> then, Lady, what's it all for?[2]

On 5 May 1972, he translated two poems by István Jánosy. In 'The Eyes of Old People', the poet exclaims

> How many things old people's eyes are true with:
> so clear, like the last phase of Bartók's music.
> So marked is every line the face has gathered,
> like an old gnarled root that twists and darkens.

And in 'The Sounds of the Night', the poet recalls a death that is both distant and local:

> Now this very sound comes from the distance
> where they have laid out a woman of eighty.
> Three years she had been choking. Today finally
> (the bird has settled!) she succeeded in dying there.[3]

Relatives thought, since he seemed closer to his mother, that her death would affect him more deeply than his father's had done five years earlier. But EM finally came to believe that the opposite was the case. His mother had no greater sympathies with his poetry and books than his father had had, it seemed to him. And although once, after he had quarrelled with John Scott, she wrote him a letter to bring about a reconciliation, there was no impression in EM's mind in old age that she was particularly sympathetic to his own sexual orientation. The action of contacting John does in itself suggest a degree of kindness and concern, and yet EM continued to stress the conservative and church-going nature of both parents. Certainly there was no open discussion of his 'difficulties with women', but that would be typical of the social norms in which she had been raised. Emotion, he was taught at an early stage, was what other people indulged in – the Morgans and Arnotts were expected to cope without tears or complaint. This developed resilience, certainly, but not much empathy for an approach to life that was suspect and dangerously different from the norm. Nor does it seem likely that, with her family and professional background in business, she would sympathise with his socialist and republican principles or his contacts and travel in Eastern Europe.

Whatever the truth is, we might now think that her death possibly intensified his memories and dreams of wartime Palestine, since that had been his first real separation from her. The 'hundred-handed Sinbad' who is EM's persona in this decade of the 'Epilogue' seems to revert to a childhood love of fantastic tales. But the poet's task was to create a long poem about war, the great epic subject: the hundred stanzas of 'The New Divan' needed to unroll 'carpets of love and blood' and raise 'tents of pain'. With such serious adult aims, EM was nonplussed that what seemed to him a major work, exploring time, history, homosexual and heterosexual relationships and the Eastern arts of storytelling and verse, did not achieve immediate recognition.

Nor has it still. I believe this has something to do with its form. EM's emphasis in interviews on its 'Arabic' method of interweaving images, echoes and quasi-autonomous delights may well have distracted attention from whatever structure this long poem actually does possess. I am biased here, since the topic of my own doctoral research with EM was on form and structure in the modernist long poem. I was focusing on the poetry of Basil Bunting, a distinguished Northumbrian modernist, whose long 'Sonatas' were underpinned by a quasi-epic structure, I argued, although this tended to be hidden by the musical analogy he used.

EM was too polite to tell me his own view of Bunting at the start – as I now learn from a letter of 20 November 1971 to Michael Schmidt, his Carcanet editor:

> Bunting is also not one of my absolute favourites, though I can see he has a gluey music all his own – but I like a verse that moves. It's not enough to have images, fine though many of his are. On the other hand, his quirky crabbitness is also a 'north-ernness' and in some moods this attracts just because at least it is not smooth. [. . .] From my window I am watching the snow fluttering past the orange streetlamps like – like – come on Bunting – like
>
> > doom-grated
> > orange-peel
> > puffed through
> > fine fans.[4]

Bunting was a conscientious objector in the First World War and an enthusiastic fighter in the Second, rising to the rank of Squadron Leader in the Intelligence services, based in Persia, Italy and North Africa. He knew the Persian language well and his long war poem 'The Spoils' (1951) deals specifically with Islamic culture and the North African campaign in its separate sections. This may have spurred EM on to emulation or rivalry with his own North African experience in 'The New Divan'.

I like to think he had altered his view of Bunting, to some extent at least, by the end of our continuing conversation on literary archetypes and plot structures. It was a protracted discussion at a distance, since I was teaching full-time in Dumfriesshire and helping to raise a young family. So I would send him parts of the thesis to read, and they would be discussed during holiday visits to Glasgow. These visits, I now know, coincided with how he wrote 'The New Divan': in bursts during the Christmas, Easter and Summer vacations between December 1973 and July 1975. On one occasion he showed me the section he had just completed, not asking for any comment but just because that was what he was working on at the time.

He thought the completed sequence was significant enough to use it as the title of his third collection, *The New Divan* (1977). As editor, Michael Schmidt needed some convincing about that, as we will see. But EM had enough confidence in the work to begin publishing sections of it in various magazines even when it was still far from completion.

TAKING OFF

EM was fortunate in his editors throughout the 1970s, but to some extent he had made his own luck. Looking at his publications list from the first two years of the decade, we see *The Horseman's Word* (Akros Publications, 1970), *Interferences* (Midnight Press, 1970), *Twelve Songs*, (Castlelaw Press, 1970), *The Dolphin's Song* (Leeds School of English Press, 1971), *Glasgow Sonnets* (Castlelaw Press, 1972), *Instamatic Poems* (Ian McKelvie, 1972) and *Wi the Haill Voice: 25 poems by Vladimir Mayakovsky* (Carcanet Press, 1972). There's an impression of phenomenal creativity, although much of it was part of his 1960s trajectory, still in flight.

Writing to the Norwegian-based poet Robin Fulton in mid-decade, in the gloom of his not-quite-end of winter in Stavanger, EM advised him to 'hold on and *get* through'. He recalled how life 'dragged its black claws' through his own bleak mid-thirties, which were then transformed in his early forties: ('it was like being shot from a gun').[5] That exhilarating energy carried him forward into the new decade, and became more evident now in the numbers of small-press pamphlets, books and special editions that began to appear. Hamish Whyte's bibliography in *About Edwin Morgan* (1990) gives a year by year account of individual poems published in poetry magazines. In this chapter, the focus will be on the role of different independent publishers in helping EM to gather his work in more permanent form.

EM had already discussed various projects with Duncan Glen in the late 1960s. There were ideas for poster versions of concrete poems; for an over-ambitious anthology of Scottish translations to be co-edited by EM, Alex Scott and Duncan Glen ('better to be safe than bankrupt,' Glen concluded after costing it); for a collection of the Whittrick dialogues; and for *The Horseman's Word* as a poster series.

One practical problem presented itself for the posters. The repetition of certain words meant that Glen did not have enough type to set up the whole *Horseman* series, so he suggested a typewriter version. EM was pleased with this idea, and sent four more poems to make a total of ten. Glen was enthusiastic: 'The sophistication allied to the primitivism of "THW" appeals to me very much and allies to the primitivism that lies behind concrete poetry'.[6] Within its small space the series of horse poems ranges across Scottish, Norse, North American, Greek, English and Hungarian sounds, images and myths. EM's 1960s travels in Hungary recalled Hortobágy, a region where the ancient ways of life of the steppes are preserved, and also its animals including the native horse (ló) which canters through the poem of that name (CP: 212).

Although Duncan Glen initially offered a hardback publication for *The Whittrick*, EM preferred a paperback 'if only because it would be cheaper and more young people would be able to buy it'. It was eventually published in April 1973 as a stapled pamphlet. Glen apologised in May 1970 for the delay with *The Horseman's Word*, as he had been swamped by orders for *Akros* 13–14. Like EM, he was combining his academic work with a remarkable range of writing and editorial tasks.

The two men also shared a frustration with Edinburgh University Press. EM was trying to get an answer from them about a second collection that he had sent for consideration. Glen had found Edinburgh University Press so unsatisfactory to deal with for the book he was then editing on MacDiarmid that he lost patience and withdrew it. His *Hugh MacDiarmid: A Critical Survey* was eventually published by Scottish Academic Press in 1972.

When *The Whittrick* eventually appeared in 1973, after initial alarm when EM discovered some upside down pages, it actually made a profit – 'unusually for one of our books' said Duncan Glen, sending him a cheque for eight pounds and fifty pence. Poet-critic and poet-publisher kept in touch throughout the 1970s, although nothing came of a plan to publish EM's *Newspoems*. These 'found poems' of subliminal messages cut from newspaper print, headlines and other ephemera, pasted on to sheets and then photographed, eventually found a London publisher much later (wacy!, 1987). Some of them dated 1965–1971 are in *Collected Poems* (CP: 119–30), with a fuller selection in the *Themes on a Variation* collection (Carcanet, 1988).

One result of EM's wider publication in the 1960s was that now small-press publishers would sometimes approach him with ideas for limited edition productions. Alex Frizzell was a bookseller who had originally worked in the paper-mill in Penicuik but, after war service in the RAF, had begun to learn the book trade in 1947. Within four years he had opened his own business in Bruntsfield Place, Edinburgh, before moving out of the city to an old farm house by West Linton. Here he continued his book-selling business, but also developed Castlelaw Press, after acquiring a treadle press in 1969, and later an antique Albion. He was an enthusiast, with a warmth and geniality that often brought the word 'Dickensian' to the minds of those who knew him. He and his wife would dispense generous hospitality in the form of wine and malt whisky fetched from within a capacious grandfather clock.

In February 1970 he wrote to EM for permission to print a limited edition of six to eight poems. Payment was to be ten per cent of sales and twenty-four copies of the booklet. Drawing on his experience with Duncan Glen and the *gnomes* production of 1968, EM suggested that Frizzell consider signed copies for the American market, where his work was becoming known in specialist bookshops. He also thought that the planned price of five shillings perhaps contrasted with Glen's Parkland Poets series at half that price, and the larger format Modern Scottish Poets series from Caithness Books at about the same price.

EM sent eight songs originally, but soon increased this by four. *Twelve Songs* contains some of his best known poems: 'The Apple's Song', 'Loch Ness Monster's Song', 'Oban Girl', 'Off Course' and 'Shantyman'. EM suggested bookshops and reviewers or editors to contact, as well as two American outlets: the Asphodel Bookshop in Cleveland, Ohio, and the Phoenix Bookshop in New York.

Fascinated with the printing process, Alex Frizzell enthused about the potential for EM's work in large type and poster poems, with the possibility (once his own skill increased) of interchange colours. EM replied immediately in July 1970:

> Tell me, what are 'interchange colours'? I always prick up my ears when I see 'colour', because a number of things I have been doing recently have been hand-written visual poems in polychrome – these have been shown in various exhibitions but so far I have found no way of getting them published. I mention it to you in case the possibility arises![7]

Had he pursued a career in design, as his parents had briefly considered in the 1930s, he would have learned that 'interchange colours' were used to print wallpaper patterns without blurring. EM would still be agitating towards publication of his colour poems in 2009. He also told Alex Frizzell about the one hundred Newspoems 'in a sort of collage or found-poem category', and about eighteen pages each of August von Platen and Leopardi translations, and about fifteen pages of Voznesenky. It was decided to go with the Platen poems. EM felt that his own versions varied in quality, because he had wanted to create a strict translation of Platen's concentration on form. Although Platen (1796–1835) belonged to a past period, EM thought nevertheless that his poetry did arouse echoes of Thomas Mann's novel, recently filmed by Visconti, in giving

> a remarkable (pre-*Death in Venice*) account of the impact of Italy on the Teutonic soul. And he is an odd forerunner of Cavafy in his interest in the clashes of histories and culture, noble barbarians versus effete sophisticates and so on.[8]

They toyed with the idea of asking David Hockney to provide a cover. More practically, EM was aware that they needed to get permission from Doubleday and Co., because some of these translations had already been published in *An Anthology of German Verse from Hölderlin to Rilke* (1960), edited by Angel Flores. The atmosphere of the Venetian sonnets has the homo-erotic tone of Platen's originals:

> Gay all around is the dear swarm of souls
> Moving in idleness, as if freed from care;
> A queer soul can feel free here as he strolls.
> Then that full chorus in the evening air –
> The Riva where the story teller calls,
> The singer singing in St Mark's great square.
>
> (Sonnet III. CT: 318)

The Platen translations were not published finally by Castlelaw Press until 1978. Various things intervened, not only *Glasgow Sonnets* (1972) but also the impact of the 1970s postal and transport strikes on Frizzell's livelihood as a book-seller. But it may be that revisiting the strict rhyme scheme of the Platen sonnets influenced EM's choice of this same form for his own *Glasgow Sonnets*. And there are psychological similarities between the erudite and multilingual German poet and himself, including war service in which he saw no action, which may well have led EM to *Ghasalen* (1821), Platen's first major collection of poems.

These are modelled on the ghazel form of Hafiz, the 14th-century Persian poet who would later be a guiding presence in EM's 'The New Divan'.

The atmosphere of Platen's Venice also led his publisher to reminisce about wartime experiences of Middle Eastern male society that both men had shared. He had also sailed out on a troopship, and had then been a wireless operator in Jerusalem. He recalled the close physical proximity of travel, much as EM did in 'War Voyage' (*A Book of Lives*: 88), and was interested in North African sexual mores. This may have stimulated EM's own memories and dreams of Palestine about this time.

Writing to Frizzell on 17 December 1970, he said that, although he had found it impossible to write poems at the time, he had been

> left with a series of strong impressions and experiences which have little to do with the war – persons, places, atmosphere, things that have since filtered at times into my poetry and will likely do so as yet.

This is the first declaration of intent of what would become 'The New Divan', and it characteristically combines boldness (it is 'likely') with hesitancy (but nothing 'as yet'). Meanwhile *Twelve Songs* made an excellent impression, with John Fuller declaring in *The Listener* of 24 December 1970 that EM was 'in top form in one of his too rare appearances', and praising his great invention and variety.

When his publisher asked in February 1972 what to print next, the Leopardi or the Platen, EM suggested neither and presented instead the 'Glasgow Sonnets'. He had written ten of these 'fairly swiftly and connectedly' between 2 and 10 January 1972, and quickly sent four off to *Stand* magazine and the rest to the *Times Literary Supplement*, who decided to print all six. His only hesitation now was that he wanted a week to consider whether he might raise this number to a more book-length total of twenty. But by the beginning of March he had concluded that 'they are a group that I cannot at the moment easily add to' and so the ten were published.

To his irritation, in the confusion of the printing process Alex Frizzell had forgotten to send him proofs, and instead of the complete accuracy EM expected 'in such a small book as this', there were four typographical errors. However, by 23 October he was describing the positive impact of the book:

> Several people, by the way, have said they think the sonnets are among the best things I've done, and if this is true it is strange that it should come from reverting to such an ancient and worked over form as the sonnet. There's absolutely no foretelling what one is going to do next.

The *Times Literary Supplement* reviewer (19 January 1973) recognised them as highly effective, and designed to stir the social conscience. Their 'dour' quality and occasional Scots words gave an authentic and unsentimental tone:

> Whether the indignation and irony will have any effect on the Ministers who decide the fate of the Clyde is another matter. But like Siegfried Sassoon's poems against war, they at least say something intelligent and human about an unbearable situation.

There was also a certain dour quality in the review of *Glasgow Sonnets* that Douglas Dunn wrote in *Ostrich* 7, a Northumbrian journal. Noting that EM's contrasting styles and restless 'post-Modern' search for the New had already led many people to see him as 'too trendy for his own good, an opportunist', Dunn then contrasted that waywardness with his latest choice of the traditional and concise sonnet form. While admiring the poems, Dunn wondered how much EM 'really knows about the "stalled lives" he tells us about. There is no "I" in the poems, no proof of testimony'. The review winds its way to the odd conclusion that the poet 'is not a poor man. There is something wrong in writing about slums if you don't live in one [. . .]'.

It is true that EM came from a wealthy family. But we have already seen his pre-war concern to speak for the poor in the blackness of the Glasgow nightscape. He also had strong emotional connections with Clydeside, both through his father's ship-breaking business and his own love of sea voyages. In 'Glasgow Sonnets' he now used the discipline of the sonnet form to channel those feelings into articulate and memorable speech. He also extended his West Coast perspective geographically, noting how 'The North Sea oil-strike tilts east Scotland up'. In the sonnet form, as in any traditional music, variation and improvisation on one basic and memorable shape is a way of linking the community of generations, the living and the dead. It is not really a way for some ego to provide 'proof of testimony'.

Dunn would later write a more positive appreciation of these poems in 'Morgan's Sonnets', his chapter in *About Edwin Morgan* (1990: 75–89), with just the occasional grouse about the science-fiction dimension of EM's later *Sonnets from Scotland* (1984). These he found sometimes 'too close for comfort to the special effects departments of the movie studios'.

In the earlier sonnets, this sense of a duty to speak for Glasgow may have come from his late mother. As he wrote in 'The Coals', published in *Poems of Thirty Years* (1982), she had shaped her son in duty:

> As once she had been taught,
> I was taught self-reliance, discipline,
> which is both good and bad. You got things done,
> you feel you keep the waste and darkness back
> by acts and acts and acts and acts and acts,
> bridling if someone tells you this is vain,
> learning at last in pain.

(CP: 421)

Of course, action or activity – of endless translation, for example, or writing series of sonnets, or triplets, as in his *Virtual and Other Realities* of 1997 – might become a substitute for something else, or a way of avoiding other thoughts. Even in old age, however, EM would continue to make a strong case for action:

> Want something done you must do it, do it.
> A never to pain and you'll always rue it.
> It comes back, it chokes, it corrodes, eschew it!

And his answer to those who are scared of the night sounds of dragons outside 'scratching in their lair' is – 'get out, you fools, and breathe the dragon's air' (*Virtual and Other Realities*: 61).

All the same, the thought occurs that the fifty-two 'instamatic poems' that he published in 1972 were in some sense a way of handling emotion by carefully keeping it in check. The matter-of-fact voice, the control of detail, the device of using a camera angle on horrific events to present them in plain sight without comment, as witness without testimony, might suggest something beyond a 'post-Modern' play with information. Or, at least, it is both playful and strange: the media world of photo-journalism is caught in its own lens. The *Times Literary Supplement* reviewer thought they were 'marvellously done; as concentrated description they could hardly be bettered'. But the blackness of the perspective, even in most of what little humour there is, led him to suggest that 'Mr Morgan seems to have set out to prove that the world of the early 1970s is a pretty ghastly place'.

A London bookseller, Ian McKelvie, had written to EM at the end of February 1972 outlining his plan to publish a series of books of contemporary verse and asking for a small collection to consider. EM replied on the first of March, offering his new 'instamatic' poems 'based on items reported in newspapers or television and visualised by me as if someone had been present and fixed the event with a camera'.[9] He had about thirty already written, but was in the process of doing more. Younger readers may need to be told that an instamatic camera was one that quite speedily developed the photographs it took, which were tugged out of a clunky tray in the base: fairly advanced 1970s technology.

The poems were all headed by the place, month and year in

217

which the image was 'captured': mainly 1971 and some from 1972. They were not in chronological order, and after some consideration it was decided to leave them that way. Because the dates gave a sense of topicality, Ian McKelvie decided in May to bring the date of publication forward to 1972, and EM worked to produce another twenty poems by the beginning of July to create 'a richer-looking book'.

There was some discussion about the order of poems, particularly the opening poem. In the end they settled on 'Glasgow 5 March 1971' ('With a ragged diamond / of shattered plate-glass [. . .]' CP: 217) which would become one of EM's best-known poems. But the final poem in the book was always going to be 'Heaven September 1971 AD'. This does not appear in the *Collected Poems*, and its satire on 1970s modernisation of the words of the Lord's Prayer, as viewed by the Trinity ('God is lying on a cloud / watching the teleprinter') has not worn all that well. It recalls now EM's play with biblical language in 'Message Clear', as his father lay dying. The order of the poems, however, travelling from Glasgow to Heaven via Nice, Chicago, Manchester, Nigeria, Vienna, Burma, Innsbruck, the Mid-Atlantic, Translunar Space and other venues, prefigures the sweep of his second collection's contents and title – *From Glasgow to Saturn*.

Instamatic Poems was very well designed, in a squarish shape with fine black lines focusing in to a small circular lens-like shape at the centre of its off-white cover. EM declared that it was 'just what I would have wanted', but noticed five misprints. He suggested magazines that might review it. The *Glasgow Herald* reviewer astutely noticed that 'the poet is not quite the camera he seems to be' and that his selection of detail, tone and rhythm all served to control the reader's responses: 'what we do not feel is a sense of the poet admitting his own responses openly'.[10] That too may be an effect of the disciplined control of the emotions learned at his mother's knee, or of EM's self-concealment, keeping himself out of the camera's gaze by focusing busily on everything outside.

Because of their clarity and black off-beat humour, however, the Instamatics proved popular as teaching texts in schools. Geoffrey Summerfield, an influential editor and enthusiast for EM's work, included seven of them in his anthology *Worlds: Seven Modern Poets* (1974, reprinted 1976, 1979, 1986) from Penguin Education. And the New Zealand Broadcasting System used four Instamatics in a Schools Broadcast in 1973. Clearly he had begun to touch both a national and an international readership.

NATIONAL AND INTERNATIONAL

EM's poetry became much more widely recognised in the 1970s. Maurice Lindsay's brief outline of his work in *Contemporary Poets of the English Language* (ed. Rosalie Murphy 1970) was updated in 1975 and then rewritten for publication by the Macmillan Press in 1980. EM had provided entries for this book too: on D.M. Black, Ian Hamilton Finlay, Robert Garioch, W.S. Graham and W. Price Turner in the 1970 volume, together with a statement on his own poetry. But a more substantial academic appreciation of his work came in Robin Fulton's *Contemporary Scottish Poetry: Individuals and Contexts* of 1974. This was published by Calum Macdonald in Loanhead, who also published *Lines Review*. Fulton edited this journal with distinction for many years, working from Stavanger in Norway where he taught English language in the university college there.

Fulton was in regular correspondence with EM from the late 1960s, when he was on the board of *Scottish International* and actively involved in Scottish editing and reviewing generally, as well as working on his own poetry and translations. He specialized in Scandinavian poetry and in October 1970 EM offered him advice on some translations of a Swedish writer's versions of Sándor Weöres. In June 1971 Fulton was gathering material for a Scottish-themed edition of *The Literary Review*, based in New Jersey, and wanted to include EM's article 'Towards a Literary

History of Scotland' that had been published in *Scottish Literary News* 1:2 in January of that year.

This shared dynamic of national and international perspectives helped to sustain over the next thirty years the correspondence of two poets whose work and temperaments were so different. Fulton's poetry is detached, meditative, lyrical and melancholy, often with a sense of deep psychological disturbance just beyond the edge of his local landscapes. We might think of this as 'typically' and gloomily Nordic, but his childhood experiences in Arran and later, after a spell in war-time Glasgow, in Helmsdale in Sutherland, to which his poetry frequently returns, do relate to a Norse and Shetlandic voice that has retained a significant presence in modern Scottish literature, as in George Mackay Brown and Neil Gunn. The poet Richard Price has written about this theme of absence and elegy in Fulton's work, and on his formal mastery of free verse (*Lines Review* 131, December 1994), as well as publishing him in his journal, *Painted, Spoken*. Although Robin Fulton may have felt side-lined by poetic fashion, the more astute of the younger generation of Scottish poets have not failed to register his presence.

EM supported Robin Fulton with references and advice. He had been the External Examiner for Fulton's PhD, and did his best to help him gain a university post as a lecturer or creative writing fellow. Stavanger was where he ended up, and replying to a gloomy letter in January of 1974, EM tried to make him count his blessings – after all, he might be in Britain:

It is a curious feeling to be living in a country which is markedly and visibly running down – ill-lit or unlit shops with many empty shelves and large areas cordoned off to avoid pilfering, terrible public transport, longer and longer delays in repairs and services (I've been waiting seven months for a thermostat for my central heating), the bland face of Lord Carrington on television saying industry might have to think of a two-day week (and a no-day week, what then? Like Beckett's people we shall all be in the cylinder, where there is neither central heating nor peripheral

heating, and the bus and the train do not come): doesn't un-
humorous Norway have its points?[11]

As a non-driver living in an all-electric flat, EM felt particularly
vulnerable. By the end of October 1974 things seemed no better:

> The dustmen are back today, but sewage still pains, and we have
> no buses or underground yet. Shoe-repairers will be [. . .] opening
> up branches in all the suburbs. Citizens who bought the Corpor-
> ation's new 'transcards' for a month's unlimited travel just before
> the strike can be seen cursing and foaming at the mouth as they
> trek through Drumchapel and Castlemilk.[12]

Travels, real and poetic, offered some respite. Sending Fulton
some poems from 'The New Divan' as a 'sequence in progress' in
early August 1974, which were published in *Lines Review* that
September, EM mentioned that he had been with a friend for a
week in Holland, with a week in Ireland coming up, and then a
poetry reading at the Theatre in the Forest at Grizedale in the
Lake District. It is not clear from his diary entries whether John
Scott was the friend involved in the Dutch or Irish trips. In early
September 1972 EM spent a fortnight in Budapest, where he had
gone to receive the Petöfi medal from the Magyar branch of PEN,
the international writer's association, for his services to Hungarian literature. Some of his translations of Petöfi, Hungary's
national poet, had appeared in *Petöfi Sándor (1823–1849)* in
Budapest in 1973, but the award was for his sustained engagement with Hungarian poetry in English translation. He had
continued to publish translations of Hungarian poetry in the
new decade, both in Hungary (Ottó Orbán, Istvan Vas and László
Kálnoky in *New Hungarian Quarterly* X1:37, 38 and 40, 1970, to
take only a single year as example) and in Scotland (Sándor
Weöres in *Lines Review* of January 1971, for example).

On his trip to Hungary, he visited Sándor Weöres again, and
brought home a book from him for Robin Fulton. The Hungar-
ian-Scottish connection was a two-way affair. Fulton co-operated

with George Gömöri of the *New Hungarian Quarterly* to produce a Hungarian issue (*Lines Review* 59, September 1976) and EM's poems 'Stobhill', 'The Old Man and the Sea' and 'From the Domain of Arnheim' appeared in the Budapest magazine *Nagvilág* 21:5 in May of the same year.

He was translating Lajos Kassák quite intensively about this time and his poem 'The horse dies the birds fly away' was the one of the six he sent to Robin Fulton at *Lines Review* that was actually published. EM commented that this poem 'is his major work and is generally regarded in Hungary as one of the important poems of early twentieth-century modernism. Versions have appeared in French and Italian but this is I believe the first in English'.

Oddly, it is not included in *Collected Translations* (1996). This poet was connected with a double disappointment early in 1976. The previous summer Penguin books had written to inform EM that, after a period of uncertainty, they intended to publish his Kassák and József translations in 1977. He had typed out fifty pages of Kassák translations in the autumn but then had somehow lost them ('impossible, you may well say, but . . .!') and so had to start over. In the event, the Penguin book never appeared.

He had better fortune with the Penguin connections of Geoffrey Summerfield. He was a lecturer in English and education at Langwith College in the University of York, and he had first contacted EM in June 1968 with some questions from junior school pupils about 'The Computer's First Birthday Card'. He declared that he wanted to collect all of EM's poetry as it appeared, 'since, for my money, you are the most interesting poet writing today'.[13] In December 1971 he was on sabbatical, teaching in schools in Chicago, Ontario and Berkeley, California, with the result that 'You must be the most popular poet in California among kids aged 7–13'.

The collection *Worlds: Seven Modern Poets* which Summerfield edited for Penguin in 1973–1974 was a crucial text in establishing EM's poetry in British schools. His work was already becoming better known and used in Scottish schools, particularly through *Twelve Modern Scottish Poets* (1971, reprinted, 1973), edited by Charles King for the English Association. Two of his more experimental poems, 'Goal!' and 'Strips', also appeared in the 1971 Penguin English Project book, *Ventures*. But the *Worlds* volume combined accessible poems with pictures of the poets in their home environments across Britain, Ireland and the US, plus a personal comment from each on the sources of their writing. The poets were Charles Causley, Thom Gunn, Seamus Heaney, Ted Hughes, Norman MacCaig, Adrian Mitchell and EM. He was asked to make a selection of his work, and so the book includes twenty-five poems selected from his own list and Summerfield's choices. 'Trio', 'Glasgow Green', 'In the Snack-bar', 'One Cigarette' and 'The Death of Marilyn Monroe' are there, as well as some of the 'Glasgow Sonnets' and 'Instamatics', and several space poems including 'The First Men on Mercury'.

The photographer Larry Herman came from London to take pictures for the book, also meeting Norman MacCaig in his favourite landscapes of Lochinver and Edinburgh. EM took him around Glasgow, including some of the new high-rise flats and the socially deprived Blackhill housing scheme on the edge of the city. Herman was so struck by the experience that in October 1973 he discussed the possibility of collaborating with EM on a photographic and poetic study of the Blackhill area and its people. Nothing came of this, but it was a forerunner of the television programmes that EM would later make, and, in another medium, of the Radio 4 combination of poetry with on-site recordings of demolition workers in Glasgow, broadcast on 19 May 1978 as 'Voices and Verses' (CP 578–85).

One of the photographs in the book features John Scott, seated slim and dark-haired in EM's living room and looking relaxed and confident. His appearance in this 'instamatic' is surely a matter of selection and inclusion, in its current socio-political sense: EM would have invited John to the flat to coincide with Larry Herman's visit. And his presence here alongside EM's early plea for gay liberation, 'Glasgow Green', as well as 'One Cigarette' and some lines from 'In the Snack-bar' ('Wherever he could go it would be dark / and yet he must trust men'), suggests that EM wanted to use the occasion of *Worlds* to make as full a statement as he could (in the legal conditions still pertaining in Scotland) about his own particular world. As mentioned earlier, EM knew that friends such as Tom Leonard and Tom McGrath had guessed that he was gay. It seems clearly hinted at in some of the imagery in his poems, And yet other colleagues such as Alex Scott were convinced that he was not, and it was possible to teach his poetry in school or university without referring to his sexuality. EM was now willing to present the truth more openly.

Perhaps something similar was happening when I met John Scott about this same time. On a weekend visit to Glasgow, I needed to find information on the American group of Objectivist poets, whose leading spirit, Louis Zukofsky, had been a friend of Basil Bunting in the 1930s. EM had an 'Objectivist Issue' of the journal *Comparative Literature* (10:2, 1969) on his shelves, and suggested I could look at it at his flat. This was a Sunday afternoon, and John was visiting as he often did then, so we were introduced in the living room and shook hands. I remember the look on EM's face as he watched me for a reaction, I supposed: amused, somewhat defiant, a bit like a boy standing up to a teacher. John was relaxed as in the photograph, but smoking.

I made my notes about the American journal at EM's desk in his study down the hall. When I was finished and came back to the living room, both men were seated on the black vinyl couch of the *Worlds* photograph, watching 'The Golden Shot' on television. This was a game show involving a crossbow attached to a television camera, operated by a blindfolded cameraman who was directed by the contestant to fire at a distant target: 'Up, up, left a bit, right a bit, down . . . Fire!'. For me, this was an unusual homely view of EM that contrasted with the book-lined walls and the papers and books on the dining table, each with a deadline for completion.

Worlds was, in fact, the final book to appear in the Penguin

Education imprint. Pearson Longman, the new owners of Penguin, decided to axe the series to save on costs, and its editor, Martin Lightfoot, resigned in protest. These uncertainties, and the three-day week, delayed production from the early summer, and EM received his two copies in mid-October of 1974.

Geoffrey Summerfield was full of ideas, and in 1976 was general editor of a new series of non-fiction for adolescents, but EM had no time to write or edit the complete book that was expected. Now in his mid-fifties, he may have had less inclination for a task that would have taken him back to his isolated teenage years. Later in the decade, Summerfield also invited EM to write for a poetry collection aimed at young listeners of six to eight years. EM sent him nine nursery rhyme variants in July 1979. I am unsure whether that book ever appeared, or whether it was transformed into his influential *Voices* and *Junior Voices* series from Penguin. He would certainly publish EM again in his *Words 3* (Cassell, 1984). Here are a couple of EM's nursery rhymes that never saw the light of publication:

> *When Mary was Unlucky*
> Mary had a little lamb,
> Its fleas were black as jet,
> And everywhere that Mary went
> Those fleas were there you bet.

> *When Mary was Bad*
> Mary had a little limb.
> She tore it from her dolly,
> And everywhere that Mary went
> She sucked it like a lolly.[14]

Geoffrey Summerfield worked regularly in the United States, ultimately resigning from the University of York and going to work as a visiting professor in New York University and Queen's College, New York. In 1990 he sent EM a close colleague's description of her students' 'unfeigned and spontaneous enthusiasm' for his poetry, an impact that she had never before encountered in thirty years of teaching.

EM had experienced such American enthusiasm right at the start of the seventies. In September 1970 he told Alex Frizzell that he was

> just back from Oxford, New College, where I was reading my poetry to two hundred American school teachers on summer school tour – cameras flashing, tape recorder and microphone, these people really know what they want![15]

Two of these members of the National Council of Teachers of English certainly wanted the poet to visit high schools in the Eastern United States. Nancy Pritchard and Mary Todt arranged funding and worked out a three-week itinerary. Leaving Scotland on the first of May, he would fly to New Jersey to teach in Red Bank and Keyport High Schools in the north-east of the state, then have a brief stay in New York to see some theatre productions before travelling by car with his hosts, Bill and Mary Todt, to Washington DC to visit the Library of Congress. He would then return to New York briefly, staying each time at the Algonquin Hotel, before teaching in Schenectady Union College, with a few days free in New York again before his flight back to Prestwick.

As on his trip to Russia in the 1950s, EM was alert to the new society he was encountering. Early on he kept notes on landscape, housing and social habits, and he collected ephemera such as *New York Times* articles on black issues ('Ceremonies held for Malcolm X') and right-wing religious publications such as the *King's News Letter*, which informed its readers that '*Jesus Christ Super Star* is blasphemous, sacrilegious, irreverent, profane, desecrating, apostate and ANTI-CHRISTIAN'. School literary magazines and theatre journals and programmes were also of interest.

He wrote in advance to Mary Todt that he 'would like to see

an American musical in its native surroundings', and wondered whether it would be possible to get a ticket for Lauren Bacall in *Applause*. It was, and he also saw a production of *Awake and Sing* by Clifford Odets, who came to prominence in the 1930s theatre of social protest in New York. EM watched the New York City Ballet at the Lincoln Centre, toured the Guggenheim and other galleries, and walked in Central Park. He saw for himself Brooklyn Bridge, which he had recently written about as a source of poetic inspiration for Hart Crane, Mayakovsky and Lorca: 'Three Views of Brooklyn Bridge' (*Akros* 3:9, 1969, reprinted in *Essays*: 43–57). He had always identified with the image of the young man in the city in the novels of Thomas Wolfe, and with Hart Crane's special feeling for New York. And to him, westward-facing Glasgow always had some of that 'American feeling of doing what you want to do, just going ahead and making your mistakes, put up a big building and if it's not liked in twenty years, we'll take it down and put up another one'.[16] Glasgow people also shared 'something of this thrusting sense Americans have', so unlike Edinburgh, 'stuck with its history'.

Prior arrangements for the trip had been complicated by a lengthy postal strike in Britain, delaying his visa from the United States Consulate in Edinburgh. The change that year to decimal currency did not help. But once he had arrived, EM was fascinated by the cultural differences: the lack of pedestrians, who according to a Washington road sign might be liable to arrest, the push-button phones, a black student sit-in at Union College, and Methodist church family services with a 'totally different atmosphere to Church of Scotland!'. In Washington he met the poet William Stafford, four years his senior, who was Poetry Consultant to the Library of Congress, and took part in a poetry workshop.

His work in various high schools mainly focused on concrete and sound poetry, and he had brought slides to illustrate his talks. Interviewed by their local newspaper, *The Key Point Weekly*, the students described him as 'A fascinating, charming man who seems so kind and sincere – very understanding, intelligent and a gentleman'.[17]

In New York, he met up with a former exchange student, Jacqui Stark, who now worked in publishing with Appleton-Century-Croft. He noted examples of computer origami in the IBM offices, and took a Gray Line tour to Lower New York and Greenwich Village. The guide pointed out Sheridan Square as a haunt of 'gay boys': 'They may not be happy but they're certainly gay'. EM noted the dozen or so, white and black, who posed and pranced as the bus went past, one of them throwing a boomerang. On one of his return stays in the Algonquin Hotel during this trip, EM found an airmail from John Scott, describing recent police entrapment activities in the Playhouse cinema in Glasgow, and warning him to be careful in New York. Whether this was genuine or a black joke is unclear. EM went to the cinema in any case to see Andy Warhol's *Trash* and *Flesh*.

Back in Scotland on 23 May 1971, EM found three weeks' mail and five novels waiting for a *Listener* review. He met the deadline. Bill and Mary Todt remained in contact with him, and travelled over to Scotland in 1973, when he organised a tour of famous places and the chance to meet not yet quite so famous people, including Iain Crichton Smith in Oban.

THE CARCANET CONNECTION

The 1970s saw the development of the key publishing relationship of EM's creative life, with Michael Schmidt of Carcanet Press. The relationship was also a creative one: heartening, supportive, amusing, sometimes at odds but always sharply engaged. It began, as so much poetry did for EM, with Mayakovsky. In the spring of 1971, he had written to Daniel Weissbort, who with Ted Hughes was editing the *Modern Poetry in Translation* series. Carcanet were the publishers for the series. There was a possibility that EM's Mayakovsky translations might join Hughes' versions of Janos Pilinsky, Weissbort's Vinokurov, and Taner Baybars' Nâzim Hikmet as one of the first books in the series.

EM was delighted, and in April he gave Weissbort a detailed outline of his decision to use Scots, after failing to match Mayakovsky's exclamatory style and abrupt changes of tone and imagery in Standard English: 'it was almost as if the spirit of the language was against me'. In Scots, however, he found it possible

> to tap a Scottish tradition both of grotesque exaggeration and fantasy and of linguistic extraversion and dash that goes back through MacDiarmid, Burns and Dunbar. And at the same time, it may be that the linking of the fantastic/wild/grotesque with the moral/political/social comes more easily to the Scottish than to the English poet.[18]

This Scottish tradition in which EM is clearly at home may help to explain the unease with his work that is sometimes expressed south of the border. There is an inability in some readers to get hold of its range confidently enough to place him securely in the canon of significant poetry. This Scottishness relates not only to his engagement with political issues in 'Glasgow Sonnets', but to his later inclination towards political, moral and social commentary in his poetry, which runs parallel with his delight in wordplay and fantastic journeys. It is significant that the Mexican-born and American-raised Michael Schmidt and EM hit if off so well, and that their most serious quarrel was over Englishness and the idea of 'the nation'.

Carcanet was at that time, by its young literary editor's own admission, 'a very small and tottering press'. Schmidt was working out of Pin Farm, in South Hinksy by Oxford, and handling almost every aspect of the operation, apart from printing, with all the aplomb of a twenty-four year old poet. He was full of ideas and multiple projects, and asked EM in early September 1971 to write on the Scots poetry revival for a book he was co-editing with Grevel Lindop: *British Poetry Since 1960: A Critical Survey*

(Carcanet, 1972). EM's contribution is reprinted in *Essays* (1974: 177–85). He thought that he could not 'with propriety' discuss his own contribution to Scottish poetry in the 1960s. Michael Schmidt responded enthusiastically to the chapter which arrived by 18 November:

> it is *exciting* to read, larded with excellent quotation, and in every sense my sort of essay. I only wish you had planted yourself in the landscape you so beautifully conjure. We'll have you later writ large.[19]

Meanwhile work on the Mayakovsky volume went on. *Wi the Haill Voice: 25 poems by Vladimir Mayakovsky* appeared in 1972, with some accommodation to EM's request for colour, which was also important to the Russian poet. Hence the red and black futurist design of the endpapers and a cover reproduction of El Lissitzsky's designs for Mayakovsky's *For the Voice*. As ever, EM was able to suggest contacts for publicity, reviews and sales: Christopher Small, the literary editor of the *Glasgow Herald*, Eric Mottram at *Poetry Review*, academic colleagues such as Thomas Crawford and W.R. Aitken in Aberdeen and Glasgow, and the Richard Demarco gallery where he was due to give a reading in July 1972.

Receiving a poem with his Christmas card from EM, Michael Schmidt suddenly realised that he knew his work only through anthologies, and wanted to buy copies of his books. EM sent him copies, including his *Beowulf*, mentioning that *gnomes* and *The Horseman's Word* were already out of print. The younger man was struck by the 'delightful lilting vitality and yet a wonderful sense of words and humour too in *Twelve Songs*'.

He asked EM if he was able to help with additional translations of Vinokurov for the translation series, but EM was plunged into work and intermittent darkness:

> Between electricity cuts I am deep in marking examination papers of which there seems no end. How Edna Saint Vincent Millay managed to get that candle of hers burning at both ends I don't

know – but perhaps being American she was able to buy a special gadget for holding it horizontally (but then what happens to the drips?). Last night I blew out one candle over vehemently and a spatter of wax spread most clingingly over the table top. [. . .] Snuffers. Every home should have one.[20]

Schmidt too was struggling to cope with disruptions to business – but also to his creative life. He had the first two lines of a poem about the dark, but couldn't get any further:

> The lights went out –
> It was like death indeed.

Then nothing. He asked EM to complete it for him. This was the start of a lively writing partnership between them, that would be published as part of *Grafts/Takes* (Mariscat, 1983), a book which combined back-to-back some hitherto unpublished Instamatics (the *Takes*) with the completed poems or *Grafts* that emerged from EM's work on his publisher's fragments of poems. The first one sent by Schmidt appears as 'Albion' on page twelve of the Grafts section.

Schmidt had various analogies for the partnership. Sometimes they were 'renga-like' in the Japanese manner of joint composition of variations and echoes, or again like Navajo sand-poems ('Which of us is the black sand and which the white?'). Other times they were like the head and tail of a dove; or like gallstones in the bladder of his own lyrical workings. In which case EM became like the doctor operating to cure his patient's discomfort: 'The clouds are in their arms' is 'our masterpiece to date', Schmidt thought in April 1972. The rhythm and imagery here recall something of 'The New Divan'. It is entitled 'Beginnings', and may well have been the first stirrings of that major work:

> The clouds are in their arms
> as if lolling with wine
> on zigzag bones,

231

> twitching a mantle, taking a kiss,
> pietas, laocoons falling
> where no bones could be, into air.

That's EM. The second stanza is the original starting point in Michael Schmidt's unfinished poem:

> The stones lie still
> like sleepers waiting for their injuries;
> and they will break, bruise
> in substance, roots
> work round them like a curious thought
> that has its logic, and its hunger too.

So the progression is from sky to stone to tangled roots. Then the cosmic shift of gear:

> Five minutes or five million years
> is relative. Hold
> the deal to your heart.
> A little swirl of hydrogen,
> and clouds and stones that have no bones,
> and men that have, begin.

The 'ending as a beginning' is a stratagem that EM would call upon again for his great poem on the opening of the Scottish Parliament in its new home on 9 October 2004. But it is that early relaxed sense of potential discoveries in geological time and human civilisations that recalls 'The New Divan'.

In their correspondence of the time it emerged that Michael Schmidt also liked the Middle East very much, enjoying Egyptian and Arabic culture. Both poets were pro-Arab, Schmidt having once been confronted at close range by an Israeli soldier with a rifle. On 14 April 1972 EM commented: 'How strange that we should both be feluccaphils. Or Middle Easters. Of all these countries Lebanon is my favourite.'

At the end of April 1972, EM complained in a letter about Edinburgh University Press keeping hold of the typescript of a second collection for eighteen months without returning it. The University Court had told the press 'to cut out fripperies like poetry – so my typescript comes back and I have to start all over again with some other publisher. This despite the fact that *The Second Life* has now nearly sold its two thousand copies [. . .]'. He was uneasily aware that Norman MacCaig was being published at Chatto and his friend, Iain Crichton Smith, at Gollancz, both established London presses.

Michael Schmidt was at that point on his way to Mexico via New York, but on his return the following month he offered to publish the collection, subject of course to perusal and some editorial role. He warned that he was not a passive editor.

The problem now was that Edinburgh University Press would not return the typescript – EM wondered whether they had lost it – despite his telephone and personal calls. He was favourably disposed to the Carcanet offer, but would have preferred a Scottish publisher. Coincidentally, a small Edinburgh-based publisher, the Poni Press, also offered to publish a collection. This press was run by Tom Buchan, who had taken over from Bob Tait as editor of *Scottish International*, shortly before the journal closed down with some acrimony about disputed sales figures. EM kept his options open with Poni Press, but said that Carcanet should have the first option on his new collection. By the end of May the manuscript was returned from EUP:

> Part of it seems to have been run over by a car, and some pages have perhaps been in the soup, and I had to extract from the middle a batch of pages of somebody else's Italian translations and send them back.[21]

In sending it on to Michael Schmidt, EM included some of his collage 'Newspoems', which he regarded as an extension of his concrete poetry, and also thirty-one Instamatics. He noted that these were shortly to be published by Ian McKelvie and suggested this might seem like parallel publication. With an editorial eye which was remarkably sure and accurate, Michael Schmidt decided to keep the 'Glasgow Sonnets' but to drop the Instamatics, which might figure in a further EM collection in 1974, and also the Newspoems, which would be too expensive to reproduce. Looking forward, he also indicated that he would like to develop a critical list at Carcanet, and suggested that they also look at publishing a collection of EM's essays.

By 21 July 1972, he sent EM an outline of the key thematic order of *From Glasgow to Saturn*, beginning with lighter, clear energetic pieces like 'Columba's Song', 'Floating off to Timor' and 'In Glasgow', then moving into more troubled love poems such as 'At the Television Set', 'The Milk Cart' and 'Estranged'. More playful 'language poems' follow: 'Blue Toboggans', 'Flakes' and 'The Loch Ness Monster's Song', for example. A long three-part poem on London came next, although Schmidt persuaded him to cut some of the less effective lines of the list-poem, 'Soho'. In the 'Interferences' sequence which follows, EM returns to an earlier theme: breakdown in communication. Each of the nine poems ends in a misprint or confusion, and the effect lies somewhere between sound and concrete poetry.

Prefiguring the strong moral ending of the collection in 'Glasgow Sonnets' and the Stobhill hospital sequence on abortion issues, about which Schmidt had editorial reservations, two poems of messianic leaders sit side by side: 'Che' and 'The Fifth Gospel'. These are followed by a poem about war in the Far East, seen through children's eyes. This last is almost an Instamatic in its clarity but with a more brooding sense of the poet's attitude. The collection then takes off into poems of time- and space-travel – the Saturn dimension of its title – together with computer poems, 'The Computer's First Dialect Poem' and 'The Computer's First Code Poem', before the surrealistic 'Rider' brings it back down to darker Glasgow in the threatening atmosphere of 'Christmas Eve', 'Stobhill' and 'Glasgow Sonnets'.

Thus the collection 'flows' in a natural-seeming but stimulating manner across the widest range of themes and styles. The above outline is the published shape of the book, of course, which took a little longer to settle in its final details. Michael Schmidt had not hesitated to cut the original collection EM had sent. He spread out across the book poems that 'used similar devices that tended to become mechanical', omitted some poems that were 'vaguer' or could 'sentimentalise' their subject. He expressed reservations about some poems, accepted late submissions that should have been in the batch, but all within a positive framework. EM liked his suggested changes: 'you have no idea how fine it is to think of things actually going forward! – I mean after my couple of years of communication-less murky brooding years of the Edinburgh University Press. "The years of the eup / May thou ne'er sup!" (old proverb)'.

By August 1972, Carcanet was in the process of moving to Manchester, two hundred miles each way between Glasgow and London, which 'must make you the hub of something,' EM thought. Professor Brian Cox at Manchester University had arranged some funding so that Michael Schmidt could do a little teaching, as he wanted to do, and also 'run the press without starving to death'. When EM returned from his Hungarian trip to collect the PEN award, the final running order of *From Glasgow to Saturn* was waiting for him, with pencil markings where his editor felt the poems were weaker. EM accepted 'many' of the suggestions, but challenged others or explained why poems should remain unchanged.

Their discussion was both amicable and sensible, and was probably helped by their continuing co-operation on the shared poems that were about eight-ninths Morgan and one ninth Schmidt, by the younger poet's reckoning: 'We are a good poet, aren't we,' he said, and suggested that they should call this new author Edmal Morgash or Medwin Sorgan. He wondered whether Castlelaw Press might be interested in publishing them, but nothing came of this.

More serious were the various financial problems of running a press when sudden credit squeezes could lead to overdraft facilities being withdrawn even when book sales were high. Carcanet's own creditors were sometimes not paying in good time, and book stocks were locked up in shops or warehouses across the country. In these circumstances, Schmidt not only worked for very little but also needed to sell his library and ceramic collection and to mortgage his archives to get collateral to keep going. At one point he had to ask selected patrons, including EM, to invest in shares in Carcanet Press in order to raise funds. It was a most unpredictable and difficult time. EM was among those who did support the press by investments or short-term loans, but he was also punctilious about the contract terms of royalty payments, seeing legal or financial complexities that had escaped his editor's eye.

They were on happier terms in dealing with design elements, such as EM's favourite colours for the book cover of *From Glasgow to Saturn*:

Yellow and red, yellow and black, yellow red and black, red and black. (Bumblebees sitting on a brick – marvellous.)

Happy too was their shared enjoyment of the book's successes, in being selected as a Poetry Book Society Summer Choice, which caused the publication date to be deferred till May 1973, and in the possibility of Scottish Arts Council awards for both this book and *Wi the Haill Voice*. The Poetry Book Society nomination would mean sales increasing by about half of the two thousand copy print-run.

There were reversals too. Philip Larkin left EM out of his *Oxford Book of Twentieth Century Verse* (1973), to some astonishment. But the publication of his second collection was a welcome arrival, when he was in need of assurance not only in the Oxford Book context but also

after receiving a long abusive letter from a disgruntled student who had not won mention in a BBC student verse competition I had been one of the judges of [. . .] such letters have a physical effect on me – headaches, loss of appetite, and phrases churning around in my mind for days.

To make matters worse, he was a first year student in Glasgow University, so EM might have to deal with him for a further three years.

However, future projects were useful in occupying the mind: Michael Schmidt offered a collection of *Essays* for 1975, Tom Buchan of Poni Press had offered a book of translations, and Routledge seemed committed to an anthology of Scottish Satirical Verse. In the same post in early May, EM was asked for poems to accompany a filmed helicopter flight from Land's End to John O'Groats and also to translate a tragedy for the new *Complete Greek Tragedy* from Oxford University Press. Whether or not these offers came to anything, he told Schmidt, 'That's what I like about life – it's so incongruous'. He signed the letter, N. Kongruss.

From Glasgow to Saturn sold 1700 copies in four months. This astonishing success would continue through further printings. A friend wrote to him to say that he had cracked 'The Computer's First Code Poem' (CP: 277) but that there were some misprints, which EM asked to be corrected in the second edition. I suppose it might be helpful to provide a partial decoding here of the poem, in case readers want to have a head start on the puzzle. I confess to never having persevered to the end, and suspect that the intellectual effort is meant to be its own reward, but there is a wild humour in the 'dirty whist fight' and 'manic tapir party' of its opening, and the very last line of the poem begins with 'ghost haiku':

PROLE	SNAPS	LIVID	BINGO	THUMB	TWICE
DIRTY	WHIST	FIGHT	NUMBS	BLACK	REBEC
MANIC	TAPIR	PARTY	UPEND	TIBIA	MOUND

Printing of the second edition was held up by the three-day week of industrial inaction, but an 'astounding' further 1500 copies were ready by December 1973. And by the start of 1974 Michael Schmidt was already editing the *Essays* and setting them in a new order. He omitted 'The Fold-In Conference' about the

Edinburgh Festival Conference argument between MacDiarmid and Trocchi and also the introduction to *Beowulf* as being different in kind, but EM admired and accepted the arrangement.

Where the two men disagreed, or radically misunderstood each other's position, was over *Poetry Nation* (later *PN Review*) which Michael Schmidt was very proud of as 'the first national literary magazine, without a London bias or a media bias'. He had co-founded it in 1973 with Brian Cox who had brought him to Manchester University. They were later joined on the editorial board by the academic and poet, Donald Davie, and the poet, C.H. Sisson. Part of the problem was that Brian Cox with A.E. Dyson had been the author of the Black Papers on education, which had achieved notoriety from their first appearance in 1969. Setting themselves against the White Papers of the Labour Government's education policy, these were polemical documents attacking the perceived excesses of progressive education, and also the introduction of comprehensive secondary schools to challenge the selective system of grammar schools and separate secondary modern schools in England. Rhodes Boyson, a head teacher and later Conservative politician, also wrote for the Black Papers, as did two of the deliberately un-experimental Movement poets: Kingsley Amis and Robert Conquest.

All of this right-wing agitation went against the Scottish and socialist grain in which EM had come to maturity. Setting aside his own secondary education in the fee-paying High School of Glasgow, he could see that their views were alien to the small-town norm of Scotland, in which most children attended the same burgh school, albeit divided into different academic streams. It seemed to EM to be aimed at entrenching social divisions whereas he sought inclusion and a progressive approach, in society as much in the arts. We remember that he had declined the offer of an Oxford Scholarship after the war.

He had met Brian Cox on a trip to Manchester in October 1973 for a poetry reading with Douglas Dunn, and got on reasonably well at a personal level. But Cox's political attitudes clearly rankled. The Black Paper ideas were, he told Michael Schmidt, 'deeply repugnant to me [. . .] he is working to bring about something I am working to prevent'. This attitude extended to *Poetry Nation*, where he was co-editor. EM declared himself 'deeply suspicious' of the journal's aims, particularly as expressed in the writing of C.H. Sisson. And he hoped that this 'neo-reactionary' stance was just a phase his young editor was going through. EM challenged him to prove him wrong by publishing more radical and avant-garde work in the journal.

Michael Schmidt replied that he was not averse to experimental writing, citing Geoffrey Hill's *Mercian Hymns*, *The Anathemata* of David Jones, and William Carlos Williams's poetry, but declared that his most profound taste was 'mainstream'. He was notably unenthusiastic about concrete poetry, which seemed to him a branch of graphics or calligraphy. But Schmidt seemed genuinely hurt that significant poets such as EM and Charles Tomlinson would write for Ian Hamilton's *New Review* – which he thought was notably against experiment and cross-fertilisation – and yet refused to write for *Poetry Nation*.

This word 'nation' was at the heart of their mutual incomprehension. Schmidt had come to England from the New World, able to shrug off (or perhaps not even to fully register) the subtle social gradations and antagonisms that pertained in Britain's culture. Scotland's place in the nation state, however, its language, identity and values, were all matters of deep concern to EM and others of his generation. So this 'national' journal which spoke for England, as EM felt, was a matter of dispute in ways that the free-wheeling and internationally-minded Schmidt could not have anticipated. Nor was EM really able to articulate it for him, despite earnest telephone and face-to-face conversations. Reading their correspondence, it is quite touching to see two such intelligent, determined, sensitive men unhappily at odds with each other, where previously communication had seemed so easy and heartening.

Projects and plans helped them work through it, to some extent. Michael Schmidt had asked EM to send him poems as he wrote them, so that the work of shaping his second Carcanet collection could go on even subliminally. Even as he was outlining his objections to *Poetry Nation*, therefore, EM also told his editor at the beginning of January 1974: 'I spent Christmas with a friend in Amsterdam and wrote twenty poems when I came back. (Short, admittedly – between ten and sixteen lines each)'. These were the opening poems of 'The New Divan', which he dated from 28 December to 3 January.

Although the three-day working week delayed the printing of EM's *Essays* from May till September, and a general slow-down forced Carcanet to put the brakes on a hoped-for twenty two titles in print by 1975, there was always the excitement of another project. In June 1972, EM had offered Tom Buchan at Poni Press the idea of a collection of his translations, in place of the second collection of poems that had now gone to Carcanet. Buchan was keen and suggested the title *Cantrips*, a Scots word meaning either a magic charm or a piece of mischief. By March of the following year EM had a collection together, and proposed *Rites of Passage* as a title, 'a sort of pun on the act of translation'. He had a clear sense of its structure from an early stage, with groups of poems from Brecht, Lorca, Michaux, Leopardi, Enzenberger, Montale, Quasimodo, Braga, Pasternak, Voznesensky, Martynov, Gomringer, Mayakovsky and some Anglo-Saxon poems, and then individual poems from others. There remained the problem of securing international copyright, although EM had at least tracked down the original publishers of the poems he had worked on.

By April, Buchan was still struggling to move forward with the book, as he had been badly affected emotionally by the debacle of the closure of *Scottish International*. By mid-June 1974 he concluded that liquidity problems made it impossible for him to publish it, and suggested that Carcanet take it over. EM proposed this, but it was now too late to include the book in Carcanet's planning budget for 1974–1976, and Michael Schmidt was in any case unwilling to rush it without building up advance orders. So he worked on the basis of 'a book a year' for EM in the following years: *Essays*, to be followed by translations, and then by a new

Family Pictures
1915 — c.1935

EM's mother's parents, the Arnotts.

EM's parents, Stanley and Madge Morgan,
on honeymoon in Torquay, July 1915.

EM, aged one, and mother.

On holiday at the beach.

His favourite toy, a sailing ship for dry land.

EM, aged six, with his father, June 1926

On holiday at Ascog, June 1926.

On holiday, possibly on Arran or at Milport.

On holiday, 1930s.

University pre-war,
national service and return
c. 1940 – 1946

As a student, prior to national service, 1940.

The raw recruit, March 1941.

Ready to embark, June 1941.

Among the snow-covered cedars of Lebanon, April 1943.

42nd General Hospital staff at Haifa, May 1945. EM is fifth from right on the top row.
His Quartermaster is at the extreme right of the second row.

Homecoming, Rutherglen.

1950s

Some of the Departmental staff, 1951.

From left to right: J.W.R Purser, K.P.A. Drew, J.F. Arnott, J.C.Bryce, J.F.Richard, E.Morgan,
T.C. Livingstone, Peter Alexander.
Absent from the group were Hannah Buchan, Jack Rillie, Charles Salter
and Ernst Honigmann.

In Dublin, July 1952.

With Thomas Livingstone and colleague, 1952.

Sydney Graham at Burnside, September 1954.

At the Lenin Memorial, Kiev, Ukraine, May 1955.

Building socialism in Moscow, May 1955.

EM in Brighton, 1958.

EM. Dumbarton, 1959.
(Iain Crichton Smith)

Iain Crichton Smith, Dumbarton 1959.

1960s

On the balcony of 19 Whittingehame Court,
September 1964.

John Scott, 1964.

On the boat to Ireland, July 1965.

EM and Marshall Walker, 1966.

With Blue Bird typewriter, late 1960s.

With George MacBeth at Nottimgham Poetry Festival,
February 1966.

New shirt. (Carcanet publicity shot)

Looking at a late Scrapbook, 1975.
(Marshall Walker)

With John Scott in Romania, 1976.

Reading at Colpitts Hotel, Durham, June 1976.
(David James)

1980s

Reading tour of Israel with Michael Schmidt et al., 1981.

With Aunt Myra and Dr Janet Hamilton at
Buckingham Palace, November 1982.

With George Mackay Brown and Peter Maxwell Davies,
St Magnus Festival, Orkney, June 1985 (Gunnie Moberg)

On the balcony, August 1986.
(Marshall Walker)

1990s

At Paisley Book Festival, 1996.
(Chris Watson)

Gagarin's voice, recorded from outer space, 1998.
(Marshall Walker)

Gael Turnbull reading at EM's 80th birthday event,
Kibble Palace, Glasgow, 2000. (Kenneth Whyte)

2000s

Checking emails on the website with Claudia Kraszkiewicz,
Whittingehame Court 2002.
(Hartmut Salmen)

With Hamish Whyte at YES restaurant, Glasgow, 2002.
(Hartmut Salmen)

Jack Rillie with *Thirteen Ways of looking at Rillie*,
Clarence Court, 2004.
(Alan Riach)

Study by Martin Capie, a student of photography at
Glasgow School of Art, c. 2004.

collection. *Essays* already had a comforting two hundred and twenty-one copies subscribed to, pre-publication. He thought that since *Rites of Passage* had already been used as a title they should look for something else. EM's suggestion of *The Black Trout* did not impress. He was thinking of one of the Montale poems in the collection, and 'the relevance would be that the elusive lively lovely trout – life, or love, or poetry, or translation could be found in the book'. His Whittrick-like enthusiasm for this title may have been rekindled by the recent publication of those eight dialogues by Akros.

Nor did Michael Schmidt much like *The New Divan* as a title for the next collection. It reminded him of Canova's painting of a mistress of Napoleon III in the Galleria Borghese in Rome. However, EM was reluctant by now to start looking for a new title for the Selected Translations, reminding his editor that there were lots of other books that used the same title: *Poems*. There is a sense here of the slight distance caused by their disagreement over *Poetry Nation*: Michael Schmidt felt misjudged and EM felt misunderstood. He dug his heels in too about a cash-flow plan by Carcanet to pay his royalties slowly and in arrears. 'I would never really catch up, would I?' he argued. The royalties for *From Glasgow to Saturn* were significant, as by September Michael Schmidt was noting 'incredible' sales of 2,274 copies.

The Scottish Arts Council was willing to subsidise *Rites of Passage: Selected Translations* (1976) to the sum of £720. Since Michael Schmidt was working single-handedly at Carcanet, he asked whether EM had any research assistants that could help with clearing the permissions. 'You must be joking!' came the response, 'My candle is well known in the window at two in the morning.' But the English Department secretary did probably help with this task. The final order of poets translated was quite different from what was originally envisaged. This was probably the result of Michael Schmidt's keen sense of the whole text and also of the look of each page, as well as of the more commercially attractive names. Russian translations frame the selection, with Voznesensky, Yevtushenko and Pasternak opening and Mayakovsky ending the volume, and with a number of other Russian voices heard briefly throughout.

Both men were busy in 1975 and the intensity of correspondence sometimes slackened, although they did meet amicably in Manchester at the end of June. Both were frequently on the move, sometimes very happily so in EM's case, encountering new experiences. In February 1975 he described how

> coming up by train from Birmingham was absolutely celestial – blue sky all the way, criss-crossed by vapour-trails from jets that seemed to be playing like whales, and all the time that hot extraordinary February sun – I had Virginia Woolf on my lap but instead I wrote a poem (poem and a half actually) [. . .] 'Dicen que no hablan las plantas, ni las fuentes, ni los pájaros . . .' but it's not true it's not true![22]

By January of 1976, Michael Schmidt stated on his return from Mexico how his visits there always 'radicalised' him, making him more anti-England than when he had departed. Perhaps this was the shift of perspective EM was looking for. By coincidence, a letter from EM was waiting for him:

> The other night I was idly scanning our joint gallstones and I must say they seem to stand up pretty well. If we could strain to produce say three or four times as many, we could have a wee buik that might really prove of some interest. I think we toyed with the idea before. [. . .] *Biodes*, we might call that book.[23]

There was no chance of Carcanet publishing Michael Schmidt's work under Charity Commission rules, however, and the matter lapsed.

WAR STORIES

Work continued meanwhile on 'The New Divan', the unwritten story of EM's war. It had been surfacing in dreams and nightmares, as well as in correspondence with other ex-servicemen, for several years. There was an artistic and personal need to make a full statement about that wartime experience, to replace his surrogate 1950s *Beowulf* tale of warrior bands against northern monsters. But how were the varied memories and experiences of this Mediterranean story to be organised?

Although EM disliked analysing his own poetry, feeling like many other poets an almost superstitious respect for its mystery, he knew how to make poems in the structural sense, out of sound and visual patterns. He had begun, as he told Michael Schmidt, with twenty poems. These were written over seven days of the midwinter season from 28 December 1973 to 3 January 1974, as noted on his original typescripts.[24] It seems at least feasible that he would use this twenty-stanza pattern as a building block.

Before even looking at his originals, where the dates of composition are given, I re-read the poem itself in the Carcanet edition of 1977 which EM had given to me in July of that year, and tried to spot the structural elements he had used. Overall, of course, he was using an 'Arabian Nights' technique in keeping with the Middle Eastern setting. There, the marvellous tales of fantastic journeys and the unrolling of many a magic coincidence are set within the life-crisis of the teller, the clever Scheherazade. In order to save herself from execution by a king who hates all humankind, every evening she tells him a story and leaves it incomplete, promising to finish it on the following night. Hence, *The Thousand and One Nights* or *The Arabian Nights Entertainment*, the alternative titles. The king, anxious to hear the ending, postpones her execution from day to day, until finally he abandons his cruelty. I am not sure when EM encountered *The Arabian Nights Entertainment*, but I do know that he was reflecting on traditional tales in 1974, because he gave my children his annotated review copy of Iona and Peter Opie's *The Classic Fairy Tales* (1974), after he had completed 'The dark side of Fairyland' for the *Times Literary Supplement* (6 December 1974). There are several comments in this book regarding the Middle Eastern tales.

I read 'The New Divan' again, looking at its stanzas not as separate stories but as a series of strong sense impressions and images of contrasting cultures in conflict – flashbacks, as it were, from several different narratives from different eras. The marvellous journey is, of course, the standard epic device, whether in Dante, Basil Bunting or Ezra Pound. The story of that journey is the poem, but with the storyteller's voice and stance brought to the fore. In 'The New Divan', the journey has an element of time-travelling, but it moves towards a combination of visionary clarity and autobiographical testament in the final stanzas, giving a sense of uplift that abides beyond the pain of wartime loss that must be endured.

But how was this positive emotion to be arrived at? Stanzas 1–20 set the scene, or rather the scenes, of the tale. It opens with the Persian poet-figure, Hafiz as the 'old nightingale' who has, in the historical past, achieved his great poetry within the 'wretched-ness' of life. The modern poet now must enter history like a masked dancer, or take on multiple identities like an actor, keeping 'no form but water' to deal with complex reality. Eastern princes, a dancing bear, rough angels in their unmade beds, slow caravans and white sails on the turquoise Gulf of Arabia are images that provide movement and a sense of unknown destina-tions. There is a ship, a voyage: 'We pound and shudder through the dark. / A drunk at my cabin door thinks it's his. / Everything's confused [. . .]'. But there is 'No going back, no one to go back with, / back to'. Then 'Halfway down the road', as Dante was at the start of his epic (although unlike Dante in the company he keeps), the speaker meets a visionary creature, possibly 'just a shade', a ragged wraith under a date-palm. He cackles that 'We're / on the same road'. '*The Scene is set*', as in a play. But this is a poetic theatre with multiple stages – possibly more like an editor's suite in a television news studio where different stories are playing simultaneously on many screens, and we are flicked from one to the other.

Nevertheless the Dante comparison is not irrelevant. The poem does end with a 'paradise in prospect', although it may be a mirage. And the violence of war has its infernal aspects, just as the pain of lost love creates a period of purgatory that must be endured. What is lacking is the certainty of Dante's medieval categories. Here the images flicker and rewind and intersect. Love has both divine and demonic tendencies in EM's modern vision of things.

Section two's Stanzas 21–42 were composed between 7–11 April 1974, when ten poems were written, and then between 28 May and 16 June 1974, fairly intensively in bursts of three or six poems. That looks as if Easter and then examination marking have interrupted the April flow. The theme of this second section is '*Exploring the Arabian world*' – striking more deeply into its weathers, markets, boats, young Arab gangs ('Real nomad cats / with nose-rings, knives, horsewhips [. . .]'). There are cockerels, calabashes, parakeets and a hunting horn, all brought on board by 'the master of ungathered things'. There are see-through demons and ruins under snow, and a desert excavation of a king's body: 'His whole retinue had been burnt like coal / to warm his afterlife'. Ancient civilisations and living crowds jostle in the same space, and within this human chaos the key question is posed: 'Where can love, in this world, ever lodge?' In an image that recalls Bunting's poem 'The Spoils', Faruz, a female Arabian singer, laments on the radio 'the final / flake and loosened quiver, winding down, of love'. This is where the journey has taken us so far.

Although he had completed stanzas forty to forty-two in that preceding period, my reading of the third section placed its starting point at forty. A frightened gerbil being stroked by a child is so anxious that 'it trusts its cage more than love, that like wax / can melt to fearful shapes and suffocate'. This third movement of the poem, forty to fifty-nine, deals in more detail with '*Dimensions of love*', both heterosexual and homosexual. Earlier images of voyage and archaeological excavation recur, floating by like the clouds 'boiling in swarms'. This is a 'speeded-up universe', a time-travelling test of endurance where we enter gardens, rooms, and lives. Looters in the market squares and desert bandits co-exist with the cosmic perspective of mysterious calm observers of human activity: 'This world, they say, has only action'.

Set against that world of impulse and desire, the fourth section, stanzas 60–80, explores more deeply '*The force of commitment*'. Commitment is seen in its political, religious and artistic forms. There is a break where EM had to begin again after a month's gap caused by the new university term. Stanzas 62–66 were written between 20 August and 18 September. Then he manages another three stanzas between 30 September and 1 October. After a month's gap, he manages to complete nine stanzas between the end of October and mid-November. The storyteller's role acts as a sort of hinge here, in stanzas 67 and 68, where stories within stories mark the place. It is almost as if he is reminding himself of what the poem is about, and what his own artistic role must be within it.

This section on commitment opens with 'an activist grown old', walking in his garden: 'the admired, / limping, white-haired child of the revolution, loved / by the soft generations smells blood, not roses, still'. Cheap religious statues for Christian pilgrims are mocked ('nothing looking / blander ever shot from the mould') and 'demons fill the cracks with smoke'. There is often a bitter cast to the results of political commitment in wartime violence: 'By searchlights men were made the maggots of / a turned furrow, each waving with his / scattered O of panic'. Somewhere there may be a recording angel, but he is only writing down a 'vast perhaps'. The final nine stanzas, completed after the month's break, are much more physical, with a sexual atmosphere and sharply observed domestic detail that may be setting the poem up for the final loss soon to come: 'That day was an onion of skins, / it came apart in temporary / hours, distinct, sweet, pungent and good'.

The last section of the poem, stanzas 81–100, was written mainly in two halves: 83–90 between 24 March and 10 April, and 91–100 between 25 June and 20 July 1975. The dates again suggest that composition is sustained in the breaks from teaching and assessment. It offers '*A final vision*': 'Paradise in prospect / after sand after sand after sand'. It may be a mirage, but the pilgrimage goes on. Sages smoking their bubble-pipes in an anteroom of heaven, recording angels, and a flying carpet snapping its fringes are all intersected with demonic images of death and torture ('in the form of dragons, worse. Winged leather, metal beat about us'). Love, unrequited but faithful, is the end of the journey, although it is 'Not in King's Regulations, to be in love'. Cosgrove is named, recreated and recalled forever: 'yesterday, tomorrow / he slumbers in a word'.

The physical fears and excitements of war are suddenly brought into full light. The poem places the individual transient life of the young soldier-poet, with its intense friendships and painful encounters with the dead and injured on stretcher duty, together with his later dream-visions and survivor nightmares, confidently but quietly alongside the work of the great Persian poet, Hafiz. The final image is of a shred of sailcloth, washed up after a shipwreck, that can still be used to bind this set of stanzas, or 'divan', in the Arabic sense of a collection of poems.

It is possible, therefore, to discover a formal structure present within this long sequence that helps explain why it is shaped as it is. But this formal presence does not of itself guarantee an enthusiastic readership. Should poems need a critical gloss? And *The New Divan* certainly sold less well than his previous collection. Sales were pretty good, his editor said, and compared with many books of poems they were excellent. *From Glasgow to Saturn*, however, remains the book by which EM is best known in England.

Michael Schmidt was probably correct in his initial reaction to the title. Three meanings of the word 'divan' are glossed opposite the book's Contents list – '1. a state council, 2. a couch or bed, 3. a collection of poems e.g. the *Divan* of Hafiz' – and each meaning has it place in the poem – but this attempt at definition gets lost among the Acknowledgements and publication details. In any case, it seems by its positioning to refer to *The New Divan* as a whole rather than to the title poem it is meant to contextualize.

247

Most readers picking it up in a bookshop might be expecting a domestic interior and puzzle over the one hundred stanzas that open the volume. They have rhetoric, colour, concern and drive, but seem hectic and confusing at first sight. Human emotion and biographical detail do not really surface clearly till the final section. Yet once the title had been accepted, it made sense to place this *magnum opus* first in the collection. Late in life EM came to think it should have been published by itself as a separate small volume. In my view, spaced sections might have helped.

Arguably the most powerful, involving and human poems in the collection are left till last. These are, first of all, the sequence of love poems 'The Divide', 'Smoke' 'The Beginning' 'The Planets' and 'Resurrections', this latter winning one of the 1976 Cheltenham Festival prizes of two hundred pounds, alongside poems by George Mackay Brown and Charles Tomlinson. They record the process of the poet's falling in love with a younger man. Perhaps he is a student – certainly someone interested in poetry, since they meet after a poetry reading in Glasgow University's Bute Hall, where EM had been contributing translations to a reading by the Russian poet, Andrei Voznesensky, on 10 November 1975.

The 'divide' is age: 'These years between us like a sea'. Common sense and cautious self-preservation seemed to have vanished:

> Any dignity that came with growing older
> would stop my pencil on the paper.
>
> (CP: 369)

The affair is complicated, confusing, unconsummated at the start but full of longing. 'I want to be born again' the poet says in 'Resurrections', as he wakes alone but filled with the exhilaration of being 'caught up in another life'. This person was Bobby C. who is recalled in 'Love and a Life', on a journey that he and EM would later take across the United States by Greyhound Bus:

> Bobby at the Grand Canyon, squinting up, on the verge,
>   fathomless purple below.
>
> (*A Book of Lives*: 99)

The sequence still seems troubled and troubling: this is a more clearly gay encounter than the love poems in *From Glasgow to Saturn*, just as the homosexual elements in 'The New Divan' are more explicit than before. For that reason, some contemporary readers may have found it less appealing than the poet's earlier work.

The sequence of 'Unfinished Poems' that ends the book is, on the contrary, immediately moving. It is, I think, among his finest works: an elegy in ten poems for Veronica Forrest-Thomson who died in 1975, her life and promising poetry cut short at the age of twenty-seven. Every poem is therefore left unfinished, and we find ourselves, as we come to the end of each one, straining to complete it. It is a remarkable sequence, where the 'tricks' of his avant-garde exploration find a human home.

Veronica Forrest-Thompson, as described in the previous chapter, was both an individualistic poet and a strong literary theorist. Her critical book *Poetic Artifice* was posthumously published in 1978, and a *Collected Poems* and then *Selected Poems* in 1990 and 1999. Her difficult, allusive poetry was influenced by the philosophy of Wittgenstein, the critical work of William Empson and by linguistic theory. She also admired the austere writing of the Cambridge academic and poet, J.H. Prynne, whom she met when she was writing her doctoral thesis there. Both Prynne and EM recalled her intensity in argument: 'a spiky, difficult character of great intelligence and wit, engaging, vulnerable and lonely', as EM describes her in his note to 'Unfinished Poems' (CP: 373). Both men were struck by her unorthodox sense of fashion and colour, and her intense use of makeup and perfume.

After she died, EM felt guilty that he had not, somehow, done more to help her. Possibly more constant contact with her might have given her the sort of support that he himself clearly got from correspondence. A combination of alcohol and an overdose of medication was considered the cause of death. Her personal relationship with the literary critic Jonathan Culler had recently broken up. It seemed accidental, and yet EM suspected suicide. But he was circumspect, or kindly, when Cavan McCarthy wrote to him, and later phoned, about her death. The 'Unfinished Poems' weave an elegiac thread through his own poetic concerns and hers: 'O blessed trivia that keep us from dying: did you not find / them – Veronica – '.

The New Divan also contains another of EM's most powerful poems, 'The World' (CP: 346–8). I often recalled its oblique final stanza in seeing EM chair-bound in the nursing home in his last years:

> I don't think it's not being perfect
> that brings the sorrows in, but being soon
> beyond the force not to be powerless.

His self-control and dignity within an undignified state seemed at this point to find the very last shred of force within a seeming powerlessness.

In preparing the collection for publication, he made a strong plea to Michael Schmidt for the inclusion of 'Vico's Song', 'A Girl', 'Three Trees' and 'On John Maclean':

> I would particularly like the Maclean poem to go in, as I think it is a good one, and it would certainly interest (a) Scottish and (b) politically-minded readers.[25]

The political differences between the two men clearly remained. EM still refused to send poems to *PN Review* because of the right-wing bias he perceived in the early issues, whereas Michael Schmidt began to tease him about his social animosity towards Mexicans and Englishmen. To Schmidt, at that age, simple left-right distinctions seemed rather silly in a country with so much history as Britain.

In old age, EM still felt disappointment at the reception of *The New Divan*. He admitted that the title was wrong (Schmidt used to call it *Nude Ivan*), and that he himself had mainly organised the book, without realising the difficulties that the opening long poem would pose. He had been misled by the ready acceptance of it in a variety of journals – but those editors were only seeing interesting fragments of a forthcoming work by a recognised poet.

What emerged was a complex whole that lacked adequate signposting for readers. There are good things in the collection. I particularly like the sound poem 'Shaker Shaken'. But there was a warning signal too, perhaps, in the inclusion of so many series of poems: 'Three Trees', 'Ten Theatre Poems', 'Five Poems on Film Directors'. There is a law of diminishing returns that can operate in poetry as much as in business, no matter the technical skill.

ENDINGS

Academically EM had moved forward, becoming a Professor in 1975, partly as a result of Carcanet, as he said to Michael Schmidt. His scholarly work had continued throughout the decade, with an Introduction to *New English Dramatists 14* (Penguin 1970), his *Essays* (Carcanet 1974), and a new Introduction and Select Bibliography for *Hugh MacDiarmid* for the British Council (1976). He lectured on 'Gavin Douglas and William Drummond as Translators' at an international conference on Medieval and Renaissance Scottish Language and Literature in Edinburgh in 1975, and he gave the Warton Lecture in English Poetry for the British Academy in 1977, later published as *Provenance and Problematics of "Sublime and Alarming Images" in Poetry* (1979). He annotated a selection of *Scottish Satirical Verse* (Carcanet 1980, although earlier destined for Routledge). He also scripted an Open University teaching film in 1975 on Modern Eastern European Poetry, focusing on Herbert, Holub and Popa.

The reality of a British Council poetry reading tour of

Czechoslovakia in late 1977 proved less engaging than reading or translating the poetry of embattled writers under Communism. He found the people he met difficult and uncooperative, with little interest in contemporary British or American writing. At Bratislava, he was lodged in a student hostel miles from the city centre, isolated and bleak. When he protested, he was grudgingly given a hotel room in town, but had to organise his own travel there by train. To be fair to the British Council, as he told his publisher, they had asked him 'to go in a missionary spirit, and to bear with frustrations'.

The summer of 1977 had also been unhappy, 'distracting and depressing . . . in both the inner and outer worlds', as he admitted to Michael Schmidt at the end of August. Cracks and bulges in two walls of his flat meant lengthy repairs, with books piled everywhere and a white plaster dust coating everything. Worse than that was a holiday with John Scott in Tenerife, which turned bitter at the end:

> a sudden flare-up [. . .] one of those tiny almost accidental things which are nevertheless very hard to undo once certain words have been said (we were both edgy after a twenty-four hour plane delay).

They would not meet again before John's death one year later.

The tensions that sparked this final quarrel may have been the sort that arise when friends or family whose working lives keep them conveniently apart are thrown as holiday makers into each other's daily presence. John had been ill with a stomach complaint, and an x-ray at Law Hospital two months previously had diagnosed a penny piece lodged in his stomach, or so he had told EM.

The holiday had been going quite well, in EM's recollection, and they had ascended to the top of the volcanic Pico de Teide, with its marvellous perspectives over island and ocean. But it could have been that John Scott, although he never read EM's poetry, sensed the poet's emotional dissatisfaction, his longing 'to be born again' and 'caught up in another life', as revealed in 'Resurrections'. His relationships with both John and Bobby C. coincided, from the evidence of his diaries, sometimes over-lapping within a single week. Whatever the cause of the quarrel, EM would be haunted by it for the rest of his life.

Academic success gave very limited satisfaction at this time. New responsibilities for academic leadership came with the professorial role, so there were many meetings to attend. These were probably concerned with developing a curriculum to cope with a significant increase in student numbers during these years. At the same time, the university study of English was becoming heavily influenced by continental literary theory. The Young Turks were setting out their various critical stalls: indeed post-structuralism and deconstruction threatened to take over the whole bazaar. Their linguistic or philosophical undermining of the role of the authorial voice may have been particularly troubling. While EM could understand the theory, and in fact taught it in the Masters course I followed, he did not feel that he had the time or real inclination for wide or deep reading around it.

Of course he 'kept up', and would make occasional later reference to Iser's work on indeterminacy in literary response, and to Bakhtin's focus on dialogic and heteroglossic texts. In the latter case, he must have felt drawn back to the Russian futurists whom he revered, and perhaps he always remained a futurist at heart. Clearly he preferred to explore such issues creatively rather than academically. Yet in this decade there was an increasing pressure on academics to publish steadily in specialist journals and university presses, whereas he was concerned to publish steadily in poetry journals and small presses.

Early in 1978, EM became friendly with a Glaswegian work-ing-class poet, William G., whose hand-written poems he typed up and whom he helped financially on occasion. But all personal and professional concerns were knocked sideways by two deaths in the late summer of that year. Hugh MacDiarmid died aged eighty-six on 9 September in Chalmers Hospital in Edinburgh. He had been suffering from bowel cancer. Two days later John

Scott died in Law Hospital, Carluke, aged sixty. He had lung cancer which had spread to his liver.

John's family had not contacted EM when his friend was dying, but they phoned to give him news of the death and the funeral arrangements:

> I was quite surprised that at the burial they gave me a cord to hold, which normally would only be the family circle, so they must have reckoned that this was something they accepted.[26]

Nothing was said openly about their friendship. It was a Catholic funeral, and a cold day. The funeral meal afterwards surprised him too, by the amount of drink and enjoyment of life – a sort of wake after the event. The family members were friendly, but he felt alien to their culture. They put him on a bus for Glasgow and went back to their gathering.

The following day he had to travel down to Lockerbie and then across to Langholm for MacDiarmid's funeral, a more literary affair. Again the day was grey and damp, 'gey dreich' in the Scots phrase. Norman MacCaig gave a eulogy, a pibroch was played and the widow, Valda Grieve, placed white roses on the coffin. As reported by Alan Bold in his biography *MacDiarmid* (1988, 1990), she was heard to comment that the people of Langholm who had rejected the poet 'will now have to live with him'.

EM had been on the receiving end of a similar sharpness of tongue at an earlier stage. When Alex Frizzell passed on to him in February 1972 a somewhat flattering remark that Valda Grieve had made, EM recalled an earlier remark of hers

> made to me in a rude moment: 'Edwin Muir wasn't much of a poet but at least he was better than Edwin Morgan!'[27]

Although he and MacDiarmid had had their differences, EM felt that there was a later reconciliation between them. They had shared an early enthusiasm for Scots language, but then differed radically over how experimental its uses should be. They were both radical socialists, but MacDiarmid's ruthless support of Russian force in the Hungarian uprising of 1956 contradicted absolutely EM's love for that country and its poetry. The younger poet became identified in MacDiarmid's mind with all that he considered tawdry and somehow 'disloyal' about avant-garde writing by Scottish internationalists. Both men were determined characters, although the younger man was less vociferously polemical. I believe that EM survived the opposition of Mac-Diarmid's supporters by continuing to work intelligently and diligently in both verse and prose, and building up a body of work that could not easily be contradicted, particularly by those who wrote less well and less widely than he did.

EM and MacDiarmid did not meet frequently, especially after the debacle of the Edinburgh Writers' Conference. But EM continued to be invited to literary functions and celebrations for the older poet, and his impression was of a thaw in their relations, and a belated recognition of what they had in common. They shared a similar realisation of the role of science and language in human development, and both aspired to create a poetry that could contain the multiplicity of science and society. EM had been working on his new bibliography of the older poet's work only two years previously, and in January 1978, when asked by the Committee of the Swedish Academy to nominate a candidate for that year's Nobel Prize for Literature, he had put forward MacDiarmid.[28] The older poet's work and example had almost from the start been a spur to his own, and one of his earliest published critical pieces in 1956 had been 'Jujitsu for the Educated: Reflections on Hugh MacDiarmid's poem *In Memoriam James Joyce*', published in *The Twentieth Century*.

In one week EM thus was twice bereaved, and took it hard. On 19 September he realized that he would not be able to take part in a radio programme on MacDiarmid, and asked Michael Schmidt to apologise on his behalf to the producer, Fraser Steele:

I am sorry I did not say this when he phoned, but I thought I would be able to deal with it. I find I can't. It is partly because the two funerals were so close together that whenever I think of MacDiarmid I think of John. And we were more than friends, so the physical separation is very hard.[29]

The loss had its effect on his work rate, and months later Michael Schmidt was still waiting for EM to complete his Introduction and Glossary for the *Scottish Satirical Verse* collection, even although three hundred advance copies had been sold.

Some of his grief poured itself into *Star Gate: Science Fiction Poems*, published by the Third Eye Centre in Glasgow in 1979 to accompany their 'High Frontier 1970–1980' exhibition and events. The collection plunges deep into outer space, but also into the inner spaces of particle theory and of time, and of personal emotion too. Within a twenty-page span it encompasses a remarkable range of tones. There is the historical 'Instamatic The Moon February 1973', the humorous 'Particle Poems' and 'Foundation', the tenderness of 'A Home in Space' which builds beautifully in linked lines to the human needs of voyagers in 'space that needs time and time that needs life' (CP: 383–8). 'The Mouth' deals with anti-matter in apocalyptic long and fearsome lines, and 'The Clone Poem' (CP: 389–90) uses sound-poem techniques to break through the truisms and clichés which human beings use to get by in the world: 'you can have too much of a good thing too much of a good thing too / much you can have too much you can you can [. . .]'. From his own perspective, this was something he had discovered too late, once the good thing had been rejected and was gone. The more intense the love, the emptier life can feel once that person has gone.

The final sequence, 'The Moons of Jupiter', sets personal grief against the cosmos. In 'Io', the surface of the planet is a scarred industrial landscape that might well be Lanarkshire (the miners are on strike after a major accident) but is also like hell (these are sulphur mines). There has been a funeral: 'Empty / though not perfunctory', and now the 'weird planet man's flute from friends in grief' rises into 'the raw thin cindery air' millions of miles from home (CP: 391). In 'Callisto', the final poem, the lunar landscape has been scarred by meteorites into a 'slaty chaos' that still cannot prevent the ongoing human quest: 'our feet, our search, our songs'. The pits and mounds remind the narrator

> of one grave long ago
> on earth, when a high Lanarkshire wind
> whipped out the tears men might be loath to show
>> [. . .]. (CP: 394)

EM had been taught not to show emotion, but to get on with life in a stoical manner. The poem about his mother, 'The Coals', was written about this time, and published in *The Listener* on 31 July 1980. It deals with the moment of seeing her cry before her hysterectomy: 'Her tears shocked me / like a blow' (CP: 421). He must rarely have seen her weep. Also shocking to some extent is what she tells him she is crying about. She will now need to depend on someone else's help, even to carry a bucket of coal into the house from the outside cellar. EM had indeed 'learned both love and joy in a hard school', but recognises that the hardest thing of all can be

> to forgive yourself for things undone,
> guilt that can poison life – away with it,
> you say, and it is loath to go away.

The same word 'loath' is used in this poem and in 'Callisto' above. It derives from an Old English root that means 'unwilling' but also 'disgust' or 'hatred'. Self-disgust may be an element in these poems too, despite the defiant final stance of onward duty and 'fierce salvage' from the wreck of life.

EM's personally fateful year of 1978 was also the time when the so-called 'Cunninghame amendment' was added to the struggling Labour Party's bill for a measure of devolution of political power to Scotland. The progress of the bill had not been smooth, because the idea of devolution raised emotional issues and divisions across party lines. The amendment, which was named after George Cunning-

hame, a Scottish Labour M.P. representing a safe London con-
stituency, stipulated that over forty per cent of the total Scottish
electorate had to vote 'yes' in a referendum before the act would be
put into effect. 'In short', as Richard Finlay points out, 'the
apathetic would be counted as voting "no"'.[30]

In March 1979 when the referendum was counted, 51.6%
voted 'yes' to devolution, but in terms of actual percentage of the
total electorate, the 32.9% who actually voted were fewer than the
36.3% who did not vote at all. Devolution came to a halt under
the forty per cent rule, and the Scottish National Party withdrew
its support from the minority Labour government. The Con-
servatives, under their new leader Margaret Thatcher, were back
in power.

The Scottish National Party lost some of its support in the
aftermath of these events. EM had always tended to vote for
them, despite some reservations:

> But it seems to me to be the only party committed to Scotland
> as an entity, so I tend to give it my support. I feel Scottish – I
> suppose it comes down to something as simple as that on a basic
> level.[31]

Despite the political let-down of the 1979 referendum, EM felt it
was important not to be downcast or pessimistic: indeed he came
to think of it as a spur to creativity in Scotland throughout the
1980s that followed:

> If you think of all that appears in the decade, with Alasdair Gray
> and James Kelman and Tom Leonard and Liz Lochhead, all of
> the kinds of books that were available. So it was a surprisingly
> good decade from that point of view [. . .] saying, well here we are,
> we may not have got our assembly but we're still here, we've got
> our writing to continue and maybe think about Scotland [. . .].[32]

As in the 1960s, creative partnerships with musicians provided
one way of moving forward. In 1976 he had worked with

composer George Newson on a multi-media piece called *Valentine*, which combined music, theatre and slides. It was performed at Glasgow University, directed by James Arnott of the Drama Department, who chose the slides. In 1979 it was revived at Queen's University, Belfast. In the same year, EM's choral piece *Call for the Hazel: A Spell for Four Voices*, was set by Martin Dalby and published by Novello.

Nevertheless he could not really move forward until he had looked back. 'Istanbul' describes something very uncharacteristic of EM. It is the last of the 'Pieces of Me' published in Colin Nicholson's critical study *Edwin Morgan: Inventions of Modernity* (2002: 201). These 'pieces' are odd – more flashbacks than instamatics, deliberately un-worked and un-posed fragments of things that had actually happened but could not be turned into artworks and left behind.

It happened when he visited Turkey for a reading tour in April 1979, as guest of the British Council and the Istanbul Turco-British Association. He had climbed a hill to look down at the city. When the full extent of it gradually rose into view as he neared the summit, he found his steps 'slowing, slowing, as if the ground was sacred, / and perhaps it was'. Then as the sight of the minarets, domes, waterways, ferries, bridges, along with the noise of traffic horns and human cries together suddenly

> crowded the very
> emptiest spaces
> of the heart
> I tried to stifle
> sobbing but could not,
> could not stop tears.

Reflecting on this 'strange moment' in old age, he thought it was partly the sense of the past that had brought him to tears. Here were so many layers of history, so many levels of ancient civilisation, both locked into and locked out of Europe. He had earlier been to the museum in the Topkapi Palace and had seen armour, embroidery – 'everything' – superior to European artefacts of the time. And the Turkish audiences had taken well to his poetry and lectures, asking interesting questions and showing wide knowledge of modern literature in both Europe and the United States.

This old city created a strong atmospheric impression beside its several seas, with lively wharves and waterways packed with astonishing life, late into the night. 'I could live here,' he suddenly thought. He felt safe in this ancient modern Eastern place, as multifarious as his own imagination. But he knew he could not stay.

CHAPTER EIGHT

Facing up to the future 1980–1990

At sixty I was standing by a grave.
The winds of Lanarkshire were loud and high.
I knew what I had lost, what I had had.
The East had schooled me about fate, but still
it was the hardest time, or more, it was
the worst of times in self-reproach, the will
that failed to act, the mass of good not done.
Forgiveness must be like the springs that fill
deserted furrows if they wait
until – until –

'Epilogue: Seven Decades' (CP: 595)

Retirement can provide, at last, the freedom to pursue personal interests. It can also open up time to brood on past events, on roads not taken. The 'Epilogue' here transposes John Scott's funeral into the early 1980s, and suggests a deal of guilt and self-reproach waiting to enter the spaces that EM's university work had previously filled: 'the will / that failed to act, the mass of good not done'.

After a month or two of savouring the luxury of not having to teach on a daily basis, EM told me, he began to feel guilty that nothing much was being achieved. His diary for 1980–1981 suggests that this period of retirement was really closer to two weeks, before activity was cranked up again. Eight years earlier in his 'Notes on the Poet's Working Day', he had concluded that, despite the disadvantages of a heavy academic workload, 'I seem to need some tension, some anxiety, some clash of responsibilities, and if I am too free I may be less creative'.[1] Now he would have to create these competing deadlines for himself. As he told the poet Peter McCarey, whose doctoral research on MacDiarmid and Russian culture and philosophy he was continuing to supervise:

> I have just been along to the Social Security and am now officially a self-employed person; so I had better get to work.[2]

The letter is dated 11 October 1980, the second week of what would have been his normal university term. He did not miss the grind of assessment and committee work, although as we have seen nightmares of academic errors would continue to disturb him in retirement. There may be an impression in his ready acceptance of speaking engagements that he missed the lecturer's podium, but in fact he had always given talks and continued to do so, and to be involved as external speaker, examiner or visiting professor in various universities. But the balance shifted to creative work.

By 27 October, EM was involved in discussions with Chris Carrell, the director of the Third Eye Centre, and Mary Baxter of the National Book League, Scotland, on a proposed 'festival of books and writers' in Glasgow. This would become the first Glasgow Bookfest, taking place over three weeks from late February to mid-March 1981. It coincided with a major exhibition organised at the Third Eye Centre, *Seven Poets*, with photographic portraits by Jessie Matthew and paintings by Sandy Moffat alongside thirty-minute films of the poets and individual poetry readings. The poets were Hugh MacDiarmid and Sorley MacLean in the older generation, and Norman MacCaig, Iain Crichton Smith, Robert Garioch and George Mackay Brown, as well as EM.

There would also be other readings planned over the length of the festival, from a wide range of Scottish and other writers including Dominic Behan, Melvin Bragg, Anthony Burgess, John Byrne, Stewart Conn, Douglas Dunn, Robert Garioch,

Christopher Logue, Norman MacCaig and Sorley MacLean. Younger Scottish writers were to include Marcella Evaristi, Alasdair Gray, Andrew Greig, James Kelman, Liz Lochhead, Tom Leonard, Tom McGrath and Alan Spence. Altogether thirty-nine events were planned, including seminars, lectures, films and book exhibitions.

EM wrote a poem for the festival's opening, but his main work was arranging and chairing three seminars on *Writers Talking*: 'Facing in or out: Attitudes to Scottish Poetry', 'Class in Scottish Fiction' and 'Critics – who needs them?'. He organised a variety of speakers, including Ron Butlin, Philip Hobsbaum, Tom Leonard, Alan Massie, Lorn McIntyre, Trevor Royle, Alex Scott, Anne Smith and Iain Crichton Smith. Overall, the Bookfest attracted around 2,300 people, and even made a slight profit of one hundred pounds or so. EM's own seminar events went 'surprisingly well', he told Michael Schmidt, with much better attendances than he had feared, given their Saturday afternoon slots in a busy programme. Indeed, the whole event seemed 'to have turned out to be a reasonably encouraging operation' – although not encouraging enough to tempt him to continue on the planning team for the following year. Financial aspects were troublesome, he felt, or intractable.

At home, EM was by now the immediate support for his mother's elderly surviving sister, Myra Parrot, whose flat at 16 Whittingehame Court was near his own at number 19. He seems to have been a dutiful nephew, going to her flat for tea every few weeks, taking her on Christmas outings and helping her on holiday journeys to Pitlochry and other Scottish towns, and also dealing with medical problems when she had a slight stroke early in the decade. She went with him to Buckingham Palace on 23 November 1982 to collect his OBE, together with Janet Hamilton, who lived next door to him. Both she and her husband John Hamilton were retired doctors, and good and helpful neighbours. However,

No sooner do I receive my OBE, and a pretty object it is too, than I read in the paper that Willie Ormond has just lost his to a burglar. My aunt says, Put it in the bank! But that seems a counsel of despair. I must say there is something to be said for Muslim fatalism as against Christian angst.[3]

His aunt would become increasingly anxious and dependent on him as the decade wore on. It may have been to gain some form of respite for himself that EM took on a time-share week in an exclusive complex on Rannoch Moor, where he went regularly in the third week of July. He may have been searching for isolation. Originally he had hoped that without distractions he would be able to do more writing there, but of course the opposite proved to be the case. He seemed to need the distraction of city life with all its contrasts to stimulate his creativity. There was also the fact that the holiday complex was designed around outdoor pursuits, and he was no sportsman.

He also found emotional support, and a sort of surrogate family, in Morven Cameron. She was Head of English at Laurel Bank, a private all-girls school very near the university. In his desolation after the death of John, she had convinced him that he would never be completely alone, although it must now feel like that. As he described her to a friend early in December 2002:

She had all of that womanly quality, and I remember her as one of my first students, a mass of blonde hair and a fine pair of legs: a character, and a wonderful person.[4]

EM was writing here shortly after her death. She was an 'inspirational' teacher, by all accounts, witty, intelligent, subjective and flamboyant. Born in Rothiemurches, she had been educated in Glasgow where her father was a doctor. She figured in the Citizens Theatre Company in 1947–1948, and after university worked as a script editor with the BBC before returning to teach in Glasgow at Whitehill and Cleveden Secondary state schools and in the private sector at The Glasgow High School for Girls and finally at Laurel Bank. As Principal Teacher of English at Cleveden in 1975, she revised Maurice Lindsay's schools anthology, *Voices of our Kind* (1971).

She was a glamorous woman, who never married but had close friendships with several poets whom EM knew, such as Hugh MacDiarmid and Norman MacCaig, so there was a shared interest in poetry, drama, art and gossip, as well as a welcome into her circle of colleagues and close family. She was talented in several areas, had written poetry and also published a drawing of EM in *The Scottish Review* 20 (December 1980: 47). Jack Rillie had earlier tried to persuade him to marry her, and that possibility seemed still to linger dangerously enough for EM to side-step a planned holiday with her in Naples in the 1990s, I believe. Or so he told me.

Alongside this retired bourgeois social life, EM's somewhat more unsettling private life of more or less casual relationships continued. Do I mean 'unsettled' rather than 'unsettling'? Probably both. After a profound emotional loss, the mind and body often cast around for sources of distraction or oblivion. Although some of these male friendships had run alongside EM's relationship with John Scott, they had never supplanted its peculiar emotional bond. That absence now haunted him, particularly as he had failed to act to bring about any reconciliation before John's death.

EM's new routine is also disconcerting because it seems a reversion to the bleak 1950s, not only in what he had described to me as

> the sense of going in search of something – maybe I'm not sure what – [. . .]. Perhaps if it's a gay poem then the quest is for the impossible perfect partner. (Quentin Crisp used to write about that.)[5]

The age gap now between EM and his partners could be seen as a lack of emotional maturation, a negative aspect, or, more positively, as the creative artist's search for new experiences in a changing world. Or both may be true to some extent. The image of old man and younger object of desire is well known in cultural and literary history: one thinks at once of Yeats or Dickens. It is also true that men quite often marry a second wife whom others can see bears a remarkable resemblance to their first. EM's preference was for dark, gallus, working-class Glaswegian males. He also enjoyed the sheer differences between ways of life, in all their variety and oddness. This was part of his search for creative tensions that might produce poetry.

Of course, I have to admit that Basil Bunting made a great poem out of a similar early fixation, and Dante too, to name a greater poet. Yet I think that this trait kept EM's poetic focus as much on the surface variety of life as on its emotional depths, and his later love poetry repeatedly explores the first heady impact of attraction. This may be why his work has always made a marked impression on young people, and why he himself retained an astonishing youthfulness of outlook and dress, which was in itself attractive.

In our conversation around these issues as I was writing this chapter in late October 2009, EM said that he was not particularly concerned about the age difference. Possibly it was a way of rejuvenating himself, and possibly there was something in the idea of a reversion to an earlier self. These relationships would often begin with an interesting conversation in a bar, and develop from there – or not. He recalled with wry amusement one such meeting with a former student from one of his seminar groups whom he failed to recognise. They had met for a drink three or four times before the ex-student asked: 'Do you not recognise me?' Clearly not.

He also reminded me that, although these relationships might seem transient, many of them kept going in 'a subterranean way' across the years. They were 'strangely lasting' and men would come back into his life in a mysterious way years later: 'I didn't give people up'. He felt that such relationships did affect his understanding of the world in which he lived, for which he was always grateful. For writing about Glasgow people or events, they created a necessary empathy that would not otherwise have existed. Glaswegian themes in his poetry were thus deeply connected with these working-class relationships.

John Scott, in particular, had taught him to be more honest, to avoid wrapping himself in 'a cloak of class' instead of getting to the truth of who he was. This helped develop maturity. Nor were his social explorations confined to working-class people. At the other extreme of the spectrum, he had met land-owning and aristocratic people through his long friendship with Colin Hamilton and Kulgin Duval, the book dealers, whose beautiful house and garden in Frenich, Perthshire, he would regularly visit. They owned four houses, one in Kerala in Southern India.

EM's 1980s diaries show regular meetings with various men who enter, depart and re-enter his life across the years: Bobby, Harry, Jimmy, Malcolm, Willie, George. There are meetings in Glasgow pubs such as the Lorne Bar or the Horseshoe Bar, and sometimes in his flat, with a sort of consistency of timing that seems accommodated to their working lives or his own. Their work was mainly casual: in garages, security firms, hotels or building sites. Sometimes meetings were abandoned with no prior warning, because of the chance of an extra shift. Or they would lose their jobs and then have to 'sign-on' or move in search of another.

As in his 1950s, EM's experiences offered a personal awareness of other lives that few among his own social class had access to. This coloured his view of 1980s politics, and the changes brought by Thatcherite economic policies. They had a major impact on the traditional industries of the West of Scotland, with consequent rises in unemployment, poverty and unrest.

In early 1982 there was a by-election in Hillhead at which Roy Jenkins, a former Labour minister, stood for the Social Democratic Party which he had helped to found. He stayed at the Pond Hotel, almost opposite EM's front window. Writing to Michael Schmidt on 23 March, and asking him to include 'The Flowers of Scotland' in his forthcoming collection *Poems of Thirty Years* because people still asked for this political poem at readings, EM described his annoyance at the real politics revealed by fringe groups in the election:

> trying to whip up their pet specialities, whether anti-Pope or anti-gay or anti- feminist or anti-Ann-Summers – they never seem to be *pro* anything except capital punishment [. . .]. There's something ominous about the Eighties, so much hatred boiling and swilling about near the surface – do you feel this?[6]

With his left-wing convictions, it may seem surprising that EM accepted the Order of the British Empire without hesitation later that year. He once tried to defend his decision to Hamish Whyte by saying that he thought he could more easily 'change the system from the inside'. That seemed evasive, even then. In old age he admitted that he thought that it was simply his 'turn' for the award. George Mackay Brown had got his in 1974, then MacCaig in 1979 and Iain Crichton Smith in the following year. One can imagine feelings of puzzled rivalry in a habitual prize winner: why not me?

Iain Crichton Smith, with whom he had discussed political matters since the 1950s, shared EM's concerns about the current state of society. Interviewed for the book published to accompany the *Seven Poets* exhibition, he complained about a sense of mediocrity in Scotland, of superficiality and a lack of professionalism. He made an exception for Hugh MacDiarmid and the Celtic Football Club. But elsewhere he found 'nothing real in Scotland that you can actually operate on to make real poetry' (p.47). This had not, in fact, prevented him from publishing ten collections of poetry with various publishers in the 1970s, as well as thirteen novels or short story collections in the same decade. Despite a laissez-faire approach to typing and an apparently careless outlook on his own creative processes, he was prodigious.

Whereas EM found George Mackay Brown too spiritually secure and not tormented enough for the good of his own poetry, his friend Iain seemed probably too conflicted and troubled. The dichotomies in such titles of his as *Thistle and Roses* (1961) or *The Law and the Grace* (1965) have often been noted. Another, *Burn is Aran* (*Water and Bread*), a 1960 collection of poems and short stories in Gaelic, demonstrates that he had access through his bilingual upbringing to the main area of Scottish experience that is missing from EM's poetry: Gaeldom. Iain Crichton Smith may have seemed to him as Sorley MacLean to MacDiarmid: a significant poetic force whose experience and art he could not fully comprehend or match. Norman MacCaig did possess, through his Gaelic mother's family, a ready access to that rural, island-centred culture, which has its own complexities. EM on the other hand was a lowlander, and saw himself as not in the least clannish but ever an individualist.

In EM's interview in the exhibition book, he emphasised his own interest in 'sheer fact', and his attempts to examine and re-imagine whatever flies past 'in the great flux of time'. This is the Scrapbook-maker's dedication again. His friend and colleague Marshall Walker conducted the interview, and was able to bring up the criticism 'sometimes levelled at your work, that you are warm – but a little icy too'. EM countered that he was present in the poems more frequently than was sometimes said, but admitted that this was often 'at a remove', through a projection into other existences:

> like the apple, or even like the hyena or the Loch Ness Monster [. . .] presumably, if the poems work at all, if I get any joy out of doing it, there must be something in me that goes out to things like this.[7]

It is interesting that the examples EM chooses here are all non-human, although he would in the 1980s and 1990s increasingly use drama to voice a range of human characters and concerns, and in the late collection *Cathures* (2002) he would employ the dramatic monologue with great energy to express the identity of his native city.

In the same book, Neal Ascherson saw EM as working

'feverishly against the dangers of provincialism by importing culture from the big world on the other side of England'.[8] He is referring to the translations, but world travel also enabled EM during the 1980s to import imagery and ideas from other cultures into his poetry, from Canada, Israel, Holland, Lapland, Italy, Albania, Germany and Yugoslavia. This constant sense of work and travel was usually connected with poetry readings in Scotland, in the United Kingdom and overseas. He began almost a second career of school and community readings, and was much annoyed to learn from the Department of Health and Social Security in April 1985, approaching his sixty-fifth birthday, that

> since I'm a self-employed person earning over seventy pounds a week (the maximum allowed) I do not qualify for a pension (which I had naively expected to start receiving later this month).[9]

The poet Robert Garioch had experienced a similar problem in the mid-1970s. His literary earnings were much less than EM's but, as he complained to Michael Schmidt, anything above £10 had to be subtracted from that week's pension.

Other paid work for EM in the 1980s included the judging of literary competitions, which was rather like the marking of examination papers that had tried him in earlier days. With Norman MacCaig he read 1200 entries for the Poetry Award of the Lancaster Festival in April 1985, and then proceeded to select the European Translation Prize with Peter Levi. By November 1986 he had joined Carl MacDougall and Hamish Whyte in co-editing the annual volume *New Writing Scotland* for the Association for Scottish Literary Studies. His engagement with new writing continued in July 1988 when he was judging the National Poetry Competition:

> Between now and November the house will gradually fill with paper, starting in a corner and creeping up the walls, spreading like ivy across the windows – help! – [10]

ON TOUR

From the start, retirement did extend his opportunity to travel. EM flew to Toronto in the first week of May 1981 for an International Poetry Conference. The journey was delayed by an air traffic controllers' strike and he had to leave a day early and travel to London by train. He found Heathrow full of stranded travellers 'sprawled everywhere on the floor – it was like one of those simulated atomic attacks'. However, he enjoyed Toronto once he got there, both the city and the poetry festival.

In November he travelled to Israel with a group of British poets, on a reading tour organised by Charles Osbourne for an organisation called Friends of Israel. The other poets were Patricia Beer, Michael Schmidt and Robert Wells. The welcome was not at all friendly. For EM, it contrasted in every respect with the earlier trip to Turkey. The first question asked at the very first reading was: 'Who are your sponsors?'. It seemed that great suspicion was aroused by any question about the Arabs. When the bus was pelted, he got no response to his: 'Are those *Arab* stones?' and was made to feel an emissary of the enemy.

On reflection, he blamed the organisers for not briefing the poets frankly about the political situation. They stayed in good hotels and he revisited tourist sites first seen in his wartime years in Galilee and Jerusalem, as well as Masada and the Dead Sea. There was, however, no engagement of hearts or minds. Instead, there was a lack of curiosity about British writing, an enduring sense of an inward-looking and embattled society, and no chance at all to meet Arab writers. Generally, he was confirmed in his preference for Islamic culture, although he never failed to realise that 'history will see things differently' as the centuries unfold.

From January to March of 1982 EM was much involved with a major Mayakovsky event. It reconstructed an exhibition organised by the Russian poet himself in Moscow in 1930. EM wrote an essay for the book of the exhibition, which opened in Edinburgh on 16 January. It then travelled in February en route to

271

Oxford, Sheffield and London, and in March EM lectured on Mayakovsky at the Museum of Modern Art in Oxford. Back in Glasgow at the end of the month, he took part in an evening of semi-dramatised readings of the poet, with Margaret Moore and Alan Riach, who was writing a thesis on MacDiarmid at the University of Glasgow.

Around this time, EM became involved with the Medieval Players, a small touring company of actors and musicians which had been formed in 1981 by Dick McCaw. They focused on classical texts and had made adaptations of two of Chaucer's *Canterbury Tales*. Now they approached EM for an acting version in translation of a 15th to 16th century Dutch play: *The Apple Tree*. It needed to be accessible to audiences and yet not sound like a medieval pastiche. He was supplied with a literal version of the text by a Dutch research student from Edinburgh. The original used rhyming couplets and some rhetorical flourishes that defied literal transposition. EM's solution, as outlined in his preface to *The Apple Tree*, published by the Third Eye Centre in August 1982 to coincide with its premiere, was 'to make the language itself modern, but set within the structure of a four-stress alliterative line which would hold associations with earlier English drama and poetry'. The alliteration was a kind of equivalent to the original's rhyming couplets. This exercise of balancing colloquial and racy language with formal patterns of sound would serve him well in his later more extended translations of drama in the 1990s.

His partnership with the Medieval Players continued in 1983 with the translation of a 15th century French farce, *Master Peter Pathelin*. This was published by the Third Eye Centre in November of that year, and the first performance was at the Crawford Centre for the Arts in St Andrew's University in early October 1983. By July of the following summer EM had finished a version in English and Scots of the *Second Shepherd's Play* from the Wakefield Cycle of medieval mystery plays. Performance was planned for Glasgow Cathedral in October 1984.

Dramatic translations were journeys through time, to make old conventions live again theatrically. Distant travel at speed might also involve a time dimension. Journeys through time and space appealed strongly to his creative imagination. In December 1985 EM took a day trip to Lapland in the Concorde jet to meet Father Christmas, who turned out to be a citizen of the most northerly town in Finland, Rovaniemi on the Arctic Circle, the centre for the Lapland area. EM saw the trip advertised shortly after winning the Soros Translation Award and decided to spend the prize money on it:

> I'd never have another chance to do it, so I went. Yes, Santa Claus is a very tall, six-foot six Finn [. . .] one thing I learned during that one-day trip is that Finnish and Lappish are different languages. They are related languages, but if you are interested in one you have to learn the other.[11]

The Concorde's elegance and speed was the real attraction. He used the experience of sudden dislocation in a 'reconstruction' of Milton's sonnet 'On Time', where he describes the

> five hours of frozen river and pine
> inside me, long or short
> impossible to say.
> Afterwards, that day seemed a week,
> a fortnight, a world, Puck's world, a puck
> birled across a void of sticks for luck.
>
> (CP: 529–30)

This poem also reveals that EM was number 102 on the civilian waiting list for a trip in the Space Shuttle. He was

> never tired of stars, always longing to sit
> in the brilliant cone, even with chance, even for a time.

Time was further dislocated by an Arctic reprise of his 'Night Pillion' experience, but on a skidoo this time, whooping over a frozen lake:

> double furry biker
> cloned centaur
> clinging and swishing
> magic circles
> Lappish flakes
> to kiss our faces.[12]

A spirit of adventure took him to Albania in early October 1988, when he booked himself on the first flight once an air link was established from London to Tirana. There already was a Scottish and artistic connection of sorts through Lord Byron, who liked the Albanian culture and had his portrait painted in their kilt-like native costume. EM found that Byron was still remembered with respect in Tirana:

> Rapid Albanian patter from a guide at
> the ethnographic museum became luminous
> as he dropped in the magic name and pointed
> at dress that might have graced Scottish bards [. . .].
> (*Sweeping Out the Dark*: 37–8)

EM liked this sturdy independently-minded state, self-isolated from both Russian and Chinese communism, a land of eagles. Here was a possible vision of an independent Scotland: 'no Hiltons and no Palaces of Culture' but only the clarity of a 'Long narrow mountain-backboned rivery country / of gorge and gully and beach, of pines and roses [. . .]'. Drawing his own contrast with the white marble statue of Mother Albania, EM

> thought of Scotland's other, shameful silence,
> and Mother Scotland like a crone in cast-offs [. . .].

This was the silence of the 1979 referendum, lost through a nervous unwillingness of a sufficient majority of Scots to take a chance on the political future of their country.

EM returned to Albania as a setting for one of the poems in his

1999 *Demon* series from Mariscat Press, later reprinted in *Cathures* (Carcanet, 2002). 'A Day Off for the Demon' finds him in Albania's main seaport:

> Dark shape on a white beach near Durrës,
> Dark yet glistening too, spreadeagled,
> Uncrumpling like a new-born dragonfly [. . .].
>
> *(Cathures*: 104)

Writing to his Mariscat editor, Hamish Whyte, at the end of May of 1988, having just returned from a British Council visit to Naples where he had read his Leopardi translations in English and Scots at a major exhibition on the poet's work, EM tried to express what it was that he liked about travelling to other cities. Naples seemed

> fairly chaotic but fascinatingly so – a pullulating street life [. . .] lots of old but peeling buildings rather like Glasgow before the ['Glasgow's miles better'] campaign [. . .]. I think it is the sense of a rich, spilling-over, uncontrolled life that attracts me so much about cities like Naples and Istanbul and (looking back) Cairo.[13]

THE MARISCAT CONNECTION

From a publications point of view, the most important new connection of the 1980s was with Hamish Whyte. He was Senior Librarian in the Rare Books and Manuscripts Department of the Mitchell Library, and had a wide knowledge of Glasgow's history as well as of modern poetry and classical literature. He had first encountered EM when he came to give a talk on Aristophanes to the Glasgow University Alexandrian Society. The poet's future editor and bibliographer was then in the Honours Classics class, and vice-president of the society. This must have been in the first term of 1968, because EM had written to Bob Tait on 29 September, in the midst of *Scottish International* business:

I have three papers to write for the next fortnight, one on Chekhov,
one on Ibsen/Shaw/Brecht, one on Aristophanes! (international? –
man!).[14]

Hamish Whyte wrote to EM in April 1980, mentioning his
interest in compiling an anthology of local poems. This would
eventually become *Noise and Smoky Breath*: *An Illustrated Anthology of Glasgow Poems 1900–1983*, published by the Third Eye
Centre and Glasgow Libraries. He was also organising an exhibition on EM's poetry in the Mitchell Library to coincide with
other sixtieth birthday celebrations of the poet's work. EM sent
him the original typescripts of poems from different decades:
'The Pond', 'Trio', 'At Central Station', 'A Girl', and 'The
Computer's First Christmas Card'.

Probably the most significant part of the letter for both men
was the idea of compiling a bibliography of EM's publications.
He immediately invited the librarian round to check out the many
books, pamphlets and journals in Whittingehame Court that
contained his work. EM sold a fair amount of material to the
Library around this time, including slides, photographs, early art
work and original manuscripts, including that of his translation of
Beowulf. When the Mitchell Library extension opened at the
beginning of June 1981, Hamish Whyte was able to draw on these
new materials for another exhibition. Some of EM's drawings
from the 1930s and 1940s were shown, including four surrealist
colour designs that had been made into table mats.

Mariscat Press first emerged as a publisher in May of the
following year, with a hand-produced edition of three copies of
EM's 'Nine One Word Poems'. These had first appeared in
November 1967 in *Poor.Old.Tired.Horse*. The first Mariscat
publication for broader distribution was a poem-card of 'Grendel'
(CP: 427–8), in an illustrated and handset edition of 300, printed
in red and black. More ambitiously, Hamish Whyte along with
Kevin McCarra, Tom Berry, David Neilson and Alasdair Robinson had decided to correct an Edinburgh bias in Scottish literary
journals. They would establish *The Glasgow Magazine* – or

technically re-establish it: the title had last been used in 1783. He asked EM for poems or an article for the first issue.

In that same summer of 1982, Mariscat published David Neilson's versions of Catullus. EM suggested that the press might be interested in *Instamatics II*, written in the ten years since the Ian McKelvie publication, or in his Newspoems, or in something he called *Joints*: 'poems written round tiny données supplied by Michael Schmidt'.

EM had also sent a copy of his sonnet 'The Solway Canal', which was the first of what would ultimately be fifty one *Sonnets from Scotland*. Hamish Whyte suggested this might be first of a series of postcard sonnets, and this may have prompted further poems:

> When I wrote 'The Solway Canal' I had a vague idea of making it
> the first of a series, and when you made the same suggestion [. . .]
> this must have given the necessary external jog.[15]

EM sent a further six sonnets for *The Glasgow Magazine* (December 1982). 'The Solway Canal' was already destined for *Akros* 17:50 (October 1982). He had also begun to publish the 'Joints' in Robin Fulton's *Lines Review* (76, March 1981 and 81, June 1982). They were prefaced by a note from EM outlining their origin:

> Examples from a collection of joint poems [by EM and Michael
> Schmidt], quantitatively about ten per cent Michael Schmidt and
> ninety per cent EM. Michael Schmidt sent EM batches of what he
> called his gallstones or chips and shavings from the workshop floor
> – short fragments of a line or two from abandoned poems. EM
> then used these fragments as starting-points – oyster-grit – for
> new poems of his own, the original material being kept intact,
> though it might appear in any part of the poem.[16]

This is carefully phrased, echoing Michael Schmidt's estimation at an early stage, and factually true except as to the line lengths of these fragments. EM claimed to have got rid of his publisher's chips and shavings once he had remoulded them into something polished. But of course enough of them survive embedded in the letters from his publisher, which he had filed by date, to show that the authorial balance was slightly different. In a sample of seven of them from March and April 1972, the approximate percentages of lines from Michael Schmidt's originals within the final poems are 50% (twice), 33% (twice), 20% and 10% (twice).[17] So the attribution of relative effort might seem ungenerous, and less than symbiotic. The proportions may well have changed in some of the later poems, of course. EM had a problem with the give and take of poetic partnerships. From his own viewpoint, he took the useless 'grit' from another poet and turned it into pearls. Another way of looking at it is to say that Michael Schmidt seeded clouds that rained on Anniesland. A certain self-centredness is often a useful quality in a major artistic talent.

EM had fewer problems with ensemble working, as we have already seen. In early 1981 he was completing the libretto for the opera *Columba*, with music by Kenneth Leighton. It was performed in the Royal Scottish Academy of Music and Drama in June of that year and in Glasgow Cathedral in 1986.

His magpie tendencies, however, led him into legal problems with the 'Alphabet of Goddesses' sequence of poems. In September 1982 he visited an exhibition of twenty-six pastel drawings and accompanying notes by the Paisley artist, Pat Douthwaite, in the 369 Gallery in Edinburgh. Entitled 'Worshipped Women: An Alphabet of Goddesses', the series was inspired by Robert Graves' work on Greek mythology, and he had even written an Introduction to the exhibition catalogue.

EM was very excited by these drawings. The combination of art, ancient myth and alphabetic sequence stimulated him into a feverish burst of writing between the 6th and the 14th of September, as he described it to Hamish Whyte:

> The poems were written quickly and with considerable excitement in a week when by lucky chance I had no readings or other engagements and was completely free – a rare occurrence. One

poem seemed to lead on to another, although there are many differences in mood and style.[18]

As usual, he sent the poems off immediately to various poetry magazines, and they soon appeared in *New Edinburgh Review* 60 (December 1982), *Literary Review* 56 (February 1983), *Poetry Review* 73:1 (March 1983), *Strata* 1 (Easter 1983), *The Poet's Voice* 3 (July 1983) and *Labrys* 9 (November 1983), with others published in 1984. Although the first four of these publications include a dedication to Pat Douthwaite, and EM had already sent her £100 for the drawing of 'Rhea', she felt that he had infringed her joint copyright with Robert Graves. EM's fear of a legal action by the Graves family cost him some sleepless nights:

> I feel very unhappy and inhibited about the Goddesses, though I am sure they are good poems; relations with Pat Douthwaite could hardly be worse [. . .]. It is all very sad, especially as she is getting much free publicity from the fact that I always if I include some of the poems in a reading mention her name and describe how the sequence came to be written. I suppose the moral is that one should not dedicate poetry to someone one does not know.[19]

Her lawyers wrote to him listing the instances where phrasing in his poems paralleled the Graves catalogue. And the drawing of Rhea finally cost him more than the original £100 he had sent her. When he came to include the sequence in his *Selected Poems* from Carcanet (1985), Michael Schmidt made sure that EM had negotiated with the original artist's lawyers and the Graves family a suitably humble, explicit and quite lengthy form of words outlining the original inspiration of his 'Alphabet of Goddesses'. EM had also agreed to pay her a proportionate share of the royalties from the book, and duly signed and sent his cheques. Despite his high estimation of them in the months after their hectic composition, the poems have perhaps not stood the test of time. They do not appear in the *New Selected Poems* (2000).

EM had more positive relations with Laura Riding (Laura Riding Jackson as she is now styled) a writer whose connection with Robert Graves tends to obscure her originality and achievement. He had known and admired her poetry since before the war. It appeared in *The Faber Book of Modern Verse* (1936) which he read carefully at the time. The rhythms and imagery of her poems printed there, such as 'Lucrece and Nara' and 'The Wind, The Clock, The We', seem to resonate with his. She had a remarkably haunting style, both in verse and prose.

EM was in contact with her between 1977 and 1989. This arose firstly out of his work as External Examiner on a PhD thesis by Mark Jacobs at Leicester University. Laura Riding persuaded EM to write an affidavit for her to prevent publication of a book by T.S. Matthews that she thought libellous. In 1978 he recommended her for a fellowship of the National Endowment for the Arts, and he also persuaded Michael Schmidt to bring out her *Collected Poems* at Carcanet. She appeared in the first issue of *The Glasgow Magazine* in December 1982, as Hamish Whyte was also an admirer of her work.

The most important publication from Mariscat in the 1980s was EM's *Sonnets from Scotland* (1984). This sequence used his favourite device of the science fiction journey through time in order to view Scotland through history and in potential futures. In place of the customary events of Bannockburn, Flodden or the Act of Union, we find Pontius Pilate at Fortingall, Matthew Paris's early map, Poe, De Quincey and Hopkins in Glasgow, the Referendum, nuclear attack and a future Glasgow – Clydegrad. From Scotland, these sonnets move outwards to connect with European learning and world culture.

This imagined Scotland had a profound effect on younger writers such as the novelist James Robertson, since it countered the shame of a failed referendum with the possibilities of an imagined future republic, and a Solway Canal that has cut Scotland free at last. The space visitors also find a coin, with *One Pound* on one side and *Respublica Scotorum* on the other. Choosing 'The Coin' for a book of fifty favourite poems by Edwin

Morgan, *From Saturn to Glasgow* (2008), Robertson explained that for him this collection

> was a hugely uplifting read during a politically frustrating time. Morgan seemed to reinvent Scotland's past, present and future. In 'The Coin' space travellers find a coin, a relic from a country that once existed – Scotland, but not a Scotland that has ever yet been. The poem asks if this is a Scotland we can attain? How long will it last? But there is a great optimism in the last lines which still fills me with hope and pleasure whenever I read them.[20]

EM's characteristic sense of poetic optimism in the midst of political frustration reminds me of a comment he made to Julia Kada, a young academic and secretary of the Hungarian branch of PEN, who was his translator during his trip there in 1968. They had been to see a play and had then discussed modern drama, the theme of her doctoral thesis:

> She said, 'What is optimism today?' And I replied 'Optimism today is anything that is not complete pessimism.' She pondered this, accepted it, laughed as she began to think about it – .[21]

Alasdair Gray was very keen to design the cover for *Sonnets from Scotland*, and sent an early sketch of one featuring that same republican coin. Another creative response came from Martin Dalby, whose settings of five of the Sonnets were performed on 17 March 1986 in Aberdeen Chamber Music Club with later performances at the Queen's Hall, Edinburgh and the Sir Henry Wood Hall, Glasgow.

Sonnets from Scotland was thus significant for the standing both of the poet and of his new Scottish publisher. The other editor at Mariscat Press was Kevin McCarra. He and Whyte had met when he was working in the book shop at the Third Eye Centre. He had begun a PhD on the dramatist Sir David Lyndsay, and was also by 1986 planning to write an introduction to EM's work in the Scottish Writers Series from Scottish

Academic Press. Kenneth Buthlay's influential book on Hugh MacDiarmid had appeared in this series in 1982. Although the project did not materialise, some of the research contributed to McCarra's very fine opening chapter in *About Edwin Morgan* (1990): 'Edwin Morgan: Lives and Work'.

Kevin McCarra went on to become a journalist and contributing editor on the *Scottish Field* magazine, and then a noted football writer, currently for the *Guardian* newspaper. His description of EM's characteristic performance at a poetry reading seems absolutely accurate and right. Many will recognise it:

> Morgan is an unassuming, unshakeably polite man but, nonetheless, his ferocious devotion to the business of writing is apparent. Watch him reading to an audience and it is obvious that he is feeding on his own nervous energy; he is never quite still, his head bobbing to emphasise the urgent rhythms of his poetry. He looks, perhaps, ten–fifteen years younger than he is but his vigour, one guesses, owes less to stalwart genes than to his own desire to keep on writing. To be even better.[22]

Thousands will have encountered that shy yet humorous and urgent presence through the hundreds of poetry readings that he gave throughout the UK in the last decades of the 20th century. To take only the three months before and after Kevin McCarra's piece appeared in *Scottish Field* in July 1987, EM was reading in Bolton, Wigan, Leigh, and Dundee University (April); Manchester, Edinburgh, Oxford and Paisley (May); five different venues in Edinburgh (August); University of Stirling (September); Edinburgh University and the Glasgow Writer's Group (October); Blackburn Academy, then three readings in Edinburgh, and four readings in Portree on the Isle of Skye, including three at the High School (November). The list is not untypical, although schools are rather under-represented compared with normal. Of course, his pattern of activity was so varied that there was no obvious 'normal'. His stamina and physical energy were considerable, and seemed even to increase in old age once freed from the burdens of daily teaching. The balance of 'stalwart genes' and determination 'to keep on writing' was possibly more equal than Kevin McCarra thought. There was also the simple desire of the clever person, child or man, not to be bored. His Scrapbook project was early evidence of that.

Reading tours provided another way of meeting new people, or of catching up with old friends. Returning from Colchester in November 1982 by plane, he was seated next to Adam Ant, the rock star, who was on his way to play at the Apollo in Glasgow. EM seemed equally impressed by his striking appearance ('black leather trousers, studded belt, black – cloth, not leather – bomber jacket, notable gold earring on the left, short-nailed left hand and long-nailed right to show occupation, black ribbon in hair at back') and by the fact that he 'took out a Menzies pad and began writing, or rather re-writing from rough notes, an article on *Video from an artist's point of view*'.[23]

At another event in Bath late in 1985, he was reading with Iain Crichton Smith, who had earlier suffered a mental breakdown after coping with his mother-in-law's painful final illness. EM was able to talk with him about this, and be happy in his recovery. Meeting new poets at such events, EM could make a strong impression. In April 2008 he was surprised to receive a card from the poet Libby Houston, who had been with him on a Manchester-based reading tour in 1983, with day-time events in schools and public readings in the evenings. They had not been much in touch since then, apart from the occasional card, but she had recently read a newspaper article about him and remembered that his birthday was some time that month. So she wrote to thank him for 'what you have unwittingly taught me', as literary hero, model and touchstone.

She had first met him at one of the cellar readings in Edinburgh in 1961, and was a bit baffled by his kilted performance of poems about the Whittrick. But on the Manchester tour of 25–28 April 1983, they had stayed in the same boarding house, and would talk at breakfast, waiting for the organisers of each day's events to appear:

He brought me up short with many of the things he said, and the way he went about readings [. . .]. He had just received [the OBE] and it was outrageous to me that he was on a three-day 'mini-tour' with me, while Andrew Motion, I think, had a week solo in the same NW Arts programme. He came across to me as a great man – I think it is the only time I have ever felt I was in the presence of a Great Man![24]

She had remembered EM's birthday month because one morning at breakfast he had received a letter, opened it and said: 'Oh it's a birthday card, from my auntie'. Libby Houston who had a noted career as a performance poet, touring with the avant-garde band Earth House in the 1980s, couldn't imagine having such a quiet birthday.

He returned from this Manchester tour to *Noise and Smoky Breath* in Glasgow: Hamish Whyte's anthology was launched by EM at the Mitchell Library on the fifth of May. *Grafts/Takes* also appeared from Mariscat in 1983, containing the Instamatic poems, or Takes, in one direction and the 'joints' or Grafts in the other. Although most of these joint poems with Michael Schmidt had been completed between February and August 1972, there was a later return to the wood shavings in August and September 1979 ('Testament' and 'French'), then in December 1980 ('Heaven', 'Snorkelling' and 'Remora'), presumably to make up poems for a future collection.

There had been some early discussion about including the *Sonnets from Scotland* series in *Grafts/Takes* instead of one of the other elements, but EM sensed that there were more sonnets to come and wanted to hold them back for another volume. He was keen on the back-to-back format, as he had on his shelves an Ace Doubles paperback similarly printed, with *Junkie* by William Lee (aka William Burroughs) sitting with Maurice Helbrant's *Narcotic Agent*, between two equally lurid cover illustrations. *Grafts/Takes* has almost the same image on each side, with some slight variations: a stark and doubly intimidating portrait of EM by Alasdair Gray.

In February 1983 a batch of EM's Newspoems turned up. They had gone missing in Kirkcaldy Arts Centre a few years earlier, and now returned via Alan Bold via Carl MacDougall. Thus he had the complete set of about 130, and still thought this might make a decent book, for Mariscat or someone else, although belonging mainly to the past of the late sixties. 'If you had a book that opened *three* ways, it could be called Grafts/Takes/Treats (i.e. treated texts)' he suggested.[25]

After discussion with Michael Schmidt, EM offered *Sonnets from Scotland* to Mariscat as an interim publication that Carcanet could later use in a full collection. He suggested to Hamish Whyte in October 1983 that he was aiming for a total of fifty sonnets:

> I'm nudging forty at the moment, and have intimations and scents
> of more in the womb of thyme. If I think in terms of the round
> figure of fifty, I can work towards a whole.

In the end, there were fifty-one sonnets in total.

Responding to a request from EM, Hamish Whyte also made some proposals for the contents of the forthcoming *Selected Poems*. He suggested the 'Night Pillion' poem, which had gained a new lease of life from its publication in *Noise and Smoky Breath* (reprinted in August 1983, and again in 1984, 1986 and 1988). He also advised the whole of 'The New Divan', which did not make it into Carcanet's final selection, and the 'Alphabet of Goddesses' which did, along with such other uncollected poems as 'From the *Dictionary of Tea*' (1966), 'Cook in Hawaii' (1974) and 'The Break-In' (1982).

The tea poem was originally from *Poor.Old.Tired.Horse.*, and the Cook poem from the libretto of EM's music-theatre composition with George Newson, *Valentine*. The break-in poem describes a real event, with smashed glass and possibly virulent blood:

> I took a mop and swabbed the burglar's blood
> from windows, walls and floor. The spray and trail

> of arteries punctured by the shards of panes
> he had himself broken, entering, and was broken on
> leaving, spread down three stairs and made the block
> of flats a Hitchcock set [. . .].

(CP: 463)

This had, naturally enough, shocked and dismayed him, especially when he cut himself clearing up the blood-stained glass. He had written to me about it, and I replied offering to help in whatever way I could, though still living at a distance. In researching this book I was surprised to find a copy of the letter he sent back, and which I had forgotten:

> When you don't have any close relatives, as I don't, it's no doubt much better to make sure that your wishes are known [. . .]. While we are on this morbid subject, and especially since you ask if there is anything you can do – and I very much appreciate it – let me put you in the picture, not to burden you with any sense of obligation but simply to let you know what the arrangements are.[26]

He then outlined the details about his books going to the Mitchell Library and his papers to the University library, as well as contact details for his aunt and neighbours. Then he characteristically shrugs off the thought of death, in his dragon imagery, and looks to the future:

> Letting the black scaly wings clatter off beyond the horizon, I must get my thoughts in order for various impending readings: with Pierre Garnier the French spatialist at the Poetry Society in London on Thursday, an Abingdon (Oxford) schools audience on Friday, Bedford College on Tuesday and Wednesday.

This was an odd premonition of what my role in his later years would turn out to be. Presumably I was one among many people in different spheres of his life whom he 'did not like to let go'.

Facing up to the future 1980–1990

Neither did he like letting go of the ancient technology of pen and paper. Photocopiers and fax machines were all right, because they could replicate script, but computers remained suspect. EM had sat on the University's Computer Committee for some years before retirement, so he knew the theory and their potential. In the mid-eighties he read about the Amstrad and wondered whether he should buy one. The thought of not having various drafts of poems in the process of composition was something to grapple with, as was this:

A darker thought that haunts me is the possibility of something disappearing for ever (as apparently can happen!). Suppose you had just finished *Finnegans Wake* and could not retrieve it. The tail-end of the carbon age is full of imponderables.[27]

By March 1986 he had finally made up his mind and ordered one, partly on the recommendation of Cooper Hay, an antiquarian bookseller in Glasgow. He cleared the desk in his study and awaited its arrival, which was delayed by problems with stock and transportation. At last the Amstrad sat on his desk, in three parts plus an instruction manual. And there it sat for months, still in three bits, before finally being given away.

Television technology was more productive. In December 1984 he had bought a video recorder for Christmas. He had been considering this 'for a couple of years, ever since the break-in gave me second thoughts about portable re-sellable objects', but had now taken the plunge. His nucleus of a video-cassette collection, he told Hamish Whyte, was *That Sinking Feeling*, *Metropolis* by Fritz Lang, *Ian Hamilton Finlay*, and Andy Warhol's gay movie, *Lonesome Cowboys*. Several months later, Whittingehame Court was converted from VHF to UHF, so he was able to watch Channel 4 for the first time.

The new channel's 'vox-pop' use of a video box to record comment on programmes and current issues from the general public, which were then shown on the programme *Right to Reply*, soon stimulated ideas for a sequence of twenty-seven poems which used the same format. This became his next Mariscat pamphlet, *From the Video Box*, published in May 1986 in an edition of three hundred copies, with a cover design by David Neilson. It used the monologue form to explore the media age through viewer comment on imagined programmes representing modern compulsions, as well as the impact of televised spectacle on those who watch it. Disturbing, ribald, emotional, revelatory – the tone alters with the programme and the person. This is instamatic technique remade for the video age:

> If you ask what my favourite programme is
> it has to be that strange world jigsaw final.
> After the winner had defeated all his rivals
> with harder and harder jigsaws, he had to prove his mettle
> by completing one last absolute mindcrusher
> on his own, under the cameras, in less than a week.
> We saw, but he did not, what the picture would be:
> the mid-Atlantic, photographed from a plane,
> as featureless a stretch as could be found [. . .].

(CP: 497–8)

From the Video Box and *Sonnets from Scotland* would both feature in EM's next collection from Carcanet, which was *Themes on a Variation* (1988). The final Mariscat publication of the 1980s appeared in the same year, *Tales from Limerick Zoo*. The sadder story behind this light alphabetic series of limericks on creatures from Amoeba and Anaconda through to Zebra and Zebu, was that EM's aunt had become slightly confused in old age, and began to accuse her nephew of stealing from her flat. A clock had gone missing – she had forgotten that it had been sent for repair – but the accusations upset EM so much that he began composing the limericks to keep his mind occupied and calm.

Through its blend of Glaswegian connections, regular and stylish publication, and congenial focus on new and unpublished work, Mariscat Press perhaps provided a similar role for him, both calming and creative, through the 1980s and beyond. Its book launches also kept him in regular touch with his Scottish readership, and they with him, so that a sense of commitment and response to their concerns was firmly established. This would not have been so possible had his poetry been published by Carcanet alone. It was the combination that worked.

THE CARCANET CONTINUATION

Carcanet's publication of *Poems of Thirty Years* in August 1982 was a major event for EM and for Scottish writing too, judging from the number and tone of the reviews. Michael Schmidt had asked him to think about a Collected Poems, possibly the work of six decades, in May 1980. By July of the following year the Scottish Arts Council had offered a grant of £950 towards production costs for such a major undertaking.

EM worked closely with his editor in selecting the material, and made a case for including the whole of *The Vision of Cathkin Braes* (1952), along with the *Dies Irae* that had remained unpublished by Lotus Press in 1951. These were to have been the tragic and comic masks of his early work. He also suggested 'Cinquevalli' and 'Jack London in Heaven', both written in 1980, as strong poems with which to end the collection. It was dedicated 'In Memory of John G. Scott (1918–1978)'.

Production at Carcanet was brought to a halt in the summer of 1981 by a Civil Service strike which withheld £6000 worth of Value Added Tax, essentially the publisher's working capital. So *Poems of Thirty Years* was rescheduled until January or February 1982. Still struggling to reduce stock and warehouse charges, Michael Schmidt offered EM some of the remaining 390 hard cover copies of *The New Divan*, 200 copies of *Essays* and 140 copies of *Rites of Passage*, both paper and hard back at twenty pence per copy. But the poet said he had no space to store more books.

Michael Schmidt invited him down to his family home in Cheadle over the Christmas period so that they could discuss the final form of the collection. EM did not take up the invitation, but

289

finally decided to travel around 12 January 1982 so that he could combine this editorial discussion with a reading to students in Manchester.

Carcanet had hired a publicity firm to co-ordinate sales and events, and they wrote to him for his upcoming public commitments, in order to avoid any clash. Excluding schools, he listed the Mayakovsky seminar at the Museum of Modern Art, Oxford, an Open University lecture and reading at their Aberdeen Day School, and a weekend poetry course at Newbattle Abbey College in March; a Leeds University conference on James Joyce, where he was to read a paper on 'James Joyce and Hugh MacDiarmid', and a reading at Forfar Arts Guild in April; a reading at the Oriel Theatre in Clwyd as part of their *Seven Poets* exhibition in May; a reading at Kirkcudbright as part of Dumfries and Galloway Arts Festival in June; and the opening night of *The Apple Tree*, prior to its Edinburgh Festival production, in August.

Carcanet also asked him for a mailing list of people who might pre-order or, better still, pre-pay to help with production costs. He sent a very long list, which helped to generate three hundred subscriptions for the book. Michael Schmidt thought it might be necessary to reprint before the end of the year. EM liked the eye-catching deep blue and turquoise cover of *Poems of Thirty Years*: 'Does the colour represent both the sea and the depths of space?' he wondered. As so often, EM noted 'a sprinkling of misprints', but his publisher felt these could be caught in the reprint. He was 'ecstatic' about the reviews coming in, but had underestimated the production costs in relation to pricing (£9.95 in my copy of August 1982), and reckoned he would need to sell eight hundred copies just to break even. But the book was selling remarkably well, and he thought he could raise the price to £12 or so when reprinting in the New Year.

Poems of Thirty Years won the Royal Bank/Saltire Society Book of the Year Award, sharing this recognition with Derick Thomson's collection: *Creachadh na Clarsach | Plundering the Harp*. He was Professor of Celtic at Glasgow University, a significant presence in Gaelic academic and cultural studies as well as poetry, and came originally from Upper Bayble, where Iain Crichton Smith was also brought up.

EM followed the reviews carefully. He found Alan Bold's in the *Scotsman* 'a poorish effort', but praised the positive profile-cum-interview by Raymond Ross in the journal *Cencrastus*. He sent Michael Schmidt a copy, as well as an extended quote from Peter Scott's review in *Gay News*, which named him as the next great Scottish poet, on a level with Burns and MacDiarmid, because of his multiplicity of voices and perspectives combined with a clear, accessible social conscience that was always open to new horizons.

Problems with reprinting coincided with a withdrawal of the first edition from the suppliers, unfortunately, and this meant that copies of the collection were hard to find in bookshops at the time of the award. He sent a tetchy letter to his publisher, who thought his complaint 'possibly in excess of the occasion'. They were already in discussion, however, about future volumes. EM had sent him 'Alphabet of Goddesses', which was felt to be too short to make a separate collection. However, Michael Schmidt suggested both a compendium of EM's Scottish criticism, prob-ably a mix of older and new material, and a *Selected Poems*. The first suggestion would eventually emerge as *Crossing the Border* (1990), but *Selected Poems* was launched as intended in 1985.

EM's irritation over Carcanet's production capabilities grumbled on. His publisher hoped that one little incident would not cause long-term damage to a fruitful relationship. He wrote in early January 1984 that Davie and Sisson were stepping down as editors of *Poetry Nation Review*, and hoped that this would make it possible at last for EM to contribute to its pages, especially as he planned a large supplement on Glasgow poetry. But there appears to have been no positive response to this. EM could be difficult to shift in his opinions: 'thrawn' is the Scots word for it.

Plans for *Selected Poems* developed. Michael Schmidt envi-saged this as the first of a series of extended paperbacks of about 144 pages, in large format with an essay by the poet introducing his own work and an accompanying cassette of readings and an interview. Iain Crichton Smith, who had changed publisher from Victor Gollancz to Carcanet with *The Exiles* in 1984 and *Selected Poems* in 1985, was next in line for the recording process. The series was partly aimed at the schools market and this to some extent affected the contents. Hamish Whyte suggested that the 'Stobhill' sequence with its emotional drama of characters involved in an abortion (CP: 284–8) might be replaced by the 'Unfinished Poems' from *The New Divan*. But this was rejected: accessibility to a young audience was a key factor.

The readings and interview for the accompanying cassette were recorded in a Watford studio at the beginning of January 1985, with Michael Schmidt conducting the interview. He was also casting around for a clear black and white image to be placed within a central circle on the cover. EM himself drew a tower crane that might suggest 'the urban theme, the actual tower cranes of *The Second Life*, the themes of construction and renewal'. He also wrote the blurb for the back cover, which ended with this summing up of his own poetic scope:

> The hopes and fears of a concern for man's fate, and a belief in its huge potential for change and renewal, give unity to these vigorously diverse creations.

Michael Schmidt liked the drawing very much, and also the fact that the advance subscriptions indicated they might sell one thousand or more copies even before publication. The bad news was that Carcanet's book distributors had gone bankrupt, owing three months in arrears. The cash-flow problem now meant that EM was asked to be patient about his royalties, which would be delayed for two months.

Nothing much could be done about this – nor about the four misprints he had noticed in the book. Michael Schmidt had already distributed three thousand copies, but said he would pick up the errors in the next edition, which might well be needed within eight to ten months. At this stage he was acting as sales manager, managing editor and production editor. A staff member who was organising the reading and promotional tour had suddenly moved, leaving everything in disarray – including the launch in Glasgow at John Smith's bookshop, which had to be cancelled at the last moment.

By midsummer, EM had cooled down sufficiently to supply Michael Schmidt with another astonishing list of academic and literary contacts to approach with publicity material. He also wondered by the autumn of 1985 whether Carcanet could publish his play *Columba*. With fifty items already scheduled for the following year, they could not, but Michael Schmidt did give him a contact to approach at Methuen. By the following year, poet and publisher were working together on the new essays on Scottish literature.

Both men also felt that a new collection of poems was due. Michael Schmidt admired the 'thrifty and tasteful' Mariscat productions, their typesetting, quality of paper and design, but his understanding was that these would feed into later and larger Carcanet collections. Both *From the Video Box* and *Sonnets from Scotland* were thus to appear in *Themes on a Variation*. The publisher was surprised, therefore, to receive Mariscat's request for £300 for copyright for the Sonnets and told EM that normally this sort of expense would be deducted from the author's royalties. In fact, EM had earlier signed a contract with Mariscat giving them publication rights, although Schmidt had not known this. Some quick re-negotiation took place, I believe, and a slightly lower figure was arrived at.

Themes on a Variation combined this recent work from Mariscat with a selection from *Newspoems* (1965–1971) and more recent poems, including some generally unhappy love poetry about M.T., the man to whom the collection is dedicated. Malcolm had met EM in 1986 just after the publication of *From the Video Box* in May of that year. He had been attending a Writers' Group run by the Glaswegian writer, Peter Kearney, who gave him EM's address. He sent a sample of stories, and was invited to Whittingehame Court to talk about them. Malcolm had a gay partner at this time, and as his relationship with EM developed there was an understandable degree of antagonism. Invited to a fortieth birthday event for Hamish Whyte, EM wanted to bring Malcolm:

> but that depends on *his* partner (a bit like G[raham] Greene, *May we borrow your husband*), at the moment my ration is one evening a week plus the very occasional weekend.[28]

Malcolm's first meeting with Hamish Whyte was disconcerting. He found him on EM's bedroom floor, surrounded by books and magazines, which he was cataloguing for the still expanding bibliography of EM's publications. There were books in every room of the flat except the kitchen and bathroom, with the long L-shaped hall being particularly useful. Some of the fitted wardrobes in the main bedroom were also needed to house books (contemporary Scottish writing and drama, I think), and poetry journals were stacked in shelves below the bedroom window.

Several times a year, EM would also select out books he no longer wished or needed to keep, and Hamish Whyte would arrive with his family and enough plastic bags to carry these to the Mitchell. He was in the process of building up there 'a poet's working library' which would eventually number some thirteen thousand books – all read, many annotated. At this first meeting on the bedroom floor, it may be that EM was deliberately bringing different aspects of his life together in order to watch the effect, as he had done earlier with me and John Scott.

Malcolm continued his friendship with EM into his final period in the nursing home, the 'most faithful' of friends. A care worker from the East End with a genuine humility and a commitment to living a 'poor' life, untarnished by money, he had gained a university degree and read as widely as possible, and so he was a kindly and interesting person to meet. But the conflicted early stages of the relationship as it developed through their first dark November and winter create a sombre mood in 'Stanzas', 'Waking on a Dark Morning' and 'Dear man, my love goes out in waves' near the start of this collection.

EM struggled a little with its overall structure, but finally took Michael Schmidt's advice:

> I had doubts about the alteration of personal and non-personal poems at the beginning, but on mulling and meditating I can see the point of what you call 'an interesting lead-in', so let us leave it.[29]

I think his editor was struggling to create a 'rhythm' for the readers of this book. It is one of EM's most diverse collections, where recent sonnets and 'reconstructions' of classic poems sit alongside the older off-concrete material of the Newspoems. Variation does seem to be the theme.

Production was less variable, however, as it was seen through the press by Robyn Marsack. She was a young New Zealand academic who combined a deep knowledge and love of poetry with an accurate editorial eye and organisational skill. She soon moved to Glasgow, and would ultimately become Director of the Scottish Poetry Library. She suggested that the book be launched in the People's Palace museum on Glasgow Green, and that it should coincide with the Mayfest city-wide arts event of 1988.

By December of the same year, EM was trying to interest Michael Schmidt in publishing the Scrapbooks. Arrangements had already been made to archive some of his papers in Glasgow University Library. He knew the Librarian, Henry Heaney, who in February 1988 had gone to London with him to advise on some Trocchi material that had become available. Before the sixteen Scrapbooks left the flat, he took photographs of enough of their 3600 or so pages to give his publisher an idea of the scope of this 'mixture of autobiography, documentary and art [. . .] I regard them very much as part of my works'. He claimed to have kept them going, on a reduced scale, during the war 'so that there is no break from 1931 to 1966'.[30]

Of course, this was all too hugely expensive, especially as colour printing and copyright permissions would be needed. The later Scrapbooks also lack the aesthetic and satirical qualities of the earlier ones. While a documentary focus remains on scientific events such as space exploration, and on cultural variety with a focus on human sexuality, the autobiographical elements remain obscure. An enthusiasm for kilted soldiers and for early Cliff Richard and Elvis Presley is persistent, but not enlightening. Michael Schmidt speculated politely about taking the war material alone, perhaps to be used as the basis of a documentary autobiography. But a more immediate and feasible task was to think of a new *Collected Poems*, aimed roughly for EM's seventieth year in 1990. EM approved this idea, and added another suggestion by January 1989: 'Philip Hobsbaum and others have urged, why don't I bring out a *Collected Translations*, either for 1990 or for your later suggested series of *Works*'.

The book of essays on Scottish literature was worked on in the first half of that year. He had no title for it, and I suggested *Crossing the Border*: *Essays on Scottish Literature*, among other more facetious ones, which he and his publisher both liked. This was published in 1990, as were *About Edwin Morgan*, which Hamish Whyte co-edited with Robert Crawford, and *Nothing Not Giving Messages*, which he edited alone. Michael Schmidt thought both of those EUP volumes most attractive, but told EM he was 'more excited by your prose book than by the book of prose about you: you are a very wonderful essayist'.

The relationship between publisher and poet is always an interesting tightrope-walk between commerce and creativity. Although EM never succumbed to what Norman Mailer once described as 'the terminal animosity of the Senior Citizen', he could be impatient or demanding where his own publication and reputation were concerned. Occasionally, as with the Scrapbooks' intrinsic worth, he could lose a sense of judgment. This led on occasion to strains in the relationship with Michael Schmidt, but never terminally. The publisher's optimism and energy seemed to create a force-shield against outrageous fortune. Somehow things worked out.

To meet one of the crises of the 1970s, he had been forced to raise money on his Carcanet archive, which was now in the John

Rylands Library in Manchester University. To celebrate twenty years of the press in 1989, it was decided to revisit this archive for *Letters to an Editor*, a volume of correspondence between Schmidt and his authors. It was edited by Mark Fisher, who wanted to use some of the correspondence around EM's differences with his publisher over *Poetry Nation*. EM agreed, suggesting only one excision of an unclear reference. He found it strange to read these again, particularly one written on hotel notepaper from Dublin, of which he had kept no copy. Despite antagonism over poetic and actual politics, the selected letters also referred to the more positive counterbalance of their joint 'Grafts' in the early days:

> we could challenge the critics to say where the join showed. (The book could be called *The Dove's Tail*.)

INFORMATIONISTS AND OTHERS

In 'Stanzas', describing his feelings for Malcolm, EM refers to the age difference between them:

> I was thirty-eight when you were born.
> You think I want a son? Of course I do –
> or daughter – but that's not it,
> not it at all. I'd rather have your scorn
> than you should never know what runs me through.
>
> (CP: 508)

In his other life as a writer, he was also gathering around himself a brood of young Scottish poets, most of whom were born within the same late 1950s to early 1960s period: Peter McCarey (b. 1956), Alan Riach (b. 1957), Robert Crawford (b. 1959), David Kinloch (b. 1959), W.N. Herbert (b. 1961), and Richard Price (b. 1966). The first and last named in this list were to remain the most esteemed by EM in old age, because most avant-garde, and I will therefore concentrate more on his contacts with those two here.

297

Richard Price invented the term by which this group became known, the Informationists. He was so excited at finding a word to encapsulate what he saw as their shared focus – the poetic exploration of the contemporary impact of information on minds, relationships and culture, at local as well as global levels – that he telephoned EM immediately to tell him. To that list could be added two poets who had clear connections with the Informationists through friendship, shared attitudes or interest in certain poetic techniques: Donny O'Rourke and Iain Bamforth, both also born in 1959.

The ages of most of these poets mirrored Malcolm's. More important was the way in which each of them took forward, and indeed extended, an aspect of EM's variousness. Basil Bunting once compared Ezra Pound to the renaissance poet Edmund Spenser, in that both these men left an 'encyclopaedia of possibilities' for other poets to develop. EM's poetry is a similar treasure-house of strategies and themes. For example, Robert Crawford's poetry explores the impact of scientific invention, as EM's does, and of a Scottish engagement with eclectic knowledge. Herbert pushes forward the use of demotic urban Scots (Dundonian, in his case) as a poetic vehicle for both anarchic humour and cultural commentary. Richard Price's lyrical poetry mixes avant-garde experimentation with a deconstruction of language and intimate relationships. Peter McCarey blends professional skills as a translator of Russian and French with experimental verse forms and serious engagement with global issues. David Kinloch extends EM's involvement with French literature and translation, as well as developing Scots language as a means of exploring gay experience.

Beyond Europe, Alan Riach explores the open forms of American poetry as well as the perspectives on Scotland that wide travel can bring. Donny O'Rourke also responds to the style and urbanity of the New York School of poets, and has a professional film-maker's eye for telling visual detail. Iain Bamforth has a multiplicity of interests – in medicine, science, philosophy, religion and central European culture – and uses poetry as a means of bringing together such contrasting human realms of knowledge and identity.

EM taught most of these poets at undergraduate or postgraduate level, and supported all of them as a mentor, generous correspondent, writer of references for jobs or fellowships, and endless encourager of experiment, effort and optimism. He had himself lived through a long and frustrating apprenticeship where recognition and publication were difficult to achieve. So he would support these young poets with advice on possible publishing outlets, with names of new authors to read and react to, with poems or reviews for the new poetry magazines they were trying to get off the ground, and even with each other's names and addresses, as like-minded writers worth knowing. Whittingehame Court was a sort of cultural sorting office, with mail arriving and being posted out on a daily basis.

Of course, these were all intelligent and hard-working people in their own right, and would have succeeded in some way or other. They went on to gain academic titles, postgraduate and honorary degrees, fellowships and leadership roles in literary studies, creative writing, translation and interpretation, media, medicine, editing and anthologising. But their lives would have been different without EM. And so, too, the lives of other writers whose work they have gone on to support in their turn.

Almost all of these poets remained in contact with EM into old age, although their own family and work commitments, as well as distance in England or Europe, prevented this in some cases as the years went by. In the 1980s, their interaction with each other's work was just beginning. A glance at their Publications lists in Donny O'Rourke's anthology *Dream State: The New Scottish Poets* (Second Edition, 2002) will reveal how frequently they co-edited, co-wrote, co-founded, co-published.

The collateral damage of their occasional fallings-out on literary or other matters is not evident from the official record. EM was mainly a sounding-board for their artistic ideas, but occasionally served as a sounding-off board. His advice in the letters he wrote back was mature and reasoned – fatherly, in a way, although as much elder-brotherly in its irony and wit. These younger poets kept the old man on his mettle.

If each of the Informationists is reminiscent of a different aspect of their mentor, Crawford was perhaps most recognisably like the younger EM. Academically bright and very ambitious, he came from a similar family background and secondary education. He grew up in Cambuslang, just beyond Rutherglen. His interest in knowledge and how it could be used poetically led EM to reflect in 1986 on his own young self:

> I loved encyclopaedias and dictionaries from my earliest reading days: I still have on my shelves, as a school prize for English, fourth form, session 1935–36, chosen by myself, Frazer's *Golden Bough* (the one-volume edition) which I remember gave me endless fascination [. . .].[31]

Academically, EM thought that he was one of the best undergraduates he had taught, and he went on to Balliol College, Oxford, to complete doctoral studies on Modern Poetry and the City. This was the same postgraduate scholarship that EM had been unwilling to take up in the late 1940s, and he was slightly worried about the possible impact of Oxford on his former student's poetry. EM encouraged him particularly in his more experimental work, and the juxtaposition of unusual facts and jargons:

> Although I think you have a good command of the shortish blank verse [. . .] meditational poem, it may well be that collage techniques will prove a useful way of dealing with the layerings and parallels and contrasts of history and geography that attract you. I'm glad to see from a few of the poems that you have not given up the use of scientific vocabulary.[32]

This was on 4 February 1985. EM need not have worried about Crawford's commitment to broader approaches to poetry. With a fellow Oxford doctoral student from the same cohort in the

University of Glasgow, David Kinloch, he had already begun to co-edit *Verse*. This would become a significant and influential journal for Scottish poetry in the 1990s. Kinloch's first degree was in French and English Literature, so an international perspective and interest in poetic translation was evident from the start.

David Kinloch's major poetic development was the discovery of Scots as a new means of expression for suppressed language – in particular of gay speech that was then coping with the devastation of Aids. His character 'Dustie-Fute', from an old Scots word for a troubadour, juggler or merchant, became a metaphor for a boisterous self-expression in defiance of death. In a sense, this ability to expand the range of Scots language was part of Kinloch's own inheritance, since William Jeffrey (1896–1946), a follower but also an extender of MacDiarmid's renaissance of Scots language poetry, was his grandfather.

MacDiarmid was also a unifying presence among the Informationists. In particular they extended his later 'poetry of fact', which EM had long championed. W.N. Herbert had gone straight from secondary school in Dundee to Brasenose College, Oxford, and then began a doctorate on MacDiarmid's poetry. This was the first doctoral work on MacDiarmid's poetry in Oxford University and EM was External Examiner for the thesis.

Alan Riach completed his PhD on MacDiarmid in Glasgow in the mid-1980s, and then took up a research and teaching fellowship in the University of Waikato in New Zealand, where EM's former colleague Marshall Walker had become Professor of English in 1981. Riach would return to New Zealand at the end of the decade for a full-time post there.

Approaching his own retirement, EM had asked Marshall Walker to be his literary executor, and had insisted that his friend's imminent departure to take up the professorship in New Zealand would make no difference. They would catch up whenever he returned on research leave or on holiday, and together they began to construct a timeline of key events that might underpin future research on EM's life and work. But Marshall became aware of the need for a 'safety-net' of other younger supporters, and eventually persuaded EM to invite Hamish Whyte and Kevin McCarra to become co-executors. Thus Mariscat became even more closely involved with EM's creative legacy.

EM's academic work continued beyond his set date of retirement, however. In 1978, two years earlier, he had taken on the supervision of Peter McCarey's Masters thesis, a comparison of twentieth-century Scottish and Russian poets with special reference to MacDiarmid, Blok, Mayakovsky and Esenin. He then continued with doctoral studies beyond 1980. Born in Paisley but educated in Glasgow, McCarey had gone to University College, Oxford for a first degree in Russian and French. He was fortunate to find in EM a supervisor who could answer his questions on the extent of MacDiarmid's actual knowledge of Russian, or on his use of Solovyov's philosophy, or on the relationship between poetry and propaganda, or on his sources in Scottish history and mythology. EM's depth of knowledge of original texts and of critical pathways to follow is impressive in some of the early letters to McCarey: if he didn't know the actual source, he knew just where his student should look to find it.

Peter McCarey's research involved travel in Russia for access to key libraries there, with EM supporting his application for a British Council Studentship. Letters sent back to Anniesland must have recalled his supervisor's own earlier experience of Soviet Russia and its paradoxes. EM was able to discuss his feelings about Albania too, on his return in October 1988. He had gone there, he said, with the negative expectations aroused by Yevtushenko's poetry, but

I now see that from the Albanian point of view [Yevtushenko] is just another Great-Power communist who can't stand small nations [. . .]. For 'the most backward country in Europe' etc. etc., the people were relaxed, friendly and curious.

EM enjoyed the early autumn heat, and seeing the men in shirtsleeves who linked arms and kissed on meeting, like Italians. Generally he gained the impression that

> It is possible to break with both America and Russia and yet make a go of it. The water might go off suddenly in the hotel when everyone is washing at the same time, and there were classically no [bath] plugs, but somehow it didn't seem all that important. Tirana, no bigger than Aberdeen, has classical ballet, symphony orchestra and film industry, though no private cars and no fifty-seven varieties of ketchup.[33]

EM tended to dislike co-writing as we have seen, but was intrigued in 1987 by Peter McCarey's 'rehabs' or rehabilitations of familiar classic poems by Pope, Byron, Shakespeare, Tennyson and Milton. He 'countered' these with his own versions or 'reconstructions', as he says in the Acknowledgements to *Themes on a Variation*. The whole sequence was published in *Verse* 4.2. He admired a man whose Russian and French were better than his own – and who would be able to offer a critique of 'Edwin Morgan the Translator' in *About Edwin Morgan* (1990: 90–104).

Peter McCarey wrote this out of his multi-lingual experience in the World Health Organisation, based in Geneva, where he would eventually become Head of Translation and Interpretation. His work there clearly involves politics, as well as travel in sub-Saharan Africa, south India and south-east Asia. This affected his poetry: his first collection was called *Town Shanties* (Broch Books, 1991). There is an acerbic, moral quality to his work that works against the 'ludic' or carelessly playful exploration of social issues by postmodern artists, who can sometimes seem to veer towards exploitation. On the other hand, his Syllabary sequence of poems based on all the possible single-syllable words in English is deliberately experimental, somewhat in the mode of the mainly French Oulipo writers, who constrain and challenge their own skills by forbidding, for example, the use of certain letters in a text.

Others of McCarey's small collections were published in 1995 and 2000 by Vennel Press, which was founded by Richard Price and Leona Medlin in 1990. Born in 1966, Price was younger than the rest of the Informationist group that he had labelled, and his educational history was different too. He had left school at sixteen, trained as a journalist, then enrolled for a joint Honours course in English and Librarianship in the University of Strathclyde in Glasgow. He already had a liking for both the variety and the useful cataloguing of knowledge.

EM came to give a series of four lectures on Modern Scottish Poetry at Strathclyde University in the week beginning 7 March 1988. This was in Price's final year, and he had already begun to win student poetry prizes. His initial reservations about the 'real' professor coming down from the 'real' University to speak to students in the technological university soon disappeared. In fact, where else should EM's poetry have been more at home?

As part of this series of lectures, there was also the opportunity for students to take their own poetry along for separate tutorials. EM retained his notes from that first meeting: 'clearly intelligent and with a good combination of visual sense and social comment . . . Poems don't always cohere'.[34] But talent was clearly there. In the week of his graduation he had a full page spread of poems in the *Glasgow Herald* as winner of the Glasgow and Strathclyde Student Writing competition, sponsored by Scottish Television. Unable to find work in Scotland, he went to London and began as a Cataloguer with the British Library. He would become its Head of Modern British Collections, and then Head of Content and Research Strategy by his early forties.

That was in the future. In the late 1980s EM would correspond with him regularly, and meet for a meal whenever Price was back in Glasgow. The sustained human communication mattered to both. There was an element of chatter, as both shared an enthusiasm for space exploration, fast flight and grand engineering projects. The younger poet was introduced to new movements in poetry, such as the 'Cambridge' poetry that included the difficult work of J.H. Prynne, and the Language poets, but

EM was also intrigued enough by Price's descriptions of the impact of Bob Dylan's songs to buy recent CDs and listen again to his work. His own enthusiasm for The Beatles in the 1960s meant that other music had passed him by.

Richard Price came to know Robert Crawford and W.N. Herbert, he recalls, through readings at Babbity Bowster's restaurant bar in Glasgow's Merchant City. These were organised by Donny O'Rourke, who was, and remains, a great enabler of new Scottish writing. He was at that time a producer and director with Scottish Television, having worked for BBC Scotland in mid-decade. He would go on to become Head of Arts and Documentaries at Scottish Television, and these responsibilities, among many other duties, included a film they were making about EM and the contexts of his poetry.

Involvement in the film-making process was highly interesting to EM, who loved cinema even more than theatre. He was also struck by the public reaction to its screening, and by the usefulness of publicity in the media. This he would employ increasingly in his later years. He told O'Rourke:

> I've had a lot of reaction to our programme, all of it favourable, though one or two thought my life 'fairly whizzed past' and would have liked a longer programme. On the phone to my milkman, I got his wife instead, and she said 'Are you the Morgan that was on TV?' – she thought it was great.[35]

EM thought it was a pity that there had been no time to comment on some of the still photographs which had been used in the film, and that 'in the Scrapbook scenes we rather lost the point of the gay "pin-ups" (I remember you used the word)'. But he was particularly pleased with the desert war scenes:

> It was a brilliant shot to move from my Cosgrove poem to the soldier with the cigarette – oddly enough he was not unlike Cosgrove, with the gallus quality that has always attracted me.

305

Donny O'Rourke eventually left his television career, becoming Scottish Arts Council Fellow in Creative Writing in the universities of Glasgow and Strathclyde in the mid-1990s, as well as teaching in the School of Art. His poetry was published by Polygon, and later by Mariscat and Richard Price's Vennel Press. Price had begun *Gairfish* magazine in 1989 with W.N. Herbert, and later founded *Southfields* magazine, which he co-edited with David Kinloch and Raymond Friel. In 1994 *Contraflow on the Super Highway*, an Informationist primer of the work and ideas of this group, was jointly edited by Price and Herbert, and demonstrated their creative engagement with language, ideas, science and culture.

A poet who did not fit easily into this networking development of a movement, but seems intellectually akin to it, was Iain Bamforth. His medical work took him to rural Scotland, the Australian outback and Central Europe, but his contact with EM, occasional but steady across the years, was significant for both. He had first contacted him in 1979, in his final year as a medical student in Glasgow University, with poems for comment. His interests were wide. He liked the pure sciences, languages, music, metaphysics, Paul Valéry, 'long-forgotten cultures and the slowly receding ideal of the Renaissance man', as he informed his mentor. EM sponsored him for a Scottish Arts Council grant in 1982, citing the young poet's 'remarkable maturity and self-definition [. . .] at a time of much specialization it would be good to give encouragement to someone who ranges over such a wide field, in such an interesting and probing way, as he does'.[36]

Iain Bamforth wrote to EM in April 1990 from West Germany, where he was working as a doctor and also travelling in 'Mitteleuropa', encountering EM's work in translation in almost every bookshop in Budapest. He would be on his way shortly to work as Medical Officer in Broken Hill in New South Wales, but wanted to wish him a happy 70th birthday before departure. He reflected on the 'unfathomable' way that EM presented himself as a modest tenant of his own poetic house, and yet how this lack of arrogance made him not only approachable but also inspirational

306

for younger poets. He and EM would correspond only intermittently during the following decade, but each time took up the
relationship after a gap of years as if it had remained a continuing
conversation of individuals who realised they were essentially
like-minded in their fascination with language, cultures and
knowledge.

OLDER GENERATIONS

EM also kept his connections open with other generations of
writers. He remained close to Gael Turnbull, another medical
man, now back in England and 'doctoring' in Malvern near
Worcester. Like the younger poets, he sometimes yearned for
a move to a Creative Writing post, and asked EM's advice about
this in early 1981. Turnbull found *Sonnets from Scotland* both
liberating and also stimulating in the ways it made him think
about his Scottish identity and language. Born in Edinburgh but
much travelled, he had come to feel that his native language and
diction had been fragmented, and to long for a move northwards
again.

Gael Turnbull was constantly experimental. In the early
summer of 1987, he was working on a 'combined text', a
composition that could be read in different ways, as two poems
or a single one. He and EM also worked together on a science
fiction prose piece called 'The Eye Opener'. It began with the
protagonist coming to a locked door. The plot then proceeded by
Turnbull writing and sending a section, leaving an empty space
for EM to complete and post back to him. He also provided ideas
for poems. An article he cut out from the *Local Government
Chronicle* of 10 January 1986 contained a spoof 'Report on Dwarf
Throwing'. In EM's hands this soon became 'Rules for Dwarf
Throwing', dated 1986 (CP: 531–2).

During the 1980s, too, EM kept in touch with poets of the
immediate pre-Informationist generation such as Alan Spence,
Ron Butlin and Andrew Greig, all of whom he had first supported
in the 1970s. He had been aware of Alan Spence since the late

1960s, in fact, when he submitted poems for *Scottish Poetry 5* (1969) and was involved with the 'Other People' group of performance poets with Tom McGrath, Anne Thomson and others. Tom Leonard and EM also participated in readings with the group at the Edinburgh Festival. In 1971, Alan Spence asked EM to sponsor him for an Arts Council grant to complete the collection of short stories that would become *Its Colours They Are Fine* (1977). Two had already been published in *Scottish International* 8 and 11. In 1975 with Stewart Conn and Tom McGrath, EM supported Alan Spence's application for the Creative Writing Fellowship at Glasgow University. Although he could never share the younger man's enthusiasm for Buddhism, EM had no doubts about Spence's creative talents. All of these writers had begun from poetry but then extended into prose and, in Alan Spence's case, drama.

EM had known Ron Butlin since September 1973. He had included one of his poems in a student verse programme, and Butlin then asked him for further guidance on other poems. EM provided a quote for the back of an early pamphlet collection, and sponsored him for a Scottish Arts Council bursary. In 1979 Edinburgh University Press Student Publication Board published *Creatures Tamed by Cruelty*, with an Introduction by EM. He liked the young writer's subtle psychological analysis both in prose and poetry and followed his progress with great interest.

With Andrew Greig, it was the breadth of his interests and experience, from philosophy to mountaineering, that EM admired and also the verve with which he was willing to tackle large subjects as well as high peaks. He had positively reviewed his *Men on Ice* (1977), in which a trio of climbers is caught in a crisis situation at 20,000 feet, and we recall that he had always taken vicarious pleasure in the beauty and terror of snowcapped mountain landscapes. EM sponsored him for the Scottish Canadian Writers Fellowship in 1979, and then for the Glasgow University Creative Writing fellowship later that year. In the mid-80s, Greig was a member of a Scottish team whose assault on the summit of Mount Everest was only beaten back by weather so bad that their oxygen tanks froze. He described the experience to EM shortly afterwards, in an airmail from Tibet written within sight of mountain and glacier.

Were there no women poets as friends? The impression is clearly one of male circles, but EM also got on very well with women writers. Jackie Kay was someone whose writing and personality he enjoyed in equal measure. He shared reading tours and platforms with Liz Lochhead at this time, and liked her use of the dramatic monologue in poetry that would eventually lead her into fuller engagement with theatre.

Both she and EM were part of a delegation of Glasgow writers to Berlin on 1–7 December 1988, with Adam McNaughton and Stephen Mulrine among others. Berlin was that year's European City of Culture, and Glasgow was soon to take on that title, so it was thought to be a useful link. EM was not really fond of such official visits but found the city worth seeing, and the readings and discussions with writers in East and West Berlin were interesting. But the meetings with East German writers were rather strained, and most likely being overseen by the security forces. Within a year, the Berlin Wall would fall.

EM's own attitude to the demise of communism over the next few years was mixed. In fact he had always found his attitude to its dogma wavering according to events. Unlike MacDiarmid who re-joined the Party at the time of the crushing of the Hungarian uprising in 1956, EM responded to the predicaments of life under communism as he encountered it, whether in the act of translation or on his quite extensive travels behind the Iron Curtain. With the eyes of a tourist he admired the independent approach of the Albanians, who deferred to no greater state. He would have had no contact with that state's system of justice, both repressive and arbitrary.

In the 1960s, EM had gained the reputation among university colleagues of being extremely left-wing. Some of them linked it to John Scott's politics, but it is unclear whether this was anything more than gossip. But by the 1980s his views were more mixed, and their ambiguity was expressed among the seventy poems on 'social themes' that he began to write about this time, looking forward to his 70th birthday. These poems would be published in their entirety by Mariscat as *Hold Hands Among the Atoms* in 1991, with a substantial selection of 58 of them in his next Carcanet volume, *Sweeping Out the Dark* (1994).

The opening two of the Carcanet selection offer opposing views of the Russian experience of communism. 'A Departure' recalls EM's long admiration for Russian technology and their exploits in space: the astronauts 'sat down like old Russians, / breathed steadily till none of us was anxious [. . .]'. Their equipment before takeoff 'seemed gold-foiled / in the low sun, like gifts' (*Sweeping Out the Dark*: 33). But the next poem, 'Difference' (p. 34), exalts variety in place of the Communist Party's system and sameness, focusing on the issue of ethnic languages crushed by Russian:

> And Iskander stopped writing in Abkhazian,
> Aigi in Chuvash, Rytkheu in Chukcha.
> So much the worse, so much the worse. You think not?
> You'd rather have the second-best as long as
> millions get it?

However, another poem 'Friday', not included in this collection, complains about the change of title of a Communist party weekly from *Hammer and Sickle* to *Friday,* which seems a poor abstraction that 'won't knock nails and rivets in', but is an illusion and a distraction

> from all the hard things that are great in hardness,
> the setbacks that still sting us crying forwards [. . .].
>> (*Hold Hands Among the Atoms*: 37)

At some level, EM maintained an emotional identification with the future possibilities he had glimpsed in the radical socialism of earlier times.

COMING OUT

EM's 1980s seem like a birl of activity. They make use of every day released from the timetable of teaching. Time was passing all the same, and he was nearing seventy years of age. His Aunt Myra died in June 1989, the last close relation and direct contact with his parents' generation, and he had to make arrangements to clear and sell her flat. Richard Price asked if he was less optimistic at this stage of life, as some readers felt from the darkness of some of the poems in *Themes on a Variation*:

> I don't *think* I'm at bottom less optimistic, but of course the 80s are not the 60s, and the unease which one reviewer detected in the volume is doubtless there. Love and war: the two ancient subjects: they return and return.[37]

Earlier in the decade he had been heartened by translating fourteen poems by Gennady Aigi, the Chuvash poet first mentioned to him by the Brazilian concrete poets, Augusto and Haroldo de Campos. This was for a new Scottish journal of Slavonic Studies, edited by Peter Henry of Glasgow University. 'Things are *happening*, aren't they,' he said to Hamish Whyte in February 1983. In November of the same year he translated six poems by Sándor Weöres, and in January 1984, and then in August and October 1985, sixteen poems by Attila József. In 1986, came translations of Ivan Blatny, Lázló Kálnoky and Pushkin, with further poems by Weöres and József.

In May of 1986 EM told Hamish Whyte that the Hungarians were about to publish a volume of his own poems in translation, and that this could then be compared with a similar Polish volume of his work, edited by Andrzej Szuba:

> I'm greatly pleased it's two Eastern European countries which are doing this, as I've always wanted my work to do a bit of East–West bridging.

Things were also happening as he approached his seventieth year. Hamish Whyte and Robert Crawford were preparing the critical study *About Edwin Morgan* for publication by Edinburgh University Press in 1990. This was the first extended study of his poetry. Hamish Whyte was also working on his own collection of interviews, articles and statements: *Edwin Morgan: Nothing Not Giving Messages*, to be published by Polygon at Edinburgh University Press.

This landmark birthday coincided with publicity around Glasgow's 'European City of Culture' events. EM was uneasily aware that a continued public silence on his homosexuality would be a 'nothing' that would likely be taken as giving a very loud message: namely, that he was ashamed of his own nature or still feared the public criticism that might follow from discussing this openly. He had been schooled for decades in the subterfuge necessary for a man in his position, in his culture. But the time had surely come to speak openly about matters that the poetry now indicated more and more clearly.

The chosen interviewer for *Nothing Not Giving Messages* was Christopher Whyte, a linguist and lecturer in literature, and a poet in English and Gaelic. He had contacted EM at the beginning of the decade from the University of Rome, where he was teaching English and translating Sorley MacLean's poetry into Italian. He had been looking for advice on possible research topics in Scottish and Gaelic literature.

The interview on his homosexuality went well, and some of it has been quoted in earlier chapters. Afterwards EM wrote to Christopher Whyte:

> I owe it to you that I found it so easy to talk about things I hadn't talked about in that way before. It was strangely liberating once I had made the decision to do it.[38]

For his part, Christopher Whyte affirmed that EM had, in his quiet and unobtrusive way, been a positive role model for gay people in Scotland. By his own warmth and creativity he had confounded the all too familiar narrative, in life and in literature, of the gay character who dies with promise unfulfilled. Knowing some of the chances he had taken at different times in his life, EM replied:

> Good or bad luck enters into the course of every life, and especially a life of risk, and that is another factor to be taken into account.

Approaching seventy, EM was now reflecting on past events in his life, and imagining other possibilities. Among the seventy poems on social themes in *Hold Hands Among the Atoms* are some that look forward and some that glance back. When he had to clear his aunt's house around the time of her final illness, he found the experience of handling the accumulation of another person's past life a difficult one, and wrote a poem about this, focusing on the detail of her dance-cards, kept from 'those far-off flirty Twenties':

> The room darkens
> with a blue lingering glow above the roof-tops
> but the man still stands there, holding up the dangling
> dance-cards by their tiny attached pencils.
>
> *(Hold Hands Among the Atoms:* 33)

Among his own life's accumulation of papers detailing a varied past, he was equally uncertain how to judge what was worth sharing with the public. It had all been written by him, so it was possibly of equal interest. He sent Hamish Whyte in 1989 some verse letters from the 1950s, which opened up 'various areas of embarrassment, not just personal details but the fact that they all come from the period before my end-of-fifties "liberation"'. These were for possible inclusion in *Nothing Not Giving Messages*. However, he added:

> I suppose there is no point in having embarrassment about things written forty years back, if someone else (i.e. you!) thinks they should be of general interest.

EM had made later amendments to these verse letters, which were written to Vivian Linacre, an Edinburgh writer and businessman, and to Ian Dallas, a promising young Scottish dramatist of the early 1950s who went to Italy and worked in the film industry there, as well as one to W.S. Graham, already quoted from. However, he suggested using the originals as 'it would give a dishonest impression otherwise'. Too different in form from the rest of the book, perhaps, and insecure in tone, none of these letters was finally included.

A similar sense of hiddenness waiting to be disclosed through art and memory is signalled by one of the epigraphs to *Hold Hands Among the Atoms*. It is a quotation from Laura Riding Jackson:

> There is something to be told about us
> for the telling of which we all wait.

The second epigraph is from *Beowulf* in the original Old English. In his own translation, the lines mean

> The men cast off
> Eager voyagers, in their tight-timbered boat.

Within the time left to him, the poet's honest exploration of experience should be unceasing, and eagerly pursued. But would he have the physical and artistic strength for this? At the very beginning of the decade, on 20–21 March 1980, EM had written one of his own favourites among all his poems, 'Cinquevalli' (CP: 432–4). He had come across his name first of all on an old postcard that he picked up in a bookshop:

> I thought he looked interesting but knew nothing about him; later I came across an article in a theatre magazine which told me something about his life and the extraordinary feats he had performed. I was struck by the fact that he had been almost forgotten, after once enjoying world fame, and that's what started the poem.[39]

The athleticism and acrobatic skill of Cinquevalli had attracted EM as he approached the freedoms of retirement. He had identified with the performer's quick and supple art, together with the determination and long hours of practice that lay behind public recognition. Fame like strength was fleeting. Ten years older, he prepared to cast off on what, with luck, might be a last decade of exploration.

CHAPTER NINE

Speaking for Scotland 1990–2000

> At seventy I thought I had come through,
> like parting a bead curtain in Port Said,
> to something that was shadowy before,
> figures and voices of late times that might
> be surprising yet. The beads clash faintly
> behind me as I go forward. No candle-light
> please, keep that for Europe. Switch the whole thing
> right on. When I go in I want it bright,
> I want to catch whatever is there
> in full sight.
>
> 'Epilogue: Seven Decades' (CP: 595)

Unlike the earlier stanzas of 'Epilogue: Seven Decades', this final one looks forward, not back. EM asserts his desire to face the future with the light of understanding clearly shining. Not for him the embattled tone of Basil Bunting's preface to his own *Collected Poems* (1968): 'A man who collects his poems screws together the boards of his coffin'. Rather, he looks expectantly for life, or perhaps the moment of death, to be 'surprising yet'.

In fact, by the end of the decade he was facing death, diagnosed with a cancer that might give him six months – or six years. The prognosis was uncertain. Thus the approaching millennium would see him writing against the clock to complete his latest project: *A.D.*, a trilogy of plays on the life of Jesus. Typically, this would seek to rewrite the Gospel narrative in ways that challenged traditional beliefs. He had just completed *Demon* (1999), a sequence of poems that presented its outsider hero speaking in his own magnetic voice.

The 1990s were a decade in which EM would indeed face surprising changes of fortune. His own self-identity in socialism had been challenged by the collapse of Communism. Now his political values were affronted by what he saw replacing it. At a civic luncheon in Glasgow's City Chambers on 27 October 1989 to inaugurate *New Beginnings*, a season of Soviet Arts, EM read a poem written for the occasion, 'New Beginnings and Old Memories'. Recalling the unknown socialist guest who in 1932 'slipped past' his conservative parents to leave what must have been propaganda magazines with astonishing photo-images of the *USSR Under Construction* for their son to look at, enthralled, and remembering also how his university friend, George Hunter, battled Arctic seas on the Murmansk convoys 'while I was scraping desert from my mess-tin', the old poet now opts for a new beginning:

> Enough of war; and let construction be reconstruction,
> watch Perestroika skimming in her troika
> like Mungo's mother over the old badlands, rocks
> of bureaucracy, sands of censoriousness,
> bogs of dogma, let the horses whinny and get a whiff
> of good broad high free blue bright heady air [. . .].[1]

That sounds confident enough. Yet just two months later, EM was dismayed to find that in Russia that old Communist dogma seemed to be being replaced by a more ancient Orthodox Christianity. In a poem written over the first and second days of January 1990, he gave a bitter response, 'A Warning':

> What makes you think you have an acclamation?
> Was it, they dragged the body of socialism
> into a common grave, quicklime, dancing,
> opening of cathedrals, minuet of

vestments as they cross the ancient incense,
ranks of dew-eyes dibbling trembling candles
in waxbound trays that never will grow freedom?

(Sweeping Out the Dark: 61)

We can see why the 'Epilogue' wants 'No candle-light please'. As he grew older, EM came to see himself increasingly in conflict with organised religion, particularly in its traditional forms. I remember him complaining to me in 2009 that the old women who ran the pensione where he stayed in Naples had never even *heard* of Presbyterianism when he tried to discuss it with them, but just retreated into the corner muttering and clacking something – their prayers perhaps. I found his surprise at their lack of interest amusing, and his latter-day Knoxian mission to these old Neapolitan souls absolutely beside the point.

But then, I like candles. As a Catholic, I tend to see the institutional Church in a more variegated way than EM could manage, and perhaps deplore some aspects of it even more deeply, while also valuing other dimensions in ways he must have found incomprehensible. We were agreed that the 'official' dogmatic line on homosexuality and AIDS was not sustainable. What I did not know until much later was that his dear friend and former student, Morven Cameron, had shocked both family and friends at a festive gathering by announcing to the assembled company that she intended to become a Catholic.

There may have been some misgivings about me on his part, although this never surfaced on the occasions when we did meet in the 1990s, perhaps four or five times a year. It was true that each of us was busier than ever, which can create a distance, with my mid-forties bringing new responsibilities at work combined with a fair amount of publication, both professional and creative. EM meanwhile was entering a much more public stage of his career, when dramatic and musical performance of his writings brought him into contact with an even wider audience than before.

CITIZEN OF CULTURES

My memories of EM in the 1990s open and close with poetry readings in places that shone with a different light. On 5 May 1990 there was a seventieth birthday lunch and readings on the Renfrew Ferry, which had been renovated and transformed into a performance venue, moored on the Clyde near George V Bridge. There was a boat-load of friends and well-wishers, and his birthday had become part of the 'City of Culture' atmosphere. There were many people present whom I would later come to know better, but it was thrilling to meet the poet Roy Fisher, a long-standing friend of Gael Turnbull and Basil Bunting as well as of EM, and with whom he had read on many occasions over more than twenty years. In October 1967, for example, they had performed at the Midland Institute in Birmingham, poems interposed with clarinet music. He was a gifted jazz pianist as well as a remarkable poet of the urban landscape, and he played on this birthday occasion.

Also present was Hamish Whyte. In fact, the other memorable incident in the Renfrew Ferry event was the arrival during the proceedings of a tribute volume for EM: *Felt Tipped Hosannahs*. This had been edited by Hamish Whyte and Susan Stewart, Kevin McCarra's wife, who was working at the time for its publisher, the Third Eye Centre. The book had been brought from the printers that very afternoon and so was almost literally 'hot off the presses'.

EM had introduced me to Hamish Whyte a month earlier, at an ASLS conference in the University's Boyd Orr Building, where the topic was 'Glasgow Poets Past and Present'. We got on well, being the same age and with similar interests in poetry and publishing. Over the following ten years we would co-write and co-edit on several projects, building up a sense of trust and understanding that would later help us work together to support EM in his illness.

These events of celebration, affection and respect for the poet's achievements took place in central venues, and were clearly part of Glasgow's City of Culture activities. But the programme as a whole had sparked controversy among some radical Glaswegian writers, who objected to what they saw as exploitative importation of 'culture' in terms of high art, drama or music while the true culture and language of Glasgow's citizens was being ignored. Looking back on the events several years later, the Ayrshire novelist Andrew O'Hagan, now London-based, recalled this factional tension in a *Guardian* article, and the paradox that both 'sides' were internationally minded. He compared the general openness to other languages and cultures in EM's reading at a *From Glasgow to Saturn* conference on 3 April 1990, and the equally admirable conviction with which Kelman, Gray and other radicals set up a 'Workers' City' in opposition to the cultural tourism and hype of the official celebrations. Tom Leonard provided his own brand of satirical dissent.

For O'Hagan, such internal quarrels of Scot against Scot seemed somehow symptomatic of the national psyche, as in Scottish Orange Walks where the focus of aggression is not international capitalism or English centralism but local Catholics. When EM looked back on the matter, he had a fair amount of respect for Tom Leonard's position, and yet he felt overall that the civic benefits and the impetus towards new architecture probably outweighed the charges of exploitation or neglect of Glasgow's citizens, in this instance.

His own 'coming out' was also a focus of media interest throughout that year. This had been prompted by his interview with Christopher Whyte, 'Power from things not declared'. A conflation of two interviews from October and November 1988, it was now published for the first time in Hamish Whyte's edited collection, *Nothing Not Giving Messages* (1990). EM was thus interviewed at home on gay poetry for *Scotland on Sunday* in late January, gave a reading at Edinburgh University Lesbian and Gay Society in February, and took part in a reading and discussion in the Queen Margaret Student Union for the University of Glasgow's Gay Awareness Day in April 1990. An interview with John Linklater for the *Glasgow Herald* on 25 April 1990 to mark his seventieth birthday turned the focus from 'literature' to 'news', with centre-page treatment of his gay identity. In the following month, he gave readings in Volumes Bookshop for 'Outward Gaze', and in the Garret Theatre in Otago Street, as part of Lesbian and Gay Glasgow events for Mayfest.

The media interest suggests that his sexuality was news to the general public. This may be so, although those who were familiar with his more recent poetry would have worked it out for themselves. But EM was aware that, even though 'Glasgow Green' and the early love poems were enjoyed and anthologised:

> They weren't *discussed*, and nobody really went into what they were actually saying. But they took them as good poems and accepted them in that sense. It was a long time before people delved into what they were actually saying – nobody has delved very much into them even yet. [. . .] I was surprised in a way.[2]

He found it very strange that 'Glasgow Green' was 'even taught in schools', but realised that a lot would depend on the teacher and the level of the class. In my experience, this poem is often taught in schools in an inexplicit way, as a poem of Glasgow's violent past, with a lot left unexplained. Young people are sharp, however:

> I have been asked at a school reading what exactly is going on in 'Glasgow Green'. I just said what it was: a homosexual rape. And the boy who had asked just accepted that all right. [. . .] Nowadays people see so much on television that they are aware of these things. He was not particularly shocked.[3]

Coming out altered his approach to poetry to some extent, compared with his earlier ambiguous or semi-coded writing. He felt that he could now write about anything he wanted to. It was just a matter of whether he wanted to do so or not:

> There are some poems I write just because of the freedom, taking up subjects that would be regarded as improper or certainly not

universal. [. . .] There is one of the poems called 'A Memorial' [*Sweeping Out the Dark*: 58] that is about 'cottaging', which is considerably disapproved of, because people who might accept a nice affair by two men living together in a house would not so easily accept someone going down toilets in search of prey (as it were), in search of partners. [. . .] But of course it goes on, it went on, and I just felt: It's part of human life, let's have a look at it.[4]

That determination to speak for outsiders, and to bring readers face to face with what is too conveniently ignored, is a feature of his later poetry, done now with a more undisguised directness. 'At Central Station' (CP: 405–6), for example, shows a middle-aged self-neglecting woman 'pissing on the pavement. / With her back to the wall and her legs spread [. . .]' – meanwhile the Glasgow crowd either hurries on past or else 'looks hard, bold as brass'. The poet's feelings are complex, 'confused as the November leaves'. In one sense he knows he is an 'accursed recorder' of the scene, and yet he is also the only one to reveal both the indignity and, somehow, dignity in her situation. The use of this poem in a Highland school's English syllabus caused complaints to the Scottish Education Department from one of the parents, a minister of religion.

This is just one of several poems from the late 1970s and early 1980s that deal with outsiders: 'Gorgon' (CP: 413), 'Caliban Falls Asleep in the Isle Full of Noises' (CP: 420), 'Iran' (CP: 420–1) which records the judicial crushing of an adulteress under lorry-loads of stone, 'Eve and Adam' (CP: 426–7), 'Grendel' (CP: 427–8), and also 'Jack London in Heaven' (CP: 430–1).

What is different now about the 1990s poems is the directness of an older poet addressing his own outsider status, as in the poems in *Sweeping Out the Dark* (1994: 23–9) that describe incidents and feelings on a trip across the United States with Bobby C. The image of the writer Jack London recurs, '– in his boat – when day is done // sailing well out to make a catch / beneath the stars', and links these poems from different decades. But in the 1990s, the poet begins to sense something of the gap between wishes and reality. Here he is, relaxing on holiday with his young friend in a revolving restaurant above twilit San Franciso Bay, eating sprouts and listening to muzak. Jack London is long gone, although longed for still.

This US trip by Greyhound bus from coast to coast lasted from 26 June to 10 July 1991. Two days after his return EM received an Honorary D.Litt. degree from Edinburgh University, to add to the one received from the University of Glasgow the previous October. Such contrasts of role and acquaintance intrigued and stimulated EM. All of this was 'him', and he refused to censor any part of its variety.

Just prior to flying to the United States of America he had given the James Cameron Commemoration Lecture in Glasgow City Chambers for the Scottish Council for Civil Liberties, taking as his theme 'From Pasternak to Rushdie: Some Thoughts on Literary Censorship'. Freedom, of course, is no guarantee of literary quality in poetry, and it may be that the 'underground' quality of EM's earlier work and his own self-censorship actually strengthened its impact. In the 1990s, in these poems from America and in his 'Virtual and Other Realities' series of 1997, he imposes on himself the discipline of a tercet form of triple-lined rhyming stanzas. But the reader may soon become impatient with this insistent juggling with rhyme, clever though it is, and long for some variety, formal surprise or lyric grace.

There were, however, emotional surprises still in wait. In March of 1994 he found himself in an unexpected situation:

> A new state in a relationship – totally unexpected – exciting – but very unsettling – I'm neglecting the things I ought to be doing ('ought' in the businessy non-creative sense) and spending much time looking out at the rain and writing poems – quite a lot in the last few weeks [. . .] and oddly enough not about the relationship but on other subjects, yet somehow the feeling that comes from a single source is busy channelling itself elsewhere, magnetising and vivifying – so the mind is one and all things are connected – [5]

He contrasted this emotional state with what might be expected of someone 'safely in his seventies', namely putting on his slippers and watching *Coronation Street* on the television.

The newly ignited relationship was with Malcolm T., and the poems being written that March were nine of the 'Virtual and Other Realities' sequence of fifty, including 'March', which he would later place at the start:

> A wilder March I never saw for sleet.
> I feed my fax, and watch the whitening street.
> I send the southern sun sheet after sheet.
>
> > (*Virtual and Other Realities*: 47)

The poem 'For Love' reveals something of the origin of this affair, and a sense of the transience of life:

> If lovers often dwindle into friends,
> friends can become late lovers, make amends
> for habit, live with beginnings and not ends.
>
> Armies of time, once summoned, are soon massed.
> We run to meet them, disappearing fast
> into a future that soon too is past.

Perhaps the tercet form here is linked to the love theme, or to the turbulence of emotional involvement which seemed to him to unify heart and mind. The insistent rhymes may be like tacks the poet uses to pin down this fleeting inspiration. Other sorts of love and loss do figure in the sequence: two especially recall his mother. In 'At the Last' he records how

> My mother's last words as she fell, 'Don't leave me!'
> have come back many times to re-bereave me [. . .]
>
> > (*Virtual and Other Realities*: 82)

and in following poem 'The Brink', as he writes at his table in the gathering dark, 'a lamp in the half-light / gleams on my mother's vase'. There are also memories of 'The Dead', haunting the older poet:

> It is not true to say they are not here,
> the dead. Never gone but never clear,
> they punctuate the room, the street, so near [. . .].
>
> (*Virtual and Other Realities*: 65)

He was also aware of the ambiguity of giving up the memories embedded in his collection of books and his files of correspondence, which were now passing to the Mitchell and Glasgow University libraries. 'To the Librarians, H.W. and H.H.' (Hamish Whyte and Henry Heaney) records a double-edged sense of casting his life away. On the one hand, he felt 'a Pasternakian lightness, kicking the cumber / into other's vaults'; but on the other hand came the sharp awareness that 'Your files are you', and that all these letters and papers of a lifetime, even could he burn them on some shore,

> no tide
> will ever wash away the ash you hide
> of pain, or love, or pain or love denied.
>
> (*Virtual and Other Realities*: 71)

The pain of aging now included the death of friends, particularly where there was a gay connection. In September 1992 he attended the funeral in Ayrshire of a friend of many decades:

> I had feelings I couldn't share, as we had had a fairly passionate affair many many years ago which settled down to an easy-going friendship – his wife knew – it was okay – we got on well together all three of us – but how strange to sit there as encomiums rolled out, not one of them mentioning the fact that he was gay.[6]

The following June he attended the funeral service in the University Chapel for Alastair Cameron, a much-admired lecturer in the Drama Department, who had died of AIDS. The family and his partner asked EM to read his poem 'When you go' (CP: 184), and he found this a very emotional occasion.

Writing to Richard Price in July 1992, EM criticised media attitudes to the disease. He was responding to an account that the younger poet had written of his own father's reaction when on a hospital visit to one of his young employees in the Goodwill Stores he managed in Glasgow, who was dying of AIDS. Scarcely able to believe the young man's suffering, he burst into tears at the bedside. He was furious that his Methodist line-manager from the Glasgow Voluntary Community Service had refused to visit the hospital 'on moral grounds'. EM replied:

> I was touched by what you wrote about your father [. . .]. That human reaction was so good and so real and so many light-years away from the moralisings of the tabloids which really make you sick. The Methodist overseer seems a poor Christian too. How can people *be* like that?[7]

In critical mood, he then noted that with the Glasgow Fair holiday approaching 'Archbishop Winning has been publicly lambasting Glasgow Airport for issuing free condoms to holiday-makers bound for the hot and sexy Costas'.

He himself flew off to Iceland in January of 1993, invited by the Icelandic Writers' Union for a Scottish Festival. Also there were Alasdair Gray, John Purser and the Whistlebinkies band, and an Ian Hamilton Finlay exhibition. EM gave lectures and readings, and had the experience of bathing in a temperature of minus twelve degrees in an open-air hot swimming pool with Alasdair Gray and his wife, Morag. He enjoyed the austere landscape of glacier and geyser, waterfall and volcano, and the seas teeming with life ('but you only see that *dead*, when the fishing boats come in').

A year earlier EM had experienced Antipodean warmth during a three-week tour of New Zealand in March 1992, giving readings and lectures in Wellington, Hamilton and Auckland, 'to which a

Maori ceremony and an honorary degree (no connection!) have now been attached'.[8] He attended Writers' Week at Wellington International Festival, and received an honorary doctorate from the University of Waikato in Hamilton, where both Marshall Walker and Alan Riach taught. With them he visited the Waitomo underground caves, descending by a rough stairway to a large lake, then being taken by boat across the dark waters, gliding in silence so that no conversation would disturb the glowworms lighting up the cavern roof. It was a thrilling sight that remained with him for many months.

He recalled this excursion at the end of the decade, in response to a request from W.N. Herbert and Matthew Hollis for an article for their book *Strong Words: Modern Poets on Modern Poetry* (Bloodaxe, 2000). Here he used the subterranean experience to try to explain why he disliked writing about his own creative process: some things should be left mysteriously shining in their own surrounding dark.

Interestingly he then reflects upon his unwillingness to keep a journal of his wartime experiences, taking the risk of leaving those images and incidents buried, until they surfaced, still fresh and clear, thirty years later. Of 'The New Divan' he complains: 'It is my hidden poem, which no one writes about!' And he then goes on to stress his own sense of identification with poets of many voices, such as Dunbar, Blake, Khlebnikov, Voznesensky, Weöres or Prigov, as compared with poets who have a single style or voice, such as Seamus Heaney.

The latter's wide popularity rather irked him. When Faber published Heaney's translation of *Beowulf* in 1999, Hamish Whyte asked EM what he thought of it: 'Too Irish' was the response. It was the rural, meditative and non-experimental quality of his poetry that EM did not rate highly, and this is reminiscent of his judgments on the poetry of Edwin Muir and George Mackay Brown. He admitted to a variety of emotions when Heaney won the Nobel Prize for Literature in 1995. These included recognition of his poetic skills, but also jealousy – EM suspected that he himself had once been shortlisted – as well as a genuine puzzlement as to the sources of the Irishman's world-wide success.

EM's reflection on his own practice in *Strong Words* ends confidently enough, with a vision of poetry as 'a brilliant vibrating interface between the human and the non-human', and with Scotland too as one part of the universe that seemed now, with its new Parliament, to be 'twinkling, however faintly' in the night sky. There is nonetheless a sense of dissatisfaction, a perception that he still lacked sufficient recognition. That seems strange at the end of yet another decade of public success, both creative and academic.

Other travels of those years had included a British Council tour of Poland in February 1998 with readings and lively student seminars in Warsaw, Krakow and Katowice. EM met the Polish translator of his poems, Andrzej Szuba, and the poet Piotr Sommer. A 'sightseeing' visit to Auschwitz on a suitably freezing day was included:

> It wasn't exactly 'shocking' to someone of my generation: my shock came with seeing the first newsreels and accounts of the liberation of the camps at the end of the war, and nothing since has matched its impact.[9]

Some of these journeys in old age influenced the poems in EM's *Demon* sequence of 1998–99, as we will see.

THE YOUNG AVANT-GARDE

In this decade, EM was in regular contact with two young poet-publishers in the next generation of the Scottish avant-garde: Richard Price who was based in London, and Alec or Eck Finlay, who was the son of his old friend, Ian Hamilton Finlay. Richard Price had made a particular commitment to write to him every ten days or so, whether EM had time to respond or not within his still busy schedule of writing, travel and performance. He stayed true to that promise and, since EM would fairly often photocopy his own replies, their correspondence builds into a detailed and sometimes touching record of artistic development across the generations. The faxes fed into his machine in the poem quoted above ('I send the southern sun sheet after sheet') were also being sent, in some sense, to a southern son.

Their close connection had been sealed in circumstances of family grief. Richard Price's mother had died on Midsummer's Day in 1990, and he had found the experience of reading EM's *The Second Life*, in its contrasting poems of optimism and vulnerability, a touchstone of constancy in the midst of mourning. EM responded quickly to this letter:

> The book was, in a way, my own recovery from a period of self-doubt, and (precarious though such recoveries always are!) the sense of release, of change, and also the pain of change, make it very much a book of feeling – I'm sure you're right about that.[10]

EM's letters show him setting up connections between like-minded young poets, for example sending Price a copy of Peter McCarey's collection *Town Shanties*. Richard Price and W.N. Herbert were planning an issue of their *Gairfish* journal to be devoted to the Scottish avant-garde (*The McAvantgarde*, 1992), and EM mentioned that there was a recurring theme of 'a vanguard' in his forthcoming Mariscat collection, *Hold Hands Among the Atoms* (1991).

But the letters also reveal something of his domestic routines or creative commitments. On the second of January 1991 he described how he always spent 'the last bits of December clearing things up, paying bills, destroying receipts more than three years old (maybe unwise), looking out books for Hamish Whyte to take to the Mitchell Library [. . .], setting up my new diary'. On the following day he was set to meet a choreographer for the TAG theatre company, about to begin rehearsals for a new show, *From Glasgow to Saturn*, in which EM had a walk-on part.

This piece had a good run at the Tron Theatre at the start of February 1991, before moving on to the St Andrew's Festival later that month. In March there were performances in North Kelvinside Secondary and Greenock Prison. EM took the whole company to dinner at the fashionable Ubiquitous Chip restaurant at the end of this run. He would meet people regularly for lunch and discussion in some of Glasgow's more expensive restaurants during the 1990s – Café Gondolfi, Yes, and 78 St Vincent Street being other favourites.

The letters also reveal EM's increasing public role as a gay writer. At the end of October 1993, he writes that his work on the 'Virtual and Other Realities' sequence has been interrupted by preparations 'for the festival *Glasgay*! which will pinken the city all next week'. He was working on his talk 'A Scottish Trawl', for an all-day University seminar on Lesbian and Gay Studies, organised by Christopher Whyte and Alastair Cameron. This would later be published in Whyte's critical book, *Gendering the Nation: Studies in Modern Scottish Literature* (1995). He was also about to give a reading with poet and novelist Jackie Kay; being interviewed by Scottish Television; and discussing recent gay fiction 'on Radio Scotland in the (gay) Blue Moon Café in Edinburgh'.

There were creative or playful elements in the correspondence too, as EM experimented with photocopy art ('photocopioids') on his machine. Several examples of these appeared in the first issue of *Southfields*, which Richard Price founded with Raymond Friel after a split with W.N. Herbert at *Gairfish*. EM kept twelve of these, and the titles of some reveal a seriousness underlying their ludic origins: 'Leviathan', 'Helen and Mephistophilis' (the reference is to Christopher Marlowe's tragedy of Dr Faustus, which EM would later adapt), 'The Exorcism', 'Two Souls in Purgatory', and 'The Edge of Hell'.[11]

Now well into his 80s, EM had occasional reminders of the vulnerability of age. At the end of May 1993 he admitted:

> I have been doing my best to overcome jitters after two Whit-
> tingehame Court burglaries, one next door and one in the flat
> above me, both too near for comfort, done in mid-afternoon by the

total non-finesse of smashing the door open, stuffing videos and other portable sellables into a large holdall, and making off into the May sunshine apparently unnoticed by anyone.[12]

His flat was more vulnerable because of the amount of time he spent away from it on various engagements. To take his itinerary from a few months earlier as an example, we find him giving readings at Belmont Academy in Ayr on the 4th of March, then travelling to University College, Aberystwyth for his annual visit to give a lecture, seminar and reading (7–10 March). He then read at the University of Glasgow with Liz Lochhead on 15 March, and at the Stirling Writers' Group on the following day. A trip to Newcastle followed on 19 March, with readings at Cramlington High School in the afternoon and Morden Tower in the evening. On 22, 23 and 24 March, he gave two readings at Ardrossan Academy, and one apiece at Tynecastle High School and Hamilton College. The pace of his engagement with the younger public, in particular, scarcely seemed to have slackened.

Travel did bring him into contact with the wider political malaise of the United Kingdom at this time. He commented in February 1995 that this seemed to be a time of 'small scale protests against veal crates while the real scandal of privatised companies and excessive rewards goes unremarked'. Within Glasgow, he lamented changes not only to the civic architecture but in the character of ordinary people. He complained of

a society which has become either cowed or indifferent when it comes to the larger issues (when a great battery of police security cameras is installed in the Glasgow area people interviewed in the street, far from doing a Kelman, nod appreciatively, 'good idea', 'makes you feel safe' [. . .] and will it be any different when identity cards come in? – I doubt it). As long as the shopping malls are open, who cares about civic liberties?[13]

As often in the past, translation served as a reminder of a different, and more revolutionary, socio-political energy. In the same letter EM notes: 'I've just given Eck Finlay my translation of Khlebnikov's 'Dragon Train' for his Morning Star book(let).' This poem, written in 1910 by Velemir Khlebnikov, is subtitled 'An Escap(ad)e' and recounts a wild encounter with a dragon that attacks a passenger train. It is part symbolist, part futurist, part apocalyptic. Before the narrator and his comrade manage to jump off and hide among the fir trees, the dragon wreaks havoc reminiscent of Grendel in *Beowulf*:

> On its haunches, its neck stretched out, a swarm
> of desires tormenting and maddening it, calling it something:
> What rites, what lustrations had come and gone?
>
> It turned back to us – I went rigid, trembling –
> Snatched a sleepy neighbour, cracked him open,
> Gobbled him up, young lawyer, snake's plaything.

(CT: 425)

But there is also something magnificent in the awe-inspiring energy of the creature that expresses a typical doubleness in EM's vision of things. This is only the latest in a poetic line of beings divided from the norm, unspeaking or with distorted speech, and presenting a radical challenge to the *status quo*. As such, it also prefigures the Demon character who would shortly be allowed to speak for himself.

'The Dragon' appeared in Alec Finlay's *Under the Moon Series*, published quarterly: these were high quality limited editions of texts accompanied by artwork. He had contacted EM from his parents' house at Stonypath, where he was spending time with his father and meanwhile kept discovering 'new' writers from the 1960s on the bookshelves. Who among the younger poets, he asked EM, might provide something different for the millennium? His current flatmate in Edinburgh was the son of Jessie McGuffie, his father's original partner in the Wild Hawthorn Press, so it may have seemed to EM that some of that 1960s creative energy was being brought to life again. The younger Finlay was also full of ideas, and keen to commission folios of new work. One of the most attractive of these would be a series of stamps for the Republic of Scotland: a republic as yet unfounded, but not therefore unimaginable.

A few months earlier, he had asked EM for help with locating and translating some letters of Attila József, and wanted to publish a selection of his translations. Again there are echoes here of *Poor.Old.Tired.Horse.*, and of fulfilling his father's hopes of three decades earlier. In the event, the publication of this Folio, *Fragments by József Attila* (Morning Star Publications: 1992) was fraught with difficulties. EM found that the artist, John Byrne, had altered some of the line divisions in his hand-written versions of the texts, and lost the rhyme or assonance. Attempts to redo the Folio also foundered at first, because of an accidental mix up of the printer's sheets, much to EM's frustration:

> Six of the fourteen József poems are still wrong – all he has to do is to write them out with the line-divisions *as in the typescript*. Why will he not do it?
> – Yours with hair torn in handfuls.[14]

Alec Finlay's abiding memory is of watching John Byrne nonchalantly redoing the drawings and texts at his kitchen table, 'just like that'.

He was also responsible for bringing EM into contact with Cecilia Vicuña, a Chilean poet, film-maker and performance artist from Santiago. She worked within the traditions of the oral poetry of the Andes, having lived and studied with women shamans there. Her work celebrated the importance of weaving (in Quechan, the word for 'language' is 'thread'). Finlay was keen to present a performance of her work in Scotland, with the Gaelic singers Flora McNeil of Barra and Margaret Bennett of Skye, Rosa Alcalá, an American poet and translator of Vicuña's work, and EM. Finally Finlay got funding to put on an event at the Centre for Contemporary Arts in Glasgow, and sent a book of hers from which EM could select some poems for translation.

This would become *Palabrarmas / Wurdwappinschaw* (1994) from Morning Star Publications. Before the performance, EM expressed some concerns about where he fitted in, since 'my translations are not for reading aloud but for the eye and inner ear'. But it seemed to turn out all right on the night.

The postage stamp project (*Imagined Lands: Volume XIV Scotland*) developed into an exhibition at the City Art Centre in Edinburgh, with subsequent publication of an album with Scottish stamps designed by six artists: Linda Taylor, Gary Hinks, Robin Gillanders, Eileen Lawrence, David Bellingham and Kate Whitford. EM and Ian Hamilton Finlay worked with the first and second of these artists respectively.

EM's first stamp combined images from two of the *Sonnets from Scotland*: 'The Coin' and 'The Summons', together with the oldest musical instrument in Scotland, the Caprington Horn, which he had read about in John Purser's book *Scotland's Music*. Linda Taylor echoed the horn sound with images of howling wolves, and linked this with lines from EM's poem 'Wolf' in the *Beasts of Scotland* poems he had written for the jazz saxophonist, Tommy Smith. The interweaving of poetry and image here, as well as musical, natural and ancient history, is typical of EM's work. There may even be an emotional echo of the unused stamp albums in which he had copied out his earliest poems sixty years before.

There were other echoes too in this relationship with the Finlay's son. In June 1993 he wrote to seek EM's support in his father's long-running legal battle with Strathclyde Regional Council, which was suing him over the Garden Temple artwork of Little Sparta. The artist and his wife, Sue, had transformed a semi-derelict shepherd's cottage at Stonypath, set in five acres of wilderness at the edge of the Pentland Hills, into an artistic landscape of natural and created forms. The Council in 1978 proposed to re-classify and tax it as a commercial gallery. Hamish Henderson, the poet and folklorist, was among other literary figures championing Finlay's resistance. In the so-called Battle of Little Sparta in 1983, supporters had successfully prevented the removal of artworks by the Council in lieu of payment. But the issue was not resolved, and it ran on into the 1990s.

This may have recalled for EM some earlier difficulties which his friend had had with bureaucracy. In the 1960s he had intervened to argue Finlay's case with the local Benefits office, when the award of an Arts Council grant triggered the suspension of other payments.

Alec Finlay admired both Hamish Henderson and EM, and tended to see a link between these writers and his father's work, and also with the folksong movement of the 1960s which Henderson did so much to encourage. In his view, all three formed a nexus against the high modernism of MacDiarmid and his followers, which, as we have seen, had tended to close down certain avenues of artistic exploration. His reading of the period was that both Henderson and EM used the secret cult of 'The Horseman's Word' – an initiation ceremony into the exclusive male world of Scottish ploughmen, to which Henderson had been given entry during his folklore research in the Highlands – as a way to hint at gay subculture.

EM and Henderson seem an odd couple, the one as dapper and the other was dishevelled, but they did as young men share some radical socialist views and a commitment to Scottish self-government. When EM received the second volume of Timothy Neat's biography, *Hamish Henderson: Poetry Becomes People (1952–2002)* as a Christmas present in December 2009, he read it quickly, and was interested in the sections on the Horseman's Word ceremonies. He also focused on its outline of the *Honour'd Shade* controversy already described in the 1960s chapter above, where MacCaig had excluded many folk elements of Scottish culture, and of Burns's poetry, as well as the work of younger more experimental poets. He was also interested in MacCaig's public mockery of Henderson for his homosexual or bisexual identity, which was widely rumoured at the time.

EM knew of the rumours, but had no direct evidence of their truthfulness. He did then ask for the first volume of Neat's biography, and was amazed at the amount of sheer action and leadership Henderson had shown in the North African and Italian campaigns, so unlike his own war experience. He had met him at several literary functions after the war, but Henderson had always been drinking, and EM had found it difficult to work out the significance of the folklore research that he was engaged in.

It was this later cruelty of MacCaig towards Henderson that most intrigued him, and what his possible motivation might have been, and the sources of an animosity which had no wit about it. EM had taken notes of several of his own conversations about MacCaig's character with Morven Cameron, who knew him personally. MacCaig was, of course, EM's rival for the title of greatest living Scottish poet in the anglophone tradition, and so a fitting subject for reflection, or self-protection.

Contact with Alec Finlay and other members of this new generation of experimental Scottish writers was important to EM in old age. It offered a continuity, and an opportunity to pass on his own sense of a hidden tradition. Thus we find him recounting to Richard Price a telephone interview in late 1994 with Sean O'Hagan for the weekend *Guardian* on the subject of Trocchi: 'Isn't it curious how Trocchi never quite lies down and disappears and yet never enters the mainstream: an endless fate?' A few years later, he wrote an introduction for a new edition of Trocchi's novel *Helen and Desire*, issued in the Scottish counter-cultural Rebel Inc. series.

In 1995, EM sent Alec Finlay photocopies of three of the letters that Veronica Forrest-Thomson had sent him, two from 1965 and one from 1970. In March 1996, he was in contact with the poet and literary theorist Drew Milne, then working at the University of Sussex, and sent him copies too. EM noted how the 'strong clear hand' of the earlier letters had altered in her final letter, written some months before she died, revealing 'the sad disintegration at work'.[15] The sight of this may have awakened the feelings of guilt that EM had experienced since her death – the uneasy sense that he might have done more to prevent it.

Many of the poets under forty who were published in *Dream State: The New Scottish Poets* (Polygon, 1994) edited by Donny

O'Rourke, were personally known to EM. In some ways it was a tribute to his tutelage, as one pro-MacDiarmid reviewer rather sourly pointed out. EM reviewed the book in *The Scotsman* (22 January 1994). He was upbeat, as the volume as a whole vindicated his sense of looking positively towards the future:

> The breaks and flaws in earlier cultural development, and indeed in Scottish history in general, are no longer nagged at, or scarted as sore places, or mistily regretted, but rather become a productive premiss, in Iain Bamforth's perceptive claim, that these disconti-nuities, time-lapses and demons are what has made us modern.

Understanding the modern might also involve a recovery of unheard voices. As the decade drew to a close, EM used the occasion of a major lecture on 'Scotland and the World' at the Edinburgh Festival in August 1999, to press the claim of an unjustly forgotten poet. This was Helen Adam (1909–1993), from the same generation as Norman MacCaig and Sorley MacLean, who had been born into a minister's family in Glasgow and brought up in the North-East, before being sent with her mother and sister to New York on the outbreak of war in 1939. Moving to San Francisco in the 1950s, she made links with the Beat movement, particularly Ginsberg and Duncan.

What attracted EM to her style is easy to see. She wrote in Scots, influenced by the starkness of the ballad tradition, and was a mesmerizing performer. Her books are decorated in a collage style, clearly influenced by surrealism. 'Her master subject is love in all its manifestations,' he wrote in a trailer for his lecture, for the *Sunday Herald* (9 August 1999), 'but especially those that were not likely to lead to a happily lasting outcome' – and he goes on to cite jilting, two-timing, adultery, unrequited passion, over-requited passion and murderous revenge. In old age, the nature of love as well as of time, both great mysteries, would become the guiding themes of his work.

MARISCAT IN THE NINETIES

While EM was weaving connecting threads between the new generation of Scottish avant-garde writers and his own history, he continued to publish regularly with both Mariscat and Carcanet. The smaller press possibly produced the better individual collections in the 1990s. Beginning with *Hold Hands Among the Atoms* (1991), and continuing with *St Columba: The Maker on High* (1997) and *Demon* (1999), there is a clear focus on EM's concerns as the century moved towards a close. These were not the *fin de siècle* themes of disenchantment and world-weariness, but rather a renewed interest in first and last things: origins, reward and punishment, willpower, strife and striving, and what remains of us

> as caskets sink with horrifying blandness
> into a roar, into smoke, into light, into almost nothing.
> The not quite nothing I praise it and I write it.
>
> (*Hold Hands Among the Atoms*: 72)

This is from 'Fires' (later re-published in *Sweeping Out the Dark*: 85) which begins with a meditation on 'my father and my mother', and of early life in Rutherglen so many years before. Such family recollections speak very strongly in this collection, because so rarely heard elsewhere in his poetry.

He had already published many of these seventy poems 'on social themes', in twenty-four journals or newspapers. The latter included the *Glasgow Herald*, *The Scotsman* and *Scotland on Sunday*, and there is perhaps a more conscious sense in this decade of using the media to connect with a wider audience than before. Of course, he had always written for newspapers, but now, with his greater involvement in the theatre, EM himself often became the feature.

The poems in this collection are varied in theme but not in form: each consists of mainly one blank verse paragraph of between six and forty or so lines, most being between about twenty and thirty lines in length. This would become EM's later tendency in writing, especially for social or performance verse: his style shifted towards unvaried form in either tightly rhymed or unrhymed blocks. Ideas, rather than formal inventiveness, drive the work forward. Beneath the range of ideas there was, however, that 'recurring theme of a vanguard'. Whether they were cosmonauts or soldiers, they represented an avant-garde outlook.

The book was launched on 2 May 1991 at Waterstone's Bookshop in Glasgow. Two days before this, EM had given the 'Town and Gown' lecture in Strathclyde University on 'The Spirit of Scotland', and five days later he was giving lectures and readings as Honorary Professor in the English Department of the University College of Wales in Aberystwyth, an annual event for the next six years. So the range of his intellectual experience did not diminish during these years, nor the quest for new knowledge of self and society.

If that book's epigraph from Laura (Riding) Jackson hints that 'There is something to be told about us / for the telling of which we all wait', few could have predicted the appearance of *The Maker on High*. Published by Mariscat in 1997, this is EM's translation of the Latin poem *Altus prosator*, from an original generally ascribed to St Columba. It is composed in driving syllabic rhythms of a post-classical Latin which 'have the effect of a new metre clamped on them by internal rhyme, half-rhyme, and echo'. EM's brief Preface praises the power of the poem:

> Anything remotely 'pious' or 'saintly' [. . .] is absent. For Columba, God is God, and the ministry of Jesus and the comfort of the Holy Ghost are firmly marginalised. Without being unorthodox, the poem is a concentrated, relentless blast of fearful praise for the *Altus prosator* of the opening line, and, friends, you better believe it.

The poem proceeds alphabetically by the opening letter of each stanza. N gives a flavour:

> No one needs to show us: a hell lies deep below us
> where there is said to be darkness worms beasts carnage
> where there are fires of sulphur burning to make us suffer
> where men are gnashing roaring weeping wailing deploring
> where groans mount from gehennas terrible never-ending
> where parched and fiery horror feeds thirst and hunger.
>
> > (*The Maker on High*: 6; CT: 391)

The Preface states that a slightly different version had appeared earlier in *Collected Translations* (1996), but the Mariscat production is a fine limited edition of 300, printed by David Hamilton at the Partick Press, Kilmacolm, in a stern and clean Scotch Roman font. EM's intention in translating this particular poem was political not religious:

> I was doing it in a sense for Scotland: to try to extend the awareness of what the people of Scotland were thinking about in writing long before the Wars of Independence in the twelfth to fourteenth centuries. Most anthologies of Scottish poetry before that time had begun with Barbour's *Bruce*, and I knew there was good poetry written in Scotland long before that, which wasn't well known. It was in Latin, in Norse and in various other languages, because the language mix in Scotland was very great in those early years.[16]

Columba and his monks were Irish, of course, but obviously not 'too Irish'. He was pleased to have his translation opening an anthology of Scottish religious poetry that I co-edited with Robert Crawford and Meg Bateman in 2000, and also *The New Penguin Book of Scottish Verse*, which Crawford co-edited with Mick Imlah in the same year.

As we have seen, EM in his lectures on *Paradise Lost* was always more on Satan's side than on that of the Maker on High. He admired Milton greatly, and considered him the greatest English poet. In *Paradise Lost* he preferred 'the strong dark dissident [. . .] poetry of the satanic part'[17] while also feeling that

Milton had caught the human tragedy and drama of the expulsion of Adam and Eve from the Garden in the final books. Once *The Maker on High* was published, EM was soon engaged in writing a sequence of twenty poems which appeared as *Demon* (Mariscat, 1999) in a suitably striking scarlet and black cover, with EM's own calligraphy. They were composed between January 1998 and January 1999.

These deliberately run counter to the vision of Lucifer as presented by St Columba:

> He Zabulus was driven by the Lord from mid heaven
> and with him the airy spaces were choked like drains with
>   faeces
> as the turgid rump of rebels fell but fell invisible [. . .]
>
> (*The Maker on High*: 4; CT: 390)

In *Demon*, in contrast, EM defiantly outfaces the traditional view by his imaginative identification with the demon's guise and voice, which is by turns seductive, mocking, knowing, witty and cruel. The character shows a remorseless drive for survival. In the last poem, 'The Demon at the Walls of Time', the demon climbs a final barrier by fingertip holds on lines of a mysterious text cut in the wall:

> [. . .] feeling and following
> The life-lines of unreadable inscriptions
> Cut by who by how I don't know, go
> Is all I know.
>
> (*Cathures*: 115)

EM's characteristic sense of a drive towards discovery, and an unwavering following-through of purpose, can be linked to what has been called a 'voluntarist' tendency in Scottish thought. This view challenges the traditional medieval vision of the mind's key role as being to recognise what is true and good. Instead it takes a more instrumental view of practical reason, where the mind's

341

function is to identify the best means to achieve a goal that is fixed by our own desires and preferences (Duns Scotus and David Hume would be of this party). In these late Demon poems, EM remains determined to wrest knowledge from what is negative, alienated and irredeemably obscure:

> I don't come unstuck, I don't give up.
> I'll read the writing on the wall. You'll see.
>
> (*Cathures*: 115)

The impetus towards exploration had long been a feature of EM's poetry, and in certain ways it intensified with aging, as if in defiance of time. In another poem of the 1990s, he describes the initial shock 'when two swans flew like spirits past my window': but what remains of their powerful passing in 'A Flypast' is merely a

> wonder that we ever thought them spirits,
> those muscles working, those webs, that eye, that purpose.
>
> (*Sweeping Out the Dark*: 74)

The Demon's determination to keep going may have been connected with EM's awareness of something being wrong with his body, even before the cancer was identified in 1999. When he told me about its diagnosis in August of that year, he admitted that he had experienced 'various pains and discomforts this year, but put it down to being seventy nine'. Typically, he was focusing his attention now on the next project:

> I hope and hope that I shall be given enough time to complete the major task I have on hand, a commission from Raindog Theatre Company to write a trilogy of plays on the life of Jesus Christ, for production late 2000.[18]

This would be a further rewriting of religious tradition and not unexpectedly create its own controversies in a West of Scotland context. However, the sources of EM's Demon are to be found less in the religious tradition of Scotland, I believe, than in Russian painting of the *fin de siècle*, and particularly in the work of Mikhail Vrubel (1856–1910).

Vrubel's work on the restoration of twelfth century icons in the Church of St Cyril in Kiev and his study of Byzantine mosaics and frescoes, led him in search of a spiritual ideal. He sought that ideal in beauty, and created many works around the image of a Demon. This was not to be identified with Satan of the Judeo-Christian tradition, a personification of evil. Instead it was linked with the Greek meaning of 'daimon' as 'divine power' or 'guardian spirit' mediating between humanity and the gods.

Vrubel's Demon is revealed as a heroic personality, an isolated rebel forever unwilling to accept social injustice and determined to oppose it in endless struggle. More particularly, Vrubel painted illustrations to a long Romantic poem by Mikhail Lermontov (1814–1841) that was also called 'The Demon'. EM knew the work of both these Russian artists well, and also the family connection of Lermontov to the Scottish family name of Learmonth, through the seventeenth-century officer and adventurer, George Learmont. Coincidentally, EM also had Learmonth ancestors through his mother's McGowan side. The 1989 exhibition of Soviet Arts in Glasgow, already referred to, may well have brought all this to mind.

EM's interest in the Scottish philosophical tradition, and in expressing his own distance from traditional Christian and Catholic beliefs, was spurred from 1994 onwards by his discussions with a Spanish priest, Gonzalo Gonzalez. Visitors to EM might sometimes be surprised by the appearance or disappearance of a tall silver-haired figure in clerical black. He had telephoned EM from London in August of that year, wanting to discuss 'Scotland', and came to Whittingehame Court in September. As EM told Richard Price:

> History, education and philosophy were his main interests but we duly expanded and expatiated for a couple of hours. Ascetic, would not take a cup of coffee.[19]

Their discussions of the Scottish philosophical tradition continued intermittently for the next fifteen years and covered a range
of topics from Marxism to Heraclitus to the role of the artist. To
some extent, Fr. Gonzalez may have been a foil in helping EM to
articulate his opposition to Catholicism. As a member of Opus
Dei, an organisation that even in Catholic circles is reckoned to be
authoritarian and moralistic in its principles and practice, he was
certainly 'traditional' in his attitudes. It may also have been the
case that EM was trying to fathom why his friend Morven wanted
to belong to such a Church. For anyone who knew the poet, it is
an unlikely relationship but it may have had its roots in intellectual combat. Whatever motivated it, the priest continued to visit
EM for the rest of his life.

He sent Gonzalo Gonzalez copies of his *Altus Prosator* translation and his *Collected Poems* (1996), as well as his trilogy *A.D.*
(2000), and received in return a copy of a Letter of John Paul II 'To
Artists' (1999), as well as various pamphlets by the founder of Opus
Dei, Josemaria Escrivá, which he found 'awful'. The poet was also
prayed for at masses said on Christmas Day 2000, and later on the
island of Iona and in Rome. Did the Demon feel embattled
perhaps? This onslaught from missionary Catholicism seems far
removed from the generosity and openness of John Scott's family.

Of course, the Demon sequence is not a theological work, and
some of its most interesting poems result from the intersection of
EM's life and the Demon's response. For example, 'The Demon
at the Frozen Marsh' revisits EM's trip to Auschwitz in 1998:

> I take my quick sharp heel and spur and smash
> That shimmer to complaining splinters.
> I'm off to where after Oswiecim. Watch.

> > (*Cathures*: 94)

The following poem in the sequence, 'Submarine Demon', recalls
a letter to Richard Price in July 1992 where EM discusses the sea
being 'full of mysteries', such as the suction marks on dead whales
that 'show conclusively that squids far larger than those known to

science are still lurking, playing and propelling themselves through the depths'. So the Demon descends to the ocean bed, and finds among its volcanic activity many creatures

> Basking, large, coiling, uncoiling, unnamed,
> Snuggling round the black smokers, alive
> In these impossible degrees.

(Cathures: 95)

It was often EM's habit when he had no other afternoon appointment to take the bus into the centre and just observe the city and its people. In 'The Demon in Argyle Street', one member of a crowd of young lads in central Glasgow (which is 'full of would-be demons') tries to give the Demon a kicking and then wishes he hadn't. This may be a pensioner's fantasy of power.

CARCANET IN THE NINETIES

Two of EM's Carcanet volumes of this decade have already been commented on: *Sweeping Out the Dark* (1994) and *Virtual and Other Realities* (1997). The earlier volume contains fifty eight of the seventy poems from *Hold Hands Among the Atoms,* and substantial selections of translations of Attila József and Gennady Aigi, mentioned in earlier chapters, as well as small groups of poems by Leopardi, Khlebnikov, Pushkin and Montale, and individual poems by others.

Two memorial poems are worth noting, as the passing years took their toll of poets whom EM had known and admired. 'In Memoriam Laura Riding' deftly uses the breakdown of half-rhyme and assonance to signal the loss of a remarkable talent. She too seems to share in EM's claim for determination and will-power:

> Florida tucks language under her wing,
> Waits for the wet true sun, the soar of will.

(Sweeping Out the Dark: 18)

On the facing page is a poem in memory of Dom Sylvester Houédard. In 'dsh: recollection of a vortex' EM recalls

> a swirling coat on great western road
> a swirling monk filling the lift
> a swirling head in drifts of coffee [. . .]
> a swirling show of spacedout typestracts [. . .].
>
> (*Sweeping Out the Dark*: 19)

When Dom Sylvester died early in 1992, the Scottish poet Thomas A. Clark, still living and writing near Prinknash Abbey and running a small art gallery, wrote to ask for EM's help. He hoped to organise a little memorial exhibition, in a twelve-day gap between other exhibitions already booked, and asked whether EM could lend anything for it. It is possible that he sent some of those 'spacedout typestracts' that dsh had given him, although no record of this exists. Thomas Clark had attended the funeral mass in the Abbey: 'Sylvester is now buried in the Monastery grounds, among some trees in a fold of the hills, a lovely place.'

The major publication of EM's poetic work in the 1990s was *Collected Translations*, which Carcanet produced in 1996. They were also publishing most of his play scripts of the 1990s, and thus fully reflecting the creative balance of his work in this decade. Edited by Robyn Marsack, this paperback volume is almost as hefty as the *Collected Poems* (1990), and the earlier volume was now reissued in paperback to partner it. Taken together, they represent a remarkable body of poetry. In some ways, I prefer the Translations as a volume. It has a clarity of vision and development that the more complex *Collected Poems* lacks, a complexity deriving not only from the range of styles and forms there, but from the necessary embedding or disembedding of parts of Mariscat or other productions reprinted in Carcanet volumes. So the sequential development of the book becomes a little blurred. *Collected Translations* on the other hand is organised chronologically by previous volumes for 370 pages, with then a further 100 or so pages arranged alphabetically by author.

The Introductions EM had written for those previous volumes are usefully included. In a brief Preface, he focuses mainly on the translations from Hungarian which 'are something of a special case', mentioning particularly József and Weöres, and his 'feeling of eager identification' with them, and paying tribute to those who had helped him with his task of translation from a language that he was not fully expert in. He had, however, picked up a good deal of the language through the work of translating, and through his own almost 'missionary desire to spread the news to the English-speaking world that there were major poets writing in Magyar' (CT: xxi).

This desire had continued in the 1990s. He had contributed a Foreword to a new volume of modern Hungarian poetry in translation, *The Colonnade of Teeth*, edited by George Gömöri and George Szirtes (Bloodaxe: 1996), as well as translations from Lörinc Szabó, Attila József, Sándor Weöres, László Kálnoky and Sándor Csoóri. In a Poetry International event on 27 October 1996, a Hungarian Day to mark the anniversary of the revolutionary uprising there in 1956, EM read his translations of some of the country's leading poets, along with George Szirtes. In May 1997, he received the Hungarian Order of Merit award, a distinguished-looking gold cross, presented in the University of Glasgow by the Hungarian ambassador.

The production of *Collected Translations* was not without its troubles. Carcanet was damaged when the Irish Republican Army exploded a 300 pound bomb in Manchester on Saturday 15 June 1996. Although prior warnings had been given, more than 200 people were injured by debris and glass. Carcanet's office was in Corn Exchange, next to the shopping centre where the bomb went off:

> it has been shattered – records lost – general chaos which it will take some time to recover from – so obviously the publication list is a shaken and moveable feast at the moment.[20]

Carcanet recovered from this adversity, as so often before, and published *Virtual and Other Realities* in the following year.

This collection begins and ends with journeys: 'A Voyage', which dramatises the progress of a sperm from ejaculation to conception in the fertilised egg; and 'Ariel Freed', in which Ariel, the spirit-servant of the magician-king Prospero in Shakespeare's last great dramatic work, *The Tempest*, speaks of the ongoing adventure of being, finally, free:

> Only to have no shore, no landfall,
> no runway, no eyrie, no goal and no fall!
>
> (*Virtual and Other Realities*: 101)

EM was determined, he told various friends, *not* to be like Prospero, not to drown his magic and return to the mundane duties of ordinary existence. So Ariel becomes a herald of this determination:

> Oh I was electric: my wingtips
> winked like stars through the real stars.

Not a particularly realistic view of things in his mid-seventies, we might think, but for him aspiration was, almost always, everything.

'A Voyage' was completed at Halloween of 1995. It had originally been commissioned by Radio Scotland for broadcasting that December, but had then been taken over by Radio Four for the following spring. It was finally broadcast in June 1996, as part of 'Arrows of Desire', a mixture of poetry, music and drama, with Bill Paterson as the voice of the sperm and Sian Phillips as the voice of the egg. EM's poem was intercut with five original monologues by Patricia Hannah describing fictional births, e.g. of Jane Eyre's son. EM's own 'mini-epic voyage' was, he said:

highly imaginative – *had* to be! – I did quite a bit of reading to make sure I got the facts right [. . .] I enjoyed this test of my nothing-not-giving-messages belief. I'm afraid it's all very pro-life, so it won't please every feminist on the block (but some, I'm sure).[21]

The 'Beasts of Scotland' sequence in *Virtual and Other Realities* shows him on firmer ground, with a knack for finding precise images or voices for Wolf, Golden Eagle, Red Deer, Midge, Conger Eel, Gannet, Spider, Seal, Wildcat and Salmon. He had finished this sequence of ten animal poems by February 1996 for Tommy Smith to set to music for Glasgow's Jazz Festival in July.

The voices are human in 'The Five-Pointed Star' which follows, where Catherine the Great of Russia, James Macfarlan (a nineteenth-century Glasgow working-class poet), James Murray (editor of what became the *Oxford English Dictionary*), Franz Kafka and An Anonymous Singer of the 21st century all give their opinion of Robert Burns. The star in the title refers to Burns's Masonic connections. EM's father had tried to interest him in freemasonry at an early stage, but the focus on Burns here may reflect the growing sense that EM had begun to have of his own potential role as a modern poet who could speak for Scotland.

This was partly connected with translation, as well as politics. The two were linked in his mind:

> if you want to change Scotland [. . .] you'll probably gain some kind of reinforcement from trying to translate foreign poets who have been in a somewhat similar position [. . .] you'll feel sympathy with them and it probably helps you to see what you could do in your own place in your own country.[22]

Later in this interview he refers to Gavin Douglas's translation of Virgil's *Aeneid*, as an early and convincing attempt to bring classical culture, at its highest and most difficult level, into Scotland's native language – which of course became in time 'the language of Burns'. To this extent, he believed that literary translation could inspire a community's self-image, bringing diversity and an international perspective to enliven more local kinds of writing.

Virtual and Other Realities led to EM being selected for the short list of the 1998 Scottish Writer of the Year in October 1998. In the same month his name, among others, was proposed by some journalists as a successor to Ted Hughes as Poet Laureate. Hughes had just died of cancer at the age of sixty eight. At the end of November 1998, *Virtual and Other Realities* shared the Stakis Prize with James Kelman's story collection, *The Good Times*. At the ceremony, an impromptu petition went round the tables for signatures, proposing EM as the first poet laureate of a devolved Scotland.

This national award, and possibly that acclamation from the guests at its presentation, made some amends for a confusion earlier in the year. EM had received a telephone call from the Poetry Book Society, informing him that the collection had won the T.S. Eliot Prize. The next day they phoned back to tell him there had been a mistake. Describing his feelings a year later, he seemed fairly phlegmatic:

> it was obviously a psychological shock to be buoyed up one day and shipwrecked the next; but I have always believed in simply going on writing, regardless of recognition or the lack of it – I have enough trust in my poetry to do that.[23]

WORDS FOR MUSIC

EM had been slow to pick up on performance poetry in the early 1960s, but once he got the point he never lost contact with his audience. In the 1990s, that relationship was expanded through staged performance of music and drama. Other artists and production companies now tended to approach him with new ideas, and his normal inclination was to accept the interest of a challenge.

In music, EM's most fruitful collaboration was with the young Scottish jazz saxophonist and composer, Tommy Smith, for whom he wrote the sequences *Beasts of Scotland* (first performed at the Glasgow International Jazz Festival in July 1996); *Planet Wave* (first performed at the Cheltenham International Jazz Festival in April 1997); and six poems for *Sons and Daughters of Alba*, commissioned for Glenmorangie International Jazz

Festival in 2000. This last sequence would be published in EM's collection *Cathures* (2002), and *Planet Wave* in *A Book of Lives* (2007). He also performed with the guitarist Carlos Bonell, for whom he created lyrics based on music by the eighteenth-century blind Irish harpist, Turlough O'Carolan, and the modern English composer, William Walton: 'The Poet, the Planxty and the Bagatelle' (June 1997).

Tommy Smith had grown up in the Wester Hailes council estate in Edinburgh. There developed between the two artists a mutual respect and affection, based on a recognition of each other's creative strength. At school, Tommy Smith had not been good at English, but remembered being struck by EM's poem 'In the Snack-bar'. His musical gifts, however, had been recognised early, and, thanks to support from his local community, he had been able to afford to go to the United States to take up a place at the Berklee College of Music, an academy of jazz education in Boston. He had repaid their trust by his unstinting support of youth jazz music in Scotland, and by his own remarkable playing and composing.

In September 1995, he had met with EM in the Café Gandolfi in Glasgow, together with the Director of Glasgow Jazz Festival, David Gorman, and a representative from Linn Records to discuss the 'Beasts of Scotland' project. EM finished his sequence of ten animal poems four months later. The initial launch took place on 10 April 1996 at the Marriott Hotel, where Tommy Smith played 'Wolf' and EM read the poem, and the premiere of the sequence was in the Old Fruit Market on 4 July, as part of the Festival, with illustrations by Neil Boyce, a student at the School of Art. There would be another performance of *Beasts of Scotland* at the Culloden House Hotel in May of the following year, together with a BBC interview on poetry and sound, linked to the sequence, on 16 June 1997.

Earlier that year there was the first performance of their combined work *Planet Wave* at the Cheltenham Jazz Festival on 4 April 1997 in the Town Hall. The idea had been suggested by Tommy Smith in a phone call in October 1996. He asked EM if he had ever read H.G. Wells's *A Short History of the World*. Indeed he had, 'a long time ago': his list of reading in *Nothing Not Giving Messages* places it quite near James G. Frazer's *The Golden Bough*, which he had chosen as a school prize at the end of his Fourth Year at the High School. They then started discussing the possibility of a 'big theme' with music, electric synthesizer and voice to be used in a more overlapping way than they had done in their *Beasts of Scotland* suite. EM then went away and devised the ten moments of history, all in different moods for musical interest, all containing the word or idea of 'wave', and all moving forward in time. They were written quite intensively in January and February 1997.

The Cheltenham Festival performance was recorded for later broadcast on BBC Radio 3 on 21 June. EM found it a strange experience:

> reading the ten poems on a high stage, standing *very* close to my microphone, surrounded by such explosive waves of sound (planet waves), but it went well, and the *Scotsman* sent Kenny Mathieson, their jazz reviewer, who gave it an excellent write up.[24]

The correspondent for *The Times* gave a less positive reaction, feeling that the music lacked sufficient variety to sustain ninety minutes, and that EM could have delivered his ten poems with more verve and sensitivity. However, EM was pleased with the work and included them in his *New Selected Poems* (Carcanet 2000) at the end of the decade. Tommy Smith was happy to ask him to extend the sequence from ten to twenty, and it was this complete set that was published in *A Book of Lives* (Carcanet 2007).

It is difficult to see how much 'sensitivity' is required in expressing the sweep of time from the formation of the solar system in twenty billion BC ('In the Beginning'), through description of 'The Early Earth' (three billion BC), 'End of the Dinosaurs' (sixty-five million BC), through the life and art sustained by human beings 'In the Cave' and 'The Great Flood', from 'The Great Pyramid' and Viking explorations to the Mongol invasion and the voyages of Magellan, up to the starry investigations of 'Copernicus' (1543 AD).

The second Planet Wave sequence of ten poems, written after the millennium, would take the human journey forward from the 'Juggernaut' of 1600 AD via the Lisbon Earthquake (1755), and Darwin in the Galapagos (1835), through Rimbaud's Abyssinia and the wartime Siege of Leningrad, the Sputnik's voice and the music of Woodstock to 'The Twin Towers' of 2001 and outwards through space 'On the Way to Barnard's Star' (2300 AD). This interstellar journey ends, characteristically, with a next step:

> 'Open the hatch', I said.
>
> (*A Book of Lives*: 43)

The composing partnership continued in 1998, when EM produced the lyrics for ten songs to form the basis of *Monte Christo*, a condensation of the 1100 pages of *The Count of Monte Christo*, by Alexandre Dumas. It was written for performance by Jeff Leyton, an uncle of Tommy Smith, who had been singing the role of Jean Valjean in the London production of *Les Miserables*. This was aiming to be different from *Planet Wave*, moving more towards a theatrical musical with large elements of both classical and jazz music, and touches of folk music, lasting about 75 minutes. The piece had a four night run at the Traverse Theatre in Edinburgh, before its Glasgow performance at the Cottier Theatre on 5 September 1998.

These jazz performances, in which words preceded music, overlapped with another series. In March 1997 EM was in discussion with the guitarist, Carlos Bonell, about a proposed work based on music already written. This became *The Poet, The Planxty, and the Bagatelle*. A 'planxty' is a slow Irish jig or dance tune, and the music was a transcription for guitar of five harp tunes by the blind Irish composer, Turlough O'Carolan (1670–1738). The 'bagatelles' were five pieces for guitar by the English composer, William Walton (1902–1983), whose *Façade* (1923), an instrumental setting of poems by Edith Sitwell, had first brought him to prominence. EM's lyrics were ready for rehearsal by the beginning of June in Southampton, with a performance in the Turner Sims Concert Hall there on 25 October 1997. Further performances followed in Portsmouth Cathedral, the Quay Arts Centre on the Isle of Wight, and the Forest Arts Centre in New Milton, Hampshire on 6–8 November. EM flew back to Glasgow on the following day, and gave a reading in Castlemilk on 10 November for the novelist Des Dillon's *Cutting Teeth* audio magazine.

The lyrics of this performance piece have not been reprinted. The bagatelle pieces are perhaps more interesting than the Irish ones. O'Carolan, in EM's recreation of him, sounds to me a bit like a stage Irishman. Both are of interest in being amongst the earliest work by EM to appear in *PN Review*, after a long refusal to contribute (his first appearance being in issue 100). Now these were published along with the first part of *Planet Wave* as 'Two Suites' in *PN Review* 119 (24:3) in January 1998.

There is some attempt in the 'Planxty' verse to connect with the contemporary politics of Northern Ireland. O'Carolan states that he plays to all those that will listen:

> In barn or castle, healthy or sick,
> Protestant or Catholic,
> And leave to others that may come
> The beating of a deadly drum.

But it is difficult to know how to respond to such lyrics on the page, separated as they are from their musical performance. The writer Alan Spence heard a performance of *Planet Wave* at the inaugural WORD festival in Aberdeen in 1999 and found it 'sublime'. Richard Price listened to the Cheltenham 'Planet Wave' broadcast on BBC Radio 3 and described it to EM as 'a sort of lap of honour as regards your poetry to date, with suggestions of new directions (as ever!) here and there, especially there!'[25] There is, it is true, a sense of familiarity about this device of a journey through time and space. On the other hand, written for a jazz accompaniment to be created in response to his words, the sequence is designed to offer contrasts of rhythm and tone. It has a great deal of interesting detail – time-lords pick up a lot of general knowledge on their travels – but there is occasionally a know-it-all tone to the narrator's voice. Of the navigator Ferdinand Magellan, for example, we hear:

> Every triumph left a trail of questions.
> Just as it should, I told the geographers.
> Don't you agree, folks, that's the electric prod
> to keep us on the move? Don't care for prods,
> put your head in a bag, that's what I say.
> Well, I'm given to saying things like that,
> I'm free.
>
> (*A Book of Lives*: 32)

On the page, the general tone here may remind us of the sermonising stance that W.S. Graham detected in EM's wartime letter instructing him how to write poetry, or a better kind of poetry. What it lacks, perhaps, is the Demon's defiant edginess, as that character later takes his own overview of the world and time.

The two sides of the spinning coin of EM's nature were nicely caught by Gael Turnbull in 'The Locospell Poem' which he sent to EM in January 1991. He had been running the spell-check program on his Amstrad, and found that it offered him a replacement for his own surname: 'Turnable'. This gave him the idea for a poem of replacements ('Mongrel' for Montreal, 'Era' for Ezra [Pound] etc). For his friend EM, the imaginary spell-check would offer:

> Stopped at: Edwin. Replacement: *Eden*
> Stopped at: Morgan. Replacement: *Moral*

This aptly combines two aspects of EM's response to life. There is the charm he found in fresh potential, an almost childlike reaction the world and its future. Also visible is a commitment to improve the human condition by asking hard moral questions in his poetry – about politics, language and identity.

POETRY, DRAMA AND POLITICS

Drama enabled EM to develop other characters, or to take some respite from his own. The theatre now provided a way of combining his highly developed technical skills in rhyme and translation with long-standing thematic interests. Thus *Edmond Rostand's Cyrano de Bergerac: A New Verse Translation* (Carcanet 1992) links gay identity with Glaswegian speech as artistic expression. *Christopher Marlowe's Dr Faustus: a new version* (Canongate 1999) explores issues of willpower and scientific endeavour. *Jean Racine: Phaedra: a translation of Phèdre* (Carcanet 2000) continues EM's early interests in French language and in Scots as a medium of translation. And his long-standing engagement with Middle Eastern archaeology and culture finds a final expression in *AD: a Trilogy of Plays on the Life of Jesus* (Carcanet 2000) and *The Play of Gilgamesh* (Carcanet 2005, but created in the 1990s).

In March 1992 he was reading Rostand's *Cyrano de Bergerac*, which he had undertaken to translate into verse for the Communicado Company. He was attracted to the play not only because it was verbally boisterous but also because there was a sadness in it too, which he found interesting. Communicado was led by Gerry Mulgrew and had developed a high reputation in the 1980s, winning regular awards for their Edinburgh Festival productions. For the opening of Glasgow's year as European City of Culture, it was Mulgrew who was called upon to create a multimedia spectacular: *Jock Tamson's Bairns*, scripted by Liz Lochhead.

This translation took EM three months or so. By 16 July the play was in early rehearsal. It was to be produced at the newly re-opened Traverse Theatre: 'an interesting drum beside the Usher Hall, and a perfect illustration of The Times We Live In, with a financial centre *above* and the theatre *underground*'.[26] The play was previewed at the Maltings Theatre, Berwick upon Tweed on 30 July–1 August 1992, with a première at the Eden Court Theatre, Inverness on 6 August. Carcanet published the text, which EM dedicated to Gerry Mulgrew and the Communicado Theatre Company 'who made it possible'.

His customary research into the background of the play informs the Foreword. First performed in Paris in 1897, it was an immediate success through its combination of romanticism, witty and colloquial verse, and with its powerful main role in the many-sided Cyrano: 'a poet, a Guards Officer, a dramatist, a musician, a writer of science fiction, a student of philosophy and physics, a freethinker and gay (which could offer the theme of frustrated love an added resonance, scarcely but perhaps just audible in the play itself)'. It delighted EM that one of his personal heroes, Jack London, had seen the play in America by 1898, 'and (not surprisingly) felt an instant identification with Cyrano's energy and individualism' (*Cyrano de Bergerac*: ix-x).

There had been various English versions of the play, but EM thought the time was ripe for one in Scots. This version should be 'unburdened by the baggage of the older Scots that used to be thought suitable for historical plays'. Instead he decided to use urban Glaswegian Scots as his medium – since it is widely spoken, able to carry contemporary references, and capable of lyric as well as comic resonances. It would be hard to find a more perfect match of character, theme and language to attract a poet/translator of his inventiveness.

The play was a tremendous success. When Alec Finlay wrote to say how breathtaking he had found the performance, with a deeply touching vulnerability in the main character in the balcony scene, EM replied:

> I was greatly pleased by your reaction to Cyrano, since so many reviewers emphasised the boisterousness at the expense of the pathos. It *is* fun, of course, but several people have told me how surprised they were to be bowled over by emotion in the last scene and the balcony scene. The play really is like that![27]

The play won a Fringe First award, and also a special prize from the Hamada Foundation, administered by the *Scotsman* newspaper. This was presented at the Balmoral Hotel in Edinburgh on 4 September 1992, a black tie occasion on which EM wore a red one: a fashion statement or a political one? He and Gerry Mulgrew shared the £5000 prize money.

The two men would soon be working together on a dramatised version of the Sumerian epic story of Gilgamesh. EM had completed the first two Acts by Midsummer's Day of 1995, at least in first draft. He had indicated four or five songs in the stage directions, but no composer was yet arranged. EM was hoping that they might use Turkish music, since the company had recently toured there. By the beginning of September, he had completed Act Three, and sent that off.

However, there were internal disagreements within Communicado, and these lasted over the next couple of years. Eventually Gerry Mulgrew resigned to pursue with distinction his own career as director and actor, with Theatre Babel and the National Theatre of Scotland, among others. By April 1999, EM realised that he was now free to do what he liked with the play, as neither Gerry Mulgrew nor the new director of Communicado planned to produce it. He hoped that some other company would emerge, or that it might squeeze a place on his publisher's full list.

In fact, it would finally be published several years into the new century by Carcanet (2005). This will be discussed in the following chapter. What its history shows is EM's continuing meditation upon Middle Eastern culture during the 1990s. This is partly connected with a hankering after epic scope, or perhaps another major long poem. We find him in November 1996 reminiscing about his earliest contact with Eastern literature in the 1930s, clearly overlapping with the ruined architecture of temples and carvings that he was then pasting into the Scrapbooks: 'E. Powys Mathers ravished me in my teens – I speak metaphorically – with his Arabic and Sanskrit translations; he was something of a pioneer'.[28]

In the W.D. Thomas Memorial Lecture he gave at the

University of Swansea in 1995, he had chosen as his topic *Long Poems – But How Long?* and he revisited some of the issues and authors in the Introduction to his Collins *Albatross Book of Longer Poems* of 1963. At the end of the lecture, however, he extends the scope to consider contemporary versions of the long poem sequence, as in Robert Lowell and Ted Hughes, and in the American avant-garde writer Lyn Hejinian, whose work he greatly admired. He does not mention in the lecture his own attempt at a long poem ('my hidden poem, the one no-one writes about!') but does restate the case for Middle Eastern approaches to poetry. In Arabic, Turkish and Persian poetry, structure may come only from the metre and rhyme, and not from any clear development of themes or from the chronology of a voyage or journey, as is typical of Western long poems. Referring to Edward Fitzgerald's nineteenth century version of *The Rubáiyát of Omar Khayyám* (1859), he notes that what would, in the original, be to us in the West 'bewilderingly unconnected' would seem instead to a Middle Eastern audience 'delightfully unconnected and in fact mysteriously and subtly connected!' (*Long Poems – But How Long?*: 16).

EM was less concerned than he might have been about the delay with Gilgamesh because he had already turned his attention to two other drama projects. In one of these he introduced new Middle Eastern materials. In early April 1999 he described himself as forging ahead with a new version of Christopher Marlow's *Dr Faustus* for TAG theatre:

> I am about to plunge into Act Four, which I am completely rewriting. I take Faustus and Mephistopheles to Constantinople, where they will interact with the Great Sultan, his vizier, and a Genie. Will they escape? Only just. There is powerful magic in the Turkish realm.[29]

By mid-April the play was complete. Richard Price had visited Paris and met with Peter McCarey and his family. They had all gone to Mass in Notre Dame Cathedral, where Price had found the liturgy 'very long'. EM replied:

> While you were with the angels in Notre Dame I was hobnobbing
> with devils in my new version of *Dr Faustus* for TAG Theatre
> Company – now finished and waiting their approval.

This was just after his completion of the *Demon* sequence in
January 1999. Marlowe's original play tells the chilling tale of a
man who sells his soul to the devil in return for worldly knowledge and power. EM's version takes up some of his own concerns,
and Marlowe's theme of alchemical magic is transformed into one
of the worth and limits of scientific knowledge. Religious teach-
ings of his time are given short shrift by Faustus:

> Black book of predestination, I close you
> With a snap. Farewell theology!
>
> (*Dr Faustus*: 3)

For him, 'only science is truly divine' and physics as much as
metaphysics offers 'powers / of prophesy, magic of imagination [. . .]' – yet these do not prevent his being hauled off to
hell at the end of the day. Of course, all this was being written in
the same year as EM was diagnosed with a terminal illness.
Whether the play came before the diagnosis, when he was just
beginning to feel more aches than normal, or afterwards when he
knew their cause with certainty, the sense of mortality and
impermanence was growing ever more insistent.

His translation of Jean Racine's classical French tragedy,
Phèdre (1677), had already been accepted for production in the
1999–2000 season by the Royal Lyceum Company in Edinburgh.
Its premiere as *Phaedra* took place on 18 April 2000. EM had
decided to use a Glasgow-based Scots language translation, with
occasional extensions into other regional dialects:

> partly hoping that the non-classical shock of it will bring the
> characters back alive, and aiming also, since the translation is quite
> close (though it may seem strange to pure Anglophones), to find
> out what there is in this remarkable play that survives and
> transcends a jolt into an alien register. (*Phaedra*: 8)

Although the jolt was a bit much for at least one newspaper reviewer, whose opinions were duly cut out and filed with the many more enthusiastic ones, most critics could sense that it was the Scots language itself, remarkably, that enabled the translation to reach to the heart of Phaedra's tragic anguish. This seems again to have been a deliberate piece of exploration on EM's part. In an interview included in the programme notes to the Lyceum production, he describes talking with Kenny Ireland, the Artistic Director of the Company, about the range of potential that Scots has as a language: 'I remember saying to him that I thought it would be interesting to take on a wholly serious play, a real tragedy, using the same kind of language I use for *Cyrano de Bergerac*'.

This remark was noted by John Corbett, a graduate of the University while EM was still teaching there, who has written widely on Scots language and translation. He sees EM's *Phaedra* (2000) and Liz Lochhead's *Medea* (2001) as part of a shift in Scotland's devolutionary and post-devolutionary relationship to the canonical texts of Western culture. Racine and Euripides are re-translated, but now into the Scots language of the 'margins' rather than the Standard English of the 'centre'. For Corbett, 'There seems suddenly to be no irony in giving the Corinthian and Athenian ruling classes Scots accents', nor even in giving them hitherto despised urban accents and dialects, instead of the rural Scots favoured by MacDiarmid and his followers.[30]

EM was still pushing against the sort of linguistic bias against Glaswegian writing and speech that he had encountered in the literary quarrels of the 1960s. This did not prevent him from receiving the Queen's Gold Medal for Poetry in the same year. Possibly those at the centre missed the radicalism implicit in the medium he had chosen for his translation. He found the queen 'very nice'. She asked him whether he thought that imagination would wilt in the age of the computer, and he answered that it would not.

The choice of *Phèdre* itself harks back to EM's student days in the Ordinary French class, where, he recalled, 'I devoured

Baudelaire and Rimbaud and (in a different way) Racine who boolversayed my ideas about poetic tragedy [. . .]'.[31] As in *Cyrano de Bergerac*, EM's own emotional life may be thought to underpin the emotion and language of this tragedy. It deals with illicit sexuality (the incestuous desire of a mother for her son, in this case) and an imagery of monsters and misogyny haunts the text. In his personal life, EM's diaries for this decade show regular, often weekly, meetings with his various working-class friends – Malcolm, Willie, Bobby, Jim – whose Glaswegian language was current and sharp.

In the broader political world of Scotland, as in the France of Racine, there was a growing resentment of autocratic rule from the centre. Louis XIV's famous, possibly apocryphal, phrase, 'L'état, c'est moi' is the flipside of Margaret Thatcher's 1987 dictum in *Woman's Own*: 'There's no such thing as society. There are individual men and women and there are families.' Both formulations ran counter to the idea of 'civic nationalism', which had gained currency in Scotland as nationalism distanced itself from ethnic identity and developed a more inclusive sense of the values that seemed to inform Scottish culture. Scots generally were very supportive of such social institutions as the National Health Service and comprehensive education, especially in response to Conservative attempts from south of the border to dismantle or privatise them. This stance may itself have been one of defiance, as Richard Finlay points out:

> That the rest of the British political nation had rejected these values that the Scots seemed desperate to cling on to meant that they had to be increasingly represented as Scottish. In this sense, it was not [the fact] that Scots had changed that drove the changes of the eighties and nineties, but rather the fact that Thatcherism had robbed Scots of an acceptable or credible vision of British identity.[32]

As ideas of Britishness declined, so ideas of Scottishness ascended, and were given voice through a new literary generation. Many of these new writers came from the West Coast; many had been given support or guidance by EM at earlier stages of their careers: Alasdair Gray, Janice Galloway, James Kelman, Iain Banks, Tom Leonard, Liz Lochhead, A.L. Kennedy. Scottish literary studies as well as Scottish literature were on the rise, and the designation of Glasgow as European City of Culture had helped to boost the role of culture in Scottish society, whatever reservations some of the actual writers might have felt. A widespread perception that Tories of the time were anti-working class became linked also to a feeling that they were anti-Scottish.

Thus EM's artistic decision to choose Glaswegian as the language of classical tragedy both shared in and extended a national movement for change. On 25 August 1997, after an Edinburgh Book Festival reading with Iain Crichton Smith and Liz Lochhead in the afternoon, he went on to give an evening performance for 'Scottish Forward', an adhoc group to encourage people to vote yes/yes in the forthcoming referendum: yes to a Scottish parliament, and yes again to enable it to have tax-raising powers.

EM voted 'yes' to both on 11 September 1997. With a turnout of over sixty per cent, and almost seventy five per cent of those voting in favour of a parliament and almost sixty five per cent in favour of tax-raising powers, devolution was finally recognised as 'the settled will of the Scottish people'.

When the Scottish Parliament was finally opened in July 1999, however, it challenged the Scots' sense of themselves. Political decision-making on complex moral and social issues was resuming after centuries of absence, with a new and largely untried cast of parliamentarians. Their differences on such issues were now visibly closer to home, recorded for daily comment on television and in other media. The reality of devolved power soon came to seem almost as fantastic as the fictions of those Scottish writers whose words had helped to make the case for it.

The first challenge involved sexual mores in Scotland. Wendy

Alexander, the Communities Minister in the new coalition Executive of Labour and Liberal politicians, announced that Section 2a of the Local Government Act of 1986 would be repealed in her new Ethical Standards in Public Life Bill. This section, which became known as Section or Clause 28, had been introduced to counter parental anxieties in some English local authorities that public money was being spent on textbooks to 'promote' homosexuality. It prohibited schools from presenting homosexual and heterosexual relationships with equal weight in lessons on personal and social values. It is unclear to what extent Scottish schools were actually engaged in such teaching.

One of the purposes of this new Scottish Bill was to prevent anti-homosexual bullying or name-calling against gay youngsters in schools. Few people would have objected to this. However, its focus on parity in relationships was perceived by some as undermining the importance of marriage and family relationships. Some Scottish faith communities felt under attack, or saw it as an attempt to impose a climate of political correctness. In retrospect, the way the conflict was handled seems to have been a major political error.

Soon various minorities were in full cry, cheered on by the media recording every move and comment. A coalition Executive attempting to represent the rights of the gay community was now in conflict with different Scottish communities keen to defend the values of their religious and moral traditions. Each group considered itself coerced by an opposing group. Schools and parents meanwhile felt increasingly vulnerable and confused.

The ability of Scot to fight against Scot with absolute conviction has a long and shameful history. No blood was spilled in this case, but much damage was done to social cohesion, at least in the short term, and also to the reputation of the new political leadership in Scotland. As Scotland's greatest living poet, and as a person who had discussed his own homosexuality openly over the last decade, EM was asked to comment.

He took issue with Glasgow's archbishop, Cardinal Thomas Winning. In the course of the conflict, the cardinal had referred to the 'perverted' nature of homosexuality. His use of the term arose specifically from theological teaching based on 'natural law'. This held that because homosexual practice 'turned aside' from the normal purposes of procreation, the act was immoral. That is not how the word was widely interpreted, however, and many people felt outraged and insulted. Both the cardinal and the poet were equally strong-willed in defence of their values. EM spoke out for the contribution of many homosexual artists to the history of Western civilization: Michelangelo, Marlowe, Wilde, Tchaikovsky, Britten and others. In his view, 'perverted' was not a word that could apply to such achievements. It seemed a poor start to devolution.

After months of acrimony and a privately-funded referendum on the issue, it finally petered out in 'a form of words' that was broadly acceptable to all parties. This settlement could not really undo the bitter words already on record, and a street-poster campaign that intimidated many gay people in their own neighbourhoods. That damage, and the reputation of the new Parliament, would take longer to heal.

The atmosphere of that brief but disorienting period in Scotland's new national life coloured part of 'The Morning of the Imminent (Millennium Suite)'. EM wrote the lyrics for Tommy Smith's composition, which was sung by Cleo Laine with The John Dankworth Group at the John F. Kennedy Center for the Performing Arts in Washington on 11 February 2000. It had been printed closer to the millennial date in S*cotland on Sunday* (2 January 2000). In a voyage through time that opens with a 'swarthy woman and her wide-eyed baby' drenched with unearthly light, we soon enough hear:

> The terrible music of the north!
> Church bells rang and knees were knelt.
> Candles guttered and spells were spelt.
> A hail of sermons battered the flock.
> Sinners were screwed into the dock.

Those lines appear to damn pre- and post-Reformation religion alike. The lines that follow extend the negative reach of such practice into the present day:

> God was not mocked.
> Nine hundred and ninety-nine by the clock
> Was very near the end of things [. . .]
> Of everything a thousand years
> Has stumbled to build,
> Left unfulfilled.

The positive is re-established in a final journey of space-voyagers and 'the morning of the imminent'. The future is ready to be born; a universe waiting to be seeded with life. The parting exhortation to these spacemen is 'to drive the king of / Death cursing back / Behind his curtains of black':

> Where you sing there is one great sound.
> Voyagers, find whatever is to be found.

LOVE AND A DEATH

As the decade drew to a close, several deaths made EM realise more clearly that his own span was limited. He had attended the seventieth birthday party event for Iain Crichton Smith on 12 December 1997, and read there with Bernard MacLaverty, Hamish Henderson, Alasdair Gray, Stewart Conn and others. Within less than a year his friend was dead, quite suddenly from inoperable cancer on 15 October 1998. At short notice, EM stood in for him at a reading he was booked to do at the Poetry International Festival that November in London's Royal Festival Hall. Writing to a friend two days after Iain's death, EM admitted the shock:

I must say it has hit me. I have known him for over forty years, and felt much closer to him than to MacCaig, Mackay Brown, or

Sorley MacLean. So please allow me just a little space, till I get myself back on track.[33]

A year later, EM gave a lecture on Iain Crichton Smith at the Schools Conference of the Association for Scottish Literary Studies on 2 October 1999. He talked about the early days of their friendship, the photograph he had taken of him outside his house in Dumbarton, 'leaning against a lamp post with a match between his teeth, looking more worldly and gallus than he really was'. He described a way of writing that was very different from his own, and yet could achieve effects that his own poetry could not:

> He wrote quickly, usually without revision, and with the risk (which he was aware of) of being careless and slapdash when he was not writing under good pressure. On the other hand, he gained a sort of unstudied, often surprising lyrical quality which he couldn't have got in any other way. His best poems often seem to slide onto the page without strain or effort; they seem natural, seem right, seem inspired.[34]

EM had attended Iain Crichton Smith's funeral in the crematorium at Dumbarton along with Hamish Whyte, and both found it a bleak occasion. Its general gloom contrasted with the blend of music, songs and anecdote at the funeral of Norman MacCaig two years previously. EM felt that MacCaig would surely have liked that lack of pomposity. The obituary which he had written for MacCaig in *The Guardian* of 24 January 1996 might not have been so welcome, as it re-affirmed the boundary between them:

> If his marked resistance to ideals and visions was a limitation for his writing, it was part and parcel of his clear-sighted and essentially modest claim for what poetry could do – help us to 'resist stock responses' and 'to have a shrewd nose for the fake, the inflated, the imprecise and the dishonest'.[35]

EM's former colleague Philip Hobsbaum wrote to him on the day that obituary appeared, as 'our senior poet in Scotland, at least among those writing in English'. EM's response characteristically referred to the work he was getting on with: 'a longish poem on conception (the biological kind)' and his work with Tommy Smith: 'Both of these were unexpected operations, and I can only hope that unexpectedness will not vanish from the scheme of things'.[36] New work, he hoped, might take care of the status, and perhaps the burden, of the 'senior poet' title. EM was not, however, expecting the lightning shock when he met Mark S. It happened at the Edinburgh Science Festival on Saturday 18 April 1998, as EM was approaching his 78th birthday. He was giving a talk on Science and Poetry. Mark came up afterwards to ask a question and talk about the poetry he himself was trying to write. As EM described it to Richard Price:

> Even from a few yards off I was hit by that old bolt, that coup de foudre, and I was shaking (like Sappho) as he began to talk to me. I never thought it would happen again at *that* age. But there it is. No rules in this life.[37]

Mark was 24 years old, as EM noted in his diary for that date, but the gap of more than fifty years seemed as nothing.

Their first meeting is described in 'After a Lecture' in *Love and a Life* (Mariscat 2003: 26), later collected in *A Book of Lives* (Carcanet 2007: 91). EM seems desperate to make the connection: '[. . .] when we talked my mind was racing like a computer to keep that contact sparking'. The image suggests a possibly dangerous overload. Nevertheless:

> I swore I would cope
> With whatever late lifeline this man, whom
> I knew I loved, picked up and threw me.

It was a lifeline that stretched back through the decades. Mark was similar in many ways to other men that EM had loved when he was younger, being dark, stocky, working-class, gallus and sharp. He was from Lanarkshire, and lived now in the same town where John Scott had worked. Unlike John, he supported Rangers Football Club. One other difference, as EM told Richard Price in 2001, was that:

> He's not gay, but we've had quite an intense relationship for three years now. He knows my feelings ('Never seek to tell thy love' wrote Blake, but sometimes you have to –) and takes them in his stride. And speaking of strides, he is very fit and physical, plays football, goes running with weights on his ankles, and cycles from Motherwell (where he lives) to see me. What else? He has a sudden dazzling smile which makes you think all things are possible.[38]

EM dedicated the *Demon* collection 'To Mark' when it was published by Mariscat in the year after they met. The Demon's restless, questing nonconformity was a quality that its creator sought to embody, in his quietly defiant way, in his personal life. This was the first time that he had used an actual name rather than initials in a book's dedication to a living person. However, the decision was mainly taken to avoid possible confusion with another M.S., the initials of his publisher Michael Schmidt.

Some of EM's friends worried that the younger man might exhaust him with his eager questioning about Beat poetry in particular and literature in general. Others feared that he might take advantage of his relationship with the aging and by now quite wealthy poet. EM had built on the inheritance of stocks and shares left by his parents, adding his own considerable literary earnings from royalties, commissions and performances.

Friends who were worried about his becoming the dupe of his emotions might have been reassured by EM's pragmatic and self-sufficient outlook, and his ever-careful attitude towards money. In 1999, looking towards a new sort of Scotland, writers and commentators often drew the contrast with Ireland, where tax breaks were given to creative artists to encourage the cultural life of the Republic. The composer James MacMillan and novelist Andrew O'Hagan complained that Scotland was a barren place for artists. EM disagreed, stating that no Arts Council had existed when he started to make his way as a poet, and that, in any case, financial backing was no guarantee of results: the current crop of Scottish writers was the equal of those in Ireland (*Scotland on Sunday*, 28 November 1999).

While the first part of that statement is correct, it is also true those were precisely the years of his lack of success, and that he and his publisher thereafter enjoyed regular Arts Council funding towards books and projects. Nor had he hestitated to recommend many young writers for bursaries and fellowships. The thought occurs that both these artists had also publicised the sectarianism they had experienced in Ayrshire Catholic childhoods, and to that extent may have been thought to be talking Scotland down.

In old age EM was willing and even eager to 'live dangerously' and to rock the boat. He quoted Plato to Mark in an early letter: 'For all things are to be dared'. He declared that he too was not interested in serenity:

> Sailing into calmer waters, writing *Tempests*, composing last quartets, taking a deckchair into the garden – no, that doesn't seem to be me.[39]

Realistically, he then wonders whether he should add in the word 'yet' to that statement; but at the moment he felt himself to be 'as open to the stimulation of change as I ever was'. So he was not interested in whatever concerns about this new relationship his friends might openly or privately express. And, despite their concerns, EM was able to enjoy Mark's company and support over the following difficult years, insofar as their different lives allowed.

Several months after they met, Mark was in Italy on a year's VSO project, working in Rieti in the Centro Peter Pan, a daycare centre for autistic children. He asked EM to send him some books: Milton, Donne, Blake, Wallace Stevens, or any interesting books being reviewed in the *Times Literary Supplement*. He also wanted an Italian Grammar book. EM kept track of the cost of books, in his normal precise manner. Adding Homer, Virgil, Pope, Wordsworth, Shelley, Burns, Keats, Melville, Dostoevsky and Dylan Thomas to the wish-list brought it to a total of more than £1100. Letters to Whittingehame Court often posed sweeping questions on literary matters that EM would answer as fully as he could, like a patient tutor.

Time passed, and soon EM was reminding him in the poem 'Plans' to 'celebrate four years of letters and talk' (*A Book of Lives*: 91). Mark eventually became a student of English and Italian at Swansea University, but was unsettled in his first year there and wanted to come back to Scotland. He wondered how a transfer between universities was actually arranged. EM wrote to Robert Crawford in St Andrew's University to enquire about current arrangements in the School of English there, and was referred to their admissions officer. EM described Mark as 'bright, hardworking, and a bit of an original'. The regulations stipulated that he needed academic references and a pass for the year. These were achieved, with much better grades in English Language and Italian than in English Literature. Mark eventually transferred to the University of Glasgow, but continued to spend study periods in Italy, with occasional financial support from EM.

His late intense relationship with a much younger person draws me back to a remark EM made about W.S. Graham. In November 1999, Hamish Whyte and I accompanied him to an evening book launch in Waterstone's of a collection of Graham's letters: *The Nightfisherman: Selected Letters* (Carcanet, 1999). EM had sent its editors copies of several of his early letters from Graham for the book. Afterwards, as we were walking back up deserted Sauchiehall Street to my car for the journey home, he told us that Graham, on one of his tours in the United States, had met for the very first time his daughter by a war-time relationship. He had told EM about the intensity of physical attachment on that first encounter with a child he had never known as she grew up.

This was an experience that EM knew he could never have, but one that he wanted nevertheless. When I used to go with him to the Beatson Clinic for his regular checkups, he would sometimes complain: 'Other people all have sons or daughters to help them – why don't I?'.

In March 1999, EM had been called in by his doctor for a check-up. He underwent some tests, and there was sufficient concern about prostate cancer to call for further tests, and then x-rays at Gartnavel Hospital on Great Western Road. Cancer was diagnosed. Later EM said he would have welcomed a more straightforward earlier mention of the word. He began hormone treatment with monthly injections of Zoladex, which were then changed to three-monthly injections, more powerful, more painful. As he described it to Hamish Whyte:

> The jag was quite a jag; but I know what to expect now and brace myself, and it's soon over. Perhaps I should explain that it's not the usual fine needle, it's a huge syringe (the nurse said on Thursday it looked like an instrument of torture) and I think maybe a lot depends on the angle at which it is pushed in. Enough of that![40]

Work continued meanwhile. The first draft of his Faustus was due by 22 April, and there were poetry readings in a Dumfries school and also for PEN on World Poetry Day in that same week. In some ways it seemed that his creative efforts intensified, with a sense of time running out. He did not want his condition to be generally known and so the invitations kept coming, and his habit was to accept.

A close friend was also diagnosed with cancer early in 1999. This was Hamish Whyte's wife, Winifred, a librarian in the University of Glasgow. She underwent treatment, but died in the autumn of that year. EM liked her very much. She was, as he told Mark, 'a lovely character'. She had been gifted with a fine voice, singing in choral groups at national level and internationally, and her temperament had blended warmth, forthrightness and good sense. EM was a Christmas visitor to the Whyte flat in Mariscat Road, along with Gael and Jill Turnbull, and often visited around his birthday too.

Winifred's family was bereft. EM kept in touch with their children, and met Hamish Whyte weekly for meals and talk during that period of confusion and grief. Where previously the two had been bonded by a love of poetry and Glasgow and publishing, expressed in a constant flow of cards and letters, now there was the deeper bond of shared suffering and anxiety. To some extent, EM too was confused. Marshall Walker had flown back to Glasgow upon hearing of his illness, to speak to his lawyer 'and other persons concerned with *future events* – you know that Van Gogh picture of the crows gathering over the cornfield [. . .]'. EM realised that his friend and literary executor was only being sensible. Nevertheless, he told Mark, 'I shall have to shoot the clatter of those wings'.[41]

A LAUREATE'S LIFE

At this point, EM's life became even busier. He was made Poet Laureate for Glasgow at the start of October 1999. It was a new post, and not paid as such, but with a £3000 commission to produce, by the end of those three years, a substantial poem or sequence about Glasgow. He wrote to Richard Price:

> Of course there should really be a Scottish Poet Laureate, and that might come, once the parliament gets through more important business. No laurel wreath, but the next best thing, a photocall in the Kibble Palace [an ornate glasshouse in Glasgow's Botanic Gardens], where I stroked a black cat that was prowling among the exotic shrubbery.[42]

This cat may have brought him luck, as he maintained strength and invention enough to complete the commission. These poems were published in his Carcanet-Mariscat collection, *Cathures* (2002), and will be discussed in the next chapter. The title of the collection comes from a medieval *Life of Kentigern* by Jocelin of Furness, in which 'Cathures' is given as the ancient name of a settlement 'which is now called Glascu'.

The Kibble Palace was also the venue for an eightieth birthday tribute to EM. Edited by Robyn Marsack and Hamish Whyte, and jointly published by the Scottish Poetry Library and Mariscat Press, *Unknown is Best* was launched on the evening of 27 April 2000 in the lush greenery of this huge yet elegant glasshouse. 'Launch' is an appropriate word for EM's poem 'At Eighty' which opens the book. It takes up the imagery of sea and ships that he loved to use:

> Push the boat out, compañeros,
> Push the boat out, whatever the sea.

Tommy Smith played the saxophone and Gael Turnbull read an affectionate poem for his friend, as no mere 'eddy' but instead 'a Niagara of invention'. Other poets read. Former university colleagues mingled with literary figures and friends. Someone arrived who had already 'pushed the boat out'. He was a dark-haired man, possibly in his late thirties, and clearly drunk. He headed straight for the drinks table. The reading was already going on and the drunk man's voice set up in competition. I was standing at the back, and moved with Gerry Loose, who was then Poet in Residence at the Botanics, to usher him out, one on each side. My parting shove was more emphatic than Gerry's, unfortunately, and the young man staggered and fell sprawling. We picked him up. He seemed unhurt, and without rancour he wandered off towards the gates of the park.

Later I learned that this was one of EM's friends, Willie G. He had written to apologise for turning up drunk and missing the reading. I was never allowed to forget this lack of charity, which EM found highly amusing. It was one of those interesting moments when several of his different worlds collided. He laughed, as a child does at the incongruity of knocking down his own carefully-constructed tower of bricks. As 'The Demon in Argyle Street' says:

> This was in Glasgow, full of would-be demons.
> An interesting place all the way.
>
> (*Cathures*: 99)

Perhaps Gerry Loose and I seemed to EM like two middle-aged archangels trying to expel his demonic pal from the Kibble's tropical Eden.

CHAPTER TEN

At Dragon's Door 2000–2010

> Push the boat out, compañeros,
> Push the boat out, whatever the sea.
> Who says we cannot guide ourselves
> Through the boiling reefs, black as they are,
> the enemy of us all makes sure of it!
> Mariners, keep good watch always
> for that last passage of blue water
> we have heard of and long to reach
> (no matter if we cannot, no matter!)
> in our eighty-year-old timbers
> leaky and patched as they are but sweet,
> well-seasoned with the scent of woods
> long perished, serviceable still [. . .]
>
> 'At Eighty' (*Cathures*: 69)

This poem opens *Unknown Is Best*, a collection of twenty three tributes from poets, friends and editors, in celebration of EM's life at eighty. His bracing address to a crew of fellow-voyagers signals one of the remarkable features of his life in the new century. Not only would he himself remain remarkably creative against the odds, but his work would increasingly be a source of creativity for others.

The collection's title is taken from the concluding lines of EM's poem:

> [. . .] in unarrested pungency
> of salt and blistering sunlight. Out,

> push it all out into the unknown!
> Unknown is best, it beckons best,
> like distant ships in mist, or bells
> clanging ruthless from stormy buoys.

His words encompass a range of tones here, from the Walt Whitman-like address to 'compañeros', through a defiant note ('Who says we cannot guide ourselves [?]'), to a not-quite-nostalgic sense of times past ('the scent of woods / long perished'). But the main impression is one of urgency, carried in the exclamation marks, and the tone of an ancient mariner who has seen much and outlived many. Did he know that he was launching himself towards the reefs of public opinion and religious controversy – and did he care? The cause was his trilogy of plays on the life of Jesus, *A.D.*

DRAMA AND CRISIS

As earlier, the frenzy was partly created by media interest and publicity gone awry. *The List* of August-September 2000 previewed *A.D.*, which had been commissioned by the Glasgow-based Raindog Theatre Company. They had won a £130,000 grant from the Millennium Festival Arts Fund to present these plays, to be written by EM. In the year 2000, a dramatic and poetic exploration of the life of Jesus had seemed a timely idea. *The List* declared that EM's trilogy would portray Jesus as a homosexual.

This seems to have been a genuine mistake by the journalist, who had confused *A.D.* with *Corpus Christi*, a controversial play at the Edinburgh Festival, in which the Jesus character had been gay. EM immediately wrote to the editor:

> Various rumours about the sexual content of the trilogy had been flying around. I didn't want people thinking that because I'm gay myself I was creating a Jesus in my own image. In *A.D.* he falls in love with a Greek woman and has a daughter by her. The only gay

reference is to his disciple John, whom I make gay. That's perhaps
where the rumours have got themselves garbled. I daresay making
Jesus an unmarried father will be as offensive to some people as
making him gay would have been![1]

EM's rather resigned tone here may be because the 'rumours' had
been making copy since January 2000. Raindog's advance publicity had led representatives of the Churches to criticise his
portrayal of Christ 'as a promiscuous teenager' and to accuse him
of 'cashing in' on Christianity. The controversy spread, and the
artistic director of Raindog wrote to the *Sunday Times* to defend
the still-uncompleted project, which was, he felt, being con-
demned unseen. Their intention was to produce a set of plays
that would be appealing and thought-provoking to Christian
believers and non-believers alike.

EM's intention was clearly stated in various newspaper interviews. He was painting Jesus as a man, not a legend, and wanted
the portrait to be credible to the present generation. In an
education pack produced for schools by the theatre company
he wrote:

Anyone writing about Jesus starts from a tiny nugget of fact and an
enormous amount of conjecture. [. . .] The gospel writers were not
biographers, and they leave large gaps if they think there is nothing
significant. [. . .] I was well-read in the Bible and in Christian
literature in general, but I wanted to get behind all that, insofar as it
was possible, to the reality of the man and his time, his struggles, his
enduring vision and sense of mission within the seething society of
first-century Palestine under Roman occupation.[2]

Interviewed for the *Sunday Herald*, he resisted the suggestion
that his struggle with cancer was drawing him towards religion as
a comfort: 'I feel I've got a strong enough belief just in myself and
in life and in ordinary human beings and what they may do in
future to satisfy me. I don't feel the desire for anything beyond
that, for some other world.'

His decision to make John the apostle gay came from the array of small details that made it 'possible, perhaps even probable' that he was. EM did admit the possibility that, as a gay person, he may have been misreading gospel references to him as 'the beloved disciple' and 'the disciple whom Jesus loved', or being swayed by the stylistic difference between John's gospel and the other three: 'That's just speculation, but it seemed to fit in with the idea that Jesus was extending the idea of love to include that kind of love'.

Speculation may shade into wishful thinking. At this point in his life, EM was much concerned with the meaning of love in human life. This included his own lack of children, whom he would like to have had:

> In a way, the only kind of solace you have from that is that your writings are the equivalent. You can't leave children, you can't leave a family, but you hope that you are able to leave some of your writings to posterity. In a way, perhaps they are my children.[3]

In *A.D.*, he seems to be taking stock of much of his own past, not only his war experience of British-occupied Palestine but also his life-long fascination with Eastern cultures. In an interview for *The Herald* (19 September 2000), he described his own sense of belief as 'floating', 'a flux', 'not a hard-and-fast tightly controlled thing'. And he cited his academic study of theology in order to lecture on Milton's poetry as one way in which he had engaged with religion: 'I was never, as it were, out of touch or out in the cold, in the wastes of atheism'.

Revisiting in old age the gospel narratives that he had rejected in his teenage years, EM had sometimes found himself shaken. Speaking at a conference in the Tron Theatre, organised by the arts group Suspect Culture ('Strange Behaviour: Exploring Connections Between Theatre and the Divine', 10 December 2000), he described *A.D.*'s connection with his own past. He had himself lived in Palestine as a soldier, he had been pelted by stones in the Via Dolorosa, and had 'passed the alarming road sign which says

"SODOM 5 km"!'. He had wanted in these plays to reflect how the stony desert can create 'a sort of sublime, meditative alienation', and also the brilliant starry night sky under which he had been on watch. These experiences helped him in the drama to bring in themes of space and time, other worlds, infinity and humanity's place in the universe. Several scenes thus ended with someone looking up at the stars, and he presented the three Magi as astronomers meeting in their mountain observatory in Persia. These moments, he thought, were 'a sort of guarantor of what I can only call the spirituality of the plays'.[4]

In the context of his life's work, we might link his Magi with the storm-battered broch of his early letter to W.S. Graham, when he felt alienated in his tower-observatory. The sages of *The New Divan* also come to mind, and the time-travellers who move through *Sonnets from Scotland* as well as earlier poems: 'From the Domain of Arnheim' in *The Second Life* (CP: 198–9), 'The Gourds' in *From Glasgow to Saturn* (CP: 261–2), or 'Memories of Earth' (CP: 330–40) in *The New Divan*.

But the writing of this trilogy, which took just over a year, was more than just a résumé of poetic themes. He found the experience 'very involving and indeed emotional. At one or two points I had to stop writing because I was sobbing or shedding tears.' The example he gives is the moment at the Last Supper when Jesus warns the disciples he will not be with them much longer, and John says, 'Comfort us a little' (*A.D.*: 189): 'That line just flew into my head, but it broke me up, and for a while I couldn't continue [. . .]'.

EM explained this emotion as arising from the dramatic nature of the writing, where he was acting out in himself what he wanted other actors to give full life to: 'It was all part of the *human* focus and emphasis of the plays'. His personal involvement possibly blinded him to the fact that Christians also regard Jesus as human. For any poet, however, particular words can themselves take on an emotional life, and the notion of being bereft of 'comfort' may have cast EM back to the desolation of Gerard Manley Hopkins's late sonnet, 'My own heart let me have more pity on':

I cast for comfort I can no more get
By groping round my comfortless than blind
Eyes in their dark can day or thirst can find
Thirst's all-in-all in all a world of wet.

The personal experience of desolation that reduced EM to tears
here may have been his comfortless months after the death of his
own beloved John Scott. There is an echo of the mood of 'The
Moons of Jupiter':

The planet man must shoulder sorrow, great sacks
of pain, in places with no solace but
his own and what the winds and days may bring.

(CP: 392)

Directly before John's words 'Comfort us a little', Jesus has used
the phrase 'my second life' to refer to his resurrection. This use of
the title of his own break-through volume might confirm, if we
did not already think so, that there is more of EM in his portrait
of Jesus than he himself knew.

The smart young boy arguing with his father, Joseph, in the
opening play of the trilogy, 'The Early Years', possibly harks back
to the Morgan household. One reviewer noted how hesitantly the
play opens, with rather stilted 'school-play' dialogue in the family
home. EM's Jesus soon establishes his own special sense of
distinction from the rest of his family:

Father, you are a fount of thought, and what you say, we hear.
Every family is a cauldron of thoughts, and it is better for that
cauldron to bubble and seethe openly than for a set of tight lips to
store up inward poison. (*A.D.*: 17)

Echoes of EM's war experience in Middle Eastern landscapes also
conjure up his favourite narratives of journeys across time and
space, in 'The New Divan' and elsewhere:

381

Night and day flash past. Now the winds have ceased, and I am sitting in a hollow of the plain with a pebble in my hand. It is brown and blue. I have the whole world in my hand. The hollow, first hard, has become soft. I lie back in it. It is like a divan. There are voices I recognise. I open my eyes, my hand is empty. (*A.D.*: 48–9)

That is the character Jesus describing his experience of taking the drug, hashish. Satan, in these plays, possesses some of the silky, steely power of persuasion that EM had already developed in his Demon's voice. And in the cadences of this Jesus we can also recognise the poet's characteristic rhythms:

> The new is here; I have it, show it, give it!
> Those who have ears to hear can always hear it.
> Reach out; think; listen; argue with me;
> Take a crossbow to the bloated belly of convention.
>
> (*A.D.*: 163)

A problem with EM's vision of 'conventional' religion is that it may turn out to be, firstly, too easy a target and, secondly, much more variegated than he gave it credit for. I am not referring to the placards and chanting of fundamentalist protestant objectors, such as Pastor Jack Glass who threw thirty pieces of silver, in 5-pence pieces, into the foyer on the opening night. In fact, EM had been paid £5000 per play, but we do not know whether or not he gave some or all of this to good causes. It is not even the familiar problem in finding the historical Jesus. The seeker, as theologians know, can end up with a reflection of his or her own face staring up from the bottom of a deep well. In this case, the radical preacher of EM's script was considered by some reviewers to have been undermined by the iconoclastic theatricality of Raindog's production, which seemed overblown, distracting, and almost camp.

EM might have thought he was writing against conventional Christianity. Another speaker at the Suspect Culture conference was David Jasper, Professor of Literature and Theology in the

University of Glasgow. He pointed out that *A.D.* was not strictly-speaking Christian drama at all, but a sort of jazz improvisation on the life of Jesus – a Jesus who is not the Jesus of Christian tradition but particular to himself in the drama of *A.D.* The play was 'a hugely creative dialogue with the Christian tradition and its assumptions', possessing the 'edge' of the Gospel tradition itself, 'which is strictly-speaking pre-theological'.[5]

Thus the play quite rightly gives us no clear answers but leaves us to think. But David Jasper then goes on to combine his academic knowledge of theology with his own liturgical experience as an Episcopalian priest and to reflect upon the dramatic nature of the Eucharist and explore some of the paradoxes of theatrical performance and religious rites.

I suppose it is *A.D.*'s (or EM's) over-simplification of such complex issues, and the opening up of, particularly, Catholic communities to media distortion that left me uneasy about the whole enterprise. Catholic schools seemed to be singled out for blame in their reluctance to involve pupils and parents in an increasingly sensationalised distortion of the plays and of their own faith. In media-speak, *A.D.* became a drama that flopped after the Catholic Church organised a boycott of it. As EM wryly noted: 'They say there's no such thing as bad publicity but in this case that wasn't true'. But on a poetry-reading visit made to a Catholic school at the height of the controversy, he told Hamish Whyte, he found the staff welcoming and 'remarkably unfazed' by the negativity which had been built up around the plays.

Carcanet had published *A.D. A Trilogy of Plays on the Life of Jesus* (2000) to coincide with the production, and EM sent a copy to Peter McCarey in Geneva. Replying, he praised in particular the way that in the final play, *The Execution* 1:4:

> the words of Jesus suddenly fall through the talk like a stone: 'Sell what you have and give to the poor . . .' and you've done what was almost impossible: you've returned the shock to those words that I'll never live up to or without, and you've also shown them as so simple and obvious [. . .] when you pare away the mystery and

authority, the iconic isolation of Jesus, the encounter is still like running into an invisible wall.[6]

He saw *A.D.* as EM's 'very own Greek and worldly and serious take on the matter'. EM's own description of what he was about was clearly linked to his own creative impulses:

> The great fascination is trying to find what he was like as a human being. Scripture gives little help, having other fish to fry. But that's good: divine imagination, as Blake said, can get to work.[7]

I am not sure whether these plays do actually offer a more imaginative insight than some of the earlier poems: 'The Fifth Gospel' (CP: 259) in *From Glasgow to Saturn*, say, or even the earlier off-Christian emergent poem, 'Message Clear' (CP: 159) in *The Second Life*. I am particularly fond of 'Testament' that ends the Grafts re-grown from Michael Schmidt's gift of fragments (*Grafts/Takes*: 28). Perhaps EM lacked a dramatist's true ear for language, and his attempt to 'translate' the Gospel narrative for a new and perhaps younger audience sometimes seems reductive or flat. Of course, I did not see it in performance. The reviews were mixed, although some of them seem more focused on the 'politics' surrounding the event than on the drama itself . EM kept several letters from teenagers who wrote to him in praise or complaint.

But he was particularly pleased that audiences responded to moments where the language is heightened, as in the great speech about love that ends the second play, 'The Ministry':

> The very presence of life is love.
> The great leviathans embrace with love.
> The cedars of Lebanon are broad with love.
> The snows of Hermon shine and melt with love.
> The sun that warms us is a furnace of love.
> If God so loved the universe, we too
> Should love it, and our neighbour as ourself.

(A.D.: 149)

He focused on this at the conference, stressing how new and startling this commandment to love one another was, with neither Hebrew nor Greek nor Roman precedents. That Jesus first spoke about this, and about the forgiveness of sins, was what made him distinctive.

The theme of love would continue to inspire EM into poetry, most notably in the intensely personal poetry of *Love and a Life* (Mariscat, 2003). His public argument with conventional Christianity would also continue in poems for the press, such as 'Moses to God, on the Second Commandment', the one about 'graven images', faxed to the *Sunday Herald* on 2 January 2001:

> Why should I not if I want to?
> It is pretty rich coming from you.
> You were the first image-maker,
> Stooping and sweating in the shadows
> With your sand and spittle, clapping your clay
> Till you had got yourself an idol – [. . .].

Defiance can easily stumble into petulance. More interesting are some of the poems in *Cathures* (2002) that deal with religion and Glasgow. But before dealing with those, it is worth taking a quick detour into Zen – a small step for a working poet.

In 2002, EM made new versions of Japanese *Kyogen* plays for the London-based Jet Theatre. These were fifteenth-century farces that provided comic interludes to the formal seriousness of Noh plays, with song and dance as a major element. Kyogen were said to represent the masculine and active yang principle, interacting with the opposite and complementary yin qualities of the Noh drama, seen as passive, feminine and dark. Presented together, they created mutual reflection and pleasing harmony. Staging was simple and stylised, the very opposite of *A.D.*, with a single folding fan often manipulated to evoke the props.

EM had been recommended to Jet Theatre by Dick McCaw, for whom he had translated the medieval plays *Master Peter Pathelin* and *The Apple Tree* in the 1980s. The company was interested in exploring with music, dance and mime the theatrical traditions of Italian *commedia del arte*, Balinese popular drama and kyogen farce, taking examples of these on tour to schools and communities. Its director, Kenneth Rea, sent EM two translated plays in February 2002 to see if he could create 'a better flow' and livelier language, but without losing their zen-like sense of progression. The translations were by an American expert on kyogen, Dan Kenny.

EM clarified first the extent to which he could depart from Kenny's original, and also copyright issues. Kenneth Rea sent him a video of the group's first workshop attempts with the texts, and advised that the plays should not be too naturalistic, but more like Beckett or Brecht. Handed down within certain families for six hundred years in a continuous acting tradition, they had become stylised and perhaps over-solemn. Jet Theatre wanted to resurrect their lightness, warmth and universal comedy, and connect with British audiences in the 14–25 age range.

'Ten Theatre Poems' in *The New Divan* (CP: 355–61) had already shown EM's interest in Japanese theatre ('The Hana-machi'), as well as shadow play with puppets in Java, and the dramatic effects of 'The Mask' and 'The Fan'. So the stylised nature of kyogen drama was attractive, and he set to work on 'The Cowardly Bandits' text that had been sent, completing it within a month. Rea was pleased with this version, which managed to catch the right tone. EM had also inserted humour lost in the American version and significantly developed the verse passages. These are where EM made the most marked changes to his original.

From a biographical point of view, a link can often be made between these Japanese farces and his own ongoing health concerns, ironically or humorously treated. The spearman and bowman in this first play are as ineffectual in fighting each other as they are in their banditry. They are like a slapstick comedy version of 'Gorgo and Beau', the dialogue between a healthy cell and a cancerous cell that EM wrote for BBC radio around this time. All set, finally, for mortal combat, they decide to leave a farewell note in verse – before agreeing in the end just to go home, hand in hand:

> Away with death, it's too absurd.
> We'll keep it, thank you, well deferred!
> We two are now in harmony,
> Our hearts are not an armoury.
> We're ready now to go ahead
> With careful steps, and so be led
> Into a land of moderation,
> Finesse and reconsideration [. . .].

There is a similar cathartic element in the next kyogen, 'Thunder'. Here the main characters are the God of Thunder and a Quack Doctor:

> I am a doctor of no skill,
> I do not have a magic pill,
> Just a packet of tree-bark tea
> (Not much use, between you and me),
> Packet of tea to keep you chee-
> ry; just a packet of tea.

Although EM was getting good medical treatment that would help him outlive the best prognosis, he was nevertheless sometimes shocked by the apparent insouciance of his doctors' comments. He had begun to be unsteady on his feet, and so asked one whether anything could be done to help: 'Not unless you get a brain transplant' was the breezy suggestion.[8]

In 'Thunder', the God of Thunder has fallen through a break in the clouds and come to earth with a bump: 'I landed on my hip with quite a thump: My hip is sore. You must treat my hip.' His head is spinning too, 'it's full of clouds. What I need is some medicine to cure my dizziness'. By chance, these plays arrived in EM's life as a writer just as he had begun to experience falls at home in his flat. The cancer which had spread to his hip weakened his attempts to stand up again. Writing to a German friend in February 2002, he says: 'I had a terrible job getting up, but fortunately there is a good solid chair in the bedroom and I managed to hold on to it and drag myself up bit by bit'.[9]

In the play, the Quack Doctor first of all offers the Thunder God some 'Thunder Head Balm', but when this has no effect on the hip, he treats it with a huge needle, which he hammers into the God's hip – first one side then the other:

> I cannot put a needle into your body without your feeling it. You must grit your teeth and think of the result.[10]

A third kyogen, 'Tied to a Pole', features a master and two servants, whom he suspects of stealing his wine. He manages to trick them into getting tied up, and leaving them at home he goes off on his journey. Their thirst and contortionist skills help the servants to get thoroughly drunk, and they sing two songs of love. The first is the song of a child,

> Calling 'Daddy!' in the street.
> 'I want my Daddy!' At seven years
> Your world is full of foes and fears. [. . .]
> But there's one place I want to go,
> One place I love, and hand in hand
> We'll wander there, and there we'll stand
> Home at last. Small muscles crack?
> Never mind the twisting track.
> Nurse will take you pick-a-back!

Against these childlike fears, and the desire for a nurse to take him safely home, the poet creates an evocation of love, spoken by a woman as her lover is leaving at dawn:

> Her soft white arms clutch at his sleeve:
> Whether you stay, whether you leave,
> Whatever you desire or do.

I'm true to you, only to you. [. . .]
My love is fathomless,
Always more, never less.
I cannot fathom it,
No one could fathom it.
It binds me to you, brain and breast!

The final word here reminds us of EM's description of John Scott in Glen Fruin forty years earlier, in 'From a City Balcony' (CP: 183): 'Your breast and thighs were blazing like the gorse'. Indeed this whole engagement with Zen in the face of death recalls the dialogue of the Buddhist sage Hakuin with Chikamatsu, 'the Japanese Shakespeare', in part VII of *The Whittrick* (CP: 106–10), at the very start of EM's poetic career.

Fathoming the nature of love would become his major endeavour in the fifty poems he would write in the autumn of that same year, to be published by Mariscat as *Love and a Life* in January of 2003.

THE CARCANET CONFRATERNITY

Over the summer of 2002, EM was working on a new collection, *Cathures*. He received the proofs from Carcanet at the beginning of August, with Robyn Marsack in charge of the editing. This was to be a joint Carcanet-Mariscat production, by way of 'warm acknowledgement of fraternity rather than a commercial arrangement', as Michael Schmidt put it. There was clear recognition here of the role of Hamish Whyte in helping to sustain EM's contact with Scottish readers through the stylish series of Mariscat books since the early 1980s. Hamish Whyte's son, Kenny, provided the cover photograph, which captures in stormy tones – but with glimpses of new buildings and cranes rising beyond dark Victorian facades – something of the threat and promise of modern Glasgow.

Cathures was an ancient name for the city, and the collection contains poems stimulated by EM's appointment as Glasgow's

Poet Laureate in 1999. At the time, he had talked about writing an epic poem of 'the dear green place' from pre-historic times to beyond the present day. He had, however, already used this device in 'Planet Wave' and the 'Millennium Suite'. The treatment finally used in *Cathures* mixes lyrical and dramatic-historical voices, and succeeds very well in anchoring his own restless cultural and philosophical interests in Clyde waters.

This signals not so much the retirement of an old sea-captain, however, as a reaffirmation of Glasgow's connectedness with a wider universe. An introductory Note quotes from Lucretius, *On the Nature of Things* (*De Rerum Natura* Book I, 965–7), beginning 'Nec refert quibus adsistas regionibus eius'. No translation is given, but EM's own version is:

> It does not matter in what regions of the universe you set yourself:
> the fact is that whatever spot anyone may occupy, the universe is
> left stretching equally unbounded in every direction.

He had used the same quotation in a talk that would later be published as an essay, 'Poetry and Virtual Realities', in *Contemporary Poetry and Contemporary Science* (2006), edited by Robert Crawford. In fact, this was the talk he gave at the Science Fair where he had first met Mark, so the quotation had personal as well as philosophical resonance.

In that talk, EM also contemplated the mystery of what happens to poems that are faxed, in those moments between sending and receiving, and quoted from his own 'Virtual and Other Realities' sequence. But in the context of *Cathures*, the quotation from Lucretius re-affirms the links between Glasgow and Saturn, and indeed Glasgow and everywhere. These 'localised' poems will thus share the epic perspectives which Glasgow's Laureate had originally intended.

As if in confirmation of that bold intent, or possibly as a reminder to Seamus Heaney about who got there first, he arranged with Michael Schmidt to republish his own translation of *Beowulf* on the same day as *Cathures*, and to launch both books at

Borders bookshop in Glasgow on 20 November 2002. Thus his latest and his earliest substantial publications are presented as an example of that Lucretian multiplicity in which EM felt most at home. He referred, in a brief new Preface, to his *Beowulf*'s previous sales of over 50,000 copies in the University of California paperback edition of 1962, and declared it was his 'unwritten war poem'. Otherwise it was left as before. He would not now wish, he said, to alter its expression of the great themes of loyalty and loss.

Cathures contains some work already discussed above: the remarkable Demon sequence, and poems commissioned for *Sons and Daughters of Alba*, set to music by Tommy Smith for the Glasgow International Jazz Festival of 2000. These last include 'Robert Burns', 'Burke and Hare', 'Janet Horne', the last woman executed as a witch in Scotland in 1727, 'Madeleine Smith', who was accused of poisoning her lover in a famous Glasgow trial of 1857, and found Not Proven, 'John Muir', the pioneer Scots-American conservationist, and 'Helen Adam', the Scots-American poet whose reputation EM's lecture at the Edinburgh Book Festival had remarkably revived.

Some social and humorous verse on 'Changing Glasgow 1999–2001' modulates into moving poems written from the indoors perspective of an elderly man. Here the 'cold inspection' of a gull at his window prefigures a stock-taking towards the end of life. The 'familiar, stranded hulk' of the West End gasometer, stark against the wildness of the sky, has been seen on so many earlier evenings from the kitchen window. 'The Freshet' of raindrops from a rhododendron, dislodged when passing it clumsily, drenches the poet's cheek as if he has been weeping. The outer world, glimpsed through windows now as EM's life becomes more cautiously circumscribed, can still be turned into poetry in 'Use of Clouds', 'Grey' and '21 June':

> The longest day, the night is not so long.
> You fling back the curtains, the morning sky
> is like a meadow. What is it you want?

391

I don't know. You cannot walk there. No.
So what do you want? The morning, perhaps,
and then I want the day, another day.

(Cathures: 50)

Cathures is a dramatic chorus of voices, in which the poet's own
voice sounds one unquiet note. It opens with a strong series of
monologues from characters from his city's history: 'Nine in
Glasgow'. These poems were written from mid-2001 onwards,
and range in time from the fourth- to fifth-century British
theologian, Pelagius, who disputed the notion of original sin,
to the semi-legendary sixth-century bard, Merlin, and Thennoch
(St Enoch), the sixth-century mother of Kentigern, Glasgow's
patron saint. The religious theme is continued in a poem on the
Quaker preacher, George Fox. Other kinds of enthusiasm drive
the scientific explorations of the Glaswegian physiologist and
surgeon, John Hunter, and the early balloonist, Vincent Lunardi,
in the eighteenth century; or the work of Louis Kossuth, the
Hungarian patriot and national leader, and John Tennant, che-
mist and industrialist, in the nineteenth. Spokesman for the
twentieth century is Enrico Cocozza (1921–1997), who taught
Italian literature and language in the University of Glasgow in the
same era as EM, although he told me he had never met him – an
instance of those isolated gay lives of the 1950s. His main interest
was amateur film-making, and the homo-erotic *Bongo Erotico* is
evoked ('Well it's not *Braveheart*, and it's not *Little Women*'), and
the dark 'Fifties forbiddenness' in which EM had sought to make
sense of his own identity.

Each of these voices conveys a dimension of the poet's mind
and experience. His supposed Welsh ancestry, love of nature and
place, passion for science and technology, for flight and Hungary
and film – EM is everywhere and nowhere among these nine, like
the dramatist who, having composed his script, allows other
actors to take centre stage. He was particularly keen on 'the
great heretic':

I had known and been drawn to Pelagius for a long time, and liked
the accidental link with myself, his name being simply a Latinised
Morgan, a Welsh seafarer, born somewhere between Wales and
Strathclyde, which of course I take to be Glasgow.[11]

EM self-identifies with Merlin too, who inhabits an observatory
on Cathkin Braes and is an astronomer-sage like those in 'The
New Divan' and *A.D.*

This collection carries a fair cargo of information about the city
and its past. It was decided that it would be useful to have a set of
biographical notes about the 36 historical characters referred to.
This seemed like a good idea, but had the unforeseen effect of
'Cardinal Thomas Winning (1925–2001), Archbishop of Glasgow' having the very last word in the collection, on page 118. His
name appears in EM's mocking 'Section 28' (*Cathures*: 35), which
has the cleric being refused a place in Heaven because the very
last one available went to the gay mathematician and code-
breaker, Alan Turing, who was hounded to death by the UK
Secret Services after the war. Rather undiplomatically, I pointed
out the irony of Winning's having the last say from beyond the
grave. That was one of the rare occasions when I saw EM angry
with me.

Another aspect of the irony was that he had actually been
seated next to Tom Winning at an official dinner in the early
1990s, and had found him likeable and charming. The two had
got on very well. He was from Wishaw, near Motherwell. Nevertheless, the resurgence of Orthodox Christianity in the former
Soviet bloc and the bitter ideological struggle in the 'new'
Scotland over repeal of Section 28 had combined to harden EM's
attitude. It may have been with them as is sometimes said of
Galileo's quarrel with Pope Urban VIII over the heliocentric
universe – as much about two powerful men locking horns as
about the ostensible differences.

Sacred music was all right, however. EM's skill in writing for
musicians is evident in 'The Trondheim Requiem' commissioned
by the Norwegian composer, Stole Kleinberg, in 2001 for per-

formance in Trondheim Cathedral in the following year. It is a requiem for victims of Nazi persecution in three main movements: 'The Yellow Triangle: Jews', 'The Brown Triangle: Gypsies', and 'The Pink Triangle: Homosexuals'. EM was disappointed not to have been able to accept the invitation to travel to Norway for the performance.

He was increasingly unsteady on his feet, and had been knocked over by a car that reversed from its parked position as he tried to take a short-cut behind it across Great Western Road, instead of going the longer route via the pedestrian lights. EM was badly grazed and shaken, and had been unable to get to his feet without the driver's help. Later he turned it into an episode for the *Sunday Times* 'Atticus' column: his doctor had told him shortly afterwards not to worry too much about the uncertainty of the prognosis for his cancer – 'After all, you could get knocked over by a car tomorrow'.

For the launch of *Cathures*, I remember fetching him by car and then helping him slowly descend the stairs at Borders to the basement venue. The crowd was large, and included many teenagers. I thought they must have studied his poetry at school, but when they brought CDs for him to autograph it became clear that they were fans of the rock group, Idlewild. EM had written a song lyric for their latest album. The old poet continued to spring surprises, even on himself. Credit for this new 'fan-base' was due in large measure to a young German research student who had created a website devoted to EM and his work.

CLAUDIA KRASZKIEWICZ

Claudia Kraszkiewicz had come across EM's poetry in 1994 on a 'contemporary Scottish fiction' course at the Ruhr-Universität Bochum. As well as EM, the students studied MacCaig, Leonard, Lochhead, Mackay Brown, Grassic Gibbon and Gunn. Now their tutor, John Pozienski, had brought his students on a study tour of Scotland. He had been a pupil at St. Modan's High School in Stirling, and remembered clearly a visit there by EM in the early

1970s. Claudia took the opportunity to make contact with the poet, and would keep in touch with him over the years that followed.

Her 1997 Masters thesis, 'Experimentalle lyrische Formen in Werke Edwin Morgans' gained high marks. She was encouraged to continue into a doctoral study of EM's poetry, and her letters to him outlined the way in which she intended to use the work of Bakhtin and Wittgenstein as well as postmodernism as an analytical framework. Was EM 'a late Modernist or a pre-Post-Modernist'?

This academic outline obscures the liveliness of her personality. She was a passionate fan of her football team, Borussia Dortmund, and persuaded EM into watching some of their televised matches. After a very brief spell in teaching, she left because creativity was 'strictly forbidden' in the German grammar school system. She supported herself by magazine writing, and editors suggested she should begin a novel. She and her husband designed the EM website, and by late 2000 she was acting as a conduit for about twenty requests per week from readers, particularly school and university students, looking for background detail on EM's life and career.

She and EM kept in touch by telephone and fax on these matters, but she also visited him in Glasgow with her husband in March 2001. Hamish Whyte took them on a photographic tour of places in Glasgow relevant to his poetry. This included the King's Café off Sauchiehall Street, the supposed scene of EM's encounter with the blind man needing to be helped downstairs to the toilet, as described in 'In the Snack-bar' (CP: 170).

Aware of his own increasing unsteadiness, EM took the opportunity in January 2001 to fly to London to visit the House of Lords, before the lords and ladies finally disappeared, he said. Scottish peers could invite guests for dinner, around the date of Burns Night. According to his diary, he was to meet Veronica Linklater (Baroness Linklater of Butterstone), who was involved in educational and prison reform, and in the Pushkin Prize writing competition for Scottish and Russian children. Parliament was a world away from the web. As he described it to Claudia:

> One lord gave us a guided tour of the premises, which are very Victorian and Puginesque, heavy but grand, or grand but heavy, loaded with pictures and roll-calls of the past.[12]

As the website was being developed, Michael Schmidt became concerned about copyright piracy on the internet, and was unwilling at first to allow complete poems to appear. EM made the case for a sampler of his work online – say, six poems of various kinds, suggesting 'Strawberries', 'The Loch Ness Monster's Song', 'Glasgow Sonnet No.1', 'A Home in Space', 'The Dowser' and 'Ariel Freed'. This last was later replaced by 'Fires' (from *New and Selected Poems*: 166) which was often requested at readings, and 'A Little Catechism from the Demon' (*Cathures*: 113) was also added. Michael Schmidt could see the argument for a website that would keep EM's poetry accessible and publicised, and agreed.

On a return trip to Scotland in October 2001, Claudia and her husband visited the installation in the National Portrait Gallery in Edinburgh of photographs, paintings and montages of EM by Ron O'Donnell and Steven Campbell. In the following year they visited and photographed the bronze 'herm' of Edwin Morgan in the Edinburgh Business Park in South Gyle, on the west of the city. Public busts of Hugh McDiarmid, Sorley MacLean and Liz Lochhead are also placed there. David Annand sculpted the head of EM, who wrote a new poem for the column on which the sculpture stands. He had several sittings in his living room, 'perched rather precariously' on a high chair. But he got on very well with the sculptor and was pleased with the result.

It was a different sort of art that had drawn young people to attend the *Cathures* launch. The Scottish band Idlewild had recorded an album, *the remote part*, in which EM's voice featured on the final track, reading a poem, 'Scottish Fiction', which he wrote after meeting the lead singer, Roddy Woomble. He had been a fan of EM's work since his teens, and had written to the poet about ideas of identity and belonging, which would become the theme of the new album. EM wrote the poem, and Woomble recorded his reading on a mini disc player and then mixed this with instruments for the CD.

A lot of Idlewild fans had been writing to the website asking to buy or download a copy of the poem. EM asked Claudia if she could feature the poem, with a link to Idlewild's website, liaising with Roddy Woomble on this. So although he was not himself an adept of the new information technology, EM was able to engage with it by proxy. He was amazed by the numbers of emails from young people, not only Scots but English and Welsh youngsters too, once some of his poems were set for GCSE English. Older people too were brought closer by the internet: a little too close for comfort, in fact, when an American woman who had read his poem 'Strawberries' on the website wrote to say that she had fallen in love with him.

Through his more serious academic correspondence with his 'webmaster', we learn a bit more about EM's preparation for 'The New Divan'. He had read Goethe's *Westöstlicher Divan* in the Penguin edition of his *Selected Verse* (1964) with prose transla-tion. He had also read Hafiz in various translations, from Justin McCarthy's *Ghazels from the Divan of Hafiz* (1893) and Walter Leaf's *Versions from Hafiz* (1898) to Arthur Arberry's *Fifty Poems of Hafiz* (1947). The word 'divan' was one he said he had heard in the Middle East during the war, and he had liked the idea of a long poem made up of fragments of stories, so that the poems seem to be sitting 'in divan' and talking together, 'without the reader being driven along by narrative linearity (wow)'.[13] So a fairly traditional approach to research had underpinned EM's apparently pre-post-modernist approach in that long poem.

There could be great charm in the German researcher's almost but not quite perfect understanding of English. EM had been championing the work of Attila József since the 1960s without his translations forming a single substantial collection. This was put right in *Attila József: Sixty Poems* (Mariscat, 2001). The collection was launched among the greenery of the Kibble Palace glasshouse. The band played polkas as the nearest thing to Hungarian music they could manage, and there was *Bull's Blood* to drink. Claudia, hearing about this but not recognising the trademark for a basic Hungarian Red, took it as a sign of Glaswegian machismo.

In working towards publication, Hamish Whyte had discovered a poem hand-written by Jozsef and wanted to include an image of this, juxtaposed with EM's own typewriting, on the back cover. Recognising that it was a poem he had never in fact translated, EM sent his version by return:

> It's last of a sequence of seven sonnets called 'My Homeland', an angry condemnation of 1930s social conditions, and one of his last poems. Fortunately he did not live to see his warning about Germany unheeded.[14]

BENNO PLASSMANN

Through the website came contact with another performing artist who would inspire new writing. Benno Plassmann shared many of EM's interests in theatre, narrative and the poet's role, and was able to blend these in performance. He was a German director, actor and researcher whose international arts group, The Working Party, aimed to bring people from different cultures and communities together, while also exploring the role of the artist in society. Established in Glasgow in 2000, the group travelled extensively, often using multi-media approaches to engage creatively with, and learn from, those who lived in deprived or difficult circumstances. In late 2000, he had been in residence at a theatre in Denmark, researching improvisation in those arts where time was central: music, dance, theatre and song. He was working with EM's poem 'Opening the Cage' (CP: 178) which presents 14 variations on 14 words of the American avant-garde musician, John Cage: 'I have nothing to say and I am saying it and that is poetry'.

Taking his performance on tour in Scotland in 2002, at the Fruitmarket Gallery in Edinburgh, then at Gilmorehill University Theatre and St Andrew's in the Square in Glasgow, Plassmann was keen to reprint EM's poem in the programme, and to invite the poet to the event. EM pleaded his ill-health, and referred the permissions request to Michael Schmidt. But he was nevertheless encouraging, and so Plassmann contacted him again with ideas for several new projects. The first was a 12-day 'Govan Gathering Light' festival in late December 2003. For this he created an outdoor image-and-sound installation which combined projection on to the facade of Govan's former Lyceum cinema, now a bingo hall, of stills from the films of Enrico Cocozza, with an audio recording he had made of EM reading his *Cathures* poem about the film-maker.

Early in January 2004, he phoned EM and described some ideas he had about a performance based around the tall tales of the Baron von Münchausen. He was an eighteenth-century Hanoverian soldier who had served in the Russian army in several countries and campaigns, fighting against the Turks. In retirement, it was said, he would recount his wartime 'experiences' for the entertainment of friends. However, the tales as published contain many folklore motifs, and were probably adapted by a German professor from the University of Cassel, who had fled to England in order to escape prosecution for appropriating items from a museum of which he was curator. That sounds like a tall story in its own right.

These tales, written quickly for money, proved highly popular and were soon widely published across Europe. This had led Plassmann to reflect on the myth of the Baron and what his fantastic stories, rooted in ordinary-seeming problems but with absolutely fantastic solutions, revealed about the reality of fiction, the social function of the entertainer-artist's creative response to real life, and the borderlines between story-telling, lies and madness. He wondered whether EM could retell the tales in a language that would work in performance, one that would be true to the voice of the Baron, seen as either the patron saint or the daemon of storytellers, a paradoxical paradigm of all writers of fiction, and around which a broader theatrical event might be developed.

By early April this had become a firm commission. From Claudia Kraszkiewicz and others, EM had already gathered photocopies of the tales in various editions in German and English, and he researched historical background detail on both the inventive Baron von Münchausen and the rascally Professor Raspe who first appropriated and then extended his tales. Meanwhile Plassmann had been developing the theatrical character of the Baron while on other work in Italy and Brazil. He had also been devising another project based on EM's poem 'Memories of Earth' (CP: 330–40), in which six time-travellers try to come to terms with their fragmentary experience of human beings, in their desolation and also their 'ordinary fortitude'. The Working Party cooperated with Stalker Teatro from Turin, which was twinned with Glasgow in an inter-urban arts exchange programme.

In this piece, Plassmann had been inspired by the creativity and solidarity of families he had met who worked by scavenging saleable objects on a huge landfill site in the city of Belo Horizonte in Brazil. Now he used the giant rubbish recycling plant at Polmadie in Glasgow as a setting, with its mazes, caves and tunnels, and built up a cast of over 100 citizens young and old from Toryglen, Govanhill and Turin, involving local schools and creative community groups in the work. Together they explored the nature of memory, and what survives when objects are thrown away. This took place over three nights at the end of October 2004. EM wrote a poem for the programme, in which he recalled the old slates and slate pencils with which he learned to write: 'It was a revelation / When words appeared / Writing on a piece of the earth / With another piece of the earth [. . .]'.

Under EM's hand, the Baron's tales also seemed to take on a new magic. He had completed his versions by mid-May 2004 and sent copies to Hamish Whyte. He could see the potential of a new Mariscat pamphlet that might be sold at performances when the developed *Adventures of the Baron* went on a Scottish tour in

September and November, reaching audiences from Dumfries to Mallaig. The performance, with Plassmann in the mesmerising role of Baron, would later tour in Italy. The pamphlet was launched at 'The Baron's Ball', as part of World Book Day events across Glasgow, in an evening of poetry, performance, music and dancing at the Britannia Panoptican Music Hall in Glasgow's Trongate on 11–12 March 2005. This early-Victorian music hall, the oldest and most originally intact in Britain, had been recently rediscovered and was in the process of restoration. It had at various times housed a zoo, a freak show, a carnival and an early cinema – a perfect venue for the Baron in its mysterious linkage of past and present human entertainment through the power of make-believe.

EM's selection of twelve of the tales was dictated partly by the demands of a performance of about 45 minutes, allowing for theatrical action and audience engagement, and partly by the quality of those particular stories. It is introduced by 'A Letter to Baron Munchausen', in which EM addresses him as a fellow creator of fictions:

> You are of course the grandest of storytellers, and that is where our paths cross. As a poet, of course, I am by definition a storyteller, whatever else I may be. But the full potential of narrative struck me only after I learned about *The Thousand and One Nights* from the lips of the enchanting Leila whom I met in Cairo during the Second World War.
>
> (*Tales of Baron Munchausen*: 8)

The tale of Leila is then embellished to include their illegitimate son, Mahmoud, who had studied folklore and archaeology at university, concentrating on the art of storytelling in Ancient Egypt, and was shortly due to retire from his post at Cairo Museum. Clearly a chip off the old block, he had inherited his soldier-father's interest in antiquities. Leaked to *The Herald*, this story was printed seemingly as news, and provided useful advance publicity.

The stories themselves are cunningly told, in a disarmingly no-nonsense soldierly voice that enhances our desire to believe the absurdities that are borne along on the brisk ten- or eleven-syllable lines, and to delight in their detail. The Baron's favourite horse is cut in two by a falling portcullis, so he resourcefully stitches the two halves together with laurel sprigs, which later grow into 'a green canopy that shaded him and me / For many a hot summer in Muscovy'. A coach-horse's hindquarters are devoured by a wolf, which the Baron then kicks forward so forcefully that it swallows the whole beast and finds itself harnessed, thus enabling a spectacular entrance for the Baron into St Petersburg in a wolf-drawn coach.

And so they go on. The chosen stories are full of verve, speed, trajectories of weaponry and flight, and often with an interlacing of animal, mechanical and human energies. The impression is one of an exhilarating journey through life and death, constantly cheating the latter. Riding an enemy cannonball 'like a celestial horse' back towards his own lines, the Baron engages in a wild chorus with a shrieking eagle, 'Between ground and sky, between friend and foe, / Between the possible and the impossible' (*Tales of Baron Munchausen*: 30). Creating these new versions of timeless narratives in his own increasingly circumscribed condition enabled EM, in some sense, to overleap it. They also recall his earliest enthusiasms as a young reader for tales of fantasy and the imagination.

In March and April 2005, Plassmann was also engaged in creating a double CD of readings of 85 of EM's poems. This became *His City Speaks to the Poet*, to be played at venues across Glasgow on EM's 85th birthday. The project was commissioned by Glasgow City Council, supported by Arts and Business Scotland, and carried out in collaboration with several Council Departments and with Mariscat and Carcanet. There were readings of chosen poems by pupils in St Mungo's Academy and St Paul's High School, by people on the streets of the city, by the then Lord Provost, Liz Cameron, by actors and other theatre workers, and friends, teachers, former students, writers, academics and broadcasters. Their voices, and the voices of EM's poems, were heard across the city on 27 April, in celebration not only of one poet but of the ways in which his work had occasioned the creativity of others.

It was a tribute, too, to Plassmann's ability to bring complex performances together by engaging with the range of people from EM's wide acquaintance. He was a remarkably positive and creative presence, on stage and in 'real life', happy to blur too strict boundaries between art and society.

KINDS OF CARE

As his physical health declined, EM's friends supported him in normal human ways, accompanying him to readings or taking him on drives, although he could not quite escape the contrast between the vivid life around him and his own serious state. Writing to Hamish Whyte at the beginning of May 2000, he describes one expedition with Morven Cameron:

> Yesterday was a perfect day for Morven and me to have a picnic lunch at the Lake of Menteith [. . .]. The ferryman's voice was clear across the still water. We fed crumbs to an inquisitive wagtail which wagged with renewed vigour.[15]

Although weakened by cancer, and by medication that aimed to control its progress, EM had remained astonishingly productive in his flat at Whittinghame Court, seizing whatever poetic opportunities came his way. His travels were constrained to a certain extent, but his thoughts could turn inwards and backwards, and he began a series of poems in the 'Cathurian' tightly rhyming but loosely flowing stanza. These would finally total 50, and become *Love and a Life* (Mariscat, 2003).

Because of renovation work to the outside of his flat at this time, his home was caped in plastic sheeting. All the metal windows in the block were being replaced. Mark was far off in Florence. So even apart from his illness, EM was driven to look inwards. His own photograph of scaffolding and flapping protective plastic sheeting adorns the cover of this collection, and the workmen's ordinary physical life runs through it as a living contrast to the poet's personal memories of many decades:

> The metal poles are hammered into place, the
> planks are laid, the brickies are at their
> sport
> Of scampering up the near-vertical ladders,
> our fort
> Bristles with a bantering excrescence of life
> which is, well, art of a sort.
>
> (*Love and a Life*: 28; *A Book of Lives*: 92)

These frank poems were written very quickly and on a daily basis between September and November 2002, with that 'considerable excitement' which so often accompanied his discovery of a new seam of poetry to be worked. They deal with past love, with present difficulties and an uncertain future. People and events are considered with a steady and sometimes amused gaze, so the effect is not sentimental. There is also consideration of the sheer variety of forms of love, from the maternal love of crocodiles for their young to the love conventions in Victorian literature, to memories of grandparents, and of John Scott, and of various other lovers already mentioned in this biography. The presence of Mark and his absence in Italy gives sharpness of emotion, and a reflective contrast to the poet's own weakening grip on life. Two poems, 'Scan Day' and 'Skeleton Day', recall his visit to a Clydebank hospital for a scan to track the cancer's progress:

> [. . .] Skull, ribs, hips emerge from the dark like a caravan
> Bound for who knows where
> Stepping through earth and air
> Still of a piece and still en route, beating out the music of
> tongs and bones while it can.
>
> (*Love and a Life*: 35; *A Book of Lives*: 94)

Weakening he may have been, but EM was not yet exhausted or dismayed. The quasi-confessional reflection on the range of others who had touched his life closes with the renovation of his walls completed: 'this rosy cliff-face telling the tentative sun it is almost as good as new'. There is also in the final line of the whole sequence, as so often in his poetry, a moral and social imperative: 'to those and to these we must still answer and be true'.

There were new friends, too, whose young company he could enjoy. Asha Kamming was a primary school teacher from Edinburgh, and they had met when EM gave a reading at the Scotch Malt Whisky Society in 2002. Her fiancé was in charge of their whisky stocks, and sent two cask-strength bottles in thanks for the performance. She would take EM on drives out to the country, or to readings further afield, and encourage her Primary 4 children to write poems in response to EM's more accessible ones. In old age the kindness of women meant a great deal to him, and they in turn seemed to respond. Carmella Vezza, a librarian in the Mitchell Library, also supported him in practical and social ways with special meals and trips to Edinburgh galleries to see his favourite Howard Hodgkin paintings and a Fabergé exhibition.

Love and a Life was launched in Borders on 27 May 2003. Exactly three months later, on 27 August, EM was admitted to the Western General hospital for deeper treatment to the bone cancer affecting his balance and strength. Two falls have already been mentioned, but he had another far worse experience late one evening in December 2002. This was shortly after Morven had died. She had been admitted to Gartnavel hospital with a lung disorder, aspergillosis. The building was only a short walk from his flat, but he had felt too unsteady to visit her before her death. Nor could he attend her funeral, in the Catholic Chaplaincy of the University. So he was already in a bad way emotionally when he fell again. Unable to make his legs give him purchase to rise, and afraid that it was too late to telephone his neighbour who had a key to his flat, he passed a long night before calling at a more appropriate hour. As he described it to Mark at the beginning of January 2003:

> my night on the floor was strange. As I was dragging myself about, trying to claw myself on to some furniture, but without success, I also at times was looking down on myself from above and thinking, What a poor creature scrabbling there, is that the best you can do, I thought the species was Homo erectus, get up man![16]

This was a moment of realisation and adjustment: 'and it's quite hard – when you are no longer independent – as I was brought up to be – and have to have help'.

Hamish Whyte and I did what we could to make his flat safer. Rugs were removed, and access to the telephone made more direct. I rigged up a box to catch the letters that came through his door each day, so that he would not have to stoop to retrieve them. He was afraid, when taking a bath, that he might not be able to climb out, so he and I went to a bathroom centre and ordered a walk-in shower. A wheeled zimmer with brakes was tried and found wanting. I bought his food, and then weekly deliveries were arranged with a local supermarket. A contract was taken with a home-alarm service that he could page if he ever should fall. When Alasdair Gray painted a late portrait of EM around this time, the bold red-buttoned pager hanging from his neck made him look like a spaceman against the gantry of the University tower.

Once when I was accompanying him down to the taxi for one of his check-ups at the Beatson clinic, he fell down the steps at the front of Whittingehame Court and could hardly rise even with help. When we arrived at the hospital, they decided to keep him in for further observation. Ongoing tests suggested the need for surgery and more acute use of radiography to slow the cancer's progress. His stay in the Western Infirmary lasted three weeks in a male cancer ward where he observed other men suffering alongside him and admired the almost maternal care shown by the nurses. I saw him frequently, making sure that he had his normal letters and journals to read. But the nights were long, and broken by the toll of the nearby University bell.

When EM came home on 18 September, he was happy to be there but still frail. It was clear to Hamish Whyte and myself that his situation was changing and that the future needed to be considered carefully. After a long period of confusion following the death of his wife, Hamish had met and fallen in love with the poet and children's writer, Diana Hendry. Originally from Liverpool, she now lived in Edinburgh. Hamish was travelling between Glasgow and Edinburgh and was increasingly inclined to make a new life in the capital. His children were now about to leave home for study and work in England. All of this obviously had an effect on EM, as both men had come to depend on each other in various ways over the previous four years, and now Hamish was going to be less available than before.

EM, Hamish and I had several discussions of the options available. EM did not want to leave his flat, but was too unsteady on his legs to be there alone, and his condition would get worse. Live-in care was technically possible, but he thought it would be too disruptive of his writing routine – he felt he just could not write when not alone. Care homes seemed fearsome, although he did not at this point tell us why. Only years later did he speak of bad family memories of an aunt who had been put into very poor accommodation and then abandoned by her husband. In any case, in a care home would he have room to keep his books and papers? I could continue to give support in various ways, but my own university work and family commitments were increasingly demanding and time-consuming, while Hamish was likely to be less immediately on hand than formerly, once he moved to Edinburgh. So, like many such discussions between the generations, we went round and round the imponderables without seeing a happy solution.

Hamish visited some care homes in Glasgow to check out the conditions there. Some seemed depressing, all their rooms appeared too small, and not all homes had rooms available in any case. Clarence Court Care Home in Broomhill was the best of them and had a nicer atmosphere, he thought. Yet EM entered Lyndoch Home in Bearsden on 4 October 2003. The choice was made mainly because of his memories of visits there to his retired colleague, Professor John Bryce. He recalled seeing him seated by a large window with a wide table, covered with books. He made no mention of his own father's connections to Bearsden. The turreted building did possess an imposing, somewhat faded but still stately grandeur ('gormenghastly', as Hamish described it, with reference to the Gothic novels of Mervyn Peake, whose writing and painting EM greatly admired), so we had some hopes of a larger room than in the more modern homes.

Lyndoch was originally the Schaw Auxiliary Hospital, built and endowed by Miss Marjorie Schaw and gifted to the Glasgow Royal Infirmary as a convalescent home. It had opened in 1896, and in 1948 was absorbed into the National Health Service as an adjunct of the Infirmary. During the Second World War, it was an overflow unit for patients requiring medical attention rather than recuperation. In the post-war period it became a geriatric hospital, and was then sold to the private sector in 1986.

The reality was more constrained than EM's earlier memories of the place. When he moved there in 2003 at the age of 83, he had a smaller albeit still lofty L-shaped room on the ground floor. There were other patients nearby, and a bathroom shared with his neighbour. Sunlight came shining in from a southern aspect across Glasgow, past the University to Cathkin Braes in the far distance. We had brought from his flat the dining table at which he always worked, his typewriter and one six-shelved Ladderax bookcase for a choice of his favourite authors: Milton, Whitman, Hopkins, Melville, Joyce and others, together with a complete set of his own publications and some reference texts. I later brought more from the flat on demand.

The windows were so tall that he could not easily see out of them, but we assembled the table below them and the light was good for writing. The walls had been repainted his favourite shade of bright yellow, and we hung half a dozen of his paintings in their new location. In this rather monastic cell-like context he produced not only his high-flying *Tales from Baron Munchausen* but also, more aptly, completed the translation of a medieval Latin poem written in a prison. This was *Metrum de Praelio apud Bannockburn*, one of several poems included in the Latin history of Scotland, *Scotichronicon*, written by Walter Bower in the 1440s. The poem on the Battle of Bannockburn was composed by a Carmelite friar and poet, Robert Baston. He had been sent north with the English army by Edward II as its official bard, ready to compose a victory poem once the Scots had been soundly defeated. Events unfolded otherwise, of course, and Baston was captured. The ransom price set by the Scots was the production of a poem celebrating England's defeat. EM admired the way that Baston had managed to fulfil this commission, criticising the flaws in the English battle plan while also universalising the human suffering involved: 'Its end is elegiac, dark, wry, self-deprecating' (*The Battle of Bannockburn*: 7).

The idea for this translation came originally from Professor G. Ross Roy of South Carolina, a champion of neglected Scottish texts. EM's Introduction is dated 2002, which places it in Whittingehame Court, but I recall discussing Baston's Carmelite spirituality with him later than this date in his Lyndoch room. St John of the Cross, the mystic and poet who founded the Discalced Carmelites, had also written poetry while imprisoned in Toledo, and his poetry was much in EM's mind at this time. He had also figured in *Love and a Life*, in the poem 'Spanish Night'.

The Battle of Bannockburn appeared in 2004, co-published by the Scottish Poetry Library with Akros Publications and the Mariscat Press. It is a fine book, beautifully designed by Duncan Glen, with a brief note on the history of its 'New Caledonia' type face, now better known as Scotch Old Face or Scotch Roman. Financial support had come from the Scottish Executive, and this poem on the great battle of independence was one of the earliest indicators of EM's new role as National Poet. As in 'The Maker on High', his technical brio manages to evoke the strange energies of the original's intricate interlacing of internal rhyme, onoma-topoeia and alliteration.

The entourage of Jack McConnell, First Minister in the Scottish Executive, as it then was, of a devolved government of Scotland, swept up the drive to Lyndoch Home on 16 February 2004. He had come to confer the title of 'The Scots Makar' on the nation's senior poet. EM had actually questioned the Executive's choice of the title 'Makar', since it had backward-looking connotations and a medieval air, whereas he wanted always to look forward. Other suggestions had been available, such as 'Poet for Scotland' or 'The Scottish Laureate' but these were not accepted.

The position of Makar was the result of several years of lobbying, particularly by the Association for Scottish Literary Studies under its then President, Alan McGillivray, and with strong support from Dr Gavin Wallace, the Director of Literature at the Scottish Arts Council. A chance conversation with the Culture Minister led to the idea suddenly taking off, particularly once a detailed submission had outlined the ways in which different strands of poetic writing in the various traditional and new minority languages of Scotland might be fostered by such an appointment. The idea of a post that might signal the Executive's commitment to an inclusive Scottish culture clearly resonated with the Ministers involved.

Their awareness had been sharpened by those representations from the ASLS and SAC. But clearly there was also the im-mediate matter of the re-opening of the Scottish Parliament at the foot of the Royal Mile that autumn, and the desire for some poetic language that might match and express not just the occasion but also the national mood. EM's poem 'For the Opening of the Scottish Parliament, 9 October 2004' was written in the unpro-pitious circumstances of the care home. He was guided by detailed descriptions and computer graphics of the design, by a life-long love of modern architecture and by his absolute commitment to the new, even if it proved expensive. For many this poem, read by Liz Lochhead on the actual day, would remain the highlight of that occasion. It had authority, humour and a sense of hope.

At a personal level, his nights were sometimes broken by a woman patient wailing in the corridor outside his unlocked door. His days, when not filled by new writing, or letters, or physiotherapy to assist his mobility, left time to brood on what he had left behind. Like other people struggling to come to terms with the changes brought about by old age, EM was often frustrated by his circumstances. Sometimes he took it out on those emotionally close to him. Hamish Whyte was for some months censured for his transfer of allegiance to Edinburgh, that suspect city. This was despite all that he had done or still desired to do to support EM and his work. There was a thrawn and unreasonable dimension to EM's attitude in this. Eventually after much discussion, there came a thaw, or an unbending, and this was good to see.

Visits from old friends pleased him. Alasdair Gray, taking a break from painting murals in the renovated Oran Mor complex in the West End, came to see EM and left his yellow hard-hat behind; later Malcolm capered across the room wearing it at a jaunty angle. EM seemed to be becoming resigned to life in Lyndoch, aided by his own sense of self-sufficiency and perhaps by his wartime experience of institutional conditions. And at least he could continue to write. As he commented in 'From a Nursing Home':

> A room is a room. As I write this
> My eye sweeps round table and typewriter,
> Bed and bookcase and good book-booty,
> *Black Marigolds, Howl, Vereshchagin,*
> *Moby Dick, Before Adam, Ulysses,*
> *You Have to be Careful in the Land of the Free.*
> Careful, careless, carefree – we are alive
> With whatever equanimity we can muster
> As time burns and bites along our veins [. . .].
>
> (*Penniless Press* 22: Winter 2005)

The poem ends with an unexpected flight of Tornadoes, 'So low-flying they make my pen bounce, / And my heart too [. . .].'.

No-one was prepared for the sudden and frightening announcement of the closure of the care home on 15 July 2004. Residents and their families were given a month to find alternative accommodation. I arrived on a visit shortly after the news broke, and was able to drive quickly to Clarence Court in the Broomhill area of the West End, feeling guilty that others were being left behind. This home had been the best alternative visited by Hamish Whyte a year before, and I was delighted to secure a place for EM there. In fact, a double room had become available, and this would allow him more space for his work. So his bookshelves and table were dismantled again and pictures taken down from the walls, and all was re-organised in the new room.

On the ground level now, EM was happier to be able to watch buses passing and get a renewed sense of city life, less than half a mile from Great Western Road. I had some old Ladderax bookcases and so he was able to have a matching one added to his for an ever-increasing stock of books, either bought by him or gifted by authors who knew him. And so the last stage of the 84 year-old poet's creative work was beginning, with some hope even yet of new things to come. Since travel to Clarence Court was easier for visitors, their numbers rose. Locally-based poets such as Sandy Hutchison and Val Thornton kept in touch, and many of the Informationists, as well as scholars such as Ian Campbell of Edinburgh who admired EM's critical work.

EM's dedicated nurse was Malou Cruz, and the care staff came to understand his self-sufficiency: that he was happier to take meals in his room and concentrate on his own reading or writing than to go to the dining- or day-room. He did however attend the birthday celebrations for residents, and went on outings to places of interest, to sail on the Forth and Clyde canal or view again the Concorde jet in its retirement in East Lothian.

The flat at Whittingehame Court was in the process of being sold at the time of this enforced move. That had seemed too final in the early months at Lyndoch, as there was uncertainty about how the care home might work out. I had a set of keys for it, as did Mark, now back from Italy and continuing his undergraduate studies in Italian. I made regular visits over the winter to check the house and collect mail or books for EM. The flat, which I had been visiting for more than thirty years, kept its peaceful and welcoming atmosphere, and a distinctive dry aroma of books. It had been a sanctuary for him and the place where his creativity had flourished, as well as being the venue for many significant meetings with friends and colleagues over four decades. Could it somehow be kept intact?

One idea was to try to retain it in public ownership, not as a monument but as a creative venue. Marshall Walker, who had flown from New Zealand to visit his old friend, was keen on that. Another aspect discussed with EM at this time was the idea of a full and 'authorised' biography, and the recognition that this might take many years to complete. However, his diaries and some personal papers, mementos and photographs were gathered with that in mind, and lodged temporarily in the University's Department of Scottish Literature.

Enquiries were made by Hamish Whyte to the City Council about use of the flat as a Writers' House for Glasgow. After all, many important European cities have such a base for visiting authors, or for residencies by local writers. But the idea encountered practical objections. For example, who would pay for renovation, upkeep and taxes? If all the books and paintings were going by prior arrangement to the Mitchell Library and the Hunterian Gallery in the University, who would see to refurbishment and keep it as a thriving place? There were also the ongoing costs of his care accommodation, which might be considerable. The house meanwhile could deteriorate.

EM's lawyer advised sale and so, reluctantly, arrangements were made around Easter 2004 for EM to sell the flat where he had lived more than forty years. Every home has its history, but this one had been the site of countless imaginings and many hundreds of poems, written or translated. It fell to me to open the flat for viewings, by young couples, gay couples, parents of students, fault-finders and out-of-our-price-rangers. To begin

413

with, I had been wary of literary tourists, but all seemed genuine. One man did ask if the owner was the actual poet.

There were other tasks too, such as arranging for staff from the Hunterian Gallery to evaluate and pack his paintings for transport to the University. They missed or ignored one of Dom Sylvester Houédard's small typestracts in a photograph frame, which I then retrieved for EM. There was a subsequent exhibition of his collection in the University, and efforts made to keep at least some of them on show. When Michael Schmidt became Professor of Poetry in the University several years later, he was surprised to see, on a 'Meet the Professors' evening, one of EM's paintings that he had last seen in Whittingehame Court now gracing the wall of the Principal's House.

Then came the removal of books to the Mitchell Library: an all-day task by a team of four staff. There were some 7000 books to be added to 6000 already gathered over the years by Hamish Whyte, who had catalogued them and their marginal comments, to make available to Glaswegians 'a poet's working library'. When Hamish was in the process of moving to Edinburgh, his own collection of books, journals, rare first editions, programmes, posters and other ephemera by and about EM, patiently built up over the 1980s and 1990s, was transported to the Scottish Poetry Library by the poet Ken Cockburn. Now he arrived in the SPL Van at Whittingehame Court to take away the G-Plan desk and designer chair from EM's study. These were ultimately to be displayed in the exhibition space of the Scottish Poetry Library that would house their Edwin Morgan Archive.

The flat was finally sold in August 2004. Before then, we arranged for it to be cleared of furniture, which mainly went to auction with the firm EM had last used in clearing his Aunt Myra's flat. The sum raised was small, although EM said he 'had no huge expectations, having gone through this process with my mother's effects a long time ago. [. . .] By far the most valuable item was the Doulton chamberpot; if you still have any chamber-pots lying around, don't throw them away!'.[17]

Mementos were chosen by neighbours. For his home-help of

many years, Margaret, who had polished the brasses and kept everything clean and bright, there was a red Versace vase. Various visiting poets took keepsakes. Mark wanted the plants he had looked after through the winter, and was also given a recliner chair and books of the Beat poetry that he and EM had so often discussed. One of the poems in *Love and a Life* had also promised him the lucky brass dragon that stood guard by the electric fire.

The files of correspondence, cuttings, poems and translations on which this biography is mainly built were stacked in the study, ready for transportation to the Department of Special Collections in the University Library. There were still last-minute decisions to make: Where to keep the honorary degrees? What to do with the vicious-looking hunting knife with the serrated edge, and what story could it tell? The files would supply one possible answer. What about the twelve varieties of expensive soap in the drawer beside the kitchen sink?

It seemed wrong to throw out or sell his parents' walking sticks, and as EM himself refused to have them they still hang in my porch, used only occasionally for chasing urban foxes. Hamish and I took some CDs (Bob Dylan and Turlough O'Carolan in my case – I thought EM never quite got the point of either artist, although he tried his best) and I also took some of the household tools: neat chisels and a hammer, each one with the Stanley mark, his father's name. Last of all, like the servants in a kyogen play with a different plot, we were instructed to split the contents of the master's drinks cabinet, which were expensive but not extensive.

THE QUEST FOR GILGAMESH

In the midst of all this turmoil, there were some signs of things slowing down, odd metaphors for EM's changing condition. Firstly, a self-winding Rolex watch that he had bought in the 1960s stopped working. It was cleaned and examined by various specialists who found nothing wrong, and it always worked fine if

I carried it around in my jacket. The reason might have been that his left arm was not active enough to keep it wound. He refused the simple expedient of giving his wrist an occasional shake. If the watch did not work as advertised then it should be cast into a dark drawer. This had already been happening in Lyndoch, but it was finally given up in his new room, and a new watch bought.

The second and more serious loss happened shortly thereafter. The platen roller on his typewriter split, leaving a gap where the keys could not print. It was an Adler Blue Bird, which he had bought in 1961 when he was still living in Rutherglen. Despite searches by specialist repairers in Glasgow and beyond, it proved impossible to find a spare part, even second-hand. And so the machine that had typed so many poems and plays was reluctantly abandoned. It was eventually taken through to the Scottish Poetry Library. A more modern alternative was bought, but its action was too light and flimsy. And it languished on its shelf.

At this point in his life EM was struggling to cope with both psychological and physical problems. Some of the morphine-based medicine used to control pain in his legs and spine had upset the balance needed for creative work: both a wide-angled openness to moods or ideas and a focused attention to words that would give those ideas new life. Yet he still had some earlier work to hand. *The Play of Gilgamesh*, published by Carcanet in 2005, helped keep his mind occupied, and raised his spirits.

EM's personal quest to see this play produced has echoes of a struggle against fate. His Introduction compares Gilgamesh to Beowulf or King Arthur, but notes too that he was a historical figure, ruling the kingdom of Sumer, in present day Southern Iraq, around 2700 BC. EM's interest in his story had its own history. The earliest reference in his file is a cutting from the *Radio Times* of 20 November 1954, where D.G. Bridson introduces his own version of the story of Gilgamesh, about to be broadcast on the Third Programme.

It is likely, however, that EM had come across it earlier, given his interests in calligraphy and ancient languages and in the buried cultures of the Middle East, guessed at through magnificent ruins and fragments of text. The original poem was in a pre-Akkadian Sumerian tongue, recorded in cuneiform. In fact, the Gilgamesh story might have vanished from history altogether; it did vanish for millennia until deciphered in the mid-nineteenth century. The role of translation had been paramount, and EM's own play of Gilgamesh re-translates the sometimes disjointed original, filling gaps with bridging scenes and songs.

There are more personal links too. In the Introduction, EM quotes the Beat poet, Gregory Corso, who read a translation in prison, learned much of it by heart, and thereafter refused to take seriously anyone who did not know the poem. The central relationship of both epic and play is that between Gilgamesh, the powerful, moody, handsome king in his city of Urak, and the opposite but equally powerful Enkidu – a wild man, untamed, living with animals in the woods, and 'almost like an animal himself with thick body hair (Gilgamesh: vi). The friendship between the two men is deep and intense:

> The word 'love' is used; even the word 'bride' is used. Does this mean that it is not only the oldest poem in the world but the oldest gay poem in the world? Both Gilgamesh and Enkidu have sex with women, but they are in love only with each other. (*The Play of Gilgamesh*: vii)

The poem does not make clear whether there was any physical relationship between the two men, but EM points to several hints, in the erotic symbolism of a wrestling match between them, and in later dreams where Gilgamesh lifts and embraces first a strange meteorite and then a man-sized axe.

It is the mother of Gilgamesh who interprets these dreams as signifying Enkidu. In terms of EM's own history, the hirsute wild man of the woods reminds me of a letter that EM wrote to W.S. Graham after the war. Graham had asked him about the line 'To see my friend in his golden fell' in the early poem 'The Sleights of Darkness' (CP: 27). EM said it referred to a fellow-soldier whose astonishingly thick fair body-hair he used to admire when the troop went swimming. (This is probably also 'the sweating / back of my favourite / blond-haired swaddy' in the late fragment 'El Ballah' published as one of the 'Pieces of Me' in 2002.) Exploring Middle Eastern culture again through *Gilgamesh* in the 1990s may have added fire to EM's argument with the institutional churches towards the end of that decade. It was a pre-Christian reality, as he was sure there would be a post-Christian one, given time and the desert winds and sands.

He began writing his version, or versions, of the play after discussions with Communicado in 1993–94. They were looking to follow up on the success of *Cyrano de Bergerac*, and EM offered them the idea of Gilgamesh and two alternatives: a drama based on the poet Sappho on Lesbos, or on James 'B.V.' Thomson's sombre exploration of the Victorian metropolis, *The City of Dreadful Night* (1874).

He had been thinking about a Gilgamesh dramatisation for at least ten years, having been struck by the BBC radio version by Michael Poole, broadcast on 21 March 1983. *The Listener* pointed out the irony of the oldest surviving story ever written being recorded with the newest technology available, 'the recently developed ambisonics system, which is set to succeed quadrophonics'. Even more intriguing from EM's point of view, was that the equipment necessary to receive this perfect sound did not yet exist! This hi-tech version of the epic built into the narrative an astonishing array of atmospheric effects, together with a chorus and jazz-based songs. EM would similarly use a chorus in his play. In Poole's version, mythic dimensions of Gilgamesh were largely replaced by the hero as a type of the romantic artist, whose 'immortality' will be assured by his story being told and re-told through time, and not by any grander power of divinity.

EM outlined his plans for the drama to Gerry Mulgrew in the autumn of 1994, and there was broad agreement that he should proceed with the writing. By September of 1995 he had completed three of the planned five acts, making changes to his earlier writing as the drama evolved. Communicado tried to develop this Gilgamesh material in workshops, but it proved difficult. The complex dramaturgy involved in reshaping epic myth as workable drama led Mulgrew by February 1997 to think that it might work better as a long dramatised poem in blank verse, rather than the rhyming couplets EM had chosen. This would be more a dramatic recitation than a play as such, in a grand but simple style, with opportunities for songs or chanting. The rhyming couplets of the play were actually suggested by EM's research on the forms of Sumerian poetry.

He was willing to go 'back to the drawing board', having struggled with the problems of his original text. He admitted that he could not think of any successful dramatic versions of the *Odyssey*, *Aeneid* or *Paradise Lost*. So the idea of a long dramatic poem in blank verse appealed.

This second version remains in his *Gilgamesh* file. At a first reading, it seems powerful, and more single-minded than the play as finally published. The novelist Ali Smith, reviewing the Carcanet volume in the *Guardian*, described the key to EM's art as 'Selflessness and open-handed anonymity'. Certainly the drama did enable him to disappear behind or among the characters in the Gilgamesh story. But the unpublished poetic text has more of himself in it, and more adventurous language, and I like it for that. One senses EM's lithe poetic strength co-existing with that of his muscly characters – which are of course the story-teller's characters, handed on from one narrator to the next across the centuries.

Neither version was produced, because of the management problems within Communicado mentioned in the previous chapter. As ever, EM still made use of the material, publishing some of the songs, such as the 'Song of the Lesbian Blacksmith' and other free-standing pieces in *Interchange*, *Metre*, *Poetry Ireland Review*, *Scotia Review* and *PN Review*. The informative Introduction to the Carcanet volume is essentially the same as 'The Quest for Gilgamesh'. He gave this talk at the British Library in August 1996, as part of their 'Mythical Quests' exhibition of books and manuscripts linked to famous epic journeys. Richard Price had suggested that EM might be willing to talk about his translation.

Thus not much was ever wasted, or willingly let go, without recycling of some sort.

BACKWARDS OR FORWARDS

In February 2006, EM had a visit from a reporter from *The Times*. She was an admirer of his work, and had come to interview him. In the course of their dialogue he confessed a writer's block. Thereafter this became the first question asked by other reporters, steered in that direction by minimal homework in the files. The makar who couldn't write verse became a story too piquant to resist.

EM had not been able to write any poetry for four months. To many writers that would not seem too bad, as blocks go, but for him, even in his 86th year, it was a serious departure from the norm. The latest poems, in October 2005, had in any case been a series of brief 'found poems', excavated from an adventure story by Edgar Rice Burroughs that he had enjoyed in his boyhood, *The Cave Girl* (1923). These were co-written with Hamish Whyte, who had hit on this device as a way to keep his old friend amused and engaged. They would send the book and their finds back and forth to each other in a sort of poetic postal chess.

EM's dismay reported in that *Times* interview contrasts with remarks he made six months earlier in a letter to Lesley Duncan, Poetry Editor of *The Herald*. He was responding to the newspaper's poll of its readers' favourite Scottish paintings:

> I seem to be in prolific mood, and send you ten poems inspired by the pictures in your competition. They are yours if you have any interest in printing them.

> (*Beyond the Sun*: 7)

The poems, which were published almost immediately, had been written 'in his neat hand (his ancient typewriter having given up the ghost)'. After that late burst of energy, the silence that followed may have driven EM into a sort of despair. Writing of the kind he liked to do no longer seemed possible. He told the *Times* reporter that he was coping and no more, through force of will, but felt that there was no joy in his existence. Something seemed missing from his character when he was not writing.

Yet poetic work was going on, if not quite the new material he wanted to be caught up in. In that Autumn of 2005, EM had corresponded with Stephen Stuart-Smith of Enitharmon Press, regarding use of 'The Computer's Second Christmas Card' for an anthology, *Light Unlocked: Christmas Card Poems*. He had then sent the publisher a copy of his poem to mark Ian Hamilton Finlay's 80th birthday, with its vision of a ship in full sail, and Stuart-Smith invited him to send more new poems for publication in a limited edition volume. This was at the beginning of October. By the 6th, EM had sent a further single poem, 'Conversation in Palestine', where a Jesus figure predicts the future impact of Wittgenstein's character ('Ferociously honest, a life pared to the bone') and thought ('give him a chance / he'll change the world'). EM had misunderstood what was being looked for, namely a short series of poems, preferably unpublished.

Casting round, finally, for further material he found 'Thirteen Ways of Looking at Rillie'. This had been written in July 2004 for a book designed and created by Alasdair Gray. It contained messages of respect for Jack Rillie, from friends and former colleagues in the Department of English Literature, where he had taught from 1948 until 1983 and then part-time until 1993. EM's poem comes first in this book. The third way of looking at him praises 'A teacher, a teacher / never to be forgotten', from whom thousands of students 'learned to listen / when Rillie said "Yes but, you see – "'.

That was true. Equally so, alas, and closer to the age of his friend now composing the tribute, was the eighth way:

> 'Old age is hell'
> said Rillie, 'I don't recommend
> being eighty-four!'

A small University delegation presented the book to Rillie at his house in Broomhill, very close to Clarence Court. EM was too frail to attend on that occasion, but his older friend called by to show him the book shortly thereafter, accompanied by Douglas Gifford and Alan Riach from the Department of Scottish Literature, and Jim McCall, a publisher who had kept in touch with his old teacher.

The 'Thirteen Ways' became the core of the Enitharmon chapbook, with the inspirational teacher flanked by the philosopher, Wittgenstein, and the poet, Finlay, each man in his own way a hero. Although slimmer than other chapbooks in the series, it went ahead. It may, however, been his inability to respond to Stuart-Smith's request for further new material as promptly as he would once have done, that forced EM to stare bleakly at a possible future without poetry.

Physically he was weaker, and suffered a series of ischaemic attacks, little strokes that diminished blood flow to the brain and further impaired his balance and grip. His characteristic handwriting lost its elegance, another affront to his own sense of the dignity of his craft. Whatever he attempted to write now looked childish and shaky. He was able to struggle through a signing session for *Thirteen Ways of Looking at Rillie* at the end of March 2006. This was necessary, as it was a limited signed edition of 95 copies, set and hand-printed by Alan Anderson of Tragara Press in Loanhead near Edinburgh. Three years later in November 2009, when I was re-placing books and papers after his room was repainted and asked where he wanted some of the copies kept, he had no recollection at all of having signed his name, so dutifully and carefully, 95 times.

Work was already proceeding to put together his last major and prize-winning collection, *A Book of Lives*, which would be published by Carcanet in 2007. He mentioned this in the interview for *The Times*, but seemed not to count it against that imagined future without words. Hamish Whyte was already gathering texts for the book, tracking down and sending EM copies of recent work. It ranged from witty occasional verse, such as 'The Welcome' written for the International Federation of Library Authorities (IFLA) conference in Glasgow in 2002, to song lyrics for Idlewild, or to his great poem 'For the Opening of the Scottish Parliament', as sharp as a trumpet blast.

He took a detailed interest in the construction of the collection, probably sensing that it would be his last major work. 'Are we including Planet Wave I [as well as II]? The full boorach?' asks Whyte on 15 February 2006. They were. For non-Scots, I should say that 'boorach' is Highland English for 'heap', 'crowd', 'caboodle', from a Gaelic word meaning 'what is turned up or over by a spade'. There was a possible danger in such excavation. The inventiveness and energy of EM's poetry is as remarkable here as the back-cover blurb asserts. There is also, perhaps, the occasional drag of an elderly or querulous tone, heard for example in 'The Twin Towers', the planet wave for 2001 AD:

> But tall towers may be arrogant, or they may not.
> I shall become very cross – oh yes, I can be –
> if I hear the word Babel. Advocates of lowliness,
> keep off, creep off. (*A Book of Lives*: 42)

It is audible again in the more recent 'The War on the War on Terror': 'Come on, I know what I'm talking about, / I have been right through life like an arrow' (*A Book of Lives*: 104).

Even so, we might still want to borrow the poet's own words as he criticises Rembrandt for his too clean and burnished portrait of 'Man in Armour': 'You are great; even a loss from you's a gain' (*A Book of Lives*: 80). The Twin Towers poem ends in an image where poetry and pity are beautifully caught, as one ruined tower is compared to 'the broken comb of a geisha girl / which she has angrily thrown onto the road', with her unbound black hair then becoming 'cascades of unbounded weeping' for 'two thousand heads and more / that never will be found'.

The collection teems with lives and loves, then, but also with loss. The 'Love and a Life' sequence is at its heart. Also republished are 'Gorgo and Beau', EM's radio flyting of healthy and cancerous cells; and half of the *Herald* series of ten poems on paintings in Scottish galleries. The poems from a personal perspective are set against seven on Scotland's national identity, including 'The Battle of Bannockburn'. There are contrasts in plenty. Three songs for Idlewild offset darker 1950s recollections of Glasgow and Moscow.

Most moving perhaps are two recent poems of old age. In 'The Old Man and E.A.P', the phantasmagoric world of Edgar Alan Poe overtakes an old man in a care home, who seems to his visitors to be having a nap, but in his own mind he is riding 'on dragonback [. . .] perched among its spikes and rolling folds' (*A Book of Lives*: 72). He resembles the poet who created him: 'He is full of questions, this man who is not sleeping'. The poem, with its echoes of Khlebnikov's and other dragons, helps overcome dread of 'the last dragon' of death in 'Love and a Life'. Facing this, the old man is still trying to translate dragon-speak, listening and questioning 'in all the languages he knows' in a last attempt to engage with heroic times. The dragon is dumb, finally, but the tale of mystery survives when the old man wakes.

This poem sits alongside one about another care home resident, a woman of ninety-four, enjoying a large Drambuie on her birthday, and recalling her wartime experience as an ambulance driver in the medical corps while waiting for her son to arrive for a visit:

> [. . .] he is old, I forget his heart is worse
> than mine, but still, I know he'll do his best.
>
> (*A Book of Lives*: 73)

Pragmatic optimism and various kinds of strength in age form part of the book of life, as well as weakness and regret.

By the end of November 2006, aged 86, EM had recovered his strength sufficiently to visit the Scottish Parliament. He travelled to Edinburgh in the care home mini-van, to be met at the doors – less easy to enter than he'd imagined, because of tight security – by Hamish Whyte and myself. A reporter from *The Scotsman* was there too and asked about his writer's block. This gave an opportunity to talk about the new collection, due for publication in three months' time. Once that negative line of questioning had been put out of the way, there was time to marvel at the architecture, and appreciate the genuineness of welcome from the Presiding Officer, George Reid, who had got to know EM when working as a broadcaster in Glasgow years before.

The poet had the opportunity to look at his parliament poem *in situ*, and learn that it was one of the most popular souvenirs bought by visitors. He could feel vindicated too in his optimism about the building itself. At the time of his visit, there was much public complaint about how far its bold structure had outstripped the original budget estimate. EM was asked about this. He pointed out calmly that such argument about expense went along with most really significant modern buildings, and that a good building was worth paying for. Although he had a wheel-chair level view, his eyes were alert to every detail, and the effects of light and architectural energy in the place were certainly uplifting.

He took a similarly broad view about his own poetry in the new collection. After the more public poetry of the 1990s, in the plays as well as in his reflections on the digital world in *Virtual and Other Realities* and on Glasgow life in *Cathures*, EM recognised that there was a more personal element in his poetry of this new decade. He was determined to keep both strands of his writing evident in *A Book of Lives*, despite the possible dangers in factual knowledge. When Claudia Kraszkiewicz had written to ask him about the word 'falemnderit' in 'A Day Off For the Demon' (*Cathures*: 104) – it means 'thank you' in Albanian – EM admitted:

> I never know about that kind of thing, you don't want to load your verses with too much information that people don't know, but if you're interested in something it's hard not to do it, it's hard to keep pulling back.[18]

An 'encyclopaedic' tendency is sometimes discerned in Scottish thought and culture, a way of using ideas and facts with an intellectual excitement and emotional complexity that also affects poetry. The Informationists are just the latest in a line that is traceable back through EM and Hugh MacDiarmid to the nine-teenth-century poet, John Davidson, whose work EM had dis-cussed in lectures and essays, and further. While there was a danger that contemporary readers might not respond as easily to his own multiple perspectives as to a single authorial voice or style, he was determined that both the intellectual and the emotional lives of its author should be present in *A Book of Lives*.

The collection was launched on 27 February 2007 in a smaller venue than normal: in the dining room in Clarence Court, with a small crowd of about 25 friends and fellow writers. He was at this point very frail after strokes, and had lost body mass, so his ability to read aloud with any confidence was impaired. He was keen to try, but struggled despite prior practice.

His chagrin at the size of the crowd was clear, however, and a month later he was all the keener to take part in the launch at Kelvingrove Art Gallery of *Beyond the Sun* (Luath Press, 2007). Here his ten poems on Scottish artworks were braced by colour plates and by introduction and commentary fore and aft. Because of the *Herald* connection, the crowd was large and the event marked his 87th birthday. Several people who attended (I did not) felt more pity than admiration, because of his evident frailty and decline. EM however loved the crowd, the long queue for signed copies, the lofty venue hung with paintings he had viewed in younger days, and the report of the event in the next day's newspaper.

Life went on, and *A Book of Lives* went on, positively reviewed in the *Times Literary Supplement* by William Wootton, who praised 'the vigour and inventiveness of a poet who has more lives than a litter of kittens'. He noted both EM's affecting lyric voice in the songs, and the angry, tough-minded quality of his optimism. A growing fondness for 'the role of the sage' was mentioned, but also the ambiguity and darkness to be glimpsed in the details of his historical imagination. The collection was a Poetry Book Society recommendation in that year, and short-listed for the T.S. Eliot Prize.

Hamish Whyte and I travelled to London for this event on 14 January 2008, with Robyn Marsack and Michael Schmidt also there from Carcanet. EM was thought by various poets and reviewers to have a very good chance of winning, but the prize went to Sean O'Brien for *The Drowned Book*. All the other short-listed poets had given a reading from their books the evening before, and I wondered whether the tape of EM's voice that had been sent on in advance had sufficient strength against the others.

The following day when I recounted to him what had happened, he found the result disappointing, but more than that, a source of puzzlement. He had studied some of O'Brien's work in the publicity materials sent out to finalists and felt 'it was all right, but nothing special'. We speculated that it was his own variety of tone, stance and persona which might have prevented an easy, or easily graspable, relationship with readers on the panel.

Little time was wasted on regrets; other events that same month signalled both local and national respect north of the border. From noon on Friday 25 February to noon of the following day, the 'Morganathon' took place in Glasgow, a continuous 24-hour Big Read from the poet's work with a team of volunteers performing in shifts. This had been organized by Jim Carruth and others from St Mungo's Mirrorball, an association of poets from Glasgow, and was based around *From Saturn to Glasgow: Fifty Favourite Poems by Edwin Morgan* (2008). Edited by Marsack and Whyte in association with Carcanet, fifteen thousand copies of this book were given out free to all city schools, to passers-by encountered by those reading its poems aloud in the streets and squares of the city, and to visitors to the basement library in the Gallery of Modern Art where the event began and ended. Given the date, and the fact that late-night returners from Burns Suppers in the city had been involved, EM wondered whether there might ever be an equivalent for him in some future Scotland. Who can tell?

There was a further warm welcome for him at the Aye Write book festival in the Mitchell Library, again based round *From Saturn to Glasgow*. An array of writers came on stage to read a favourite poem and talk about the impact of his work on theirs. Most memorable for me were James Robertson on the way 'The Coin' sustained him in confidence about his country's future; David Kinloch on gay elements in 'Canedolia'; Michael Schmidt on the early Grafts companionship with the poet; and Bernard MacLaverty's wonderfully vindictive reading of 'Midge'. These were only some of the lives touched by his long life in words. Beyond the hall too were many he had helped. For instance, Donny O'Rourke later told me of talking to a taxi-driver whose wife had phoned EM in the 1980s, asking him to help her husband with his own poetry-writing, which EM did with patience and sincerity.

A Book of Lives had meanwhile been nominated for the Scottish Arts Council Sundial Book of the Year Award. The overall winner was to be announced at the Borders Book Festival in Melrose on 20 June 2008, from winning entrants in the fiction, non-fiction, first book, and poetry sections. That seemed worth travelling for, and appeared to have an additional good omen. The search for transport to carry him there turned up a company called Glentress Ambulances, their name recalling his early military life in the Glentress camp.

All went well on the journey down, and at the photo-shoot in Melrose Abbey with Rory Bremner, who was compere for the event, and poet and critic Rory Watson, who had known EM since his own student days in Aberdeen University. In fact, Watson told Bremner that 'Aberdeen Train' (CP: 152) had been written when EM gave a reading to the undergraduate Poetry Society there, and had been posted to them on his return to Glasgow. Everything continued well with the event itself, where EM read a short poem from the collection and his book finally won the main award, to sustained applause.

As the crowd was dispersing, however, EM began to experience extreme nausea and a sudden collapse of energy. His routine of meals had been disrupted and he seemed now alarmingly weak.

His journey back was difficult. I followed on with Robyn Marsack, fearing the worst. However, once back in his own room and with tea and toast to revive him, he was able to rest. Next day he was back at his desk, and keen to analyse the event in retrospect. He retained an inner toughness, even as his body became less dependable. He did not forget to remind me to take the £25000 prize cheque from his jacket pocket and bank it as soon as possible.

He was an original. One of the paradoxes of his old age was that while those in the crowds at literary festivals and launches had personal memories of his poems, his readings, school visits or advice, he himself continued to judge success partly by his parents' standards. The yearly total of royalties mattered: 2009 was 'a poor show'. Perhaps this was just a normal matter of seeking security in age. Another unusual attitude was his view that wolves should be released back into the Scottish mountains, despite the dangers, or indeed because of the dangers. He admitted that this might be an echo of his boyhood reading of Jack London's *The Call of the Wild*. Time and continuity continued to fascinate him. After a slight disagreement with Christopher Whyte in 2003, over whether or not he was tending to act like the Grand Old Man of Scottish Letters, he wrote about how well aware he was of the 'precarious and provisional nature of reputation':

> The only thing that matters is to be able to leave at least a few
> poems that will be remembered and read with pleasure, and who
> can guarantee that? – unless perhaps they are hammered into the
> fabric of the universe (I really believe that) and will someday
> somehow be able to be accessed.[19]

Such paradoxical thinking does not close things down but leaves them problematic and alive. He too remained unpredictable. For instance, on 'Bloomsday', Tuesday 16 June 2009, in celebration of James Joyce's novel *Ulysses*, the Department of English Litera-ture in the University presented a re-creation of the amateur musical evenings of Joyce's Dublin. The poet Hayden Murphy arrived late and sat beside me at the back. He had just come from seeing EM; he was always in touch with him by letter or in person on Bloomsday, and now was quite distraught at having found him 'much diminished'. The two old friends had not communicated but had 'communed'.

Hayden Murphy has about the softest voice in Christendom, and I knew how deaf EM had become recently, though he stubbornly refused to wear the hearing aids that had been prescribed. So, probably, he could not hear a word Hayden was saying – a later and more desperate instance of the failure of communication that figures so amusingly in his poetry. To his visitor, EM's mind must have seemed a poor fragment of what it once had been.

Yet on the following day I witnessed him give an impromptu commentary on Mayakovsky that lasted more than ten minutes and was compellingly coherent. Nick Fells of the University's Department of Music and George Burt, both of the Glasgow Improvisers Orchestra, had come to tape his comment for the CD they were making of an improvised performance of 'Schweben: Ay, But Can Ye'. This was created by the English composer Barry Guy, based on the patterns in a painting by Kandinsky and on EM's translation of Mayakovsky's poem (CT: 37). It had taken place in the Royal Scottish Academy of Music and Drama in Glasgow on 19 March 2009.

EM had been invited to the rehearsals in the hope that he could discuss the meaning of the poem, which was in Scots, but at that point he had been ill in hospital and was not able to attend. He was fascinated by the links with Futurism in Guy's painterly score, itself a work of art. The piece was shortlisted for a music award later that year. EM spoke on tape of Mayakovsky's commitment to making everything in social life speak; in the poem, every scale on the painted fish hanging outside the fish-monger's shop becomes a mouth. EM had seen such shop-signs in Moscow in the 1950s. Again we see how early in his creative life (it was published in *Sovpoems*, 1961) EM had hit upon his central

430

concern with giving all things their voice, a concern found in the fellowship of translation before he could manage it alone. His talk was astonishing, and we burst into applause when he ended.

The hospital stay, just mentioned, was frightening. EM had suddenly been taken into the Western Infirmary with breathing difficulties from a chest infection, and I was called there at 8pm, staying with him till he had been seen and settled after midnight. He was soon transferred to Gartnavel General, with a view from his ward of Great Western Road and the edge of Bingham Pond. In his poem 'A Sunset' almost twenty years earlier, he had looked out from his balcony and observed the hospital's nine storeys as 'a blazing / cage for prisoner-patients to shout out from'. The poem ends by leaving the real patients 'a little warmth, a little healing' (*Sweeping Out the Dark*: 67).

For the first time, he spoke to me about dying. It was rather like one of Woody Allen's Jewish jokes. 'Yes, this would be quite a good place to die,' he said seriously, ' – you have every facility to hand!'. He had, but thankfully did not. Instead he returned to Clarence Court more than a fortnight later, with more energy after antibiotics, blood transfusions, altered medication and follow-up care. His clothes had been lost on the transfer between the Western and Gartnavel, but that seemed unimportant in the wider scheme of things. Poets and friends called to see him or were in contact: Valerie Thornton, David Kinloch, Doreen Black, Asha Kamming, Mark and Malcolm, to name a few. Hamish Whyte had just gone through an operation and was unable to travel, but kept in touch with EM's progress.

Michael Schmidt and Robyn Marsack also visited, and both were anxious to see whether he would, when recovered, attend the opening of the Edwin Morgan Archive in the Scottish Poetry Library. This was scheduled for his birthday on 27 April 2009. He was well enough, or would be; but he was not inclined to go, and could be stubborn. He thought the archive, which was essentially Hamish Whyte's collection of original materials and texts, should have been based in Glasgow. It was only after I bought him a defiant T-shirt to wear under his jacket, showing a

Tunnock's Caramel Wafer with the logo 'Glasgow Takes the Biscuit', that he finally agreed. In Edinburgh his silent protest was noted, as EM drew their attention to it!

On the day itself he enjoyed the event hugely, meeting and talking with old friends and newer ones. Mike Russell, the Culture Minister, and Ron Butlin, now Edinburgh's Poet Laureate, made stirring speeches. Everything went well. Asha brought her baby. Also attending was Paul Batchelor, who had just won top prize in the Edwin Morgan Poetry Competition, sponsored by the University of Strathclyde and Vital Synz, a non-profit-making poetry organization set up by David Kinloch, Donny O'Rourke and others in 2007. Paul Batchelor, a free-lance writer for *The Times* and *The Guardian*, was able to visit EM in Glasgow the next day and write a positive article that balanced any doubts left over from earlier articles featuring writer's block.

His successes should not distract us from the fact that EM had difficulties, and strove to conceal these as many old people do. A contract for some new translations of Anglo-Saxon poetry for a Norton anthology remained unsigned. The offer had come in 2007 from Greg Delanty, an Irish poet now teaching in Vermont. He remembered as a teenager showing EM round Cork on one of his reading tours there in the early 1980s, and requesting, and being sent, a poem for his student magazine, *Quarryman*. EM volunteered to translate 'The Whale', a substantial allegorical poem in the Anglo-Saxon Bestiary. Yet despite being provided with dictionaries and several earlier prose and verse translations, he lacked the focus or the strength to move forward. Eventually that poem went to the American, Robert Pinsky.

But Delanty persisted, offering some of the shorter riddles in 2009, once he realised something of EM's current situation. I made a concerted effort to push him towards translation of two of these. Both were well done. I deciphered his extremely shaky handwriting as best I could, and added in any additional phrases he provided from memory. Then he worked from this draft, in a manner that was sharply aware of any changes to his intentions. This gave a sense of joint achievement. My own scribbled handwriting and his, and both of our 'senior moments' (though I had less excuse), occasionally made our dialogue like that of two characters out of a Beckett play, poring over their scraps.

An ancient kind of poetry, the riddle is also a most human form of speech. It combines child-like wonder at the puzzle of this world with adult ingenuity in its own making. It gives the mind something to work on. EM's own mind was a remarkable one, and seemed designed for poetry: responsive, adept, caught up in the range of language that shapes and expresses our existence. It gave him fixity of purpose and flexibility in achievement – both vital on life's voyage.

One of these translations would bring to a close what was likely to be his final collection, *Dreams and Other Nightmares* (Mariscat, 2010). *Likely* to be the last, but not definitely. It contained most of the dream poems described at the start of this book, as well as other poems from Mariscat collections that had not found their way into the *Collected Poems* or subsequent Carcanet books. There were poems, too, that I had come across during research in Glasgow University Library's rich archive of the poet's letters, papers, pictures and poems. There was the poem to W.S. Graham, for example, sent by way of apology for the cool reception he got in Rutherglen in 1954. There was a poem in memory of Morven Cameron, written in the stanza form of the 'Love and a Life' sequence but marked *hors série*, one of a kind. And there was another poem, 'Happiness', that described one of EM's friends threatening to kill him, jabbing his chest in a drunken rage. Possibly this was a reference to the vicious-looking knife in Whittingehame Court, an odd memento of dangers run, kept in the hall cupboard next to his clutch of honorary degrees.

Time will be the judge of the greatness of EM's poetry. He was, as we have seen from his remark to Christopher Whyte, fairly content to abide by that historical verdict. Some poets I have talked to in his city tell me that they go to EM for technical brilliance, narrative skill and breadth of inspiration, but to W.S. Graham for depth of emotion and lyrical grace. Readers, ordinary people in the streets, shops, classrooms and bedrooms of that city, might be of the opposite opinion. In writing his life, I have been struck by the number of people who were moved to contact him because of the words he had found for their own personal situations. They wrote to him because it seemed he wrote to them. That is a rare kind of conversation between writer and reader, and many more stories will emerge from it than I have scope for here.

A remarkable dimension of these last years of the decade was EM's continuing support for the creativity of others. Naturally I am aware mainly of those projects where I gave direct assistance. I recall in particular the poetry animation project for schools in Dumfries and Galloway, organized by Jules Horne. Children could enjoy poems that were recreated on screen, using sophisticated computer graphics and sound effects, and learn to work on their own versions. Thus EM's translation of 'one fly' by the Brazilian concrete poet, Edgar Braga, seemed an appropriate choice (CT: 302).

There was also the Burns project 'As Others See Us' by the Broad Daylight photography team. Here, portrait studies of well-known Scots were exhibited along with their choice of a Robert Burns poem, and an explanation for it. The exhibition was launched in the Scottish Parliament on 21 January 2009, as part of the 'Year of Homecoming' celebrations. It was also the 250th anniversary of Burns's birth. EM chose as his poem 'The Address of Beelzebub to the Rt. Hon. John, Earl of Breadalbane', favouring the Demon's voice. The explanation which he dictated was clear and cogent: all I had to do was keep up, then type up. In it, he praised aspects of Burns which, many people would agree, might equally apply to himself: 'Burns is the great example of a thinking man, gradually learning how many things he could do well, looking round the society of his own time and responding to it'. EM went to the Parliament Building for the launch.

Another photographic project was the 'Sonnets from Scotland' series by a young archivist from Ayrshire, Alex Boyd. This is a haunting series of Scottish landscapes with a single figure, not seeking to illustrate EM's work in any sense but to respond to it in a different medium. Similar structural elements in each picture play the role of octave/sestet or rhyme in the sonnet form of which the poet was so fond. Boyd had also booked his hour on the Plinth, a communal artwork set up in Trafalgar Square by the sculptor, Antony Gormley, over 100 days of the summer of 2009. From the Plinth, he declaimed EM's selection of his own poems, as well as taking photographs of the crowd. In Boyd's profile shot of EM, exhibited in the Scottish Parliament early in 2010, there are clear echoes of the Burns likeness by Alexander Reid.

'Sonnets from Scotland' also provided inspiration for the composer, Gavin Bryars, who from 2006 onwards wrote settings of several, and these were recorded in performance by the Estonian National Male Choir.

Fascinating, if less immediately successful, was the visit of Andy Lowings. He and his colleagues had rebuilt the Lyre of Ur, using Sumerian sources and traditional African instruments and materials to guide them in recreating an instrument that could now be played for a contemporary audience. He had recently come across EM's *Gilgamesh*, and came north to meet its author. The story of the lyre's reconstruction in the midst of the war in Iraq was inspirational, and led to thoughts that this might be a spur to the play's performance. With the support of Gavin Wallace, the National Theatre was approached, although without response. EM had earlier enlisted Liz Lochhead in lobbying, unsuccessfully, for a production.

Poets came to visit EM. Seamus Heaney arrived for morning coffee on 13 July 2006, with novelist Andrew O'Hagan and Karl Miller, the critic and editor who had worked with EM in the 1960s. They were on a satnav-guided tour of places in Scotland that had particular personal connections. They had just driven up from the Borders, where Miller's critical work on James Hogg, the Ettrick Shepherd, had taken them.

There was talk of the poetic generation recorded in Sandy Moffat's painting, 'Poets Pub'. EM's manner was reserved, possibly because he was never part of that hard-drinking Edinburgh scene, but perhaps also because of his earlier reservations about O'Hagan, on Scottish cultural life, and Heaney, on rural poetry and his 'Irish' *Beowulf*. Heaney presented him with his recent Faber volume, *District and Circle* (2006), and inscribed it: 'For Eddie – District Grand Master – Circle Centre – with highest regard, Seamus'. They each received a copy of the Enitharmon chapbook in return.

Another memorable visit was by Adrian Mitchell, a counter-cultural figure in the 1960s, poet, playwright and peace activist. Both he and EM had been active in the experimental and public poetry of the 1960s, and Mitchell had been one of the forces behind the 'International Poetry Incarnation' in the Royal Albert Hall in June 1965. EM had written his declamatory poem beginning 'Worldscene! Worldtime! Spacebreaker! Wildship! Starman!' for this event (CP: 199), although degree-marking at the time prevented him from attending. Now Mitchell had called in to see EM in February 2008, on his way north to readings in Fife. He was a most engaging personality, and revered EM's work: 'If there is any poetry in the world I wish that I had written, it would be yours,' he said. He was 12 years younger than EM, but died suddenly not many months later. For a memorial volume published by Markings Publications in 2009, EM again dictated a fine prose piece, 'Remembering Adrian Mitchell'. By a strange synchronicity, that 'Worldscene!' poem was also selected for *A Century of Poetry Review*, edited by Fiona Sampson (Carcanet, 2009) around the same time.

A sad coincidence occurred when Jack Rillie was suddenly admitted to Clarence Court in November 2009. While EM's room was being redecorated, he had been 'decanted' to another, just along the corridor, but had now returned to his own place. I had been busy putting books and folders back on his shelves in approximately the same order. As I was leaving, the manager, Jody MacKinnon, told me that an old gentleman had been admitted who used to work with Professor Morgan. He was now in the room that EM had just vacated. Jack Rillie was very weak at this point. He had signed himself out of hospital, determined to pass away at home, but had been unable to cope. His elder daughter was there, and we reminisced briefly about her father's positive impact on those he taught.

I let EM know what was happening, and hoped that his old friend would regain strength enough for them to meet. This did not happen; Jack Rillie passed away within a short time. At the end, however, the old colleagues had once again, if very briefly, shared a room. EM was sad at the news. He was also worried about whether he would be expected to write a memorial poem; but he had already done that in 'Thirteen Ways'.

In February 2010, EM was very ill and in great pain, and thought he might die. As I left him he said, 'Thank you for everything'. But this was more than his normal old-fashioned politeness. He was gaunt. His reticence about complaining made it hard for medical staff to work out how much he was suffering. His doctor responded promptly to my concerns, and there was a serious review of the possible sources of his pain. His medication was changed, to target the nerves. Again he recovered against expectation, and looked forward once more to the day when he would reach 90 years of age on the 27th of April.

His new book *Dreams and Other Nightmares* was to be launched on that date in the Mitchell Library, with other tributes. The last poem in it is his translation of the Anglo-Saxon riddle.

> Up beyond the universe and back
> Down to the tiniest chigger in the finger –
> I outstrip the moon in brightness,
> I outrun midsummer suns.
> I embrace the seas and other waters,
> I am fresh and green as the fields I form.
> I walk under hell, I fly over the heavens.
> I am the land, I am the ocean.
> I claim this honour, I claim its worth.
> I am what I claim. So, what is my name?

Is there an answer? A 'chigger' (or 'chigoe') is a tropical flea, the female of which burrows under the skin. But that doesn't help us much. The solution is thought to be 'Creation' – but it could equally as well be 'Creativity', or 'Morgan'.

AND FINALLY

Where a riddle conceals, the poetry reveals. EM himself was not a riddle. To know him, go to the work, original and translated. There is his voice, at home in a world of voices; and there too the watchful, singular man, who is also our representative. In the multiplicity of his work are signs of who and what he was and is. Even fragments can speak.

I want to bring this study of EM to a close with two 'Fragments' found among the papers of a poet he revered, and who died too young:

> Up like a rocket and down like the stick –
> a poet's love is greedy and quick.

And

> It will astonish
> me – to vanish.[20]

Epilogue

(January 2012)

A great artist does not vanish. Not only do the works survive but also, somehow, the spirit of their creator, expressed in a style or stance, in artistic strategies chosen or refused. Edwin Morgan died in the mid-morning of Thursday 19 August 2010. Spirit is a word to be used cautiously with someone of such complex mind and scientific commitment. Although he had rejected organised religion in his teens and hated hierarchy, he remained fascinated by all that pushed at the boundaries of experience, whether this involved space travel or mysticism. He considered John Milton the greatest of English poets (not only in his verse but also for his combative prose) and remained deeply interested in religion. He once told me quite sternly that he himself believed in the spirit but not the soul, and that I should learn to tell the difference between them.

In an information-technology culture whose implications he had explored early with ingenuity and wit, if not always much practical skill, details of his death made instant news. His passing registered a definite shock across his country, for he was a poet whom many Scots had actually encountered. Whether in poems read in primary or secondary classrooms, or seeing him on one of the many hundreds of school and community visits he had made, or through attending his lectures, plays and performances over the years, readers felt connected to him. Apart from media interest in the poet and his impending funeral, there was a flurry of Internet comment from across the generations, giving personal reactions to his special combination of vitality, creativity and charm.

Courage too. Professor Ian Campbell had visited the poet just a few days earlier and was impressed once again by this quality:

> Edwin Morgan is a brave man, and with every visit to him in Crow Road it becomes clearer and clearer. As deafness closes in a world cruelly narrowed by pain and incapacity, you might expect a drooping of the spirit, but nothing doing. A few months ago he said in my hearing that he left pessimism to others, he himself was still an optimist.

He had singled this out in *Eddie@90*, a collection of eighty tributes published by Scottish Poetry Library and Mariscat Press to mark the poet's birthday four months earlier The collection had been launched at his ninetieth-birthday celebration in the Mitchell Library alongside *Dreams and Other Nightmares: New and Uncollected Poems 1954–2009* (Mariscat, 2010). That had been a happy occasion, with the poet, although confined to a wheelchair, still looking younger than his years and pleased to meet colleagues, friends, children, editors and fellow poets: 'A good turnout,' he said, being wheeled into his homeward taxi.

What was not known was that the cancer had spread to his lungs, making him prone to infections and breathlessness. Yet his mind retained flexibility and strength not always evident from a weakened appearance. The last piece of 'writing' he managed to complete is dated 7 July 2010. A dictated response to a request from Edinburgh's LGBT Centre for words that they could use to publicise a new helpline for isolated elderly gay people, it reveals something of the sources of that courage which impressed Ian Campbell:

> [. . .] Being very old is fine if you are not in too much pain. I have experienced pain over the last few years. It would be good to have someone to talk to about this. I do not mean 'tea and a chat' with the old women who outnumber the men in the care home where I now live. Old women and old men don't generally get on well. Interaction and attraction between the sexes is *usually* over by our

advanced stage. You can't artificially make people enjoy talking to each other.

The most important thing now is to see things clearly, and to discuss things openly with one person or group. This is where the LGBT Age Project will be very helpful. If the problem can then be dealt with, fine. If not, it must be coped with. There are also positives about old age, of course, if you are not hospitalized. Age encourages you to think about your condition, and to see if it can be made any better.

It is also quite important for old people to have contact with younger people. In my care home, the age range is from 72 to 102. In my experience, I get on better with younger people than with those of my own age. This can be a chance to look back over your life, and to convey that experience to younger people. Such contact might be difficult to organize [. . .]. But telephone contact with an interested listener can also work well. [. . .] My own advice at ninety years of age is not to expect too much – but definitely to expect something!

The role of inter-generational friendships in his life is empha-sized. Most recently, he had been involved in a project run by the University's Hunterian Museum, in which young people from local schools interviewed the elderly about their experience of war and national service. In poetry, his friendship and continued contact with a range of younger male and female writers meant a great deal to him – and his inability to reply to their letters was a source of real frustration.

Also evident is a determination not to despair, but to find something of interest which might still give the mind something to work on, 'to think about your condition'. He had been a dutiful son and nephew, but was essentially someone who had developed self-sufficiency. As an only child, he must have had to depend upon his own resilient mind and imagination to invent ploys to stave off boredom. High spirits and emotionality attended his relationships with young mainly working-class men, and I came to see them partly as a company of pseudo-brothers, a subversive source of fun, dare-devilry and risk-taking. But the adapted behaviour of the only child would soon re-establish itself with the next inspiration or commission, and he would get down again to the lonely business of writing, a serious one even where its content was witty and strange. For him, the imagined experience was still a real experience, his experience.

The biography had provided a similar focus of interest. He and I discussed the decades as they were researched and written. He had the chance to read the text in draft form, but preferred not to look back. It lay on his desk for a month and then I removed it. By the end, however, he was calling it 'our book', and looking forward to the story it would tell. Visiting just three days before his death, I told him that *Beyond the Last Dragon* had finally been dispatched to the printers, after several of the last-minute emergencies to which publishing is prone. He himself had had much experience of these in a writer's life. He seemed content that we had reached this stage at last.

On the evening before he died, I was called to Clarence Court because a persistent lung infection was now causing him serious distress in breathing. Despite this, he paid alert attention to the medical care he received to relieve it. His doctor had recently joined the practice from Northern Ireland, where she had been friendly with Sinéad Morrisey, an award-winning Carcanet poet. So our talk by the bedside was of poetry and poets as we waited for him to settle into sleep.

During one of the poet's health scares several years earlier, Hamish Whyte and I realised that the death of such a national figure called for a public funeral that would challenge our capabilities. Edwin Morgan's refusal to discuss the matter left us unclear on most things, except for his preference for live music and no religion. In terms of space, co-ordination, liaison with the Scottish Government and the media, as well as his almost life-long connection to the institution, the University of Glasgow seemed the best choice. The Chaplain, Stuart McQuarrie, welcomed our approach, and with Susan Stewart, Director of

Corporate Communications, held meetings with us to discuss the broad outlines. We made lists of people to contact and assigned responsibilities. When David Kinloch joined us later as an executor, further meetings took place both before and just after the poet's death.

Gradually the funeral arrangements took shape. George Reid, former Presiding Officer of the Scottish Parliament, would give a eulogy from the national perspective and Robyn Marsack would speak from the world of poetry and publishing. Both had known Edwin Morgan personally as well as professionally for many years. The readers were poets who were also friends. The University Organist and Choir, Christina Whyte and Tommy Smith provided music by Peter Maxwell Davies, Robert Burns, the Beatles and jazz improvisation on the Wolf poem in 'Beasts of Scotland'. Since many students and Glaswegians might want to pay their respects but be unable to attend the funeral, his coffin was laid out in the University Chapel from early morning until midday, with a commemorative book for comments and a display case of some of the poet's writing from the Library's Special Collections.

Then the coffin was taken to the imposing Bute Hall, filled to near capacity. Present were Scotland's First Minister and his Cabinet Secretary for Culture, the University Principal, Glasgow's Provost and many others from political, literary and academic life, friends and former students, former neighbours and care-home staff. An enlarged version of the 1970s Carcanet publicity photograph of the poet in a Paisley pattern shirt reminded us of him in his prime. On the coffin Hamish Whyte had placed a flowering thistle, cut from near his house. Someone else, during its hours in the Chapel, had placed a small crocheted cross on the coffin. Was this a test of our secularism, David Kinloch wondered. We left it there in any case.

Because the structure of powerful readings, music and life reflections had demanded such attentiveness from those present, the impact of the final singing together of 'A Man's a Man for a' That' brought a perceptible sense of emotional release. After the service, a smaller group went on to the crematorium in nearby Maryhill. With no family connection to guide us, we had simply chosen the funeral directors and final arrangements that Edwin Morgan had used for his own parents. There his friends Malcolm and Mark spoke movingly and humorously of the sheer various-ness of the poet's company, and Benno Plassman spoke as Baron Munchausen, his final alter ego. Mark read from a list of the aphorisms that Morgan had included in the margin of letters written to him when in Italy:

One power alone drives the poet: Imagination. (William Blake)

What actually happens is so far ahead of our thoughts, our intentions, we can never really catch up with it or ever really come to know it. (R.M. Rilke)

Never be careless with ancient but still formidable weapons. (Vladimir Mayakovsky)

For all things are to be dared. (Plato)

The attraction of these for the poet is obvious. He had made a small collection of them, reminiscent of his Scrapbook days.[1] There were also humorous lines, intentional or otherwise, from Morton Feldman ('You cannot eat a fish with a Latin name') and from the baseball player Yogi Berra (of 'It was déjà vu all over again' repute): 'When you come to a fork in the road, take it'.

When we arrived back at the Chapel, the crowd had mostly dispersed. Welcome fumes of whisky and shortbread warmed its lofty spaces. Basing his plea on Edwin Morgan's 1972 self-description in 'Notes on a poet's working day' as perusing the latest part of the *Dictionary of the Scottish Tongue* over a late-night whisky and nibble of shortbread,[2] the University Chaplain had persuaded Glenmorangie and Tunnocks to supply these free for the funeral. And thoughtfully he had held some back for the crematorium returners at the end of an emotional day.

On the following Monday, a crowded event took place at the Edinburgh International Book Festival to celebrate the poet's life, with some fourteen Scottish poets and novelists gathered to honour him. Unknown to almost all of those present were the political and creative intentions of the poet's last will and testament. These would not emerge until the following summer – when once more his name would be making headline news, refusing to vanish.

The real legacy of Edwin Morgan will include not only his own work but his impact on the creative life of others working in a range of media. These are all ways of un-vanishing. His room in Clarence Court was gradually cleared, with more books for the Mitchell Library, boxes of literary papers stacked for Special Collections and paintings destined for the University's Hunterian Gallery. Jazzy jackets and shirts were dispersed to various charity shops, with the indelible laundry-labels of institutional life carefully cut out. We did not want to find the poet's clothes the following week on eBay. I thought it worth making a record of the books on his desk, and this appears in Appendix D. Some of these books were gifts from friends, but others he had ordered, with or without help. He continued to scan catalogues from booksellers. The desk also held piles of newspapers and letters, which we had tried to keep under control without obvious success. Most recently, he had taken out a subscription to *Scientific American*.

One day I came home to an email from Katri Walker, a young visual artist and film-maker working between Glasgow and Mexico City. She was reporting on the progress of her 'The City is the Film', commissioned to mark the forthcoming Commonwealth Games. She had based this film of interviews with Glaswegian residents who had all been born in individual countries of the Commonwealth on Morgan's poem 'The City' (*New Selected Poems*: 163–4 but originally from *Hold Hands Among the Atoms*). The poem itself reflects the interplay of reality and artifice in film:

> What was all that then? – What? – *That*. – That was *Glasgow*.
> It's a film, an epic: lasts for, anyway

keep watching, it's not real, so everything is
melting at the edges and could go, you have to
remember some of it was shot in Moscow,
parts in Chicago, and then of course the people
break up occasionally, they're only graphics,
look there's two businessmen gone zigzag [. . .].

The poet and I had discussed this project not long before his death and he had asked me to email his approval.

Also imminent were two creative reactions to his poetic and dramatic work on Gilgamesh, with another in the following year. Actor and director Tam Dean Burn had visited the poet in the last months of his life to discuss a production of *The Play of Gilgamesh* at the Royal Scottish Academy of Music and Drama. Communication with the poet had been difficult by that stage because of his deafness. Robyn Marsack had now put us in contact, and I was able to provide some background on the play's history and its link with Morgan's thinking on the Green Man myth, together with a copy of the poetic version that followed from Communicado's difficulties with the dramatic text. His production in early November 2010 won praise for the energy of its young actors and musicians (third year drama students and musicians from jazz and traditional music courses), the verve of its rhyming lines and the effective use of video footage from Gulf War conflicts, fought over the same Babylonian or Iraqi soil.

The second response to Gilgamesh was to the poem version, published in the *Long Poem Magazine* (Issue 5, Winter 2010/11). Visiting Edwin Morgan some months before his 90th birthday, Lucy Hamilton, one of its editors, asked whether he had a poem suitable for the magazine. She was married to the son of his old neighbour in Whittingehame Court, Dr Janet Hamilton. He thought that yes, there was a long piece somewhere in his papers, though he could not recall precisely what or where. The poem version came to light in one of the files, to be published in full alongside the work of Adnan al-Sayegh, a poet in exile from modern Iraq. Still intended for performance and declamation by different voices to a modern audience (hence its deliberate anachronisms), these lines are the second thoughts of a major poet intent on responding to epic themes of kingship and power, male friendship and bonding, ancient cultures, and the mysteries of suffering and death. It has a haunting masque-like quality.[3]

Both of these Gilgamesh productions came together, as it were, when a special launch of the 'Edwin Morgan Issue' was organised in the Scottish Writers' Centre in Glasgow in March 2011. Tam Dean Burn gave a mesmerising performance of the poem's opening sections, leaving those who heard it convinced of the power of a remarkable work unearthed from a care-home book-shelf.

Thoughts of Gilgamesh and the Green Man myth of life-force were also crucial to the development of Liz Lochhead's play *Edwin Morgan's Dreams – And Other Nightmares*, which played to packed houses in the Tron Theatre in early November 2011 during the Glasgay! Festival. At the funeral, she had given a composed yet powerful reading of 'Cinquevalli', the poem that perhaps comes nearest to encapsulating Morgan's life and art in its evocation of the life of a remarkable acrobat and juggler, a 'bundle of enigmas', who had declined in age. Few in the Bute Hall would have known that she was grieving for her husband, who had recently died of an aggressive cancer, as well as for a poet who had been her friend and mentor of many years.

In the following months she could barely read or write any-thing, but eventually began *Beyond the Last Dragon*. Its opening description of the poet's nightmare visions suddenly presented itself to her as a theatrical scene, fully formed. This would be the germ of what became a moving work for four characters: 'Edwin', 'James', 'Mark' and the 'Lady', the elegant lesbian whom the very young Edwin Morgan had seen and admired in a Glasgow tearoom. Reading and responding to several versions of the play as it developed in discussion with its director, Andy Arnold, and others, I was struck by its contrasting emotions, the bold com-bination of fact and imagination, its good humour, energy and dramatic realisation of a complex life. In performance, David

McKay playing both Edwin and his Life Force caught the rhythms and timbre of the poet's speech with uncanny accuracy.

The haunting quality of this play came in part from its use of Morgan's poetry, including work from *Dreams and Other Nightmares*. This final collection was well received, although it was perhaps overshadowed by his death. In discussion with the poet, a fairly stringent approach had been taken as to what should be excluded: it would not be a rag-bag selection. Reviewing it in *The Guardian* (20 November 2010), Paul Batchelor commented that it definitely did not present the dead-ends of uncollected work but instead revealed, in its half-century sweep of years, how this poet had embraced experimentation from the very start. He praised 'the speed and fluency of his line: his cadences emerge from a nervy self-correcting responsiveness that keeps the world on the bounce'. The poem for Morven Cameron was one he selected from 'several previously unpublished gems'. This brief, beautiful elegy for a friend ends with the poet inviting us to examine one of his own tears:

> Love go with her yet
> Love forget to forget.
> Open this tear: a seed, a shine, a glow:
> that's what you'll find.

The cover image by Kenny Whyte was of a wrought-iron gate in the wintry grounds of Castle Howard, Yorkshire, its spider webs caught in frost. It seemed, at first sight, a touch funereal. But is the viewer entering this place or leaving it, the poet wondered, and chose this image over others.

Morven was someone he had known and loved since the 1950s. The birthday tributes of *Eddie@90* convey something of his life-long gift for friendship. Alan Spence, for instance, evokes the poet's benign inspiration over forty years, recalling a public reading style that, no matter the size of the crowd, had 'that same humility and poise and wisdom and humour' (p. 80). More privately, Jackie Kay describes 'A Birthday Tea' in his care home, with bantering word-play around 'meringue / harangue / wrang', but talk too about the

Turkish writer Orhan Pamuk's novels, and love, and the work of translation. 'And what is age', she asks, 'but another translation / From curious boy to astounding man' (p. 34).

Gavin Wallace, Head of Literature at the then Scottish Arts Council, evokes both love and a sort of fear in his piece, the nicely entitled 'A Spelling Mistale' (p. 85). Edwin Morgan was External Examiner for his PhD thesis on the novelist Compton Mackenzie, and from that occasion Wallace vividly recalls three things:

> The first was the contrast between his peacock-proud colour-scheme – pink jacket, orange tie – and the gentle self-effacement of the man wearing them. The second was the powerful yet understated authority of his erudition and his generosity in sharing it. The third was his professional and creative obsession with accuracy and precision.

Morgan's final rebuke, pointing up several repeated spelling mistakes, '*You'll have to watch that, you know*', was mild but unforgettable, still resounding 'every time I put pen to paper or fingers to keyboard'.

It is time to admit some 'mistales' by Edwin Morgan. These mainly involve wishful or wilful thinking. The first was one I simply took the poet's word for, and should have known better. Gonzalo Gonzalez, his visiting Opus Dei priest, phoned me offering to review the biography in a Catholic periodical, and mentioned in his mild-mannered way that he was not, as the book reported, a Jesuit. The two organisations are quite separate and distinct, of course. The poet himself had decided that this ascetic priest must be a Jesuit, describing him as such to me and others. Why should this have been? I believe it reflects the lasting influence of his early self-identification with Gerard Manley Hopkins: in his poetic isolation, his sensitivity and troubled sexuality and his radicalism. He seems even to have conscripted him into the ranks of concrete poetry activists, alongside the Benedictine Dom Sylvester Houédard. Recently examining Morgan's papers on the international concrete movement, I came across a scribbled note where he quotes from Hopkins's theory of 'inscape', the inner design or pattern in the natural world that gives each object its distinctive shape:

> All the world is full of inscape, and <u>chance left free to act falls into an order</u> as with a pupose.[4]

It is possible here that Morgan was associating inscape with concrete poetry's notion of the graphic space as a structural shaper of meaning, and of the poem as quasi-3-dimensional sign rather than a linear sequence of ideas.

Sometimes a tale could get out of control. This seems to have been the case with the story of Edwin Morgan's son by a war-time liaison in Egypt. As Mark tells it, this was uncovered in 2002 when he and the poet were having a long conversation about Cairo in the Whittingehame Court flat, both of them slightly drunk. The talk turned to the city's museums and Morgan, looking out the window and up Great Western Road towards Anniesland Cross, suddenly said: 'My son works over there' (meaning Cairo not Anniesland). A frightened look then passed over his face and he immediately began to back-pedal on this remark. Over the next few months Mark was persistent in worrying at the story, winning a few further details of the son's name, age and occupation. Now nearing retirement from his post as an archaeologist in Cairo Museum, he was the child of the poet's wartime affair with an exotic woman called Leila.[5]

Sworn to secrecy about these events, Mark was shocked to find the whole story published in the introduction to *Tales from Baron Munchausen* (Mariscat, 2005). Claudia Kraszkiewiecz believed it too. Both were young people and perhaps the poet enjoyed teasing them, and also the Scottish newspaper-reading public when it made the news. What interests me most now is that first look of panic on the poet's face at his uncalculated revelation of the fantasy of a son, and the way in which that error of judgement was gradually teased, turned and crafted into a piece of fiction that found a safe home at last in a collection of tall tales.

His powerful imagination could lead him easily into intense identification with others. This applied not only with other writers in the act of translation, but also with animals. In 'Afterwards', a prose poem of the Vietnam War, the thought of a pet grasshopper still caged in a little bamboo box beside the skeleton of the boy who had owned it, 'alive yet and scraping the only signal it knew from behind the bars of its cage' (CP: 261), could reduce him to tears in the reading of it – and so was to be carefully handled in performance. Powerlessness and victimization moved him; he longed 'to reach out' to those who felt trapped. His late selection of *Poets' Poems* (2000, see Bibliography, Section D) included the last song of Robert Burns, 'Oh Wert Thou in the Cauld Blast':

> My plaidie to the angry airt,
> I'd shelter thee, I'd shelter thee [. . .].

In early April 1967 he was judging an island schools writing competition organised by the Arran Film Society, and gave first prize in the 15–18 category and overall first prize to an untitled 16-page autobiography, 'I was lying in my bed'. He kept his notes on the entry:

> [. . .] suffering from dyslexia & a lisp, self-conscious, teased by other boys, misunderstood by teachers – emotional – a strong passionate ill-written sensitive plea for greater understanding – whole thing raw, rings true terribly – 'I often feel I'm useless and stupid and no good at anything' [. . .].[6]

He told me about this as we discussed his 1960s, very much as he had described it to Ian Hamilton Finlay in a letter of 11 April 1967,

> The dyslexic boy (whom I met) is clearly talented and is interested in art as well as writing but is still very mixed up and uncertain about what he will do – school has had a horrible influence on him which he will find hard to shake off – has left an inarticulacy and sort of fierce withdrawnness [. . .]. It tears my heart to see someone like this.[7]

451

What he also recalled with displeasure was the lack of any expenses or fee whatsoever for all his work, apart from 'one local pottery salt-bucket filled with heartfelt thanks' – and also having to sit through a speech by a local grandee, the Lord Lieutenant of Bute.

Young Scottish writers were a particular focus of Edwin Morgan's will. He left an estate of about two million pounds. There were some thirty small bequests to individuals and organisations, of either two thousand or one thousand or five hundred pounds. Other gifts of paintings or posters had already been given to individuals when he left Whittingehame Court to enter the care home. The remainder was to be divided equally between the Scottish National Party and a 'Prize Fund' for an annual award for a published or unpublished collection by a Scottish poet under thirty years of age.

The estate was complicated to wind up. Some valuation had to be provided for his paintings, papers and the books already gifted to Glasgow University and the Mitchell Library. Individuals or amalgamated organizations had to be traced. The poet had continued to build on the legacy of stocks and shares inherited from his parents, adding his royalties and other earnings. He had wisely included his accountant, Andrew McBean, as an executor. Marshall Walker continued in his role from New Zealand, although constrained by illness. His literary executors were more concerned to be ready to argue further for the charitable nature of a prize that seemed to favour only one poet per year. But the case was accepted without fuss, and no Inheritance Tax fell due. Since the Prize was to be funded by dividends from the remaining shares, we watched the depressed Stock Market with unwonted concern.

Of the smaller bequests, the largest sums went to the Association for Scottish Literary Studies, Shelter, and the Scottish Youth Theatre – a summation perhaps of his literary, social and creative concerns. Bequests also went to two special schools in Glasgow, the gay support group Outright, and Friends of

Epilogue

Glasgow University Library. Scottish Youth Theatre decided to name a new rehearsal studio in his honour. The Edwin Morgan Room was accordingly opened by Liz Lochhead while her play was in rehearsal, and celebrated by an impressive dramatization of some of the poet's 'Ten Theatre Poems' (CP: 355–62). She had by now succeeded Morgan as Scotland's National Poet. This donation had come as a surprise to SYT, but perhaps originated in their production of *Cyrano de Bergerac* at the Cottier Theatre in August 1998. The poet had written in praise of the performance to Mary McCluskey, the Artistic Director. Because of a gender imbalance in the company, the production had used girls in the male and boys in the female roles:

> I was there with a couple of young chaps in their twenties, and they had not seen the play before; they simply took it as it came, and liked it a lot. It took me longer to adjust to the changed gender, simply because I knew the play with the original characters, but it worked on me as it went on, and I found myself happily accepting the changes. There are, in any case, sexual ambiguities lurking in the play [. . .].[8]

The letter ends by expressing confidence in directorial freedom, another aspect of the creative life.

Finally the will was confirmed and became public. News broke on 19 June 2011 in the *Mail on Sunday*, which must have had a reporter in the local Court on the lookout for newsworthy estates. Other newspapers and broadcasters tried to catch up. Next day *The Guardian* pointed up the irony of the size of Edwin Morgan's bequest being matched only by donations from Brian Souter of the Stagecoach transport group, who in 2000 had funded the unofficial referendum to uphold Section 28 in Scotland. Funds from both men would now contribute to an SNP 'war chest' for a referendum on Scotland's independence, planned for 2014.

Both the size of Morgan's estate and the political use to which it would be put aroused surprise, and also elements of criticism or begrudgery. Some felt that the poet was trying to shape the future from beyond the grave. Others savoured the contrast between the impoverished lives of poets past and present and the munificence of this accumulated wealth. In fact, given his wealth, the poet had lived comfortably but relatively sparely. He had been determined to preserve his inheritance, to enhance it through his own efforts and then devote it to causes in which he passionately believed. Our work as executors was now to put these funds to best use, not only for one lucky poet annually but through widening the impact of the award (as a clause in the will permitted us to do, within the spirit of his intentions) to sustain the development of Scottish poetry more generally.

I would still tease the great republican socialist poet about his account at Harrods and his two (!) American Express cards, but as the poet Richard Price reminded me recently, Harrods is after all preferable to Herods. And he did give almost all of it away in the end, with some style.

Developing her play, Liz Lochhead turned around the question put to me by the anxious poet in his care home: Did I ever wonder whether a person could lead two utterly different lives, without either being aware of the other? She posed a similar question about Glasgow: Was it possible for different groups to spend their lives in the same city without either really being aware of the other? Morgan's life as a member of the gay minority is at issue here. What did I really know of the realities of his life in that context?

The executors decided to scatter his ashes on Cathkin Braes, above Burnside and Rutherglen. These hills provide both title and setting for his first collection, *The Vision of Cathkin Braes* (1952). They were a vantage point from which he viewed the city of Glasgow in his dark 1950s and also in the brighter 1960s, when the Castlemilk scheme took shape on its western slopes, providing new housing as the Gorbals slums came down. Not knowing the wooded terrain, I decided to make a reconnaissance a few days in advance. It was late afternoon and I was out of sight of the road. Two young men approached me through the trees, looking casual but with identity tags around their necks and a purposeful step.

They were policemen. The place was a well-known cruising ground. What was I doing there? My story about forward planning for scattering the ashes of a national poet they had never heard of rang false even to my ears, though it was not. My place of work? (Thankfully retired.) My address? There had been complaints from local residents about homosexual activity in the vicinity, and they were monitoring the situation. Good afternoon, sir. Mind how you go.

My wife, who has a strong sense of justice, was incensed by the incident. She insisted that I write to the Chief Constable about harassment of gay people, or any people, walking on public ground. There was also the possibility that this incident might have been some sort of blackmail operation: they had my address, after all, which I had provided as an overly compliant and definitely nervous citizen. A reply came quite promptly from the Area Commander. They were indeed his men, there in response to complaints from the community and local MSP about heterosexual as well as homosexual activity. Also pertinent was the fact that Cathkin Braes were being considered as a venue for biking events in the forthcoming Commonwealth Games, and hence the need to determine that they were 'a suitable and safe sporting location'.

Och well then. . . . Someone should write a poem about it. In retrospect there was a humorous side to this. My fellow executors certainly laughed when I told them. David Kinloch knew of the place's reputation, and I had some suspicion, gained partly from the erotic imagery of the opening of 'The Vision of Cathkin Braes'. But I now knew with greater clarity what the poet meant about entrapment, and living 'a life of risk'.

Various other odd happenings delayed the scattering of the poet's ashes. But that, as they say, is another story. Sometimes it almost seemed as if he had become one of the friendly ghosts that throng the opening of 'Love and a Life' – tingling, tangling, pinning us, pulling our ears. I recall it as a fresh blue generous day in good company. Malcolm and Mark were both there. We found a burn whose clear waters would run down through Rutherglen, into the Clyde and out to the Firth. Mark scratched the poet's initials with a key on a nearby stone. A final farewell toast in Highland Park whisky or water. Then we all drove back home to the city.

Michael Schmidt, his Carcanet publisher, has described Edwin Morgan as 'a poet happy in the present tense: his elegies are themselves about presence'. He also declares that 'when the full range of his work is finally mapped, it will be seen that one of his greatest achievements is epistolary, and his letters addressing such a range of people, from Brazil to Poland, from China to Peru [. . .] are themselves a map of the age'.[9] His own heartening correspondence with the poet from the 1970s onwards sparkles with energy, friendship and respect. Work has already begun on a *Selected Letters*. But as Morgan told him on 2 April 1972,

> I am really a very native Glasgow-loving root-clutching person, and the mechanics of travel fill me with angst, yet I seem to be meant or doomed or prodded to go to place after place, city after city (but cities I love in any case, all cities) – Paris, Amsterdam, Cologne, Innsbruck, Stockholm, Bergen, Helsinki, Leningrad, Moscow, Kiev, Tripoli, Tel Aviv, Durban, Washington, New York [. . .].[10]

He would add considerably to that tally of cities over the next quarter century, a far-travelled and internationally-minded man. But Kevin McCarra brings us nearer home, knowing him better by recognizing the importance of both place and privacy:

> While the poems deal with a great range of places in time and space, Morgan keeps coming back to Glasgow like a man turning the key in his lock late in the evening.[11]

Then at last the great unknown of writing could be glimpsed, an unmapped land, and the words begin.

References

CHAPTER ONE

1 *The Dark Horse* 1997: 41.
2 *Nothing Not Giving Messages*: 112.
3 *Guardian*, 26 January 2008: 11.

CHAPTER TWO

1 *Footsteps and Witnesses*: 12.
2 *Nothing Not Giving Messages*: 118.
3 *Guardian* 26 January 2008: 11.
4 *Nothing Not Giving Messages*: 118.
5 *Nothing Not Giving Messages*: 120.
6 *Footsteps and Witnesses*: 11.
7 *Footsteps and Witnesses:* 12.
8 *About Edwin Morgan*: 1–2.
9 *Modern Scotland 1914–2000*: 70.
10 *Modern Scotland 1914–2000*: 38.
11 *Modern Scotland 1914–2000*: 95.
12 *Edwin Morgan. Inventions of Modernity*: 195.
13 *Edwin Morgan. Inventions of Modernity*: 195.
14 *Footsteps and Witnesses*: 12.
15 *Nothing Not Giving Messages*: 106.
16 *Nothing Not Giving Messages*: 106.

CHAPTER THREE

1 *Nothing Not Giving Messages*: 94.
2 *Nothing Not Giving Messages*: 104.
3 SpecColl MS Morgan 917
4 *Collected Poems 1934–1952* [1952]: 96.
5 *Nothing Not Giving Messages*: 136.
6 *Nothing Not Giving Messages*: 146.
7 *Modern Scotland 1914–2000*: 219.

8 *Edwin Morgan: Inventions of Modernity*: 196.
9 *Nothing Not Giving Messages*: 92.
10 *Nothing Not Giving Messages*: 92.
11 Tape 1.
12 *Ethically Speaking*: 143.
13 *Nothing Not Giving Messages*: 152.
14 *Nothing Not Giving Messages*: 153.
15 *Nothing Not Giving Messages*: 93.
16 SpecColl MS Morgan 1–68.
17 SpecColl 4848/102.
18 *Footsteps and Witnesses*: 13.
19 *Nothing Not Giving Messages*: 94–5.
20 *Nothing Not Giving Messages*: 147.
21 *Nothing Not Giving Messages*: 125.
22 *Nothing Not Giving Messages*: 121–2.
23 *Edwin Morgan: Inventions of Modernity*: 196.
24 *Footsteps and Witnesses*: 15.
25 *Edwin Morgan: Inventions of Modernity*: 197.
26 Tape 1.

CHAPTER FOUR

1 Tape 1.
2 SpecColl 4848/4 Garioch. From a review of Robert Garioch's memoir of life as a prisoner of war, *Two Men and a Blanket* (1975).
3 Tape 1.
4 *Official History of New Zealand in the Second World War*: 225–6.
5 Tape 1.
6 Tape 1.
7 *Nothing Not Giving Messages*: 146.

8 *Ethically Speaking*: 147.
9 *Nothing Not Giving Messages*: 144–87.
10 *Nothing Not Giving Messages*: 150.
11 See, for example, Paul Jackson's *One of the Boys*: McGill-Queen's University Press, 2004, written from a Canadian army perspective.
12 SpecColl 4848/47 and 49.
13 *Nothing Not Giving Messages*: 168–9.
14 SpecColl 4848/102.
15 *The Nightfisherman*: 14.
16 See, for example, the BBC archive *WW2 People's War*.
17 *Nothing Not Giving Messages*: 97.
18 SpecColl 4580/42.
19 SpecColl 4848/102.
20 SpecColl 4579/26.
21 *About Edwin Morgan*: 108.
22 SpecColl 4498/8.
23 SpecColl 4579/26.
24 SpecColl 4579/26.
25 SpecColl 4848/102.
26 *Strange Likeness*: 127.
27 SpecColl 4579/26.
28 *Strange Likeness*: 125.
29 *Ethically Speaking*: 150.
30 SpecColl 4848/51.
31 SpecColl 4848/102.

CHAPTER FIVE

1 *Ethically Speaking*: 142.
2 *Ethically Speaking*: 141.
3 *Nothing Not Giving Messages*: 156.
4 *Nothing Not Giving Messages*: 156.
5 *Nothing Not Giving Messages*: 171.
6 *Edwin Morgan: Inventions of Modernity*: 200.
7 *Nothing Not Giving Messages*: 171–2.
8 *Ethically Speaking*: 141.
9 *Nothing Not Giving Messages*: 165.
10 E-mail to the author, October 2009.
11 SpecColl 4848/99.
12 *Further Letters of Gerard Manley Hopkins*, ed. C.C. Abbott, 1956: 184–5.
13 SpecColl 4581/47(a).
14 *Edwin Morgan: Inventions of Modernity*: 199.

15 *Modern Scotland 1914–2000*: 220.
16 SpecColl 4848/46.
17 SpecColl 4848/46.
18 SpecColl 4579/26, 1949-50.
19 SpecColl 4848/46.
20 SpecColl 4579/26.
21 SpecColl 4579/26, 1949-50.
22 SpecColl 4848/47.
23 SpecColl 4574/26.
24 SpecColl 4848/49.
25 'Migrant the Magnificent': *PN Review 174, Vol. 33 No.4*.
26 SpecColl 4579/27, 1960.

CHAPTER SIX

1 *Modern Scotland 1914–2000*: 292.
2 *Footsteps and Witnesses*: 19.
3 *Nothing Not Giving Messages*: 178–89.
4 *Nothing Not Giving Messages*: 191.
5 *Nothing Not Giving Messages*: 173.
6 *Nothing Not Giving Messages*: 173.
7 *Footsteps and Witnesses*: 20–1.
8 SpecColl 4848/21.
9 SpecColl 4848/21.
10 SpecColl 4848/1.
11 SpecColl 4580/42.
12 SpecColl 4848/19.
13 SpecColl 4580/42.
14 SpecColl 4580/42.
15 SpecColl 4580/42.
16 *Nothing Not Giving Messages*: 246–7.
17 Spec Coll 4848/35.
18 Spec Coll 4848/35.
19 SpecColl 4848/21.
20 SpecColl 4848/1.
21 SpecColl 4848/1.
22 SpecColl 4848/35.
23 SpecColl 4848/101. It was finally published in *Dreams and Other Nightmares* (2010).
24 SpecColl 4848/1.
25 SpecColl 4848/30.
26 SpecColl 4848/30.
27 *Albatross Book of Longer Poems*: 728.
28 SpecColl 4848/47.
29 SpecColl 4498/4.
30 Reprinted in *Nothing Not Giving Messages*: 194.

References

31 SpecColl 4848/10.
32 SpecColl 4848/10.
33 SpecColl 4848/10.
34 *Beyond Identity*: 51–2.
35 SpecColl 4848/35.
36 *Beyond Identity*: 174.
37 Letter to the author, September 2009.
38 SpecColl 4848/4.
39 *Scottish International* 1: 3.
40 SpecColl 4498/9.
41 SpecColl 4498/9.
42 SpecColl 4498/10.
43 SpecColl 4848/2.
44 *Ethically Speaking*: 142.
45 SpecColl 4848/101.
46 SpecColl 4498/12.

CHAPTER SEVEN

1 SpecColl 4848/44.
2 SpecColl 4848/103.
3 SpecColl 4848/103.
4 SpecColl 4579.
5 SpecColl 4848/32.
6 SpecColl 4848/10.
7 SpecColl 4848/68.
8 SpecColl 4848/68.
9 SpecColl 4848/62.
10 SpecColl 4848/62.
11 SpecColl 4848/32.
12 SpecColl 4848/32.
13 SpecColl 4848/27.
14 SpecColl 4848/27.
15 SpecColl 4848/68.
16 *Nothing Not Giving Messages*: 182–3.
17 SpecColl 4581/47.
18 SpecColl 4579.
19 SpecColl 4579.
20 SpecColl 4579.
21 SpecColl 4579.
22 The line is from the Galician poet and novelist, Rosalía de Castro (1837–1885): 'They say that plants don't talk, nor springs of water, nor the birds . . .'
23 SpecColl 4579.
24 SpecColl 4848/103.

25 SpecColl 4579.
26 *Nothing Not Giving Messages*: 173–4.
27 SpecColl 4848/68.
28 SpecColl 4848/107.
29 SpecColl 4579.
30 *Modern Scotland 1914–2000*: 338.
31 *Nothing Not Giving Messages*: 142.
32 Tape 5.

CHAPTER EIGHT

1 *Nothing Not Giving Messages*: 199.
2 SpecColl 4848/44.
3 SpecColl 4848/51.
4 SpecColl 4848/27.
5 *Ethically Speaking*: 147.
6 SpecColl 4579.
7 *Seven Poets*: 81.
8 *Seven Poets*: 31.
9 SpecColl 4582.
10 SpecColl 4848/52.
11 *Beyond Identity*: 37.
12 *Edwin Morgan: Inventions of Modernity*: 201.
13 SpecColl 4848/52.
14 SpecColl 4498/9.
15 SpecColl 4848/51.
16 See *About Edwin Morgan*: 231.
17 SpecColl 4579.
18 SpecColl 4848/51.
19 SpecColl 4848/51.
20 *From Saturn to Glasgow*: 21.
21 EM's Hungarian Journal: author's possession.
22 *Scottish Field* Vol 133/102.
23 SpecColl 4848/51.
24 Letter to the author.
25 SpecColl 4848/51.
26 SpecColl 4848/21.
27 SpecColl 4848/51.
28 SpecColl 4848/52.
29 SpecColl 4582.
30 SpecColl 4582.
31 SpecColl 4848/31.
32 SpecColl 4848/31.
33 SpecColl 4848/44.
34 SpecColl 4848/14.
35 SpecColl 4848/19.
36 SpecColl 4848/30.

37 SpecColl 4848/14.
38 SpecColl 4848/30.
39 SpecColl 4848/48.

CHAPTER NINE

1 SpecColl 4848/104.
2 *Ethically Speaking*: 144.
3 *Ethically Speaking*: 144.
4 *Ethically Speaking*: 145.
5 SpecColl 4848/14.
6 Marshall Walker timeline, c.1980.
7 SpecColl 4848/14.
8 SpecColl 4848/14.
9 SpecColl 4848/14.
10 SpecColl 4848/14.
11 SpecColl 4848/17.
12 SpecColl 4848/14.
13 SpecColl 4848/14.
14 SpecColl 4848/19.
15 SpecColl 4848/30.
16 *Beyond Identity*: 38.
17 SpecColl 4848/80.
18 SpecColl 4848/21.
19 SpecColl 4848/14.
20 SpecColl 4848/19.
21 SpecColl 4848/14.
22 *Beyond Identity*: 38.
23 SpecColl 4848/27.
24 SpecColl 4848/14.
25 SpecColl 4848/14.
26 SpecColl 4848/14.
27 SpecColl 4848/19.
28 SpecColl 4848/14.
29 SpecColl 4848/14.
30 *Ethically Speaking*: 25.
31 SpecColl 4848/14.
32 *Modern Scotland 1914–2000*: 375.
33 SpecColl 4848/27.
34 SpecColl 4848/4.
35 SpecColl 4848/4.
36 SpecColl 4848/4.
37 SpecColl 4848/14.
38 SpecColl 4848/14.
39 SpecColl 4848/27.
40 SpecColl 4848/26.
41 SpecColl 4848/27.
42 SpecColl 4848/14.

CHAPTER TEN

1 SpecColl 4848/37.
2 SpecColl 4848/37.
3 SpecColl 4848/37.
4 SpecColl 4848/37.
5 SpecColl 4848/37.
6 SpecColl 4848/44.
7 SpecColl 4848/44.
8 SpecColl 4848/80.
9 SpecColl 4848/80.
10 SpecColl 4848/22.
11 SpecColl 4848/14.
12 SpecColl 4848/80.
13 SpecColl 4848/80.
14 SpecColl 4848/26.
15 SpecColl 4848/26.
16 SpecColl4848/27.
17 Letter. Author's possession.
18 SpecColl 4848/80.
19 SpecColl 4848/30.
20 *Attila József: Sixty Poems*: 73.

EPILOGUE

1 SpecColl 4848/8.
2 *Nothing Not Giving Messages*: 198. In the following months, the poet's favourite biscuit was reported as a Tunnock's wafer, teacake and chocolate snowball.
3 SpecColl 4975/5.
4 SpecColl 4848/69. EM's underlining of Hopkins's *Journal* entry for 24 February 1873.
5 This version of the Arabic name 'Layla' was popularized by Byron in *Don Juan* (1819). It means 'night', as in *Alf Layla*, 'The Thousand [and One] Nights', or 'The Arabian Nights' – perhaps a clue to Morgan's stratagem here.
6 SpecColl 4580/34.
7 SpecColl 4848/35.
8 SpecColl 4848/22.
9 *Eddie@90*: 76.
10 SpecColl 4579/32.
11 *Eddie@90*: 52.

Bibliography

For ease of cross-reference between the chapter endnotes and this bibliography, Section A is organised alphabetically by book title rather than by author. Books with the most useful bibliographies for further study of Edwin Morgan's work or influence are asterisked.

A list of his publications then follows in Section B, by date of publication. This list is a selection from a fuller list compiled by Hamish Whyte, omitting 10 limited editions. Whyte's original also includes details of interviews with and articles on the poet since 1988, supplementing the information in *About Edwin Morgan* (1990). Lastly, a short list of useful websites is included in Section C, and in Section D a list of the books on the poet's desk at the time of his death.

A: SELECTED CRITICAL AND OTHER WORKS

About Edwin Morgan.* Robert Crawford and Hamish Whyte, eds. Edinburgh: Edinburgh University Press, 1990.

Beyond Identity: New Horizons in Modern Scottish Poetry.* Attila Dósa. Amsterdam: Rodopi, 2009.

British Poetry Magazines 1914–2000: A History and Bibliography of 'Little Magazines'.* David Miller and Richard Price. London: British Library, 2006.

Dream State: The New Scottish Poets.* Donny O'Rourke, ed. Edinburgh: Polygon, 1994, 2002 (second edition).

Eddie@90. Robyn Marsack and Hamish Whyte, eds. Edinburgh: Scottish Poetry Library and Mariscat Press.

Edwin Morgan: Inventions of Modernity.* Colin Nicholson. Manchester: Manchester University Press, 2002.

Ethically Speaking: Voice and Values in Modern Scottish Writing.* James McGonigal and Kirsten Stirling, eds. Amsterdam: Rodopi, 2006.

Footsteps and Witnesses: Lesbian and Gay Lifestories from Scotland. Bob Cant, ed. Edinburgh: Polygon, 1993.

Modern Scotland 1914–2000. Richard J. Finlay. London: Profile, 2004.

Nothing Not Giving Messages: Reflections on work and life. Hamish Whyte, ed. Edinburgh: Polygon, 1990.

Seven Poets. Christopher Carrell ed. Glasgow: Third Eye Centre, 1981.

SpecColl 4579/26 (for example). This refers to material in Accession 4579, Box 26 of the Edwin Morgan Papers, located in the Special Collections Department, University of Glasgow Library. Similar references appear throughout the text. Most refer either to boxes of correspondence organised by year, e.g. File 1953, or to files organised by correspondent, e.g. Iain Crichton Smith or Gael Turnbull, with papers arranged chronologically within. Relevant dates of letters are usually made clear in the text. Researchers should contact Special Collections in advance, as re-cataloguing of the Papers is under way.

Strange Likeness: The Use of Old English in Twentieth-Century Poetry. Chris Jones. Oxford: Oxford University Press, 2006.

The Dark Horse. No. 5, Summer 1997. Gerry Cambridge, ed.

The Nightfisherman: Selected Letters of W.S. Graham. Michael and Margaret Snow, eds. Manchester: CarcanetPress, 1999.

Unknown Is Best: A Celebration of Edwin Morgan at Eighty. Robyn Marsack and Hamish Whyte, eds. Edinburgh and Glasgow: Scottish Poetry Library and Mariscat Press, 2000.

B: EDWIN MORGAN: A SELECT LIST OF PUBLICATIONS

The Vision of Cathkin Braes and other Poems. Glasgow: William MacLellan, 1952.

Beowulf: A Verse Translation into Modern English. Aldington, Kent: The Hand and Flower Press, 1952 / Los Angeles and London: University of California Press, 1962 / Manchester: Carcanet Press, 2002.

The Cape of Good Hope. Tunbridge Wells: Peter Russell, The Pound Press, 1955.

Bibliography

Poems from Eugenio Montale. Translated by Edwin Morgan. Reading: The School of Art, University of Reading, 1959.

Sovpoems. Worcester: Migrant Press, 1961.

Collins Albatross Book of Longer Poems: English and American Poetry from the Fourteenth Century to the Present Day. Edited by Edwin Morgan. London and Glasgow: Collins, 1963.

Starryveldt. Frauenfeld, Switzerland: Eugen Gomringer Press, 1965.

emergent poems. Stuttgart: Edition Hansjorg Mayer, 1967.

Poems by Alan Hayton, Stephen Mulrine, Colin Kirkwood, Robert Tait: Four Glasgow University Poets. Selected by Edwin Morgan. Preston: Akros Publications, 1967.

gnomes. Preston: Akros Publications, 1968.

The Second Life. Edinburgh: Edinburgh University Press, 1968; paperback ed. 1981.

Proverbfolder. Corsham, Wiltshire: Openings Press, 1969.

The Horseman's Word: A Sequence of Concrete Poems. Preston: Akros Publications, 1970.

Twelve Songs. West Linton: Castlelaw Press, 1970.

Glasgow Sonnets. West Linton: Castlelaw Press, 1972.

Instamatic Poems. London: Ian McKelvie, 1972.

Wi the Haill Voice: 25 poems by Vladimir Mayakovsky. Translated into Scots with a glossary by Edwin Morgan. South Hinksey, Oxford: Carcanet Press, 1972.

From Glasgow to Saturn. Cheadle: Carcanet Press, 1973; 2nd impression 1974 / Chester Springs, Pennsylvania: Dufour, 1973.

The Whittrick: A Poem in Eight Dialogues 1955–1961. Preston: Akros Publications, 1973.

Essays. Cheadle Hulme: Carcanet New Press, 1974.

Fifty Renascence Love Poems. Translated by Edwin Morgan. Reading: Whiteknights Press, 1975.

Rites of Passage: translations. Manchester: Carcanet New Press, 1976.

Hugh MacDiarmid. Edited by Ian Scott-Kilvert. London: Longman for the British Council, 1976) (Writers and their Work series).

The New Divan. Manchester: Carcanet New Press, 1977.

Colour Poems. Glasgow: Third Eye Centre, 1978.

Platen: Selected Poems. Translated by Edwin Morgan. West Linton: Castlelaw Press, 1978.

Provenance and Problematics of 'Sublime and Alarming Images' in Poetry. London: The British Academy, 1979. (Warton Lecture).

Star Gate: Science Fiction Poems. Glasgow: Third Eye Centre, 1979.

Scottish Satirical Verse: an anthology. Edited by Edwin Morgan. Manchester: Carcanet New Press, 1980.

The Apple-Tree: A medieval Dutch play in a version by Edwin Morgan. Glasgow: Third Eye Centre, 1982.

Poems of Thirty Years.Manchester: Carcanet New Press, 1982.

Noise and Smoky Breath: Glasgow Poems and Visual Images 1900–1983. Glasgow: Third Eye Centre and Glasgow District Libraries, 1983 (pamphlet of launch speech).

Grafts/Takes. Glasgow: Mariscat Press, 1983.

Master Peter Pathelin. Translated by Edwin Morgan. Glasgow: Third Eye Centre, 1983.

Sonnets from Scotland. Glasgow: Mariscat Press, 1984; 2nd impression 1986.

Selected Poems. Manchester: Carcanet Press, 1985.

From the Video Box. Glasgow: Mariscat Press, 1986.

Newspoems. London: wacy!, 1987.

Themes on a Variation. Manchester: Carcanet Press, 1988.

Tales from Limerick Zoo. Illustrations by David Neilson. Glasgow: Mariscat Press, 1988.

Collected Poems. Manchester: Carcanet Press, 1990; paperback edition 1996.

Crossing the Border: Essays on Scottish Literature. Manchester: Carcanet Press, 1990.

Hold Hands Among the Atoms. Glasgow: Mariscat Press, 1991.

Edmond Rostand's Cyrano de Bergerac. A new verse translation by Edwin Morgan. Manchester: Carcanet Press, 1992.

PALABRARmas / WURDWAPPINschaw by Cecilia Vicuna. Translated by Edwin Morgan. Edinburgh: Morning Star Publications, 1994.

Sweeping Out the Dark. Manchester: Carcanet Press, 1994.

Collected Translations. Manchester: Carcanet Press, 1996.

The Maker on High by St Columba. Translated by Edwin Morgan. Glasgow: Mariscat Press, 1997.

Virtual and Other Realities. Manchester: Carcanet Press, 1997.

Christopher Marlowe's Doctor Faustus in a new version by Edwin Morgan. Edinburgh: Canongate, 1999.

Demon. Glasgow: Mariscat Press, 1999.

New Selected Poems. Manchester: Carcanet Press, 2000.

A.D.: a trilogy on the life of Jesus Christ. Manchester: Carcanet Press, 2000.

Bibliography

Jean Racine's Phaedra: a tragedy. Translated by Edwin Morgan. Manchester: Carcanet Press, 2000.

Attila József: Sixty Poems. Translated by Edwin Morgan. Glasgow: Mariscat Press, 2001.

Cathures: New Poems 1997–2001. Manchester: Carcanet Press, in association with Mariscat Press, 2002.

Love and a Life. Glasgow: Mariscat Press, 2003.

Metrum de Praelio apud Bannockburn | The Battle of Bannockburn by Robert Baston. Translated by Edwin Morgan. Edinburgh: Scottish Poetry Library, with Akros Publications and Mariscat Press, 2004.

The Play of Gilgamesh. Manchester: Carcanet Press, 2005.

Tales from Baron Munchausen. Edinburgh: Mariscat Press, 2005.

Thirteen Ways of Looking at Rillie. London: Enitharmon Press, 2006.

A Book of Lives. Manchester: Carcanet Press, 2007.

Beyond the Sun: Scotland's Favourite Paintings. Poems by Edwin Morgan. Edinburgh: Luath Press, 2007.

From Saturn to Glasgow: 50 favourite poems by Edwin Morgan. Edited by Robyn Marsack and Hamish Whyte. Manchester and Edinburgh: Carcanet Press and Scottish Poetry Library, 2008.

Dreams and Other Nightmares. New and Uncollected Poems 1954–2009. Edinburgh: Mariscat Press, 2010.

C: SOME USEFUL WEBSITES

Carcanet Press: http://www.carcanet.co.uk/

Special Collections Department, University of Glasgow Library: http://special.lib.gla.ac.uk/

Edwin Morgan website: http://www.edwinmorgan.com/

Mariscat Press: http://www.mariscatpress.co.uk/

Scottish Poetry Library Archive: http://www.edwinmorgan.spl.org.uk/

D: BOOKS ON THE POET'S DESK, AUGUST 2010

And The Land Lay Still James Robertson
Edinburgh Companion to James Kelman ed. Scott Hames
Edinburgh Companion to Irvine Welsh ed. Berthold Schoene
Highlands and Islands ed. Mary Meiers
Sophie's World Jostein Gaarder
The Losing Game R.V. Bailey

Beyond the Last Dragon

Beyond Identity: New Horizons in Modern Scottish Poetry Attila Dósa
An Egyptian Reading Book for Beginners Sir E.A. Wallace Budge (1896)
The Posthuman Dada Guide: tzara and lenin play chess Andrei Codrescu
Rays Richard Price
Sonnets for My Mother Lucy Hamilton
Journey to the Centre of the Earth Jules Verne
The Gift of Words ed. Aileen Ballantyne
Poets' Poems 1–8 EM's choices:

Anon 16thC, 'Westron Winde'; Andrew Marvell, 'The Garden'; Percy Bysshe Shelley, 'Ozamandias'; William Blake, 'The Tyger'; Robert Burns, 'O Wert Thou in the Cauld Blast'; Gerard Manley Hopkins, 'Inversnaid'; Hugh MacDiarmid, 'The Bonnie Broukit Bairn'; W.H. Auden, 'Lullaby' ('Lay your sleeping head, my love').

Kieron Smith, Boy James Kelman
Mansoul or The Riddle of the World C.M. Doughty (1920)
As Others See Us, Burns volume, photographs by 'broaddaylight'
Bho Leabhar-Latha Maria Malibran / From the Diary of Maria Malibran ed. Christopher Whyte
Homecoming Alan Riach
Finding Merlin: The Truth Behind the Legend Adam Ardrey
Gay Icons: National Portrait Gallery
Access to the Silence Tom Leonard
The First Person and Other Stories Ali Smith
This Is Not About Me Janice Galloway
My Discovery of America Vladimir Mayakovsky
Lost Languages: The Enigma of the World's Undeciphered Scripts Andrew Robinson
We Yevgeny Zamyatin
Tommy's War: A First World War Diary 1913–1918 Thomas Cairns Livingstone

Index

467

Index

Index

Index

Index

Index

Index